Servant-Leadership
and Forgiveness

Servant-Leadership and Forgiveness

How Leaders Help Heal the Heart of the World

Jiying Song,
Dung Q. Tran,
Shann Ray Ferch,
Larry C. Spears

SUNY
P R E S S

Published by State University of New York Press, Albany

© 2020 State University of New York

For information, contact State University of New York Press, Albany, NY
www.sunypress.edu

Library of Congress Cataloging-in-Publication Data

Names: Song, Jiying, 1976– editor. | Tran, Dung Q., 1979– editor. | Ferch, Shann Ray, 1967– editor.
Title: Servant-leadership and forgiveness : how leaders help heal the heart of the world / [edited by] Jiying Song, Dung Q. Tran, Shann Ray Ferch, Larry C. Spears.
Description: Albany : State University of New York, 2020. | Includes bibliographical references and index.
Identifiers: LCCN 2020000970 (print) | LCCN 2020000971 (ebook) | ISBN 9781438479217 (hardcover : alk. paper) | ISBN 9781438479224 (pbk. : alk. paper) | ISBN 9781438479231 (ebook)
Subjects: LCSH: Leadership. | Organizational effectiveness. | Empathy. | Forgiveness.
Classification: LCC HD57.7 .S4587 2020 (print) | LCC HD57.7 (ebook) | DDC 303.3/4—dc23
LC record available at https://lccn.loc.gov/2020000970
LC ebook record available at https://lccn.loc.gov/2020000971

10 9 8 7 6 5 4 3 2 1

Contents

PART II

SERVANT-LEADERSHIP, FORGIVENESS, AND SOCIAL ISSUES

PART III

SERVANT-LEADERSHIP, FORGIVENESS, AND FAMILY

PART IV

SERVANT-LEADERSHIP, FORGIVENESS, AND PERSONAL APPLICATIONS

PART V

SERVANT-LEADERSHIP, FORGIVENESS, AND CONTINUING RESEARCH DEVELOPMENT

Foreword

The World of Servant-Leadership

LARRY C. SPEARS

This collection of essays, *Servant-Leadership and Forgiveness: How Leaders Help Heal the Heart of the World*, represents a compelling gathering of perspectives on the intersection of servant-leadership and forgiveness. The chapters in this compilation offer up deep wisdom, powerful questions, and helpful practices for those of us who desire to grow as aspiring servant-leaders who also understand what it means to forgive others, and to be forgiven in return.

The term *servant-leadership* was first coined in a 1970 essay by Robert K. Greenleaf (1904–1990), titled *The Servant as Leader*. Greenleaf spent most of his organizational life in the field of management research, development, and education at AT&T. Following a forty-year career there, he founded the Center for Applied Ethics in 1964 and enjoyed a second career that lasted another twenty-five years. In 1985, the Center for Applied Ethics was renamed the Robert K. Greenleaf Center, where I served as executive director from 1990 to 2007.

During those years, I edited or coedited five volumes of writings by Robert Greenleaf: *On Becoming a Servant-Leader* (1996), *Seeker and Servant* (1996), *The Power of Servant-Leadership* (1998), *Servant Leadership: 25th Anniversary Edition* (2002), and *The Servant-Leader Within* (2003). Together with others, I have also coproduced a series of seven servant-leadership anthologies, including *Reflections on Leadership* (1995), *Insights on Leadership* (1998), *Focus on Leadership* (2002), *Practicing Servant-Leadership* (2004), *The*

Spirit of Servant-Leadership (2011), *Conversations on Servant-Leadership* (2015), and this latest volume, *Servant-Leadership and Forgiveness*.

Since 1970, more than a half million copies of Robert Greenleaf's books and essays have been sold worldwide. Slowly but surely, his writings on servant-leadership have helped to transform both people and organizations around the world. In many ways, it may be said that the times are only now beginning to catch up with Robert Greenleaf's visionary call to servant-leadership. The idea of servant-leadership, now in its sixth decade as a concept bearing that name, continues to create a quiet revolution around the world.

But what does servant-leadership entail? Who *is* a servant-leader? Greenleaf said that the servant-leader is one who is a servant first and a leader second. In *The Servant as Leader,* Greenleaf (2002) writes,

> The servant-leader is servant first. It begins with the natural feeling that one wants to serve first. Then conscious choice brings one to aspire to lead. The difference manifests itself in the care taken by the servant—first to make sure that other people's highest priority needs are being served. The best test is: Do those served grow as persons; do they, while being served, become healthier, wiser, freer, more autonomous, more likely themselves to become servants? And, what is the effect on the least privileged in society? Will they benefit or at least not be further deprived? (p. 27)

The words *servant* and *leader* are usually thought of as being opposites. In deliberately bringing those two words together in a meaningful way, Robert Greenleaf gave birth to the paradoxical term *servant-leader*. His writings on the subject of servant-leadership helped to get this global movement started, and his views have had a profound and growing effect on many organizations and thought leaders. Organizations such as Aflac, Chick-fil-A, The Container Store, Starbucks, Southwest Airlines, Synovus Financial Corporation, and TDIndustries are recognized today for nurturing servant-led cultures. These institutions and many others have been encouraged and supported by a long list of servant-leadership thought leaders such as James Autry, Cheryl Bachelder, Warren Bennis, Ken Blanchard, Peter Block, John Carver, Stephen Covey, Max DePree, Shann Ferch, Don Frick, John Horsman, James Kouzes, Parker Palmer, M. Scott Peck, Peter Senge, Margaret Wheatley, and Danah Zohar, to name but a handful of today's cutting-edge authors and advocates of servant-leadership.

In 1992, I conducted a study of Robert Greenleaf's writings. From that analysis, I was able to codify a set of ten characteristics that Greenleaf wrote about in various writings, and which he considered as being central to the development of servant-leaders. These include listening, empathy, healing, awareness, persuasion, conceptualization, foresight, stewardship, commitment to the growth of people, and building community. My analysis showed these to be the characteristics Greenleaf mentioned most often in his writings, which led me to codify them into a list and to begin to write about them. While these ten characteristics of servant-leadership by no means form an exhaustive list, they do serve to communicate the power and promise that servant-leadership offers to people who are open to its invitation and challenge. Like Robert Greenleaf, I am convinced that it is possible to become an increasingly authentic servant-leader through the conscious development of these and other characteristics.

It is helpful to understand that servant-leadership starts within each one of us, and that it is first and foremost a personal philosophy and commitment that we can choose to practice in any environment. If we understand Greenleaf's best test as the fundamental understanding of servant-leadership, then it becomes clear that the choice to seek to practice servant-leadership is ours to make. Our personal embracing of servant-leadership does not require the approval of our supervisor or of our organization's chief executive. We don't need anyone's permission to personally do our best to act as a servant-leader. It is our choice.

The same can also be said of forgiveness. When we consider the inspiring examples of forgiveness demonstrated by well-known servant-leaders such as Martin Luther King Jr., Nelson Mandela, and Archbishop Desmond Tutu, it is empowering to realize that each of them made a conscious choice to forgive their oppressors. As the authors in this anthology make clear, the decision to seek forgiveness, or to grant forgiveness to others, is to be found within ourselves. It is our choice.

Servant-Leadership and Forgiveness reveals many pathways available to people, institutions, and countries desiring a better way of overcoming disagreements, pain, and traumatic events. This book also shows how the servant-leadership attributes of healing, listening, awareness, community building, and others can be used as antidotes to an increasingly polarized and troubled world. So many caring people are working to break down negative beliefs and to infuse our relationships through serving and leading, forgiveness and love.

Servant-Leadership and Forgiveness is a wise and hopeful book.

Preface

The Forgiveness Ethos of Servant-Leadership

JIYING SONG AND SHANN RAY FERCH

The modern father of servant-leadership, Robert K. Greenleaf (1977/2002), effectively embodied lesser-known servant-leadership aspects such as prophesy, foresight, and the will to better society, often through personal and collective sacrifice. Through this embodiment, a profound ethos comes to the fore: the dynamic, steadying, and fiercely graceful notion of forgiveness as part of the central core of servant-leadership. In his telling essay on Robert Frost's (1947) poem "Directive," Greenleaf showed not only his strengths in linear thinking but also his uncommon gifts with regard to nonlinear, mystery-based, and more circular aspects of wisdom more readily associated with poets and painters than with business practitioners or social scientists, and in so doing, he opened the door for leaders to take greater responsibility for their own humanity and for humanity as a whole. To be a leader responsible for the healing so vitally important to the wholeness of individuals and society, the mystery of forgiveness comes forth from the shadows, bearing light.

Greenleaf's (1977/2002) essay "The Inward Journey" from his *Servant Leadership: A Journey into the Nature of Legitimate Power and Greatness* contains an elegant, artistic, and in many respects, qualitative, look at the nature of the servant-leader. In the essay, Greenleaf relates how his reading Frost's "Directive" deepened his understanding of the courageous and wise presence of the servant as leader. In this book and in this introduction, we present the elegance and power of cutting-edge research and thinking on servant-leadership and forgiveness.

Notably, the burgeoning quantitative research in servant-leadership conducted by Liden (Hu & Liden, 2011; Liden et al., 2015; Liden et al., 2016; Liden et al., 2014; Liden et al., 2008; Panaccio et al., 2015), van Dierendonck (Sousa & van Dierendonck, 2016, 2017a, 2017b; van Dierendonck et al., 2017; van Dierendonck & Nuijten, 2011; van Dierendonck et al., 2014), and many others has revealed weighty implications for servant-leadership across many dimensions of human experience. This body of research significantly fortifies and brings to the fore the new quantitative frontier of servant-leadership understandings, leading the field in unforeseen directions while contributing invaluable new knowledge.

That said, qualitative studies in servant-leadership perform a different function—again, a function aligned less with linear or superrational knowledge than with poetic or symbolic knowledge. Quantitative research, in its emphasis on numerical reliability, validity, and generalizability at the expense of more intimate individual and collective expressions of human capacity, cannot, by definition, draw on the empirical grounding in lived experience found in qualitative research (Crotty, 1998; Denzin & Lincoln, 2011; van Manen, 1990, 2016). Quantitative research typically disallows, or rather occludes, the researcher from acknowledging and challenging personal biases, a research practice that is a common requirement for qualitative studies. This refusal to acknowledge and detail personal bias can often prevent the servant-leader from true self-knowledge, and thus it can be a shadow force or unknown frailty in much quantitative research. At times this results in calcification, brittleness, and eventual fracture of the knowledge base. Certainly, research using qualitative, quantitative, and mixed methodologies is necessary for more complete and robust understanding of servant-leadership. The gift of in-depth, well-designed, and deeply informed qualitative studies in servant-leadership offers the opportunity to expose our blind spots as people and leaders, and to bring us to a more intimate understanding of ourselves, others, and the world.

To understand the world more intimately, a move toward greater wholeness and healing, and deeper understanding of forgiveness, is required. Both poets and researchers can lead us there.

Though the extent of Greenleaf's personal connection with Pulitzer Prize–winning poet Robert Frost is unknown, they did know each other, and spent time in each other's presence. The possibility that they directly influenced one another's thought is apparent, and becomes a compelling thread in the history of leadership studies. Consider this moment, relayed by Greenleaf (1977/2002):

> In a group conversation with him [Frost] one evening, he digressed on the subject of loyalty. At one point I interjected with: "Robert, that is not the way you have defined loyalty before." He turned to me with a broad friendly grin and asked softly, "How did I define it?" I replied, "In your talk on Emerson a few years ago, you said, 'Loyalty is that for the lack of which your gang will shoot you without benefit of trial by jury.'" To this man who had struggled without recognition until he was forty, and then had to move to England to get it, nothing could have pleased him more in his old age than to have an obscure passage like this quoted to him in a shared give-and-take with non-literary people. (p. 326)

In Greenleaf's (1977/2002) "engagement" with Frost's poem, he affirmed the necessity of a prophetic, circular orientation in going further into the depths of human awareness: "Our problem is circular: we must understand in order to be able to understand. It has something to do with awareness and symbols" (p. 329). Symbolic understanding is formless, cannot be linearized, and cannot be understood by simple 1-2-3 progressions. Rather, it is absorbed; it is an element of life and leadership in which the servant-leader chooses to become willingly submerged.

> Awareness, letting something significant and disturbing develop between oneself and a symbol, comes more by being waited upon rather than by being asked. One of the most baffling of life's experiences is to stand beside one who is aware, one who is looking at a symbol and is deeply moved by it, and, confronting the same symbol, to be unmoved. Oh, that we could just be open in the presence of symbols that cry out to speak to us, let our guards down, and take the risks of being moved!
>
> The power of a symbol is measured by its capacity to sustain a flow of significant new meaning. The substance of the symbol may be a painting, a poem or story, allegory, myth, scripture, a piece of music, a person, a crack in the sidewalk,

or a blade of grass. Whatever or whoever, it produces a confrontation in which much that makes the symbol meaningful
comes from the beholder.

The potentiality is both in the symbol and in the
beholder. (p. 329)

From the foundations of qualitative research, philosophers of human
nature such as Heidegger (1962), Husserl (1970), Gadamer (1975/2004,
1976), and Ricoeur (1981) have spoken to the impossibility of knowing
humanity without knowing oneself. Qualitative research helps us find a
more accessible avenue toward increased self-awareness: through symbol,
depth, and meaning. The need to name, articulate, and bracket one's own
biases in the attempt to show the lived human experience more clearly is
inherent to qualitative research, even as it generally remains obscured in
quantitative research. By extension, the person with a leader-first mentality,
often mired in self-aggrandizement without foreknowledge, ambition at the
expense of love and service, and an inappropriate power drive obscuring
or negating authentic intimacy, generally lacks healthy self-awareness. The
leader-first leader has limited or no capacity to name his or her own faults,
let alone invite others to influence, challenge, or help correct them. In
this light, Greenleaf's (1977/2002) prophetic truths—warning individuals,
communities, and nations against the leader-first mentality—take on pivotal
and, in fact, crucial meaning.

Each chapter in *Servant-Leadership and Forgiveness: How Leaders Help
Heal the Heart of the World* first appeared in the *International Journal of
Servant-Leadership*. We are grateful to Gonzaga University and SUNY
Press for support over the years in publishing the *International Journal of
Servant-Leadership*. In this introduction, we have chosen to speak directly to
two of the chapters in this book (chapters 2 and 7), and to two additional
servant-leadership explorations (McCollum & Moses, 2009; and Reynolds,
2013, 2014), in order to illumine the book itself, and reveal the richness
of human understanding associated with in-depth studies of human nature
in light of servant-leadership. Servant-leaders—aligned with the ancient
history of servant-first leading, rather than leader-first leading—seek greater
self-awareness and greater awareness of others. They seek the essence of
what it means not only to lead and follow but also to live. In so doing,
they embody great will, considerable modesty, active engagement with a
circular world, and devotion to the great mystery of forgiveness.

The Forgiveness Ethos

At the outset of my research I was unsure, even questioning the
heart of humanity. I can now say a life for others, a servant-led life,
exists, heals the world, restores us to one another, and gracefully
makes us whole.

—Marleen Ramsey, *Servant-Leadership and Unconditional Forgiveness*

Chapter 2 of this book considers servant-leadership and forgiveness in
the presence of some of the most fraught conditions of human existence.
In 2002, Marleen Ramsey set out to interview six political perpetrators
from the apartheid era in South Africa who were found guilty of murder and other gross human rights abuses. South Africa, in the midst of
political turmoil and tormented by violence, held its first democratic
elections in 1994. Nelson Mandela became the country's president and
initiated the process of investigating human rights abuses and negotiating
national reconciliation through the Truth and Reconciliation Commission
(TRC), which was chaired by Desmond Tutu. Mandela and Tutu modeled
servant-leadership through the process of the TRC. The TRC employed
public truth-telling hearings to give voice to the victims who had been
silent about the suffering they had endured and to let political perpetrators be honest about their violent deeds. Through this process, truth was
revealed, suffering was acknowledged, forgiveness was given and received,
and lives were transformed. Ramsey's (2006) hermeneutic phenomenological
study depicted a particular and fine-grained picture of this movement a
decade after the fall of apartheid. Among Ramsey's six participants, two
were responsible for the death of Amy Biehl in 1993, one was tried for
the Heidelberg Tavern attack in 1994, one was responsible for the Saint
James Church massacre in 1993, one commanded the attacks on the
Heidelberg Tavern and the Saint James Church in Cape Town, and one
ordered the attack on a house in the village of Trust Feed in 1988. In
each case, lives were taken and innocent blood was shed.

Amy Biehl, an American Fulbright scholar, had been helping black
South Africans complete registration forms so that they could vote in the
forthcoming democratic elections, which were to be held in 1994. Her
work was a powerful example of servant-leadership. Increasing black-on-
white violence took place in South Africa in the years 1993 and 1994

under the influence of the slogan "One settler, one bullet, we want our country right now, liberate" (Ramsey, 2003, p. 124). What happened to Amy in the black township of Gugulethu on July 25, 1993, was the result of one of these uprisings. The crowd saw a government truck, and behind it Amy driving a yellow car. Someone spotted Amy's white face and shouted that there was a settler, and the crowd began throwing stones at Amy's car. They caught her, stabbed her multiple times, and stoned her to death. Two of Ramsey's participants were found guilty of Biehl's death.

In another set of interviews, focusing on a different but likewise traumatic set of events, Ramsey interviewed a white commander of the South African State Security forces. This commander was in charge of controlling the region and thwarting activities against whites in a remote corner of the KwaZulu-Natal midlands. The commander's forces, all white, oversaw a village—Trust Feed—with seven thousand black people. On December 3, 1988, the commander ordered an attack on a house in Trust Feed. He thought he was destroying an ammunition holding house and a location where petrol bombs were being manufactured. When he walked into the house the morning after the attack, blood covered the room and eleven bodies lay still, mostly women and children. He realized that the wrong house had been targeted and innocent people had been killed. In order to protect the image of the State Security forces, he and his superiors planned a cover-up of the atrocity by blaming the attack on the black United Democratic Front forces.

Ramsey's data come not from a questionnaire distributed to hundreds of people but from in-depth interviews on the lived experiences of six participants. Her questions sought the heart of the matter: "Please describe what it was like to face your victim or victim's family and to receive empathy and forgiveness from them"; "If it came as a surprise to you to receive empathy and forgiveness from the victim's family, please describe [your] response"; "Please describe the thoughts, feelings, and perceptions you experienced"; "Please describe the most transforming moment you experienced throughout the ordeal" (Ramsey, 2003, p. 261). By using a phenomenological approach, Ramsey (2003, 2006) gave space to the participants and let them share what they had experienced, which formed the starting point for inquiry, reflection, and interpretation. Hermeneutic phenomenology goes beyond merely describing the foundations of lived experience and looks for meanings embedded in the essences of the lifeworld (Lopez & Willis, 2004; van Manen, 2016). Reflecting on her work, Ramsey (2006) said,

Time and again, during the interviews and during the interpretation of these men's stories, I was struck by the enormity
of the psychological pain that we often cause others and
ourselves. I was also struck by the realization of how healing
the experience of forgiveness can be to both victims and
perpetrators. It is through the stories of these six men that
greater understanding may be gained regarding the transforming
powers of empathy and forgiveness. It is also through their
stories that we can see how the practices of servant-leadership
can restore community to people deeply separated by violence
and brutality. (p. 120)

Ramsey (2006) found five themes through her study: (a) violence
harms both victim and perpetrator, (b) denial and arrogance are self-
protections used to shield the perpetrator from shame, (c) empathy creates
an environment whereby the perpetrator can ask for and receive forgiveness, (d) the gift of forgiveness increases the ability to forgive oneself, and
(e) forgiveness is a bridge to the future. Facing violence and tragedy,
we learn some of the details of the damage through news reports and
the number of deaths, but in order to know the impact on victims' and
perpetrators' hearts and souls, we have to listen to their stories. Ramsey
pointed out that labeling perpetrators as "evil" or "inhuman" does not
help us understand them. All of her participants revealed intense pain, such
as "I felt a pain in my heart," "I felt pressed with a huge weight," "I felt
as if I was being suffocated," and "There was a poison that needed to be
released" (p. 124). However, many amnesty seekers appeared unbroken,
unrepentant, or arrogant, or showed no sign of remorse as they were
testifying before the TRC. Ramsey developed a deeper understanding of
human blame shifting through her interviews. One participant said, "I was
not prepared to make myself appear weak because it would create more
shame than I could bear" (p. 125). Five of the six participants mentioned
the need to maintain their dignity and self-respect in an environment
they felt was extremely hostile. After capturing the human side of the
perpetrators, Ramsey found that perpetrators' feelings of empathy for
their victims and their receiving empathy from victims' families were
emotional bridges that they could use to ask for and receive forgiveness.
She showed the long and torturous journey toward self-forgiveness each
of these participants faced. In the attack on Trust Feed, one participant's
action resulted in the death of eleven innocent people. Years later, in

response to Mandela's and Tutu's servant-leadership, the people of Trust Feed brought that participant back for reconciliation and forgiveness and invited him to live with them. He said, "I was dead until that day. . . . And after that day I lived" (pp. 135–136). Today he has succeeded in helping raise the funds to build a community center, hand in hand with those whose family members he killed.

All six participants received empathy and forgiveness from victims' family members or loved ones, but only four developed close relationships with the people they had harmed. These four participants expressed a greater feeling of self-forgiveness and hope for the future than the two who did not have such relationships with their victims' families. Today, after years of developing profound relationships, the men who killed Amy Biehl call Amy's mother their mother, and she calls them her sons. They all see this as a miracle, and the world echoes their sentiment. Together, these men and Amy Biehl's parents have worked to improve quality of life for families and children of South Africa.

The conclusions of Ramsey's (2006) study contribute to understanding the role of empathy and forgiveness in the healing of wounded interpersonal relationships. Even for the most hardened and unrepentant perpetrators, the practice of the principles of servant-leadership—empathy, forgiveness, and healing—has the generative power to bring hope for redemption and the restoration of community. Servant-leaders help those who have been lost in the wilderness find their way home.

For Reynolds's (2013) study through a feminist perspective, she used a mixed-methods content analysis to study commencement messages delivered by fifty of the top female and male American business leaders based on the ranking of their organizations on *Fortune* lists from 2005 to 2012. Her purpose was to understand gender differences between expressions of leadership in the constructs of servant-leadership and expressions of decision making in the constructs of the ethic of care. She also explored whether gender differences among prominent American business leaders support the conceptualization that servant-leadership is a gender-integrative mode of leadership. She found this to be intuitively and qualitatively true. In other words, no overall gender distinction was found in the main servant-leadership characteristics, but some gender differences were observed. For instance, women spoke more about humility and standing back in leadership, whereas men highlighted accountability; female speakers considered the motivation to lead as an ethical drive and a choice, whereas male speakers articulated it as an obligation (Reynolds, 2013). She stated that gender differences found in the qualitative analysis could serve to reify gender congruency expectations if read without critical gender understanding. To counteract such reification, her study presented evidence of female leaders combining care orientation and relationality (typically feminine aspects of leadership) with courage and contrarian thinking (typically masculine aspects) and evidence of male leaders combining accountability and risk taking (typically masculine aspects) with forgiveness and being attuned to others' needs (typically feminine aspects). Reynolds concluded that servant-leadership combines both feminine and masculine aspects of leadership.

Furthermore, Eicher-Catt (2005) proposed that the serving aspect of servant-leadership is associated with submissive femininity, and the leading aspect with oppressive masculinity. Reynolds (2014) challenged Eicher-Catt's framework, revealing her conclusions with regard to servant-leadership to be largely based on her perception of the words *servant* and *leader* and not on Greenleaf's own interpretations of these words. Greenleaf's interpretations serve to deconstruct the words and return them to their original meanings, affirming their value across gender, culture, time, and context. Reynolds analyzed Spears's (2002) 10 characteristics to examine servant-leadership constructs in terms of gender. She argued that six of the 10 characteristics distinguish servant-leadership from other forms of leadership, whereas the other four characteristics are more in line with traditional notions of leadership (Reynolds, 2014). These six distinguishing characteristics are stewardship, listening, empathizing, healing, commitment to the growth of people, and building community; the other four are foresight, conceptualization, awareness, and persuasion. Reynolds asserted that foresight, conceptualization, awareness, and persuasion can be characterized as leader behaviors, and are often associated with the more traditionally masculine aspect of leadership. The six distinguishing characteristics of servant-leadership, on the other hand, are predominantly needs-focused and other-oriented, and thus, for Reynolds, comprise the feminine-attributed aspects of leadership.

Eicher-Catt (2005) claimed, from her particular feminist perspective, that the apposition of *servant* with *leader*, associated with subjugation and domination, respectively, instantiates a paradoxical discourse game that perpetuates male-centric patriarchal norms rather than neutralizing gender bias. Reynolds (2014) agreed that Eicher-Catt's (2005) critique reveals otherwise obscure discursive and behavioral meanings and hidden cultural assumptions in servant-leadership. However, Reynolds (2014) exposed how Eicher-Catt lacked the will to go deeply into Greenleaf's original texts in order to find a more central discursive and deconstructive essence that can be ascribed to Greenleaf's sense of "making things whole" across gender, culture, and context. Reynolds (2014) argued that the combination of servant facets and leader facets of servant-leadership does not automatically confirm the negatives Eicher-Catt associated with gendered notions but, on the contrary, provides a model of ethical and gender equity-enhancing leadership: "Servant-leadership espouses a nonhierarchical, participative approach to defining organizational objectives and ethics that recognizes and values the subjectivity and situatedness of organizational members" (p. 57). Servant-leadership can serve as "a driving force for generating discourse on gender-integrative approaches to organizational leadership" (p. 51).

Reynolds proposed that the paradoxical linguistic term *servant-leader* is not a disguise for male-centric norms, as Eicher-Catt (2005) claimed, but a complementary and harmonious dualism. This dualism resonates with the concepts of *yin* and *yang*, which represent female and male, respectively, in ancient Chinese literature.

> As for yin and yang, they are the Way of heaven and earth, the fundamental principles [governing] the myriad beings, father and mother to all changes and transformations, the basis and beginning of generating life and killing, the palace of spirit brilliance. (Unschuld, Tessenow, & Zheng, 2011, p. 95)

Lao Tzu (2005) said, "All the myriad things carry the Yin on their backs and hold the Yang in their embrace, deriving their vital harmony from the proper blending of the two vital Breaths" (p. 49). *Yin* and *yang* cannot exist without each other. They are a contradictory yet complementary unit. Women were degraded in ancient China based on the ascendancy of patriarchy, the focus on the contradictory aspect of *yin* and *yang*, and the elevation of *yang* (Bao, 1987). The same kind of degradation still exists in the leadership field today. Having stressed the equally and mutually complementary character of *yin-yang*, some scholars paved the way for the women's egalitarian movement in nineteenth-century China (Bao, 1987). Likewise, this is what Reynolds (2013, 2014) and many other servant-leadership scholars are doing—elevating complementary aspects of gender without neglecting the contradictory aspects. Carrying *yin* and holding *yang* in intimate embrace, leaders learn to forgive more readily and more deeply, and help others gain the vital harmony so often missing in today's families, organizations, and nations.

Through a discussion of the complementary character of *yin-yang* and servant-leader elements, without ignoring the contradictory aspects, leaders may establish harmony and gender-integrative models wherever they serve. Although the results of Reynolds's (2013) study indicated that gender stereotyping continues to affect conceptualizations of leadership, her study also provided evidence of servant-leaders crossing gender boundaries and integrating gendered traits and behaviors. As Reynolds (2014) noted, by integrating the female perspective with a male perspective, a paradigm shift in leadership theory (through avenues inherent to servant-leadership) could move organizations from hierarchy-driven, rules-based, and authoritative models to value-driven, follower-oriented, and participative models with gender balance.

In chapter 7, Campbell (2017) deepens the field of servant-leadership by building a theoretical foundation upon which leaders can integrate forgiveness and reconciliation as an organizational leadership competency to resolve conflicts and sustain peace and harmony in the face of local and global challenges. First, the author introduced definitions and conceptualizations of forgiveness and reconciliation within transitional justice and organizational leadership disciplines. Second, the author compared religious themes of forgiveness in Hinduism, Islam, Judaism, and Christianity. Third, the author discussed the necessity of integrating forgiveness and reconciliation as an organizational leadership competency. Finally, Campbell suggested that servant-leadership can serve as a theoretical framework to facilitate forgiveness and reconciliation within organizations.

Enright, Freedman, and Rique (1998) defined *forgiveness* as "a willingness to abandon one's right to resentment, negative judgment, and indifferent behavior toward one who unjustly injured us, while fostering the undeserved qualities of compassion, generosity, and even love toward him or her" (pp. 46–47). Forgiveness is a process of replacing complex negative emotions with positive other-oriented emotions, and it requires empathy, sympathy, compassion, and love, along with clear understanding in the face of social tensions and injustice (Worthington, 2006).

A study conducted in Uganda by the Refugee Law Project and the Center for Civil and Human Rights from 2014 to 2015 found that the practice of forgiveness, combined with transitional justice measures, such as judicial accountability, truth telling, governance, and reparations, can be a strong asset for peace building (Shaffic, 2015). Campbell (2017) claimed that transitional justice practitioners, who may be called to lead victims through the emotional and intellectual process of forgiveness, need to develop leadership capacities such as empathy, emotional intelligence, accountability, humility, and compassion. Within an unforgiving organization, Campbell stated, leaders may employ dishonesty, power politics, and manipulative measures; employees may be afraid to speak out and may be hiding their feelings; and such organizational climates are definably toxic. He asserted that forgiveness plays a principal role in restoring relationships, rebuilding trust, nurturing healthy work climates, improving organizational performance, and transforming organizations. Campbell discerned that forgiveness in the context of servant-leadership is "a social interaction among individuals designed to resolve intrapersonal and interpersonal conflicts toward organizational and national peaceful coexistence" (p. 151). Furthermore, he pointed out that forgiveness not only frees victims and perpetrators from guilt and pain but also fosters personal, organizational, and global reconciliation.

Campbell (2017) claimed that the process of forgiveness focuses on individual healing, while the process of reconciliation fosters social healing. Brouneus (2007) defined *reconciliation* as "a societal process that involves mutual acknowledgment of past suffering and the changing of destructive attitudes and behavior into constructive relationships toward sustainable peace" (p. 6). Reconciliation involves changes in emotion, attitude, and behavior; social healing among victims and perpetrators; and an ongoing process in which relations are rebuilt for sustainable and peaceful coexistence (Brouneus, 2007). Campbell (2017) proposed two levels to the conceptualization of reconciliation: the micro level, where reconciliation is both a leadership competency and an interpersonal endeavor, and the macro level, where reconciliation redresses the physical, emotional, and spiritual wounds generated by abusers at organizational, communal, national, and global levels. For Campbell, the best example of this two-level reconciliation is found in the process of the TRC in South Africa. Tutu (1999), the leader of the TRC, said, "Forgiveness will follow confession and healing will happen, and so contribute to national unity and reconciliation" (p. 120). Furthermore, Tutu claimed that South Africa had to move "beyond retributive justice to restorative justice, to move on to forgiveness, because without it there was no future" (p. 260). Campbell (2017) proposed that restorative justice through servant-leadership builds a narrative toward reconciliation, facilitates forgiveness and societal reconciliation, and has a therapeutic effect on the society.

Campbell (2017) compared religious themes of forgiveness in Hinduism, Islam, Judaism, and Christianity and found that forgiveness is accompanied by moral virtues, benevolence, and reliance on leaders' spirituality. Perpetrator accountability and psychosocial healing is impossible without a spiritual component, Campbell concluded. Thus, he confirmed that "forgiveness is an integral ingredient of individual psycho-social healing, facilitates restoration of individual and community healing, and necessitates spiritual strength as societies heal from human rights atrocities in a post conflict environment" (p. 164).

Campbell (2017) pointed out that organizational conflicts may come from the misperceptions generated from a lack of dialogue, listening, empathy, and understanding between leaders and the fellow workers. Leaders' decisions and actions based on misperceptions may produce an environment that lacks forgiveness and hinders peacebuilding. In order to avoid misperceptions, Campbell proposed that communications at individual and organizational levels take place by building an atmosphere of trust, collaboration, and dialogue. Integrating forgiveness within an organization can not only free victims and perpetrators from their wounds but can also nurture and sustain such an atmosphere, further increasing retention and productivity. Thus, by fostering forgiveness and reconciliation, servant-leaders "create a supportive environment where individual growth toward emotional, relational, and spiritual maturity strengthens" and organizational performance increases (p. 174).

Yergler (2005) asserted that "a servant-leader must incorporate forgiveness as a leadership competency if the benefactors of that leadership are to experience true transformation into servant-leaders themselves" (para. 3). When Mandela laid down his vengeance after 27 years in jail, a spirit of forgiveness was kindled in the whole nation. Campbell (2017) argued that servant-leadership has essential ingredients that end up fostering an organizational climate of forgiveness and reconciliation. He compared the characteristics of unforgiving leaders with forgiving leaders at different levels—individually, dyadic, in teams, and organizationally—and listed the servant-leadership competencies needed to nurture forgiveness and reconciliation within organizations. To form the formless and to chart the uncharted, servant-leadership scholars such as Campbell strive to shift the stereotypical paradigms in leadership. We believe encountering, engaging, and embodying forgiveness, through the process of asking forgiveness, making atonement, and seeking in-depth reconciliation, can become a hallmark of authentic servant-leadership worldwide.

The above servant-leadership studies, as well as all the chapters we are honored to present in this book, find some of their roots in Greenleaf's original research shown in McCollum and Moses's (2009) discoveries. In their work, McCollum and Moses presented Greenleaf's legacy at AT&T in the shaping of the contemporary development of assessment centers as naturally qualitative, personal, and communal in nature and paired with certain quantitative understandings. After college, Greenleaf was hired by the AT&T subsidiary Ohio Bell in 1926. Three years later, he was moved to the headquarters of AT&T in New York. In the 1920s, Bell initiated a comprehensive study to evaluate the success of college recruits. Through the study of 3,800 college hires, it concluded that college grades and class standing could predict salary and job success (McCollum & Moses, 2009). A thriving program had been developed to attract and retain these talented graduates within AT&T when Greenleaf came to New York.

In the 1950s, Greenleaf spearheaded the Bell Humanities Program, developing executives through exposure to the humanities. The program provided opportunities for a year-long liberal arts curriculum from 1953 to 1958, and later a series of shorter programs until 1970 (Frick, 2004). Greenleaf incorporated these programs into the Initial Management Development Program (IMDP) for the development of potential managers early in their careers (McCollum & Moses, 2009). In order to better understand how these programs had been developed, we have to look at Greenleaf's Management Progress Study (MPS), which explored the factors in the shaping of managers' development. The roots of MPS were planted in World War II. The Office of Strategic Services (OSS) was responsible for selecting spies who could work in Europe in resistance to Nazi Germany. In 1943, Dr. Henry Murray, given his groundbreaking research in the field of personality development in the 1920s, was assigned the task of developing a special school to select and train spies (Frick, 2004). After the war, the results of Murray and his colleagues' efforts were published in a 1946 *Fortune* article called "A Good Man Is Hard to Find" and in a 1948 book titled *The Assessment of Men*. Greenleaf saw the relevance of formal assessment in the OSS and in a business such as AT&T. He brought the article and the book to the attention of executives at AT&T, and eventually launched a highly visionary project—MPS—a 25-year longitudinal study.

In 1956, Greenleaf hired Douglas Bray to design and deliver the first AT&T assessment program. During the first four years, the program assessed 422 high-potential new recruits or beginning managers. The initial assessment was conducted over the course of one week at an assessment center, where psychologists and managers observed the participants and rated them according to 26 specific assessment dimensions (Bray, 1982).[1] A second assessment was conducted eight years later, and a third twelve years after that. The same set of dimensions was used for years zero and eight, while 21 new dimensions were added at year 20 to reflect the challenges of middle age (Bray, 1982). Yearly follow-up interviews were used to learn about participants' work and life activities. Two hundred and sixty-six out of 422 participants went through all three assessments; the rest left AT&T at some point (Bray, 1982). This landmark study has had a great impact on the identification and development of leaders. Its success kindled the creation of thousands of corporate assessment centers all over the world.

Keeping this longitudinal qualitative and quantitative study viable in the long term did not hinder Greenleaf from transferring the results from the research to operational programs or sharing with others as early as possible. McCollum and Moses (2009) pointed out that a key finding of MPS is that more challenging job assignments early in one's career could help a manager progress faster and further regardless of his or her assessed potential. Thus we see the seeds of Greenleaf's deep-seated affinity for developing the autonomy of others. Based on this finding, participants were provided with rotational assignments and formal training. Paralleling with MPS, Greenleaf developed IMDP to provide a framework for manager development during their early years in the company. The program integrated classroom learning with job experience and contributed to the development of thousands of managers at AT&T. It continued for many years after Greenleaf's retirement in 1964 and spawned a new industry in adult learning and development.

Another key finding of MPS, as mentioned by McCollum and Moses (2009), is the strong correlation between assessment center predictions of participants' managerial potential and the actual progress of the participants. Assessment centers were used to select and develop leaders. Following Greenleaf and Bray's idea, the research model of MPS was modified into an operational program in 1958 that soon spread throughout various AT&T subsidiaries (Frick, 2004). IBM, Standard Oil, and Sears were among the first companies to adopt the process of operational assessment centers after AT&T (McCollum & Moses, 2009). Alverno College, a Catholic liberal arts women's college, was the first educational institution to integrate assessment centers into an educational curriculum (McCollum & Moses, 2009). Today, assessment centers are widely studied and used in various settings all over the world to identify and develop potential leaders. As McCollum and

Moses pointed out, this is mainly due to Greenleaf's pioneering, prophetic, and foresight-oriented vision regarding human development.

Greenleaf's innovations in human development were and remain radical. Bartlett and Ghoshal (2002) described a strategic shift from financial resources to human and intellectual capital in the late 1980s and early 1990s. Without Greenleaf's mental construction of foresight, and behavioral, emotional, and spiritual construction of narrative servant-leadership, a paradigm shift in the field of management development may not have happened, and certainly would have been dampened. McCollum and Moses (2009) said of Greenleaf's MPS, "Among behavioral research conducted over the last 100 years, the Management Progress Study stands out as one of the luminary events in the development of managers" (pp. 104–105). The authors stated that "Greenleaf left a major mark on contemporary business practices" not only because of his leadership roles and impact on management development but also through his embodiment of the concept of empowerment (p. 108). Greenleaf's modeling of servant-leadership not only nurtured this 25-year longitudinal qualitative and quantitative study but also contributed to its paradigm-shifting fruit.

According to Bray (1982), "the most significant single finding from the Management Progress Study is that success as a manager is highly predictable" (p. 183). Thus the 26 assessment dimensions used by MPS offer a tool to assess abilities, motives, traits, and attitudes and to predict potential managers' success. These assessment dimensions include administrative skills (organizing and planning, decision making, and creativity); interpersonal skills (leadership skills, oral communication skills, behavior flexibility, personal impact, social objectivity, and perceptions of threshold social cues); cognitive skills (general mental ability, range of interest, and written communication skills); stability of performance (tolerance of uncertainty and resistance to stress); work motivation (primacy of work, inner work standards, energy, and self-objectivity); career orientation (need for advancement, need for security, ability to delay gratification, realism of expectations, and Bell System value orientation); and dependency (need for superior approval, need for peer approval, and goal flexibility) (p. 184).

Two interesting discernments emerge after comparing these 26 dimensions with the 10 characteristics of servant-leadership. First, three of the initial four areas of these dimensions—administrative skills, cognitive skills, and stability of performance—resonate with Reynolds's (2014) notion of traditionally masculine aspects of leadership—conceptualization, persuasion, awareness, and foresight. For example, organizing and planning, decision making, and general mental ability relate to conceptualization; leadership skills, oral and written communication skills, and personal impact are necessary for persuasion; while creativity, general mental ability, and tolerance of uncertainty may help generate foresight (Bray, 1982; Reynolds, 2014). Meanwhile, interpersonal skills, including social objectivity (the degree to which one is free from prejudices) and perceptions of threshold social cues are associated with more circular or feminine attributes such as awareness listening, healing, empathy, commitment to the growth of others, and community building (Bray, 1982; Reynolds, 2014).

Second, the next three areas of the MPS' assessment dimensions—work motivation, career orientation, and dependency—relate to personal motivation and needs rather than the needs of others as embodied in servant-leadership's characteristics of stewardship, commitment to others' growth, and building community (Bray, 1982). Throughout MPS' 26 dimensions, listening, empathy, and healing are less noticeable yet were likely subtly present in the successful mentoring of future servant-leaders (Bray, 1982). For instance, in the case of oral and written communication skills in MPS, the goal was to convey information and thus persuade others rather than to articulate the element of listening with openness as a key element (Bray, 1982). After AT&T, Greenleaf further developed his understanding of the servant-leader. Therefore, we find it likely that the notions of listening, empathy, and healing were present to him but not yet fully articulated. For example, being that the six distinguishing characteristics of servant-leadership—the more feminine aspects of leadership (Reynolds, 2014)—are present but not specifically named in the MPS' assessment dimensions, we see Greenleaf's personal growth in later life lending to the growth of others in more unified and far-reaching ways. Greenleaf's later developments in servant-leadership, after he left the corporate environment, appear to have bloomed in the direction of the greater gender balance found in the 10 characteristics of servant-leadership.

As Bray (1982) pointed out, MPS has its own historical and social limitations, such as lack of representation by women and members of minority groups. Bray questioned whether the characteristics underlying their successful performance would be different from those for white males. Yes, Greenleaf's vision of servant-leadership was far ahead of his time; and yes, it was also bound by blind spots associated with the dominant white and male corporate culture of his day. The 10 characteristics

xxx   JIYING SONG AND SHANN RAY FERCH

that eventually showed the symbolic wholeness of servant-leadership as a more rounded and holistic female-honoring and male-honoring form of leadership are abstract principles, hard to measure, and even more difficult to embody. Greenleaf (2003) himself offered a practical example of a fictional character in his "Teacher as Servant." Through the story of Mr. Billings, Greenleaf portrayed a true servant-leader, who cares deeply about his students, nurtures the servant motive in them, and lives out his beliefs. Therefore, the quest to be a servant-leader, like the quest to be an authentic and whole person, sustains itself in the commitment to seek to understand life in all its mystery, abundance, and grace—tested in the furnace of human relations.

Crucial Discernment in Forgiveness

Greenleaf, in leading others to transcend the human furnace through listening and grace, through gentle strength and unique wisdom, was imperfect, a man with feet of clay, a devoted husband, father, and friend. He was not unlike the rest of us: imbued with gifts and faults. That said, he was, in the truest sense, a believer: one who believes. To believe in the betterment of humanity, to seek a greater good, there is a garment of praise that exists in order to relieve the spirit of despair; this garment, radiant, made by servant-leaders who are artisans of human compassion, authentic care, and legitimate power, is forgiveness. In his explication of Frost's (1947) poem "Directive," one of the very latest writings of his life, Greenleaf (1977/2002) again warns against the too rational mind:

> Those of us who undertake the journey must accept that, simply by living in the contemporary world and making our peace with it as it is, we may be involved in a way that blocks our growth. Primitive people may have suffered much from their environment, but they were not alienated; the Lascaux cave paintings attest to this. They probably did not articulate a theology, but they may have been religious in the basic sense of "bound to the cosmos." With us, sophistication, rationality, greater mastery of the immediate environment have taken their toll in terms of a tragic separation from the opportunity for religious experience, that is, growth in the feeling of being bound to the cosmos. (p. 330)

Greenleaf calls servant-leaders to follow wise people, guides who have in mind the opportunity to be lost, to lose oneself, in order to be found, in order to find oneself. Qualitative studies take us into the powerful gravity of human experience, laced as it is with losses beyond our comprehension, in order to gain greater compassion, greater fullness, and greater wholeness with others through forgiveness. Greenleaf (1977/2002) speaks beautifully of our need to be humble, to be willingly lost:

> We already feel lost. Why then would we want a guide who only has at heart our getting lost?
>
> This is the ground on which the great religious traditions of the world have always stood. The tradition built around the ministry of Jesus of Nazareth, the one in which I grew up and which has the greatest symbolic meaning to me now, seems especially emphatic on this point. Jesus seemed only to have at heart our getting lost; he was mostly concerned with what must be taken away rather than with what would be gained. We find clues to what must be lost in such sayings as "Unless you turn and become like children you will never enter the kingdom of heaven," "It is easier for a camel to go through the eye of a needle than for a rich man to enter the kingdom," "Cleanse the inside of the cup, that the outside also may be clean," and "Unless one is born anew, he cannot see the kingdom of God."
>
> A few general terms describe what will be received: heaven, eternal life, salvation, the kingdom of God. The believers of the literal word know what these terms mean; they have to. But seekers who are responding to symbols don't know, don't have to know, wouldn't be helped by knowing. They are not too interested in meaning as bounded by the vagaries of language. Rather they seek a guide who only has at heart their getting lost. (p. 331)

Those who lead us into a blessed sense of being lost—lost in love, lost in service to others—lead us to the kind of servant-leadership Greenleaf envisioned. Having escaped the ever-indulgent desires of ego, need, power, and ambition, we are free to be lost in the best sense of being lost.

Lost, we are found.

Greenleaf (1977/2002) reminds us that the journey is beautiful, and fraught with suffering. Servant-leaders are required to help guide us into the ultimate sense of what it means to forgive and be forgiven, and in so doing, to be a person who lives with and for others.

> To be on with the journey one must have an attitude toward loss and being lost, a view of oneself in which powerful symbols like *burned, dissolved, broken off*—however painful their impact is seen to be—do not appear as senseless or destructive. Rather the losses they suggest are seen as opening the way for new creative acts, for the receiving of priceless gifts. Loss, *every loss one's mind can conceive of*, creates a vacuum into which will come (if allowed) something new and fresh and beautiful, something unforeseen—and the greatest of these is *love*. (pp. 339–340; emphasis in original)

Notes

1. These 26 dimensions were described as 25 attributes in Bray, Campbell, and Grant (1974) because oral communication skill and written communication skill were combined as one attribute in Bray et al. (1974).

References

Bao, J. (1987). Yin yang xue shuo yu fu nv di wei [The idea of *yin-yang* and women's status in China]. *Han Xue Yan Jiu, 5*(2), 501–512. Retrieved from http://ccsdb.ncl.edu.tw/ccs/image/01_005_002_01_07.pdf.

Bartlett, C. A., & Ghoshal, S. (2002). Building competitive advantage through people. *MIT Sloan Management Review, 43*(2), 34–41.

Bray, D. W. (1982). The assessment center and the study of lives. *American Psychologist, 37*(2), 180–189.

Bray, D. W., Campbell, R. J., & Grant, D. L. (1974). *Formative years in business: A long-term AT&T study of managerial lives*. New York, NY: John Wiley & Sons.

Brouneus, K. (2007). Reconciliation and development. *Dialogue on Globalization* (Occasional paper no. 36), 3–19. Retrieved from http://library.fes.de/pdf-files/iez/04999.pdf

Campbell, A. (2017). Forgiveness and reconciliation as an organizational leadership competency within transitional justice instruments. *The International Journal of Servant-Leadership, 11*(1), 139–186.

Crotty, M. (1998). *The foundations of social research: Meaning and perspective in the research process*. London, England: Sage.

Denzin, N. K., & Lincoln, Y. S. (2011). Introduction: The discipline and practice of qualitative research. In N. K. Denzin & Y. S. Lincoln (Eds.), *The Sage handbook of qualitative research* (4th ed., pp. 1–20). Los Angeles, CA: Sage.

Eicher-Catt, D. (2005). The myth of servant-leadership: A feminist perspective. *Women and Language, 28*(1), 17–25.

Enright, R. D., Freedman, S., & Rique, J. (1998). The psychology of interpersonal forgiveness. In R. D. Enright & J. North (Eds.), *Exploring forgiveness* (pp. 46–62). Madison, WI: The University of Wisconsin Press.

Frick, D. M. (2004). *Robert K. Greenleaf: A life of servant leadership.* San Francisco, CA: Berrett-Koehler.

Frost, R. (1947). *Steeple bush.* New York, NY: Henry Holt and Company.

Gadamer, H. (1976). *Philosophical hermeneutics* (D. E. Linge, Ed. & Trans.). Berkeley, CA: University of California Press.

Gadamer, H. (2004). *Truth and method* (J. Weinsheimer & D. G. Marshall, Trans.). (2nd, rev. ed.). London, England: Continuum. (Original work published 1975).

Greenleaf, R. K. (2002). *Servant leadership: A journey into the nature of legitimate power and greatness* (25th anniversary ed.). L. C. Spears (Ed.). New York, NY: Paulist Press. (Original work published 1977).

Greenleaf, R. K. (2003). *The servant-leader within: A transformative path.* H. Beazley, J. Beggs, & L. C. Spears (Eds.). New York, NY: Paulist Press.

Heidegger, M. (1962). *Being and time* (J. Macquarrie & E. Robinson, Trans.). Malden, MA: Blackwell.

Hu, J., & Liden, R. C. (2011). Antecedents of team potency and team effectiveness: An examination of goal and process clarity and servant leadership. *Journal of Applied Psychology, 96*(4), 851–862. doi:10.1037/a0022465

Husserl, E. (1970). *The crisis of European sciences and transcendental phenomenology: An introduction to phenomenological philosophy* (D. Carr, Trans.). Evanston, IL: Northwestern University Press.

Lao Tzu. (2005). *Tao teh ching* (J. C. H. Wu, Ed. & Trans.). Boston, MA: Shambhala.

Liden, R. C., Fu, P., Liu, J., & Song, L. (2016). The influence of CEO values and leadership on middle manager exchange behaviors: A longitudinal multilevel examination. *Nankai Business Review International, 7*(1), 2–20. doi:10.1108/NBRI-12-2015-0031

Liden, R. C., Wayne, S. J., Liao, C., & Meuser, J. D. (2014). Servant leadership and serving culture: Influence on individual and unit performance. *Academy of Management Journal, 57*(5), 1434–1452. doi:10.5465/amj.2013.0034

Liden, R. C., Wayne, S. J., Meuser, J. D., Hu, J., Wu, J., & Liao, C. (2015). Servant leadership: Validation of a short form of the SL-28. *The Leadership Quarterly, 26*(2), 254–269. doi:10.1016/j.leaqua.2014.12.002

Liden, R. C., Wayne, S. J., Zhao, H., & Henderson, D. (2008). Servant leadership: Development of a multidimensional measure and multi-level assessment. *The Leadership Quarterly, 19*(2), 161–177. doi:10.1016/j.leaqua.2008.01.006

Lopez, K. A., & Willis, D. G. (2004). Descriptive versus interpretive phenomenology: Their contributions to nursing knowledge. *Qualitative Health Research, 14*(5), 726–735. doi:10.1177/1049732304263638

McCollum, J., & Moses, J. (2009). The management development legacy of Robert Greenleaf. *The International Journal of Servant-Leadership, 5*(1), 97–110.

Panaccio, A., Henderson, D. J., Liden, R. C., Wayne, S. J., & Cao, X. (2015). Toward an understanding of when and why servant leadership accounts for employee extra-role behaviors. *Journal of Business and Psychology, 30*(4), 657–675. doi:10.1007/s10869-014-9388-z

Ramsey, I. M. (2003). *The role of empathy in facilitating forgiveness: The lived experience of six political perpetrators in South Africa* (Doctoral dissertation). Retrieved from http://foley.gonzaga.edu/

Ramsey, I. M. (2006). Servant-leadership and unconditional forgiveness: The lives of six South African perpetrators. *The International Journal of Servant-Leadership, 2*(1), 113–139.

Reynolds, K. (2013). *Gender differences in messages of commencement addresses delivered by Fortune 1000 business leaders: A content analysis informed by servant-leadership and the feminist ethic of care* (Doctoral dissertation). Retrieved from http://foley.gonzaga.edu/

Reynolds, K. (2014). Servant-leadership: A feminist perspective. *The International Journal of Servant-Leadership, 10*(1), 35–63.

Ricoeur, P. (1981). *Hermeneutics and the human sciences: Essays on language, action, and interpretation* (J. B. Thompson, Ed. & Trans.). Cambridge, England: Cambridge University Press.

Shaffic, O. (Ed.). (2015). Forgiveness: Unveiling an asset for peacebuilding. Retrieved from http://refugeelawproject.org/files/others/Forgiveness_research_report.pdf

Sousa, M., & van Dierendonck, D. (2016). Introducing a short measure of shared servant leadership impacting team performance through team behavioral integration. *Frontiers in Psychology, 6*, 1–12. doi:10.3389/fpsyg.2015.02002

Sousa, M., & van Dierendonck, D. (2017a). Servant leaders as underestimators: Theoretical and practical implications. *Leadership & Organization Development Journal, 38*(2), 270–283. doi:10.1108/LODJ-10-2015-0236

Sousa, M., & van Dierendonck, D. (2017b). Servant leadership and the effect of the interaction between humility, action, and hierarchical power on follower engagement. *Journal of Business Ethics, 141*(1), 13–25. doi:10.1007/s10551-015-2725-y

Spears, L. C. (2002). Introduction: Tracing the past, present, and future of servant-leadership. In L. C. Spears & M. Lawrence (Eds.), *Focus on leadership: Servant-leadership for the twenty-first century* (pp. 1–16). New York, NY: Wiley.

Tutu, D. (1999). *No future without forgiveness.* New York, NY: Doubleday.

Unschuld, P. U., Tessenow, H., & Zheng, J. (Eds. & Trans.). (2011). *Huang Di nei jing su wen: An annotated translation of Huang Di's inner classic—basic questions* (Vol. 1). Berkeley, CA: University of California Press.

van Dierendonck, D., & Nuijten, I. (2011). The servant leadership survey: Development and validation of a multidimensional measure. *Journal of Business and Psychology, 26*(3), 249–267. doi:10.1007/s10869-010-9194-1

van Dierendonck, D., Sousa, M., Gunnarsdóttir, S., Bobbio, A., Hakanen, J., Pircher Verdorfer, A., . . . Rodriguez-Carvajal, R. (2017). The cross-cultural invariance of the servant leadership survey: A comparative study across eight countries. *Administrative Sciences, 7*(2), 1–11. doi:10.3390/admsci7020008

van Dierendonck, D., Stam, D., Boersma, P., de Windt, N., & Alkema, J. (2014). Same difference? Exploring the differential mechanisms linking servant leadership and transformational leadership to follower outcomes. *The Leadership Quarterly, 25*(3), 544–562. doi:10.1016/j.leaqua.2013.11.014

van Manen, M. (1990). *Researching lived experience: Human science for an action sensitive pedagogy*. Albany, NY: SUNY.

van Manen, M. (2016). *Phenomenology of practice*. London, England: Routledge.

Worthington, E. L. (2006). *Forgiveness and reconciliation: Theory and application*. New York, NY: Routledge.

Yergler, J. D. (2005). Servant leadership, justice and forgiveness. Retrieved from http://www.refresher.com/Archives/!jdyservant.html

Introduction: Love and Forgiveness

The Cornerstones of Servant-Leadership and Social Justice

DUNG Q. TRAN

Investigating the intersection of servant-leadership and forgiveness is an inherently humane and interdisciplinary endeavor. Although both concepts are paradoxically perplexing and painful processes, scholars, practitioners, and public intellectuals across many academic disciplines, art forms, organizational sectors, and wisdom traditions have examined each phenomenon (Blessinger & Stefani, 2018; La Caze, 2018; Rushdy, 2018; Selladurai & Carraher, 2014; Voiss, 2015). While the broad array of insights on servant-leadership and forgiveness has furnished a vast and varied corpus of perspectives, it has also generated conceptual confusion and ambiguity (Eva et al., 2019; Letizia, 2018; Smith, 2017; van Dierendonck, 2011).

Despite this perceived limitation, "The large metropolis of the human sciences exposes its inhabitants to opportunities of exotic travel" (van Manen, 2014, p. 13). On behalf of this anthology's diverse tapestry of thought partners, we thank you for the opportunity to explore with you the canyons of the complex yet interconnected human phenomena of servant-leadership and forgiveness. We hope (y)our travels take you to new and uncharted territories that disturb, awaken, and hopefully heal your heart and, in turn, the heart of humanity.

In their book *Love and Forgiveness for a More Just World*, noted humanities scholars, Hent de Vries and Nils Schott (2015) highlighted the importance of innovating enduring ideas: "In an age of ever exponentially

1

expanding economic markets and technological media, in which exchange and information, commerce and communication form the real currency of the day, novel approaches to old concepts and practices become more and more operative . . . [and] necessary" (p. 7). Exacerbated by the economic and technocratic paradigms of our era are myriad insidious and systemic social ills that have consumed our world (Francis, 2015). They include widespread poverty, homelessness, mental illness, emboldened racism, sectarian violence, environmental degradation, ethical scandals, political polarization, cyberbullying, the sexual abuse of minors, and so much more. Reflecting on these realities from the intellectual vista of leadership studies, it is our view that every planetary creature has a vested interest in the development of a more innovative and comprehensive understanding of servant-leadership and forgiveness. These life-affirming ways of becoming more fully alive "go hand in hand" (Ferch, 2012, p. 7) and belong to the same family as joy, wisdom, and love (Ricoeur, 2006). Underscoring the urgency for further investigation of the intersecting and "interconnected issues" (Griswold, 2010, p. 547), Martin Luther King, Jr. (1963/2010) contended, "We must develop and maintain the capacity to forgive. [The one] who is devoid of the power to forgive is devoid of the power to love" (p. 44).

Although a relatively unknown figure, Cardinal Francis Xavier Nguyen Van Thuan (1928–2002), a nephew of the slain South Vietnamese president Ngo Dinh Diem (1901–1963), is one exemplary servant-leader, among many others, who concretized King's call to (re)develop and (re)discover the capacity to forgive and love within the isolating confines of a damp, windowless, and narrow prison cell (Nguyen, 2003). Following the Fall of Saigon in 1975, then Archbishop Thuan was arrested by the Vietnamese government and subsequently held without trial for thirteen years, including nine years spent in solitary confinement (Nguyen, 2001).

Although Thuan was a Catholic leader who believed in the notion of (Christian) forgiveness, prior to his arrest and imprisonment, Thuan found it difficult to forgive those who had murdered five members of his family during the Vietnam conflict (Keith, 2008; Taylor, 2013). As Nguyen (2003) noted, Thuan "was full of bitterness" and "his heart felt closed to such an act of forgiveness" (p. 83). However, during the darkest days of his captivity, which included interrogation, torture, and isolation, Thuan heard a mysterious voice from within urging him to "distinguish between God and the works of God" (Nguyen, 2000, p. 42). He suddenly realized "that even if he could not do God's work, he could still love God, and that loving God was more important than loving God's work" (Nguyen, 2003, p. 207). It was a moment of clarity—a "transforming revelation . . . [that] loving God was the most important thing in his life, and no one could take that away from him. No prison cell could ever isolate him from God" (p. 207).

Thuan gradually realized that his mission as a servant-leader was no longer limited to the people of a particular geographical territory: "Yes, Lord, you are sending me here to be your love among my brothers, in the midst of hunger, cold, exhausting labor, humiliation, [and] injustice. I choose you; your will; I am your missionary here" (Nguyen, 1997/2003, p. 20). Eventually, Thuan discovered that despite his unjust treatment, he was being called "to transmit a message of love, in serenity and truth, in forgiveness and reconciliation" (p. 3).

However, "not all people have experienced the abiding loveliness of being welcomed back to community after having gravely wronged others" (Ferch, 2012, p. 71). Thuan's guards were among these, and they constantly questioned the sincerity of his love. Despite Thuan's reassuring responses, the guards refused to believe him: "Even when we have treated you so badly? When you have suffered in prison for so many years without ever having a trial?" (Nguyen, 1997/2003, p. 53). Thuan's captors could not conceive of such a possibility. Appealing to their lived experience, Thuan said, "Think about the years we have been here together. You have seen for yourselves that it's true. I really love you" (p. 53). Unconvinced, they inquired, "When you are freed you won't try to take revenge on us or our families?" (p. 53). Thuan replied, "No[,] I will continue loving you, even if you want to kill me" (p. 53). When asked why, Thuan offered the following response: "Because Jesus has taught me to love you; if I do not, I am no longer worthy of being called a Christian" (p. 54).

As evidenced by the preceding conversation between Cardinal Francis Xavier Nguyen Van Thuan and his captors,

> dialogue cannot exist . . . in the absence of profound love for the world and for people. The naming of the world, which is an act of creation and re-creation, is not possible if it is not infused with love. Love is at the same time the foundation of dialogue and dialogue itself. . . . Because love is an act of courage, not of fear, love is a commitment to others. . . . If

> I do not love the world—if I do not love life—if I do not
> love people—I cannot enter into dialogue. (Freire, 1970/2018,
> pp. 90–91)

For both Cardinal Thuan and Paulo Freire, love is more than a "senti-mental exchange between people, but rather love constitutes an intentional spirit of consciousness that emerges and matures through our social and material practices, as we work to live, learn, and labor together" (Darder, 2017, p. 96). As van Dierendonck and Patterson (2015) postulated, there is a "deep connection between servant leadership and compassionate love" (p. 128) that results in an outgrowth that includes forgiveness. Consequently, the world would discover that the lessons Thuan learned about love and forgiveness in prison would form, inform, and ultimately transform his spiritual life, and serve as the cornerstones of his global servant-leadership.

Following his release in 1988, Francis Xavier Nguyen Van Thuan was permanently exiled from Vietnam in 1991. Given his newfound availability, compelling story, and leadership potential, Pope John Paul II named Thuan a cardinal and appointed him vice president (1994–1998) and then president (1998–2002) of the Pontifical Council for Justice and Peace (Nguyen, 2003). This Vatican committee is charged with collecting "information and research on justice and peace, about human development and violations of human rights," and cultivating partnerships with international organizations that "strive to achieve peace and justice in the world" (John Paul II, 1988, Article 143, #2).

For consequential thought leaders such as Cardinal Francis Xavier Nguyen Van Thuan, Paulo Freire, bell hooks, Martin Luther King Jr., Robert Greenleaf, and many others, the theory and practice of servant-leadership and forgiveness is more than just an endeavor toward the healing of an individual, an organization, or a society. A servant-led way of life characterized by a compassionate ethic of love and forgiveness can evolve human consciousness toward the common good and contribute to the fashioning of a more just, humane, and sustainable world (Boyle, 2017; Ferch, 2012; Freire, 1970/2018; hooks, 2000).

References

Blessinger, P., & Stefani, L. (2018). Inclusive leadership in higher education: International perspectives and approaches. In L. Stefani & P. Blessinger (Eds.),

Inclusive leadership in higher education: International perspectives and approaches (pp. 1–13). New York, NY: Routledge.

Boyle, G. (2017). *Barking to the choir: The power of radical kinship.* New York, NY: Simon & Schuster.

Darder, A. (2017). Pedagogy of love: Embodying our humanity. In A. Darder, R. D. Torres, & M. P. Baltodano (Eds.), *The critical pedagogy reader* (pp. 95–109). New York, NY: Routledge.

De Vries, H., & Schott, N. F. (Eds.). (2015). *Love and forgiveness for a more just world.* New York, NY: Columbia University Press.

Eva, N., Robin, M., Sendjaya, S., van Dierendonck, D., & Liden, R. C. (2019). Servant leadership: A systematic review and call for future research. *Leadership Quarterly, 30,* 111–132.

Ferch, S. R. (2012). *Forgiveness and power in the age of atrocity: Servant-leadership as a way of life.* Lanham, MD: Lexington Books.

Francis. (2015). *Laudato Si'.* Retrieved from http://w2.vatican.va/content/francesco/en/encyclicals/documents/papa-francesco_20150524_enciclica-laudato-si.html#_ftn90

Freire, P. (2018). *Pedagogy of the oppressed.* (M. B. Ramos, Trans.). (50th Anniversary ed.). New York, NY: Bloomsbury. (Original work published 1970).

Griswold, C. L. (2010). Debating forgiveness: A reply to my critics. *Philosophia, 38,* 457–473.

hooks, b. (2000). *All about love: New visions.* New York, NY: Perennial.

John Paul II (1988). *Apostolic constitution: Pastor bonus.* Retrieved from http://www.vatican.va/holy_father/john_paul_ii/apost_constitutions/documents/hf_jp-ii_apc_19880628_pastor-bonus-index_en.html

Keith, C. (2008). *Catholic Vietnam: Church, colonialism, and revolution, 1887–1945* (Unpublished doctoral dissertation). Yale University, New Haven, CT.

King, Jr., M. L. (2010). *Strength to love.* Minneapolis, MN: Fortress Press. (Original work published 1963).

La Caze, M. (Ed.). (2018). *Phenomenology and forgiveness.* Lanham, MD: Rowman & Littlefield.

Letizia, A. J. (2018). *Using servant leadership: How to reframe core functions of higher education.* New Brunswick, NJ: Rutgers University Press.

Nguyen, A. C. V. (2003). *The miracle of hope: Life of Francis Xavier Nguyễn Văn Thuận, political prisoner, prophet of peace.* Boston, MA: Pauline Books & Media.

Nguyen, F. X. T. V. (2000). *Testimony of hope: The spiritual exercises of John Paul II.* (J. M. Darrenkamp, F. S. P. & A. E. Heffernan, F. S. P., Trans.). Boston, MA: Pauline Books & Media.

Nguyen, F. X. T. V. (2001). *The road of hope: A gospel from prison.* (P. Bookallil, Trans.). Boston, MA: Pauline Books & Media.

Nguyen, F. X. T. V. (2003). *Five loaves and two fish.* (Tinvui Media, Trans.). Boston, MA: Pauline Books & Media. (Original work published 1997).

Ricoeur, P. (2006). *Memory, history, forgetting.* (K. Blamey & D. Pellauer, Trans.). Chicago, IL: University of Chicago Press.

Rushdy, A. H. (2018). *After injury: A historical anatomy of forgiveness, resentment, and apology.* New York, NY: Oxford University Press.

Selladurai, R., & Carraher, S. (Eds.). (2014). *Servant leadership: Research and practice.* Hershey, PA: Business Science Reference.

Smith, S. L. (2017). Forgiveness. In R. Koonce, P. Robinson, & B. Vogel (Eds.), *Developing leaders for positive organizing: A 21st century repertoire for leading in extraordinary times* (pp. 121–134). Bingley, UK: Emerald Publishing.

Taylor, K. W. (2013). *A history of the Vietnamese.* New York, NY: Cambridge University Press.

van Dierendonck, D. (2011). Servant-leadership: A review and synthesis. *Journal of Management, 37*(4), 1228–1261.

van Dierendonck, D., & Patterson, K. (2015). Compassionate love as a cornerstone of servant leadership: An integration of previous theorizing and research. *Journal of Business Ethics, 128*(1), 119–131.

van Manen, M. (2014). *Phenomenology of practice.* Walnut Creek, CA: Left Coast Press.

Voiss, J. K. (2015). *Rethinking Christian forgiveness: Theological, philosophical, and psychological explorations.* Collegeville, MN: Liturgical Press.

Part I

Servant-Leadership, Forgiveness, and World Context

Chapter 1

Awareness, Healing, and Forgiveness

Servant-Leaders Help Heal the Heart of the World

JIYING SONG

Servant-leadership was not a leadership theory developed through empirical studies but a philosophy of life first articulated by Robert Greenleaf (1904–1990) (Beazley, 2003). Scholars and writers have criticized servant-leadership as soft (Ebener, 2011; Nayab, 2011) and lacking a coherent conceptual framework (Eicher-Catt, 2005), as an integrated theoretical development (van Dierendonck, 2011), and as empirical support (Northouse, 2016). In response to these critiques and public interest, some scholars and writers have organized servant-leadership into a variety of elements: characteristics (Liden, Panaccio, Meuser, Hu, & Wayne, 2014; Spears, 2002), behaviors (Liden et al., 2014), pillars (Sipe & Frick, 2009), dimensions (van Dierendonck & Nuijten, 2011), practices (Keith, 2008), attributes (Russell & Stone, 2002), subscales (Barbuto & Wheeler, 2006), subscores (Laub, 1999), and virtues (Patterson, 2003). Furthermore, Laub (1999), Liden et al. (2014), Patterson (2003), Russell and Stone (2002), and van Dierendonck (2011) have proposed theoretical models for servant-leadership.

However, these models have not fully addressed three characteristics of servant-leadership: awareness, healing, and forgiveness. The importance of awareness cannot be denied in Greenleaf's (1966, 1996a, 2002, 2003) writings. When one is intensively aware, foresight and serving others become possible (Greenleaf, 2002). In addition, healing has been underappreciated in leadership (Barbuto & Wheeler, 2006); it is "the most rare and perhaps the most needed characteristic of leaders today" (Ferch, 2012, p. xi). Furthermore, forgiveness serves as an indispensable part of developing the kind of wisdom, freedom, autonomy, and health espoused by Greenleaf (Ferch, 2004). The significance of this chapter is to address a deficit in the literature; to add to the understanding of the concepts of awareness, healing, and forgiveness; and to build a theoretical model of servant-leadership. In this chapter, I will review (a) the concept of servant-leadership, (b) the 10 characteristics of servant-leadership, (c) servant-leadership and awareness, and (d) servant-leadership, healing, and forgiveness. I conclude that awareness, healing, and forgiveness are essential leading practices for servant-leaders. This chapter ends with a servant-leadership model developed through literature review.

The Concept of Servant-Leadership

Servant-leadership is not a new idea. In ancient China, the best leader was regarded as the least visible and least wordy. As Lao Tzu (2005) said, the best leader is "one of whose existence the people are barely aware . . . self-effacing and scanty of words. When his task is accomplished and things have been completed, all the people say, 'We ourselves have achieved it!'" (p. 35). Servant-leaders are not leaders who stand over people and control them but servants who keep their feet on the ground and benefit all things. Thus Lao Tzu said,

> The highest form of goodness is like water.
> Water knows how to benefit all things without striving with them.
> It stays in places loathed by all men.
> Therefore, it comes near the Tao.
> In choosing your dwelling, know how to keep to the ground.
> In cultivating your mind, know how to dive in the hidden deeps.
> In dealing with others, know how to be gentle and kind.
> In speaking, know how to keep your words.
> In governing, know how to maintain order.
> In transacting business, know how to be efficient.
> In making a move, know how to choose the right moment.
> If you do not strive with others,
> You will be free from blame. (p. 17)

With this same spirit of servant-leadership, Jesus said to his disciples,

> You know that among the Gentiles those whom they recognize as their rulers lord it over them, and their great ones are tyrants over them. But it is not so among you; but whoever wishes to become great among you must be your servant, and whoever wishes to be first among you must be slave of all. For the Son of Man came not to be served but to serve, and to give his life a ransom for many (Mark 10:42–45, *New Revised Standard Version*).

As the son of God, Jesus emptied himself and took the form of a servant (Philippians 2:6–7). Preaching the kingdom of his father, Jesus led the way as a teacher, a sage, and a servant (Morse, 2008).

Sun Yat-sen (孙中山, 1866–1925) is the forerunner of the Democratic Revolution in China and the founding father of the Republic of China. He proposed the concept of *public servants* (公仆) (Sun, 1927), which is still widely used in China today. In the old days of the autocracy, an official was the servant of the monarch but the master of the rest of the people; after the Revolution of 1911, "the people has become its own master and lord, and the officials should be the servants of the people" (p. 165). Sun claimed, "The State officials, beginning with the President and ending with an ordinary sentry, are all *public servants*" (pp. 136–137; emphasis added).

Robert K. Greenleaf was a Quaker thinker and servant-leader. When he retired from his career as director of management research at AT&T, he founded the Center for Applied Ethics in 1964 and devoted his life to leadership studies. In 1970, he published "The Servant as Leader," a landmark essay that included the phrase "servant-leader" (for original 1970 edition, see Greenleaf, 2003). Drawing from his experiential leadership practice and deep Quaker spirituality, he coined the term *servant-leadership* and defined it as follows: "The servant-leader *is* servant first. . . . It begins with the natural feeling that one wants to serve, to serve *first*. Then conscious choice brings one to aspire to lead. That person is sharply different from one who is *leader* first" (Greenleaf, 2002, p. 27; emphasis in original). With regard to discernment of a servant-leader, Greenleaf writes,

> Do those served grow as persons? Do they, *while being served*, become healthier, wiser, freer, more autonomous, more likely

themselves to become servants? *And*, what is the effect on the least privileged in society; will they benefit, or, at least, not be further deprived? (p. 27; emphasis in original)

The Center for Applied Ethics changed its name to Greenleaf Center for Servant Leadership in 1985. In 1990, Larry Spears was named CEO of the Greenleaf Center, and he visited Greenleaf eight days before he died. One year later, Spears discovered the existence of Greenleaf's unpublished writings and established a committee to read through them. In 1992, Spears identified the 10 most frequently mentioned characteristics of servant-leadership by Greenleaf. Since then, Spears has devoted his life to introducing Greenleaf's writings to the public (Spears Center for Servant-Leadership, 2018).

Greenleaf's concept of servant-leadership is neither a set of procedures on how to lead well nor a quick-fix method but "a state of mind, a philosophy of life, a way of being" (Beazley, 2003, p. 10). Thus, it is necessary to bridge the gap between the philosophy and the practice of servant-leadership. Greenleaf (2003) himself offered a practical example of a fictional character in his "Teacher as Servant." Through the story of Mr. Billings, Greenleaf portrayed a true servant-leader, who cares deeply about his students, nurtures the servant motive in them, and lives out his beliefs. In order to teach servant-leadership, leaders, scholars, and researchers have offered various characteristics, formulations, or models of servant-leadership. Through my literature review, I provide a summary of these contributions in table 1.1. This is not an exhaustive summary. For more information, please see Eva et al. (2018), Laub (1999), van Dierendonck (2011), and Wong (2015).

As shown in table 1.1, authors have chosen to describe servant-leadership from different angles: characteristics (Liden et al., 2014; Spears, 2002), behaviors (Liden et al., 2014), pillars (Sipe & Frick, 2009), dimensions (van Dierendonck & Nuijten, 2011), practices (Keith, 2008), attributes (Russell & Stone, 2002), subscales (Barbuto & Wheeler, 2006), subscores (Laub, 1999), and virtuous constructs (Patterson, 2003). All of these authors broke servant-leadership into smaller elements to demonstrate or measure the components of this leadership style. For example, through their literature review, Russell and Stone (2002) provided a theoretical model of servant-leadership with values as independent variables, nine functional attributes as dependent variables, and 11 accompanying attri-

Table 1.1. Servant-Leadership Studies and Models

Contributors	Element	Theoretical Models	Research
Laub, 1999	Subscores: • Develops people • Shares leadership • Displays authenticity • Values people • Provides leadership • Builds community (including healing in the prefield test)	Laub, 1999	Quantitative: Laub, 1999
Russell & Stone, 2002	Functional attributes: • Vision • Honesty • Integrity • Trust • Service • Modeling • Pioneering • Appreciation of others • Empowerment Accompanying attributes: • Communication • Credibility • Competence • Stewardship • Visibility • Influence • Persuasion • Listening • Encouragement • Teaching • Delegation	Russell & Stone, 2002	Quantitative: design with variables: Russell & Stone, 2002

continued on next page

Table 1.1. Continued.

Contributors	Element	Theoretical Models	Research
Spears, 2002	Characteristics: • Listening • Empathy • Healing • Awareness • Persuasion • Conceptualization • Foresight • Stewardship • Commitment to the growth of people • Building community		Qualitative: Ebbrecht & Martin, 2017; Mixed-method: Chan, 2017
Patterson, 2003	Virtuous constructs • Agapao love • Humility • Altruism • Vision • Trust • Empowerment • Service	Patterson, 2003	
Barbuto & Wheeler, 2006	Subscales: • Altruistic calling • Emotional healing • Persuasive mapping • Organizational stewardship • Wisdom (including awareness)		Quantitative: Barbuto & Wheeler, 2006
Keith, 2008	Key Practices: • Self-awareness • Listening • Changing the pyramid • Developing your colleagues • Coaching not controlling • Unleashing the energy and intelligence of others • Foresight		

Contributors	Element	Theoretical Models	Research
Sipe & Frick, 2009	Pillars: • Person of character • Puts people first • Skilled communicator • Compassionate collaborator • Foresight • Systems thinker • Moral authority		Qualitative: Caldwell & Crippen, 2017; James, 2017
van Dierendonck, & Nuijten, 2011	Dimensions: • Empowerment • Humility • Standing back • Authenticity • Forgiveness • Courage • Accountability • Stewardship	van Dierendonck, 2011	Quantitative: van Dierendonck & Nuijten, 2011
Liden et al., 2014	Characteristics: • Desire to serve others • Emotional intelligence • Moral maturity and conation • Prosocial identity • Core self-evaluation • (Low) narcissism Behaviors: • Empowering • Helping subordinates grow and succeed • Putting subordinates first • Emotional healing • Conceptual skills • Creating value for the community • Behaving ethically	Liden et al., 2014	Quantitative: Liden et al., 2008

Source: Song, 2018.

butes as moderating variables. They hoped to offer a structural foundation for future research. As van Dierendonck (2011) pointed out, the biggest problem of their model is the lack of differentiation between functional attributes and accompanying attributes. Van Dierendonck and Nuijten (2011) identified 99 items to measure servant-leadership. Through factor analysis with eight samples totaling 1,571 individuals from the Netherlands and the United Kingdom, they developed the Servant Leadership Survey with an eight-dimensional measure of 30 items.

In total, five groups of writers have theorized about servant-leadership and established theoretical models (Laub, 1999; Liden et al., 2014; Patterson, 2003; Russell & Stone, 2002; van Dierendonck, 2011). Most of these servant-leadership formulations and models are designed or employed for quantitative research (Barbuto & Wheeler, 2006; Laub, 1999; Liden et al., 2008; Russell & Stone, 2002; van Dierendonck & Nuijten, 2011). Some qualitative studies are built upon Sipe and Frick's (2009) seven pillars (Caldwell & Crippen, 2017; James, 2017) and Spears's (2002) 10 characteristics (Ebbrecht & Martin, 2017). Chan (2017) employed mixed-methods study and analyzed her data through Spears's (2002) 10 characteristics of servant-leadership.

Servant-leadership research has also been done in China. In their study of antecedents of team potency and team effectiveness, Hu and Liden (2011) employed Liden et al.'s (2008) formulation to measure servant-leadership. Through the survey study with 304 employees from five banks in China, the authors found that team goal clarity, process clarity, and team servant-leadership serve as three antecedents of team potency and team effectiveness; meanwhile, servant-leadership moderates the relationship between goal clarity and team potency, and the relationship between process clarity and team potency. In addition, using data from a survey of 239 civil servants in China, Miao, Newman, Schwarz, and Xu (2014) found that servant-leadership leads to an increase in officials' affective commitment and normative commitment. Furthermore, Chan (2017) conducted a mixed-methods study in a Hong Kong K–12 school and concluded that the practices of servant-leadership by teachers meet the needs of the learners.

Some writers noted in table 1.1 touched on the topics of awareness and healing: Laub (1999) and Liden et al. (2008, 2014) mentioned healing; Keith (2008) discussed self-awareness; and Barbuto and Wheeler (2006) included both but merged awareness into wisdom. Spears (2002) presented both awareness and healing as two of 10 main characteristics of servant-leadership. Only van Dierendonck and Nuijten (2011) included forgiveness as one of their servant-leadership dimensions. I will explore Spears's 10 characteristics of servant-leadership in the next section, and this will be followed by a discussion of awareness, healing, and forgiveness.

The Ten Characteristics of Servant-Leadership

Based on Greenleaf's writings, Spears (2002) has identified ten character-istics of a servant-leader. Servant-leadership is not new to Chinese culture, and neither are these characteristics. Yet at different times in history they have been more or less popular.

Listening. In Chinese culture, hierarchy is highly valued, and people usually do not challenge their leaders. According to traditional leadership paradigms, leaders are persuaders and decision makers. Leaders have to talk and others have to listen. This stands in stark contrast to ancient China, when it was praiseworthy for the king to "listen to the representations of all in the kingdom" (Legge, 1893, p. 184).[1] Although communication is an important skill for servant-leaders, "intense and sustained listening" (Greenleaf, 2002, p. 235) is even more important because "true listening builds strength in other people" (p. 31) and can help people find that "wholeness . . . only achieved by serving" (p. 235). Servant-leaders listen not only to what is being said and unsaid but also to their inner voices (Spears, 2010). They often ask, "Are we really listening?"

Empathy. While having empathy for others, many Chinese leaders view pointing out their members' mistakes as one way to help them grow. I would argue that improvement will be better achieved if it is not done at the price of acceptance. Empathy interwoven with acceptance is the opposite of rejection (Greenleaf, 2002). There are no perfect people for us to lead, and leaders are far from perfect themselves. Servant-leaders lead wisely and distinguish between people and their performance. "People grow taller when those who lead them empathize and when they are accepted for what they are" (p. 35). Servant-leaders demonstrate empathy, understanding, and tolerance for imperfection, because it is part of our human condition (Williams, 2002).

Healing. Spears (2010) proclaimed, "One of the great strengths of servant leadership is the potential for healing one's self and one's relationship to others" (p. 27). At first glance, it might seem as if healing has nothing to do with leadership, especially in organizations with profit as their sole goal. Also, the idea of healing is challenging for Chinese leaders, because according to traditional leadership, leaders are not supposed to bring emotions into their work, so that they can be objective. But if leadership is construed as happening among people within socially constructed settings, it becomes clear that the background of leadership is broken or imperfect people coming together and searching for wholeness, for oneness, and for rightness (Greenleaf, 1998). Servant-leaders see the impediments in organizations as "illness," and they enter the relationship to heal rather than to change or correct (Greenleaf, 1996b, p. 92). As healers, they lead toward the healing of themselves and others, because all humans share the search for wholeness (Greenleaf, 2002). Forgiveness, as an essential component of healing (Ferch, 2000, 2012; Fitzgibbons, 1998; Hope, 1987; North, 1987, 1998; Ramsey, 2003), challenges servant-leaders to forgive and to ask forgiveness.

Awareness. Both awareness of the situation and self-awareness strengthen servant-leaders (Spears, 2010). Lao Tzu (2005) praised self-awareness: "He [or She] who knows [people] is clever; He [or She] who knows himself [or herself] has insight. He [or She] who conquers [people] has force; He [or She] who conquers himself [or herself] is truly strong" (p. 67). The losses we sustain and the errors we have inherited from our culture, our own experience, and our learning block our conscious access to our awareness (Friedman, 2007; Greenleaf, 2002; Scazzero & Bird, 2003). Awareness is tricky. While it is easy for us to believe that we are aware, deep in our belief system or stereotypical framework lie assumptions that even we do not know. "We do not see the world around us. We see the world we are prepared to see" (Greenleaf, 2002, p. 354). Some leaders tend to tightly control their perceptions and emotions so that they can make the "right" decision without being emotionally moved. Servant-leaders build up their tolerance for awareness and "take the risks of being moved" (Greenleaf, 2002, p. 329). They are brave enough to widen their awareness so that they can make more intense and meaningful contact with their situation (Greenleaf, 1998).

Persuasion. In a hierarchical culture, leaders often wield power through position, in order to enforce their decisions. However, in ancient China,

Confucius (2014) said, "A ruler who has rectified himself [or herself] never gives orders, and all goes well. A ruler who has not rectified himself [or herself] gives orders, and the people never follow them" (p. 101). Servant-leaders persuade through word and deed rather than by positional authority. They surrender their positional authority and seek to persuade people by role-modeling and "gentle non-judgmental argument" (Greenleaf, 2002, p. 43).

Conceptualization. Conceptual thinking is based on day-to-day realities yet goes far beyond them. In recent years, many Western management theories have become popular in China without contextualization (Chen, 2008). While some able leaders have moved into different roles, they are prone to "make any position fit one's habitual way of working" (Greenleaf, 2002, p. 81). Leaders with the ability for conceptualization should not be overtaken either by popular management theories or their own habits. Servant-leaders are not consumed by the needs of short-term operational goals but strive to provide visionary and suitable concepts for an organization (Spears, 2010). Conceptualization requires servant-leaders' love for the people, clear vision for the future, long-term dedication, and well-communicated faith in people's worth (Greenleaf, 2002).

Foresight. "If things far away don't concern you, you'll soon mourn things close at hand" (Confucius, 2014, p. 121). Foresight requires a leader to live at two levels of consciousness—the real world and the detached one (Greenleaf, 2002). "Foresight is the 'lead' that the leader has" (p. 40). A lack of foresight in the past may result in an unethical action in the present (Greenleaf, 2002). Foresight enables servant-leaders to understand the lessons from the past, see and rise above the events in the present, and foresee the consequences of a decision for the indefinite future (Greenleaf, 2002; Spears, 2010). Since ancient times, foresight has been recognized as the most important virtue for leaders in China. Chinese historian Sima (1993) wrote between approximately 145 BCE and 86 BCE, "An enlightened [person] sees the end of things while they are still in bud, and a wise [person] knows how to avoid danger before it has taken shape" (p. 294).

Stewardship. The understanding of stewardship disarms the will to misappropriate power because stewardship reminds leaders that we are here to serve others instead of seizing power to pursue our own benefits. Servant-leaders, like stewards, assume "first and foremost a commitment to serving the needs of others" (Spears, 2010, p. 29). Hsü (2005) regarded political stewardship as an integral part of Confucianism. In ancient China, when Emperor Yao chose Shun to sit on the throne, he reminded Shun that Shun was the steward of Heaven (Hsü, 2005).

Commitment to the growth of people. Emperor Yao said to Shun, "If you let this land of the four seas fall into poverty and desperation, the gift of Heaven is lost forever" (Confucius, 2014, p. 151). This is an admonition regarding the commitment to the benefit of people. Today, however, under the influence of capitalism, leaders tend to use all resources to maximize the benefits for the organization, and at times for themselves. People have been treated as resources—as cogs and wheels. In contrast, servant-leaders commit to the growth of each individual within the organization. They help individuals to develop their personal and professional skills, give them opportunities to practice their learning, invite them into decision making, and assist laid-off employees (Spears, 2010).

Building community. Confucianism emphasizes community and has defined the societal realm for Chinese people over the millennia. One of the disciples of Confucius said, "The most precious fruit of Ritual is harmony" (Confucius, 2014, p. 22). For Tutu (1998), the harmony of the group is an essential attribute of community because "a person is a person through other persons" (p. 19). According to Greenleaf (2002), building community requires servant-leaders to demonstrate their own "unlimited liability for a quite specific community-related group" (p. 53). Community is experienced as a real home of love, a healing shelter, a place where trust and respect can be found and learned, and a kind of power that can lift people up and help them grow (Greenleaf, 2002).

Next we will focus on the concepts of awareness, healing, and forgiveness within the framework of servant-leadership.

Servant-Leadership and Awareness

Many people think servant-leadership is a soft leadership style (Ebener, 2011; Nayab, 2011); however, Greenleaf regarded servant-leaders as "functionally superior" because they must be fully human and grounded so that they hear, see, and know things (Greenleaf, 2003, p. 66). Their doors of perception are wide open; they are aware of themselves, others, relationships, and situations.

Barbuto and Wheeler (2006) collected data from 80 American community leaders and 388 colleagues or employees of these leaders. Through factor analyses, they reduced 11 potential servant-leadership characteristics to five unique subscales. One of these, wisdom, is understood as the combination of awareness and foresight. They measured wisdom through five items in their questionnaire: being alert to what is happening (awareness of the situation), having great awareness of what is going on (awareness of the situation), being in touch with what is happening (awareness of the situation), being good at anticipating the consequences of decisions (foresight), and knowing what is going to happen (foresight).

In addition, Keith (2008) proposed self-awareness as one of the key practices of servant-leaders: servant-leaders should be aware of their strengths and weaknesses, and of the impact of their words, deeds, and moods; self-awareness arises from reflection. Butler, Kwantes, and Boglarsky (2014) studied the effects of self-awareness on perceptions of leadership effectiveness in the hospitality industry. They collected survey data from 696 managers of an international hotel chain, and each manager selected three to five other individuals to complete a description of their leadership. The researchers concluded that self-awareness results in increased perceptions of leadership effectiveness.

The word *aware* has two main meanings in the *Oxford English Dictionary* (*OED*): "watchful, vigilant, cautious, on one's guard" and "informed, cognizant, conscious, sensible" ("Aware," 2017). Therefore *to be aware of* can be "to be on one's guard against" or "to know" ("Aware," 2017). In "The Servant as Leader," Greenleaf (2002) said, "When one is aware, there is more than the usual alertness, more intense contact with the immediate situation, and more is stored away in the unconscious computer to produce intuitive insights in the future when needed" (p. 41). Greenleaf built his concept of awareness on the first meaning of *aware* in the *OED*. He also linked awareness to foresight (Greenleaf, 1966, 1996a, 1996b, 2002).

In the *OED*, *awareness* is defined as consciousness ("Awareness," 2017). Consciousness is always consciousness of something or an object (Husserl, 1983). The awareness of a servant-leader, as a vigilant type of consciousness, can be aware of self, others, relations, spirit, situation, and time. Thus I propose four conceptual dimensions of awareness: (a) upwardness—spirit-awareness; (b) inwardness—self-awareness; (c) outwardness—

other-awareness, relation-awareness, and situation-awareness; and (d) onwardness—time-awareness.

Parker Palmer (1998) emphasized the importance of a leader's self-awareness: a leader "must take special responsibility for what's going on inside his or her own self, inside his or her consciousness, lest the act of leadership create more harm than good" (p. 200). Outward awareness moves a leader toward stewardship, which includes persuading people through word and deed, committing to the growth of people, and building community. The awareness of time lies in every dimension of awareness, with the awareness of the future transitioning into the domain of fore-sight. This point of view does not separate time into discrete sections but regards it as a process. The progressing events move from the past to the present and into the future. Awareness of the future requires us to nurture the awareness of the past and the present (Greenleaf, 1996a). A leader with awareness sees himself or herself as being "in the center of a time span that extends back into the past and forward into the future" (Greenleaf, 1966, p. 28).

Greenleaf (2003) believed that the growth of entheos in a person can lead to awareness. By *entheos*, Greenleaf meant "the power actuating one who is inspired" (p. 118). *Entheos* was originally a Greek word, ἔνθεος, which literally means "in God." *The Oxford English Dictionary* defines it as "an indwelling divine power" and "inspiration" ("Entheos," 2017). It is in the center of upward awareness. Greenleaf (2003) suggested six misleading indicators of the growth of entheos: "status or material success," "social success," "doing all that is expected of one," "family success," "relative peace and quiet," and "compulsive business" (pp. 118–119). Furthermore, he pointed out eight valid indicators of the growth of entheos: "a concurrent feeling of broadening responsibilities and centering down," "a growing sense of purpose in whatever one does," "changing patterns and depths of one's interests," "the minimum of difference between the outside and inside images of the self," "conscious of the good use of time and unhappy with the waste of time," "achieving one's basic personal goals through one's work," "a sense of unity," and "a developing view of people" (pp. 119–121). In short, the ultimate test of entheos is "an intuitive feeling of oneness, of wholeness, of rightness" (p. 121).

I suggest that the growth of entheos can be achieved through the practices of reflexivity, listening, and healing. Reflexivity has similarities with reflection. Reflection is "the process or faculty by which the mind observes and examines its own experiences and emotions" ("Reflection,"

2017). It is "an increasing awareness of thoughts and feelings that allows a person to see things in a new light and more complete light" (Welch & Gilmore, 2011, p. 99). In ancient China, one of Confucius's disciples said, "I daily examine myself on three points: whether, in transacting business for others, I may have been not faithful; whether, in intercourse with friends, I may have been not sincere; whether I may have not mastered and practiced the instructions of my teacher" (Confucius, 1893, p. 139). This kind of self-examination has been one of the virtues for a noble Chinese for two millennia. Autry (2004) also recommended daily reflection for leaders to overcome their own egos.

Furthermore, reflexivity is being reflexive, which is "of a mental action, process, etc.: turned or directed *back upon the mind itself*" ("Reflexive," 2017; emphasis added). Stacey (2012) distinguished reflexivity from reflection because the subject and the object in this introspective process should be simultaneously present rather than separate. He went on to illustrate that reflexivity is the activity of thinking about not only our participation in social interactions (first-order reflexivity) but also about *how we are thinking about* our participation (second-order reflexivity). Second-order reflexivity requires both the conceptualization of the situation and the examination of our self-examination. Conceptualization provides vision for the organization beyond daily practice. Reflexivity is the practice of pondering and living out our interrelatedness. The practice of reflexivity leads to oneness, wholeness, and rightness—the growth of entheos.

Reflexivity can be done individually and collectively. Lyubovnikova, Legood, Turner, and Mamakouka (2017) examined how authentic leadership influences team performance through the mediator of team reflexivity. Using survey data from 53 teams with 206 participants in the United Kingdom and Greece, they found that team reflexivity is positively related to team productivity and team effectiveness.

Reflexivity, especially second-order reflexivity, will disturb and awaken a leader's heart. According to Greenleaf (2002), servant-leaders take in more information from the environment than people normally do and make more intense contact with the situation. "Remove the blinders from your awareness by losing what must be lost, the key to which no one can give you, but which your own inward resources rightly cultivated will supply" (p. 340). Low tolerance for awareness will make leaders miss leadership opportunities (Greenleaf, 2002). When our doors of perception are wide open, we are facing the stress and uncertainty of life. Awareness helps us develop detachment, the ability to stand aside and examine ourselves, and the serenity to stand still amid alarms (Greenleaf, 2002). It is necessary to be aware of our moves among interactions: move away by withdrawing, move toward by complying, or move against by being aggressive (Horney, 1992). Apparently, awareness is "not a giver of solace" but "a disturber and an awakener. Able leaders are usually sharply awake and reasonably disturbed. . . . They have their own inner serenity" (Greenleaf, 2002, p. 41).

Listening also can lead to the growth of entheos not only in oneself but also in others, because it builds strength in others. First, listening can lead to better awareness. Through both quantitative and qualitative approaches, Lau (2017) studied the listening strategy usage of 1,290 seventh-grade and 1,515 ninth-grade students in Hong Kong. She concluded that high-proficiency listeners have a better awareness of listening problems and more problem-solving strategies, and use these strategies more frequently and effectively than low-proficiency listeners.

Second, listening takes willingness, vulnerability, and responsibility. Koskinen and Lindström (2013) elucidated the essence of listening through a hermeneutical analysis of Emmanuel Lévinas's writings and uncovered seven themes: (a) listening gives humans joy, strength, and satisfaction; (b) listening is a choice to open to and welcome the Other; (c) with the willingness for otherness, listening is to put oneself into question; (d) listening is to allow oneself to see and be moved by vulnerability and compassion; (e) listening is an infinite responsibility to answer to the Other by saying here I am; (f) listening is to welcome the vulnerability and holiness in the Other; and (g) listening is to embrace each other in a communion.

Third, listening is neither a tool nor an action but an attitude that is toward other people and the understanding of them (Greenleaf, 2002). "Anyone who listens is fundamentally open. Without such openness to one another there is no genuine human bond" (Gadamer, 1975/2004, p. 355). Listening is connected to living quality through listening as silence, listening as dialogue, and listening as ethics with openness (Bunkers, 2015). Listening is openness to communication, openness to others, openness to risk and excitement, openness to wisdom, openness to the wholeness of oneself and others (Greenleaf, 2002). Openness to the other "involves recognizing that I myself must accept some things that are against me, even though no one else forces me to do so" (Gadamer, 1975/2004, p. 355). A servant-leader listens, reads, and obeys "the rhythms of creation" and dwells "in communion with the Creator" (Wangerin, 2002, p. 257). A servant-leader perceives numerous possibilities because he or she decides to listen instead of react. A servant-leader listens to his or her people's concerns and asks them what they think needs to be done and what he or she can do to help (Moxley, 2002). A servant-leader listens and accepts people for who they are (Greenleaf, 2002). "The power of feeling we are heard is what heals us" (Wheatley, 2004, p. 267). Together, we build our oneness, wholeness, and rightness.

Servant-Leadership, Healing, and Forgiveness

Barbuto and Wheeler (2006) have pointed out that healing is underappreciated in leadership. They included it in their servant-leadership subscales, and through research they concluded that leaders' emotional healing is most related to followers' satisfaction. Emotional healing, as a subscale, describes "a leader's commitment to and skill in fostering spiritual recovery from hardship or trauma" (p. 318). It was measured through four items that stated that this person is the one (a) "I would turn to if I had a personal trauma," (b) who is "good at helping me with my emotional issues," (c) who is "talented at helping me to heal emotionally," and (d) "that could help me mend my hard feelings" (p. 322). In addition, the authors claimed that listening and empathy contribute to emotional healing and wisdom (i.e., awareness and foresight).

Laub (1999) generated characteristics of servant-leadership through a three-round Delphi process with 14 experts who had written on or taught servant-leadership. He used these characteristics to construct the items for the Servant Organizational Leadership Assessment (SOLA) instrument. He conducted a prefield test of the instrument with 22 people, revised the instrument, and then conducted the field test with 828 people from 41 different organizations. After analyzing the reliability and correlation of the results, the SOLA instrument was developed. Laub included healing as one item of the subscores of the SOLA instrument in his prefield test. After receiving feedback from judges and participants, he changed "work to bring healing to hurting relationships" to "work to maintain positive working relationships" because the original item was considered "to be too strong of a statement" and " 'hurting' needed to be changed" (p. 142). One example of participants' responses on the item of healing was " 'healing' is a term that, to me, implies mending or fixing something that is broken. While this is something servant leaders do, I see other competencies being more essential" (p. 135). Thus healing was actually removed from the SOLA.

Liden et al. (2008) identified nine dimensions of servant-leadership and reduced them to seven factors through factor analysis of the data from 298 college students. Then the authors verified these seven factors through confirmatory factor analysis of the data from 182 workers. Later, these seven factors were included in the model of servant-leadership by Liden et al. (2014) as servant leader behaviors. Liden et al. (2008) employed emotional healing as one of their seven factors of servant-leadership. They defined emotional healing as "the act of showing sensitivity to others' personal concerns" (p. 162). They created four items to measure emotional healing: "I would seek help from my manager if I had a personal problem"; "My manager cares about my personal well-being"; "My manager takes time to talk to me on a personal level"; and "My manager can recognize when I'm down without asking me" (p. 168). These four items are similar to the ones defined by Barbuto and Wheeler (2006). Barbuto and Wheeler (2006) emphasized the ability of healing, whereas Liden et al. (2008) focused on the act of showing concern. In addition, Liden et al. (2014) have contended that, through awareness and empathy, a leader can iden- tify a need for emotional healing; providing emotional healing requires a leader to be aware and capable of managing his or her own emotions.

If we accept entheos as involving oneness and wholeness, healing is indispensable. Healing is the "restoration of wholeness, well-being, safety, or prosperity" ("Healing," 2017). Greenleaf (2002) pointed out that servant-leaders are "*healers* in the sense of *making whole* by helping others to a larger and nobler vision and purpose than they would be likely to attain for themselves" (p. 240; emphasis in original), and healers do this also for their own healing. Ferch (2012) emphasized, "A hallmark of servant leaders is that they heal others, and they do so through mature relationship to self, others, and God" (p. 72). Thus healing is the commitment to and capability of making whole oneself, others, organizations, and relationships. Servant-leaders are wounded healers "who must not only look after their own wounds, but at the same time be prepared to heal the wounds of others" (Nouwen, 1979, p. 88).

Sturnick (1998) observed six stages of healing leadership: con- sciousness of health, willingness to change, a teachable moment, healthy support systems, immersion in our inner lives, and returning to service in leadership. She also pointed out that "releasing obsessive and destructive perfectionism" can lead to healing (p. 190). As Greenleaf (2002) said, the acceptance of a person requires tolerance of imperfection; acceptance and empathy can lift people up and help people grow.

Barbuto and Wheeler (2006) and Liden et al. (2014) concluded that empathy, listening, and awareness can lead to healing. Another essential component of the healing process is forgiveness. Having discussed listening and awareness, I focus on empathy and forgiveness here. Empathy is "the ability to understand and appreciate another person's feelings, experience, etc." ("Empathy," 2017). Empathy is the core theme of Hopkins's (2015) five-step model of restorative interaction: Allow everyone to share (a) what has happened, (b) what was in their minds and how they felt, (c) the impact of what has happened, (d) what needs had been unmet or ignored, and then (e) discuss and find mutually acceptable ways forward. Tutu (1999) also points out that forgiveness "involves trying to understand the perpetrators and so have *empathy*, to try to stand in their shoes and appreciate the sort of pressures and influences that might have conditioned them" (p. 271; emphasis added). In addition, Elliott, Bohart, Watson, and Greenberg (2011) summarized three major subprocesses of empathy from the perspective of psychotherapy: an emotional simulation process, a perspective-taking process, and an emotion-regulation process.

Coplan (2011) proposed a narrow conceptualization of empathy and focused on three principal features: affective matching, other-oriented perspective taking, and self-other differentiation. Her three features of empathy lie in the major subprocesses of empathy as mentioned by Elliott et al. (2011), but in a narrower sense. She argued that affective matching occurs only when a person's affective states are qualitatively the same as those of the target. Thus rich experiences of the leader and his or her deep awareness are necessary for affective matching to take place. According to Coplan (2011), taking an other-oriented perspective is imagining oneself *being the target* in the target's situation rather than *being oneself* in the target's situation. This requires "greater mental flexibility and emotional regulation" (p. 10). In addition, a leader's unconditional acceptance and healing presence are crucial in this other-oriented, perspective-taking process. Furthermore, Coplan claimed that self-other differentiation is essential for empathy; empathy enables deep engagement with others while protecting one from personal distress and false consensus effects. This requires self-awareness, other-awareness, and relation-awareness.

Enright, Freedman, and Rique (1998) adopted the definition of *forgiving* as "a willingness to abandon one's right to resentment, negative judgment, and indifferent behavior toward one who unjustly injured us, while fostering the undeserved qualities of compassion, generosity, and even love toward him or her" (pp. 46–47). Incorporating both decisional

forgiveness and emotional forgiveness, Worthington (2006) pointed out
five concepts at the center of forgiveness theory: first, there are different
types of forgiving; second, forgiveness suggests changes over time; third, it
is related to perceived injustice; fourth, emotional forgiveness is the major
barometer of change over time; and fifth, emotional forgiveness happens
when we replace "negative, unforgiving stressful emotions with positive,
other-oriented emotions" (p. 17). Thus Worthington's understanding of
forgiveness is "a process of replacing the complex negative emotion of
unforgiveness by any of several positive other-oriented emotions" (p. 106).
He appealed for empathy, sympathy, compassion, and love along with
rational understanding in the face of social tensions and injustice.

The Truth and Reconciliation Commission in South Africa is a painful
yet encouraging and hopeful example of forgiveness. When Nelson Mandela
laid down his vengeance after 27 years in jail, the spirit of forgiveness was
kindled in the whole nation. Mandela and Tutu convinced their followers
through their own suffering and their willingness to forgive for the sake of
others (Tutu, 1999). Tutu (1999) said, "Forgiveness will follow confession
and healing will happen, and so contribute to national unity and reconciliation" (p. 120). He believed that we have to move "beyond retributive
justice to restorative justice, to move on to forgiveness, because without
it there was no future" (p. 260). We forgive not only for the sake of the
perpetrators but also for our own best interests. We are humanity in one.
Whenever we dehumanize others, we dehumanize ourselves. After being
stabbed by Izola Curry, Martin Luther King Jr. said, "Don't do anything
to her; don't prosecute her; get her healed" (C. King, 1969, p. 170). For
King, forgiveness was "not an occasional act" but "a permanent attitude"
(M. King, 1963, p. 26). As Gibran (2007) said, "The strong of soul forgive,
and it is honour in the injured to forgive" (p. 268).

Forgiveness has been recognized as an essential component of the
healing process (Ferch, 2000, 2012; Fitzgibbons, 1998; Hope, 1987; North,
1987, 1998; Ramsey, 2003). Through hermeneutic phenomenological inquiry
with six Christians concerning touch in the context of forgiveness, Ferch
(2000) found five main themes: "restoration of a loving bond," "restoration of character," "lifting the burden of past relational pain," "lifting
the burden of shame," and "restoration of oneness" (p. 161). These themes
reflect not only the notion of forgiveness but also its effects on healing
the people involved and their relationships. Similarly, using a hermeneutic
phenomenological approach, Ramsey (2003) interviewed six perpetrators

who committed crimes against humanity during the apartheid era of South Africa and received empathy and forgiveness from people they had harmed. She found that forgiveness heals the psyche of the perpetrator and creates opportunities for the healing of interpersonal wounded relationships. Servant-leaders help build a bridge that "takes us from power that destroys to power that heals" (Ferch, 2012, p. 15). If we are to truly serve and bring healing to others, we have to learn to forgive and ask for forgiveness from others.

> Forgiveness is embodied first by asking forgiveness and restoring one's integrity through necessary change, as well as by granting forgiveness and working toward a just resolution. Just as the servant leader is servant first, the servant leader asks forgiveness first and does not wait for the "other" to take the initial steps toward reconciliation. (p. 139)

In order to do so, we have to embrace what is natural to a child: "vulnerability, tenderness, openness, vitality, and the desire to grow" (p. 100).

Conclusion

Servant-leaders lead through awareness, healing, and forgiveness. Empathy, listening, awareness, and forgiveness contribute to healing; healing, listening, and reflexivity (with conceptualization) lead to the growth of entheos; and the growth of entheos results in better awareness. These characteristics of servant-leadership interweave with one another to bring out better awareness in a servant-leader, in order to tackle whatever issues are in front of him or her. Inward awareness (i.e., self-awareness) can help leaders understand their own strengths, weaknesses, emotions, concerns, and the impacts of their actions. Upward awareness (i.e., spirit-awareness) can shape a leader's entheos and nurture his or her oneness and wholeness. Outward awareness, that is, other-awareness, relation-awareness, and situation-awareness, can move a leader toward stewardship, including persuading people through word and deed, committing to the growth of people, and building community. A person with relation-awareness and situation-awareness is able to identify situational, historical, religious, cultural, and social elements in a complex situation. All of these forms of awareness take place with onward awareness (i.e., time-awareness); and the awareness of the future leads to foresight. A model of servant-leadership is shown in figure 1.1. Adopting an organic, rather than a mechanistic, view of people and organizations, servant-leaders can become healers of themselves and others, as did every contributor did in this book. In conclusion, the three characteristics of servant-leadership—awareness, healing, and forgiveness—are essential leading practices for servant-leaders because a vision full of hope is ahead of us: "True leadership heals the heart of the world" (Ferch, 2012, p. 194).

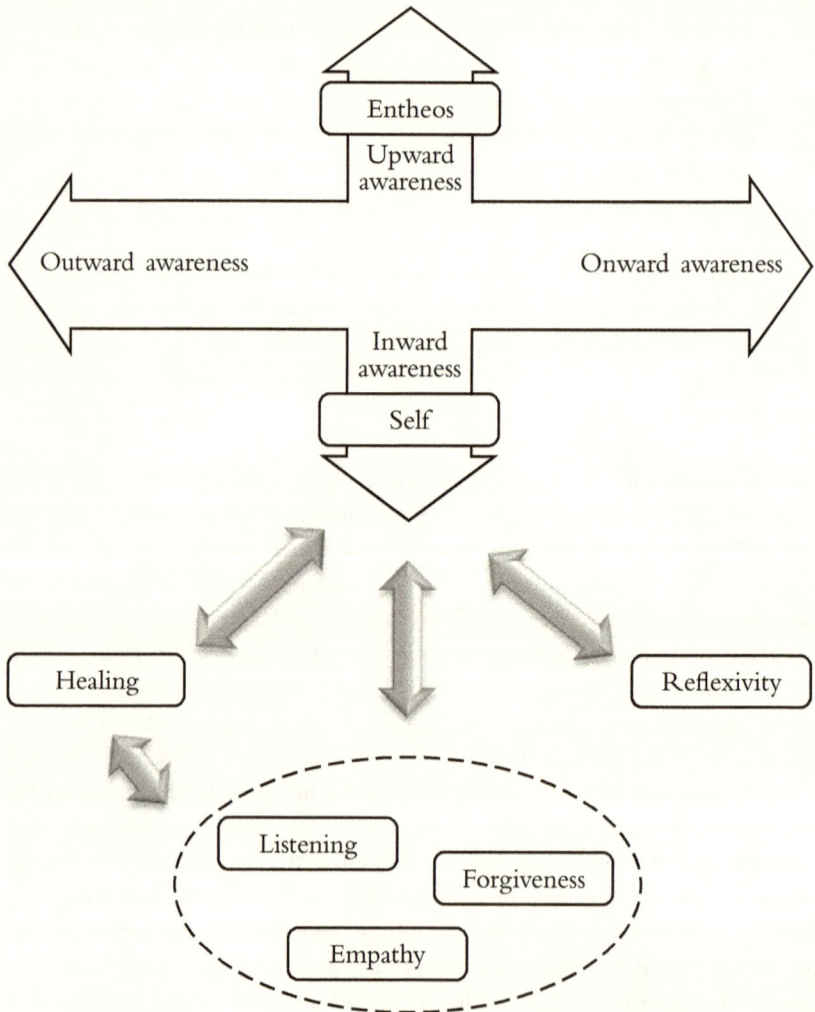

Figure 1.1. Servant-leadership model. *Source:* Song, 2018.

Notes

1. The original Chinese phrase is "圣人南面而听天下," which is in *The I Ching*. It was translated as "the sages [i.e., monarchs] to sit with their faces to the south, and listen to the representations of all in the kingdom" by James Legge in the footnote on page 184 of *The Chinese Classics*, volume 1, published in 1893. But he translated the same phrase as "The sages turn their faces to the south when they give audience to all under the sky" on page 426 of *The I Ching* published in 1899. The former translation is closer to the original Chinese meaning, which is the one I use in the text.

References

Autry, J. A. (2004). Love and work. In L. C. Spears & M. Lawrence (Eds.), *Practicing servant-leadership: Succeeding through trust, bravery, and forgiveness* (pp. 47–70). San Francisco, CA: Jossey-Bass.

Aware. (2017). In *Oxford English dictionary online*. Retrieved from http://www.oed.com

Awareness. (2017). In *Oxford English dictionary online*. Retrieved from http://www.oed.com

Barbuto, J., & Wheeler, D. (2006). Scale development and construct clarification of servant leadership. *Group & Organization Management, 31*(3), 300–326.

Beazley, H. (2003). Foreword. In H. Beazley, J. Beggs, & L. C. Spears (Eds.), *The servant-leader within: A transformative path* (pp. 1–11). New York, NY: Paulist Press.

Bunkers, S. S. (2015). Listening: Important to the stuff of a life. *Nursing Science Quarterly, 28*(2), 103–106. doi:10.1177/0894318415571606

Butler, A. M., Kwantes, C. T., & Boglarsky, C. A. (2014). The effects of self-awareness on perceptions of leadership effectiveness in the hospitality industry: A cross cultural investigation. *International Journal of Intercultural Relations, 40*, 87–99. doi:10.1016/j.ijintrel.2013.12.007

Caldwell, J. I., & Crippen, C. (2017). The leadership philosophy of Mary Parker Follett (1868–1933). *The International Journal of Servant-Leadership, 11*(1), 187–228.

Chan, K. W. (2017). Learners' perceptions of servant-leadership in classrooms. *The International Journal of Servant-Leadership, 11*(1), 373–410.

Chen, X. (2008). Independent thinking: A path to outstanding scholarship. *Management & Organization Review, 4*(3), 337–348. doi:10.1111/j.1740-8784.2008.00124.x

Confucius. (1893). Confucian analects. In J. Legge (Ed.), *The Chinese classics: Confucian analects, the great learning, and the doctrine of the mean* (2nd ed., pp. 137–354). Oxford, England: Clarendon Press.

Confucius. (2014). *Analects.* (D. Hinton Trans.). Berkeley, CA: Counterpoint.

Coplan, A. (2011). Understanding empathy: Its features and effects. In A. Coplan & P. Goldie (Eds.), *Empathy: Philosophical and psychological perspectives* (pp. 3–18). Oxford, England: Oxford University Press.

Ebbrecht, A., & Martin, B. N. (2017). The mentoring experiences of four Missouri teachers of the year through the lens of servant-leadership characteristics. *The International Journal of Servant-Leadership, 11*(1), 337–372.

Ebener, D. R. (2011). On becoming a servant leader. *Sojourners Magazine, 40*(2), 32–34.

Eicher-Catt, D. (2005). The myth of servant-leadership: A feminist perspective. *Women and Language, 28*(1), 17–25.

Elliott, R., Bohart, A. C., Watson, J. C., & Greenberg, L. S. (2011). Empathy. *Psychotherapy, 48*(1), 43–49. doi:10.1037/a0022187

Empathy. (2017). In *Oxford English dictionary online.* Retrieved from http://www.oed.com

Enright, R. D., Freedman, S., & Rique, J. (1998). The psychology of interpersonal forgiveness. In R. D. Enright & J. North (Eds.), *Exploring forgiveness* (pp. 46–62). Madison, WI: University of Wisconsin Press.

Entheos. (2017). In *Oxford English dictionary online.* Retrieved from http://www.oed.com

Eva, N., Robin, M., Sendjaya, S., van Dierendonck, D., & Liden, R. C. (July, 2018). Servant leadership: A systematic review and call for future research. *The Leadership Quarterly,* 1–22. doi:10.1016/j.leaqua.2018.07.004

Ferch, S. R. (2000). Meanings of touch and forgiveness: A hermeneutic phenomenological inquiry. *Counseling & Values, 44*(3), 155–173.

Ferch, S. R. (2004). Servant-leadership, forgiveness, and social justice. In L. C. Spears & M. Lawrence (Eds.), *Practicing servant-leadership: Succeeding through trust, bravery, and forgiveness* (pp. 225–240). San Francisco, CA: Jossey-Bass.

Ferch, S. R. (2012). *Forgiveness and power in the age of atrocity: Servant leadership as a way of life.* Lanham, MD: Lexington Books.

Fitzgibbons, R. (1998). Anger and the healing power of forgiveness: A psychiatrist's view. In R. D. Enright & J. North (Eds.), *Exploring forgiveness* (pp. 63–74). Madison, WI: University of Wisconsin Press.

Friedman, E. H. (2007). *A failure of nerve: Leadership in the age of the quick fix.* M. M. Treadwell & E. W. Beal (Eds.). New York, NY: Seabury Books.

Gadamer, H. (2004). *Truth and method* (J. Weinsheimer & D. G. Marshall, Trans.). (2nd, rev. ed.). London, England: Continuum. (Original work published 1975).

Gibran, K. (2007). *The collected works of Kahlil Gibran.* New York, NY: Alfred A. Knopf.

Greenleaf, R. K. (1966). Choosing to be aware. *The AA Grapevine, 23*(1), 26–28.

Greenleaf, R. K. (1996a). *On becoming a servant-leader.* D. M. Frick & L. C. Spears (Eds.). San Francisco, CA: Jossey-Bass.

Greenleaf, R. K. (1996b). *Seeker and servant: Reflections on religious leadership.* A. T. Fraker & L. C. Spears (Eds.). San Francisco, CA: Jossey-Bass.

Greenleaf, R. K. (1998). *The power of servant-leadership.* L. C. Spears (Ed.). San Francisco, CA: Berrett-Koehler.

Greenleaf, R. K. (2002). *Servant leadership: A journey into the nature of legitimate power and greatness* (25th anniversary ed.). L. C. Spears (Ed.). New York, NY: Paulist Press. (Original work published 1977).

Greenleaf, R. K. (2003). *The servant-leader within: A transformative path.* H. Beazley, J. Beggs, & L. C. Spears (Eds.). New York, NY: Paulist Press.

Healing. (2017). In *Oxford English dictionary online.* Retrieved from http://www.oed.com

Hope, D. (1987). The healing paradox of forgiveness. *Psychotherapy: Theory, Research, Practice, Training, 24*(2), 240–244. doi:10.1037/h0085710

Hopkins, B. (2015). From restorative justice to restorative culture. *Revista de Asistenta Sociala, 14*(4), 19–34.

Horney, K. (1992). *Our inner conflicts: A constructive theory of neurosis.* New York, NY: W. W. Norton.

Hsü, L. S. (2005). *The political philosophy of Confucianism: An interpretation of the social and political ideas of Confucius, his forerunners, and his early disciples.* London, England: Routledge.

Hu, J., & Liden, R. C. (2011). Antecedents of team potency and team effectiveness: An examination of goal and process clarity and servant leadership. *Journal of Applied Psychology, 96*(4), 851–862. doi:10.1037/a0022465

Husserl, E. (1983). *Ideas pertaining to a pure phenomenology and to a phenomenological philosophy: First book: General introduction to a pure phenomenology* (F. Kersten Trans.). The Hague, Netherlands: Martinus Nijhoff.

James, M. F. (2017). Servant-leadership in crisis: A case study of the 2002 evacuation of the international Christian academy in Cote d'Ivoire. *The International Journal of Servant-Leadership, 11*(1), 411–436.

Keith, K. M. (2008). *The case for servant leadership.* Westfield, IN: The Greenleaf Center for Servant Leadership.

King, C. S. (1969). *My life with Martin Luther King, Jr.* New York, NY: Holt, Rinehart and Winston.

King, M. L. (1963). *Strength to love.* New York, NY: Harper & Row.

Koskinen, C. A., & Lindström, U. Å. (2013). Listening to the otherness of the other: Envisioning listening based on a hermeneutical reading of Lévinas. *International Journal of Listening, 27*(3), 146–156. doi:10.1080/10904018.2013.813259

Lao Tzu. (2005). *Tao teh ching.* J. C. H. Wu (Ed.). Boston, MA: Shambhala.

Lau, K. (2017). Strategy use, listening problems, and motivation of high- and low-proficiency Chinese listeners. *Journal of Educational Research, 110*(5), 503–514. doi:10.1080/00220671.2015.1134421

Laub, J. A. (1999). *Assessing the servant organization: Development of the servant organizational leadership assessment (SOLA) instrument* (Doctoral dissertation). Retrieved from http://foley.gonzaga.edu/

Legge, J. (Ed.). (1893). *The Chinese classics: Confucian analects, the great learning, and the doctrine of the mean* (2nd ed.). Oxford, England: Clarendon Press.

Legge, J. (Ed.). (1899). *The sacred books of China: The I ching* (2nd ed.). New York, NY: Dover Publications.

Liden, R. C., Panaccio, A., Meuser, J. D., Hu, J., & Wayne, S. J. (2014). Servant leadership: Antecedents, processes, and outcomes. In D. V. Day (Ed.), *The Oxford handbook of leadership and organizations* (pp. 357–379). New York, NY: Oxford University Press.

Liden, R. C., Wayne, S. J., Zhao, H., & Henderson, D. (2008). Servant leadership: Development of a multidimensional measure and multi-level assessment. *The Leadership Quarterly, 19*(2), 161–177. doi:10.1016/j.leaqua.2008.01.006

Lyubovnikova, J., Legood, A., Turner, N., & Mamakouka, A. (2017). How authentic leadership influences team performance: The mediating role of team reflexivity. *Journal of Business Ethics, 141*(1), 59–70. doi:10.1007/s10551-015-2692-3

Miao, Q., Newman, A., Schwarz, G., & Xu, L. (2014). Servant leadership, trust, and the organizational commitment of public sector employees in China. *Public Administration, 92*(3), 727–743. doi:10.1111/padm.12091

Morse, M. (2008). *Making room for leadership: Power, space, and influence.* Downers Grove, IL: IVP Books.

Moxley, R. S. (2002). Leadership as partnership. In L. C. Spears & M. Lawrence (Eds.), *Focus on leadership: Servant-leadership for the twenty-first century* (pp. 47–52). New York, NY: John Wiley & Sons.

Nayab, N. (2011). Servant leadership theory: Strengths and weaknesses. Retrieved from http://www.brighthub.com/office/home/articles/73511.aspx

North, J. (1987). Wrongdoing and forgiveness. *Philosophy, 62*(242), 499–508. doi:10.1017/S003181910003905X

North, J. (1998). The "ideal" of forgiveness: A philosopher's exploration. In R. D. Enright & J. North (Eds.), *Exploring forgiveness* (pp. 15–34). Madison, WI: University of Wisconsin Press.

Northouse, P. G. (2016). *Leadership: Theory and practice* (7th ed.). Los Angeles, CA: Sage.

Nouwen, H. J. M. (1979). *The wounded healer: Ministry in contemporary society* (2nd ed.). New York, NY: Image Doubleday.

Palmer, P. J. (1998). Leading from within. In L. C. Spears (Ed.), *Insights on leadership: Service, stewardship, spirit, and servant-leadership* (pp. 197–208). New York, NY: John Wiley & Sons.

Patterson, K. A. (2003). *Servant leadership: A theoretical model* (Doctoral dissertation). Regent University, Virginia.

Ramsey, I. M. (2003). *The role of empathy in facilitating forgiveness: The lived experience of six political perpetrators in South Africa* (Doctoral dissertation). Gonzaga University, Washington. Retrieved from http://foley.gonzaga.edu/

Reflection. (2017). In *Oxford English dictionary online*. Retrieved from http://www.oed.com

Reflexive. (2017). In *Oxford English dictionary online*. Retrieved from http://www.oed.com

Russell, R. F., & Stone, A. G. (2002). A review of servant leadership attributes: Developing a practical model. *Leadership & Organization Development Journal, 23*(3), 145–157.

Scazzero, P., & Bird, W. (2003). *The emotionally healthy church: A strategy for discipleship that actually changes lives.* Grand Rapids, MI: Zondervan.

Sima, Q. (1993). *Records of the grand historian: Han dynasty II* (B. Watson Trans.) (Rev. ed.). Hong Kong, China: Columbia University Press.

Sipe, J. W., & Frick, D. M. (2009). *Seven pillars of servant leadership: Practicing the wisdom of leading by serving.* New York, NY: Paulist Press.

Song, J. (2018). Leading through awareness and healing: A servant-leadership model. *The International Journal of Servant-Leadership, 12*(1), 245–284.

Spears, L. C. (2002). Introduction: Tracing the past, present, and future of servant-leadership. In L. C. Spears & M. Lawrence (Eds.), *Focus on leadership: Servant-leadership for the twenty-first century* (pp. 1–16). New York, NY: Wiley.

Spears, L. C. (2010). Character and servant leadership: Ten characteristics of effective, caring leaders. *The Journal of Virtues & Leadership, 1*(1), 25–30.

Spears Center for Servant-Leadership. (2018). Larry C. Spears and Robert K. Greenleaf. Retrieved from http://www.spearscenter.org/about-larry/larry-a-robert-greenleaf

Stacey, R. D. (2012). *Tools and techniques of leadership and management: Meeting the challenge of complexity.* London, England: Routledge.

Sturnick, J. A. (1998). Healing leadership. In L. C. Spears (Ed.), *Insights on leadership: Service, stewardship, spirit, and servant-leadership* (pp. 185–193). New York, NY: John Wiley & Sons.

Sun, Y. (1927). *Memories of a Chinese revolutionary: A programme of national reconstruction for China.* Philadelphia, PA: David McKay Company.

Tutu, D. (1998, February). Desmond Tutu (Z. Jaffrey, Interviewer). *The Progressive, 62*, 18–21.

Tutu, D. (1999). *No future without forgiveness.* New York, NY: Doubleday.

van Dierendonck, D. (2011). Servant leadership: A review and synthesis. *Journal of Management, 37*(4), 1228–1261. doi:10.1177/0149206310380462

van Dierendonck, D., & Nuijten, I. (2011). The servant leadership survey: Development and validation of a multidimensional measure. *Journal of Business and Psychology, 26*(3), 249–267. doi:10.1007/s10869-010-9194-1

Wangerin, W. (2002). One man on a tractor far away. In J. Wilson (Ed.), *The best Christian writing* (pp. 252–264). San Francisco, CA: Harper.

Welch, D. V., & Gilmore, V. D. (2011). Coaching for servant-leadership: Expanding the capacity to reflect from the heart. In S. R. Ferch & L. C. Spears (Eds.), *The spirit of servant-leadership* (pp. 98–112). New York, NY: Paulist Press.

Wheatley, M. J. (2004). The servant-leader: From hero to host. In L. C. Spears & M. Lawrence (Eds.), *Practicing servant-leadership: Succeeding through trust, bravery, and forgiveness* (pp. 241–268). San Francisco, CA: Jossey-Bass.

Williams, L. E. (2002). Fannie Lou Hamer, servant of the people. In L. C. Spears & M. Lawrence (Eds.), *Focus on leadership: Servant-leadership for the twenty-first century* (pp. 65–88). New York, NY: John Wiley & Sons.

Wong, E. K. O. (2015). *"How am I going to grow up?" An exploration of congregational transition among second-generation Chinese Canadian evangelicals and servant-leadership* (Doctoral dissertation). Retrieved from https://search.proquest.com/docview/1681561062

Worthington, E. L. (2006). *Forgiveness and reconciliation: Theory and application*. New York, NY: Routledge.

Chapter 2

Servant-Leadership and Unconditional Forgiveness

The Lives of Six South African Perpetrators

M<small>ARLEEN</small> R<small>AMSEY</small>

Servant-leadership practices are becoming increasingly more important as modern humanity makes desperate attempts to heal from the atrocities of war, interpersonal violence, and injustices that destroy the human spirit. Laub (1999) conceptualizes servant-leadership in the following way:

> Servant-leadership is an understanding and practice of leadership that places the good of those led over the self-interest of the leader. Servant-leadership promotes the valuing and development of people, the building of community, the practice of authenticity, the providing of leadership for the good of those led and the sharing of power and status for the common good of each individual. (p. 83)

The broadening view of servant-leadership embeds holistic leadership practices not only in the corporate boardroom but also in social and political interactions that rely on, even demand, the need for people who are dedicated to making the world a better place for all to live (Ferch, 2005; Howatson-Jones, 2004; Spears & Lawrence, 2004).

The focus of the present study is on research I conducted with six political perpetrators of the apartheid era who were found guilty of gross human rights abuses, were then imprisoned, and finally applied for and

received amnesty. It also explores how former South African President
Nelson Mandela and Archbishop Desmond Tutu modeled servant-leadership
principles in negotiating a restorative justice process through the Truth
and Reconciliation Commission to deal with the atrocities that occurred
during the apartheid struggle. The truth hearings gave victims the opportunity to make public statements regarding the human rights abuses they
experienced from state security forces and liberation combatants. It also
allowed political perpetrators the opportunity to be truthful and to request
amnesty. Finally, the truth hearings created an environment in which
victims and political perpetrators could bestow and receive forgiveness.

The idea of servant-leadership is an ancient one, and many of its
themes are seen in the writings of Holy Scripture. Jesus made it very
clear that servant-leadership was not about power, but about serving
others. He stated, "You know that those who are regarded as rulers of the
Gentiles lord it over them, and their high officials exercise authority over
them. Not so with you. Instead, whoever wants to become great among
you must be your servant" (Mark 10:43, *New International Version*). The
term *servant-leadership* has its modern origins in a 1970 essay by Robert
Greenleaf titled "The Servant as Leader" (Spears, 1998). An executive at
AT&T, Greenleaf originally discussed the concept within the context of
a corporate or organizational leadership style. Although Greenleaf never
actually defined *servant-leadership*, he identified some central characteristics
that describe the servant-leader. These characteristics reflect a universal
ethic of empathy, forgiveness, honesty, trust, healing, community, and service
that goes beyond the corporate world and adapts well to many different
types of human environments (Bowman, 2005; Sendjaya & Sarros, 2002;
Smith, Montagno, & Kuzmenko, 2004; Tatum, 1995).

Servant-Leadership, Forgiveness, and the Truth and Reconciliation Commission

An extraordinary example of servant-leadership practices was enacted in
the restorative justice process of the Truth and Reconciliation Commission of South Africa. It has been nearly three decades now since the first
democratic elections took place in South Africa on April 27 and 28, 1994.
At the time of these elections, South Africa was a deeply divided society
tormented by a violent legacy. Hope for a peaceful co-existence among

the people of South Africa seemed an impossible dream (Burton, 1998). Apartheid had alienated South Africa from the larger global community; the threat of civil war and racial bloodbath was imminent. The social and political situation in South Africa was at a crisis (Sparks, 1994).

According to Greenleaf (1977), servant-leaders are leaders who put other people's needs, aspirations, and interests above their own. The servant-leader's deliberate choice is to serve others. In one of the most stunning examples of servant-leadership in modern times, Nelson Mandela, on being released after twenty-seven years of imprisonment, made the deliberate choice to forgive his captors and refused to bring retribution upon his political enemies. As the newly elected president of South Africa, Mandela now had the power to punish those who had injured him, his family, and his people for decades. But being a truly great servant-leader, Mandela put the people's needs and interests above his own. He committed himself to end the violence, to heal the injustices, and to forgo the settlement of old scores. Mandela's approach was revolutionary in concept. The nearly overnight regime change from apartheid, or legalized racism, to a democratic society must be credited to the servant-leadership of Nelson Mandela and his fellow leaders within the African National Congress. Through negotiations with the apartheid regime, the National Party, a compromise was reached. The African National Congress, led by Mandela, wanted to reveal the truth regarding the atrocities that had taken place during the apartheid era, and the National Party wanted amnesty for the people who had perpetrated these violent acts. The establishment of the Truth and Reconciliation Commission was the end product of these negotiations (Sparks, 1994). The Truth and Reconciliation Commission was created by the terms of the National Unity and Reconciliation Act 34 in December 1995. The Act focused on six main objectives:

1. To generate a detailed record of the nature, extent, and causes of human rights violations in South Africa during the period 1960–1994.

2. To name the people, organizations, and political parties responsible for gross violations of human rights.

3. To provide victims of gross human rights violations a public forum to express themselves in order to regain their human dignity.

4. To make recommendations to the government on how to prevent the future occurrences of human rights violations.

5. To make recommendations to the government regarding reparations and the rehabilitation of victims of human rights violations.

6. To facilitate the granting of amnesty for individual perpetrators of human rights violations. (Lax, Unpublished paper)

In 1996 the commission, chaired by Nobel laureate Archbishop Desmond Tutu, began the arduous task of reviewing over 21,000 statements from victims and examining 7,000 applications for amnesty (Terrell, 2004).

    Although truth commissions have been conducted in a number of other countries (e.g., Chile, Argentina, Uganda, and Sri Lanka), no country has undergone the type of public truth telling that South Africa underwent during the period of time that the Human Rights Violations Committee conducted their hearings (Villa-Vicencio & Verwoerd, 2000). The hearings were open to the public; they were televised, reported on the radio, and published in the newspaper. Every revealed secret, every disclosed atrocity, was made known to the public (Krog, 1998). The hearings gave voice to victims who had long been mute about the suffering they had endured during the long siege of apartheid. The permission to speak of their experiences and to share their pain was the beginning of healing for many silent sufferers (Amnesty International, 2003; Byrne, 2004). The commission recognized that human beings live in a world in which both victims and perpetrators must reside alongside one another. In the spirit of servant-leadership, the commission not only empowered victims through giving them the opportunity to speak of their suffering but also gave political perpetrators a means by which they could bridge the crevasse of separation that their violent deeds had created (Tutu, 1999). The hearings gave transgressors against human rights the opportunity to be honest, to be filled with humility, and to come to the fountain of forgiveness where healing could begin. Spears (2005) states,

> One of the great strengths of servant-leadership is the potential for healing one's self and others. Many people have broken spirits and have suffered from a variety of emotional hurts. Although this is a part of being human, servant-leaders rec-

ognize that they have an opportunity to 'help make whole' those with whom they come in contact. (p. 33)

The world watched in amazement as the hearings progressed. How could a people so deeply divided risk so much in their truth telling, be so transparent with revelations of torture and brutality, and be so generous in their forgiveness? These are questions not easily answered. Indeed, there are many who challenge the ultimate success of the Truth and Reconciliation Commission process. It may take generations before the impact of the Truth and Reconciliation Commission's hearings on South African society completely unfolds. However, even for those who doubt the commission's authenticity, there is little question that lives were changed forever, often in undeniably powerful ways, both for those who witnessed these events and for those who lived the experience of giving and receiving forgiveness.

My Journey to South Africa

Along with the rest of the world, I watched in awe as South Africa demonstrated the servant-leadership principles of empathy, forgiveness, and healing through the Truth and Reconciliation Commission process. Did the receiving of forgiveness transform people, even perpetrators, making them healthier, wiser, freer, more autonomous, and more likely themselves to become servant-leaders? The search for the answer to this compelling question led me to South Africa. I chose South Africa primarily to investigate one of the primary principles of servant-leadership, the commitment to establish a sense of community among people. I wanted to see if this principle held true for amnesty recipients—if indeed they experienced a sense of acceptance, and community, even among the people they had deeply injured. Finally, I sought the answer to Greenleaf's (1977) genuine test of a servant-leader. He states,

> The best test, and difficult to administer, is: Do those served grow as persons? Do they, while being served, become healthier, wiser, freer, more autonomous, more likely themselves to become servants? And, what is the effect on the least privileged in society; will they benefit, or, at least, not be further deprived?" (pp. 13–14)

PERSONS INTERVIEWED

Six political perpetrators were interviewed for this study. Of these six, five were found guilty of human rights violations, imprisoned, and then given amnesty after appearing before the Truth and Reconciliation Commission and giving testimony to their violations. One of the six persons, a former Azanian People's Liberation Army (armed wing of the Pan-African Congress) commander, was never taken to trial and withdrew his application for amnesty. All of these persons were male, ranging from twenty-six to forty-five years of age. Five were black South Africans and former members of the Azanian People's Liberation Army. One man was a white South African and a former police captain with the state security forces. These men each received empathy and forgiveness from their victim or victims, or from family members of their victim or victims. All of the interviews took place in Cape Town, South Africa, during September and October 2002.

Making contact with political perpetrators was a difficult process. The nature of the violations committed by both state security force personnel and members of the liberation movements were such that most amnesty recipients were unwilling to expose themselves to further external or internal scrutiny. In addition, not all political perpetrators who submitted applications for amnesty to the Truth and Reconciliation Commission expressed a brokenness of pride and spirit, and it was such persons that were needed for the study. Through the cooperative networking of people involved in such organizations as Black Sash, the Centre for the Study of Violence and Reconciliation, the Institute of Justice and Reconciliation, and the Cape Town Press Club, as well as courageous persons who willingly came forth to assist in this study, political perpetrators who had received empathy and forgiveness from someone they had injured were located in Pollsmoor Prison, Gugulethu, Khayelitsha, Langa, and the KwaZulu-Natal.

Two of the four perpetrators who received amnesty for the 1994 murder of American Fulbright exchange student Amy Biehl agreed to be interviewed for this study. Although the story of Amy's death on August 25, 1993, and her parents' response of forgiveness to the four men tried for her death have been well publicized, I have given these men the pseudonyms of Nepi and Khali to allow them a semblance of anonymity. Stone is the pseudonym for one of three perpetrators tried for the December 30, 1994, Heidelberg Tavern attack in Observatory, Cape Town. Khaya is the pseudonym for one of three perpetrators responsible for the July 25, 1993, Saint James Church massacre in Cape Town. More than 20 people were severely injured in this attack, and 11 people were killed. Khaya was found guilty and sentenced to prison, where he applied for and received amnesty during the Truth and Reconciliation Commission hearings. In September 2002 he was again arrested as a suspect in an armored car robbery outside of Cape Town and incarcerated. I interviewed Khaya in Pollsmoor Prison, where he awaited trial.

Letlapa Mphahlele (not a pseudonym) was the only political perpetrator I interviewed who did not receive amnesty. He was a commander of the armed wing of the Pan-African Congress known as Azanian People's Liberation Army and gave the orders to attack the Heidelberg Tavern and the Saint James Church in Cape Town. On October 21, 2002, I attended the Cape Town Press Club luncheon where Letlapa was invited to give a presentation to launch his new book, *A Child of the Soil*. Ginn Fourie also attended the luncheon. Her daughter, Lyndi Fourie, a 23-year-old civil engineering student at the University of Cape Town, was slain in the 1994 Heidelberg Tavern assault. During this public forum, Letlapa revealed that he was the commander who had ordered the attack on the tavern. He was initially unaware of Mrs. Fourie's presence, but when he became aware of who she was, he stopped his discourse and apologized for Lyndi's death. After addressing the press, Letlapa stepped down from the podium and went directly to Mrs. Fourie's table, where they embraced. The meeting between Letlapa and Mrs. Fourie was a profoundly moving moment, and through her tears, she said, "My tears are not for my daughter today but for the realization that the man I thought so long was a monster has shown me his human side. I am moved by his humanity."

The final man interviewed for this study was Brian Mitchell (not a pseudonym), a former police station commander in the KwaZulu-Natal midlands, who ordered an attack on a house thought to be an African National Congress terrorist cell in the village of Trust Feed on December 3, 1988. The wrong house was attacked, and 11 innocent people, primarily women and children, were killed in this massacre. Brian was convicted and sentenced to eleven counts of death for ordering the attack. On April 24, 1994, President Willem de Klerk commuted Brian's death sentence to 30 years, which opened the way for Brian to make application for amnesty.

Time and again, during the interviews and during the interpretation of these men's stories, I was struck by the enormity of the psychological pain that we often cause others and ourselves. I was also struck by the realization of how healing the experience of forgiveness can be to both victims and perpetrators. It is through the stories of these six men that greater understanding may be gained regarding the transforming powers of empathy and forgiveness. It is also through their stories that we can see how the practices of servant-leadership can restore community to people deeply separated by violence and brutality.

Findings

The six men interviewed for this study perpetrated violent acts against other people, resulting in serious physical injury, maiming, and, in most cases, the death of their victims. Each man believed at the time that his violence was merited in order to bring about justice and stability in the midst of a chaotic political situation. Initially, these men defended and justified their actions as necessary, but as the amnesty hearings went on, they began to feel confusion, doubt, and a sense of shame for their violent deeds. This occurred only after experiencing an "awakening" or realization of the humanity of their victims, a concept that Gobodo-Madikizela (2004) discusses in her observations of Eugene de Kock:

> Typically, the perpetrator starts off with rationalization, to con-
> vince himself of the legitimacy of his acts. . . . De Kock knew
> that what he had done as commander of covert police activity
> at Vlakplaas was simply beyond what most human beings could
> understand, it was beyond what he could understand . . . the
> cloak had now been removed to reveal what had been hidden
> before, not only from the public eye but from himself as well.
> This presence of an inner stirring within de Kock is what
> marks the fundamental difference between him and his former
> colleagues who appeared before the TRC. (p. 23)

All six men received empathy and forgiveness from the family members or loved ones of their victims. However, four developed close, warm relationships with family members of the people they had injured. In the cases of these men, they received not only forgiveness but also an invitation to form a relationship with the very people they had harmed. Such unconditional forgiveness is difficult to grasp, but the invitation to become a member of another's inner circle is astounding. Greenleaf (1977) believed that the servant-leader uses every opportunity to serve others and to help them develop to their full potential. Through the bestowal of forgiveness and the invitation to develop an inclusive relationship, these four political perpetrators were given the opportunity to live legitimate lives. These four men expressed a greater feeling of self-forgiveness and hope than the two who did not develop such close relationships with family members of their victims.

The study was conducted using hermeneutic phenomenological methods. Five themes emerged from the interviews: (a) violence harms both victim and perpetrator; (b) denial and arrogance are used to protect the perpetrator from shame; (c) empathy creates an environment whereby the perpetrator can ask for and receive forgiveness; (d) the gift of forgiveness increases the ability to forgive oneself; and (e) forgiveness is a bridge to the future. The forthcoming section discusses each theme and explores the psychological experience of receiving forgiveness and its implications for healing, as well as for creating opportunities for reconciliation. I must point out that forgiveness, reconciliation, and the opportunity for political perpetrators to live legitimate lives were made possible through South Africa's decision to follow the practices of servant-leadership as embodied in the principles of restorative justice. Finally, I discuss the role of forgiveness in helping both victims and perpetrators create a more hope-filled future.

VIOLENCE HARMS BOTH VICTIM AND PERPETRATOR

It is common for most people to assume that a perpetrator who commits an atrocity has a serious psychological abnormality or dysfunction. They may even describe the person who has committed an atrocity as being evil or somehow inhuman. Gilligan (1996) states, "Our horror can lead us to distance ourselves from violence. Many may already have concluded that it is only a few crazy, abnormal, and freakish people who are violent" (p. 30). Social psychologists refer to this as the fundamental attribution error and define it as the "tendency for observers to underestimate situational influence and overestimate dispositional influences upon others' behaviors" (Myers, 1999, p. 83). Although there is little support for claims that psychopathology, dysfunction, or deficiencies constitute useful explanations, the first reaction to an atrocity is often to vilify or demonize the perpetrator (Kressel, 1996; Staub, 1989). Some psychologists believe that this reaction may be a way of protecting ourselves from our own internal fears that we may have the potential to act in such horrific and heinous ways (Gilligan, 1996; Gobodo-Madikizela, 2002). However, labeling perpetrators as "evil" or "inhuman" simply describes the behavior but does not give us a clear explanation or understanding as to why the person engaged in the violent deed. Gilligan (1996) states, "It is easier and less threatening to condemn violence (morally and legally) so that we can punish it, rather than seeking its causes and working to prevent it" (p. 24). Foster (2000) supports Gilligan's views in his study of perpetrators of the apartheid era, stating,

> The weight of literature on atrocities finds little evidence to support the notion that severe abnormality is the cause of bad deeds. Even regarding sadism, the general view is that while it cannot be dismissed, only about five percent of all types of perpetrators (serial killers, torturers, rapists) may be classed as sadists and furthermore even this motive is not inherent but gradually acquired over time; a consequence of serial acts of violence. (p. 6)

Foster (2000) also suggests, "Perpetrators may experience severe stress and anxiety along with denial, disassociation, doubling, and other defense mechanisms" (p. 7). Several psychological reports that the Truth and Reconciliation Commission reviewed indicated that some amnesty seekers suffered from posttraumatic stress disorder as a result of the atrocities they engaged in and witnessed. Other psychologists have indicated the need for further research on the effects of trauma on the psychology of perpetrators within the South African apartheid struggle (Foster, Davis, & Sandler, 1987; Fourie, 2000; Nicholas, 2000; Orr, 1998).

Each of the men interviewed revealed that the memory of the violent acts in which they had engaged created internal cognitive dissonance and pain. Nepi revealed,

> I find it too difficult to accept that early in my life I happened to be involved in a murder. I was trying to be more militant but it was very difficult because your soul is not militant, it is not a machine, it is human. Your soul feels, it feels things strongly, it remembers, and the memories, they never leave you. (interview, October 3, 2003)

Stone also revealed,

> There is still pain in my heart. Maybe Mrs. Fourie has pain in her heart too. If we talk together, maybe the pain will be

less for both of us. This would be a good thing to do. I am
ready to talk with her. (interview, October 23, 2003)

Several of the men described the violent memory as a heavy weight
that they carried inside them. Brian Mitchell described the horrific scene
he witnessed as a weight that seemed to suffocate him:

> I was in absolute shock as I walked through the house and
> it became clear that the wrong house had been targeted and
> innocent people had died. As a police officer I had witnessed a
> number of violent deeds and death was common. But nothing
> I had ever seen in my life readied me for that moment. Blood
> was everywhere and the bodies of women and children lay
> where they had fallen. I think all sorts of things go through
> your mind, but once a person has moved beyond disbelief and
> reality sinks in, then fear descends upon you like a heavy black
> tarp that makes you feel like you are trapped and unable to
> breathe. (interview, October 26, 2002)

Khaya also experienced a sense of suffocating weight when he allowed
himself to recall the events of the Saint James Church massacre. He stated,
"I remember the horror of bodies flying in the air from the explosion
of the hand grenades. These memories haunt and weigh me down. The
weight is inside haunting me. It is like a poison that needs to get out"
(interview, September 27, 2002).

Each of the six men revealed intense internal pain, fear, and depression.
They described this pain in several ways: "I felt a pain in my heart"; "I
felt pressed with a huge weight"; "I felt as if I was being suffocated"; and
"There was a poison that needed to be released." Although they attempted
to hide that pain and used various emotional fortifications to alleviate the
suffering, it persisted. Among the coping strategies these men used were
denial, justification, and arrogance. The use of these defenses to protect
their ego structure from shame will be discussed in the next section.

USE OF DENIAL AND ARROGANCE AS PROTECTION FROM SHAME

Prior to my departure for South Africa to begin this study, I viewed
several videotapes of political perpetrators testifying before the Truth and
Reconciliation Commission. Although the commission had not included
remorse or repentance as criteria for amnesty, I was surprised and even

puzzled that the majority of amnesty seekers viewed on the tapes appeared to be untouched by their experiences. Many showed stoic faces that revealed no repentance or remorse. Most justified their actions as simply following orders, or maintained that it was a war and that in war there are casualties. Particularly disturbing was the apparent lack of emotion in several amnesty seekers as they described the torture they had perpetrated on others. From all outward appearances they seemed unbroken, unrepentant, and even arrogant. Gobodo-Madikizela (2004) writes,

> Some people, when faced with their evil deeds, understand the moral implications of their actions, but to maintain some dignity to protect their sense of identity as respectable human beings, they cling to the belief that what they did was morally correct. One can get a sense that they are struggling with their denial of the truth. (p. 23)

Foster (2000) concurs that this type of psychological stance creates difficulties in attempting to understand perpetrators:

> It produces something of a problem for those who constitute a third perspective—observers, social scientists, the Truth and Reconciliation Commission—since their efforts to understand perpetrators adopting their detached minimalist styles, comes across as insensitive to victims. (p. 3)

Several of the men interviewed indicated that they experienced anger, frustration, and fear during the Truth and Reconciliation Commission hearings. They felt that they needed to take a defensive, protective stance. If they didn't divulge the complete truth they would be denied amnesty, yet they were fearful that what they said might betray other comrades. Khaya revealed that he felt sympathy for Dawie Ackerman, a church member who lost his wife during the Saint James attack. "I felt sympathy for him because I knew I was the cause of his pain" (interview, September 27, 2002). However, Khaya believed that if he showed that sympathy, it would expose his weakness, guilt, and shame to the people at the hearing and to the commissioners. He stated, "I was not prepared to make myself appear weak because it would create more shame than I could bear."

Erikson (1963) gives an insightful understanding of the fear of being shamed in public settings. He says,

Shame supposes that one is completely exposed and conscious of being looked at. One is visible and not ready to be visible, which is why we dream of shame as a situation in which we are stared at in a condition of incomplete dress—with one's pants down. (pp. 252–253)

Gilligan (1996) also touches on this deep internal fear of exposing one's weakness and the level of shame that it creates when he states,

The family of painful feelings called shame and humiliation, which, when they become overwhelming because a person has no basis for self-respect, can be intolerable, and so devastating as to bring about the collapse of self-esteem and thus the death of the self. (p. 64)

After his amnesty hearing, Khaya asked to have the opportunity to request forgiveness from the people he had injured. He was taken to a small room where about 25 people were sitting in a circle and was told to go to each one and ask for their forgiveness. He said it was a humiliating experience because it was so public; he was dressed in prison clothes with a chain around his waist that extended to his ankles and up to his wrists. It was difficult to walk, he could only shuffle and extend both hands, as if begging to shake the hands of the people from whom he sought forgiveness. Khaya felt he had no dignity or self-respect. He felt threatened and perceived an overwhelming need to protect himself. He said that the "eyes of some of the people had pity, some of the eyes had fear, and some of the eyes still wanted justice" (interview, September 27, 2002).

Five of the six men interviewed spoke of this internal need to maintain a sense of dignity and self-respect in an environment they perceived as extremely hostile to them. They used words such as "protect myself," "keep my public face," and "I could not show weakness" to describe the emotions they were experiencing while testifying before the Truth and Reconciliation Commission. Even when the environment was not hostile or denigrating, it was difficult to let down their defenses and be open to the kind overtures of their victims.

Nepi described his first encounter with the parents of Amy Biehl, when he, along with the other three defendants, was being transported to a conference room. They were in manacles and shackled together when they literally came face-to-face in the corridor with Linda and Peter Biehl. The couple recognized the defendants and offered to shake hands with them. Nepi said, "They offered to shake hands and all three guys shook, but I couldn't. I don't know why, but I told myself I just couldn't. I shifted to one side, but they did not notice and I bypassed them" (interview, October 3, 2002). At that time he wanted to shake hands but felt overcome with shame, and it was easier to hold on to his prideful face than to accept their gesture of reconciliation.

At this point in the research several questions emerged. How do we move beyond our fear of the perpetrator and the need to vilify him or her? How do we break through the perpetrator's defenses, specifically, the need to protect himself or herself from public shame? Finally, what deeds, words, attitudes, or acts facilitate the breaking down of ego defenses, allowing the perpetrator to experience remorse and a brokenness of spirit in response to asking for and receiving forgiveness?

Empathy in Asking For and Receiving Forgiveness

If we accept the premise that there may be a deeply human side to perpetrators (Gobodo-Madikizela, 2004) that they cover up with defense mechanisms to protect themselves from shame and humiliation, then there must exist emotional bridges or psychological passageways that perpetrators can safely use in order to ask for and receive forgiveness. Evidence of this came forth as the men revealed their feelings of empathy and connection that arose from being forgiven. Each talked about their feelings of empathy for their victims as well as receiving empathy from victims or their families. Stone stated, "During the Truth and Reconciliation hearings I felt that I was sharing the pain along with family members of the victims. That day I felt pain for the victims." Stone also revealed, "I said to myself that I must not be difficult. I must be open to what Mrs. Fourie is feeling so that she can understand what I am feeling—so we can share, person-to-person" (interview, October 23, 2002).

Khali indicated that he initially thought of Amy as just another white person, a "white settler." However, at the Truth and Reconciliation Commission hearings he had the opportunity to hear Linda and Peter Biehl speak about Amy and suddenly he saw her as a real person, a real woman with parents who loved her just as his parents loved him. Each of the men in this study indicated that as they saw their victims as people—with subjectivity, humanity, and personhood—it was more difficult to maintain a façade of pride, arrogance, or indifference. These men indicated that it was only as they felt empathy with their victims that they were able to ask for and receive forgiveness.

The Gift of Forgiveness and the Ability to Self-Forgive

Arendt (2000) shares profound insights into the redemptive qualities of forgiveness:

> The possible redemption from the predicament of irreversibility . . . is the faculty of forgiving. The remedy for unpredictability . . . is contained in the faculty to make and keep promises. The two faculties belong together in so far as one of them, forgiving, serves to undo the deeds of the past . . . ; and the other, binding oneself through promises, serves to set up in the ocean of uncertainty, which the future is by definition, islands of security without which not even continuity, let alone durability of any kind, would be possible in the relationships between men. (p. 237)

A primary difficulty in healing interpersonal injuries for both victims and perpetrators lies in finding a way to reconcile the past in order to move into the future (Borris, 2003; Holloway, 2002). Without forgiveness, both victim and perpetrator are locked together in the past without a pathway to the future. Arendt (2000) states,

> Without being forgiven [and] released from the consequences of what we have done, our capacity to act would, as it were, be confined to one single deed from which we could never recover; we would remain the victim of its consequences forever, not unlike the sorcerer's apprentice who lacked the magic formula to break the spell. (p. 237)

Brian Mitchell revealed that upon receiving amnesty he requested the opportunity to return to Trust Feed to ask forgiveness from the survivors and family members of his victims. However, the people of Trust Feed rejected his request for forgiveness. Brian spent a year in limbo, deeply depressed and mentally running away from who he was and what he had done. The turning point came when he received a telephone call asking him to return once again to the village and join the community in a day of reconciliation and forgiveness. The son of a woman who had died in the massacre revealed to Brian that in a dream his mother told him, "You must forgive my killer and not seek revenge." This message brought Brian comfort and took him to a place where he could forgive himself.

> One can pray and ask God to forgive you for what you have done. You can understand why you did certain things, but it seems to haunt you all the time until the stage where the other party comes and accepts your wish for forgiveness. If there is no acceptance from the offended party, forgiveness, self-forgiveness, isn't a reality. (interview, October 26, 2003)

Nepi revealed that without the forgiveness of Linda and Peter Biehl, he could not have forgiven himself. He stated,

> I've always wanted to be myself, but just couldn't get there. Linda and Peter were sort of a bridge over the trauma that I, not the militant, killed this lady and ended her life. I somehow have come to forgive myself because I have been forgiven for what I did and I can go on. (interview, October 3, 2002)

The theme of self-forgiveness appeared throughout the conversations with the men in this study. Each wrestled with the overwhelming task of moving his life beyond the violent event. Even though the attitude of the public and the larger community was centered on the men's acts of violence, they were storied as killers, these men believed themselves to be in possession of other dimensions that people were not aware of because the public could not see beyond the stigmatizing label of murderer.

Holloway (2002) speaks movingly of the burden of carrying past transgression around and the difficulty that the perpetrator has in ridding himself or herself of this stigma. He states,

> This is the cause of the greatest pain our humanity carries, the fact and remembrance of our own failures, those acts that can never be undone or reversed, which now turn the past into a great weight of regret that we bear everywhere with us and cannot lay down. (p. 32)

The men I interviewed revealed that the act of receiving forgiveness freed them from the public and psychological stigma of being a perpetrator. It lifted their overwhelming sense of guilt in such a way that they could forgive themselves, which they indicated was by far the most difficult barrier to overcome. I must emphasize that for each of these men the journey to self-forgiveness was a long and torturous one filled with doubt and moments of self-loathing. When telling the story of Amy Biehl's death, Nepi took me to the marble cross in Gugulethu commemorating the place where Amy died. He spoke about the incident in the third person, and when I asked him why, he said, "It is the only way I can talk about Amy's death without experiencing overwhelming feelings of shame and self-loathing" (interview, October 17, 2002).

The final theme of this study addresses the role of forgiveness, one of the principles of servant-leadership, in constructing the bridge that the perpetrator can cross to return to the community of people from which violence has alienated him or her.

FORGIVENESS AS A BRIDGE TO THE FUTURE

Holloway (2002) speaks of the difference between conditional forgiveness and pure forgiveness, or what I believe to be unconditional forgiveness. He believes that various aspects of conditional forgiveness, no matter how practical or creative, are structured in such a way that they simply "limit or manage the damage we do to one another whereas pure forgiveness has an intrinsic good, a pure gift with no motive of return" (p. 78). It is this pure forgiveness, or what Enright (1991) also calls forgiveness as love, that when offered may move the perpetrator toward genuine repentance. Enright's forgiveness as love constructs a bridge by which the transgressor can move from isolation to community and to a future. Holloway (2002) supports this idea:

> When true [pure] forgiveness happens it is one of the most astonishing and liberating of the human experiences. The tragedy of the many ways we trespass upon each other is that we can damage people so deeply that we rob them of the future by stopping the movement of their lives at the moment of injury, which continues to send out shock-waves of pain that swamp their existence. The real beauty and power of forgiveness is that it can deliver the future to us. (pp. 12–13)

Nepi, Khali, Letlapa Mphelele, and Brian Mitchell developed very close relationships with the people who forgave them. These four men indicated that these relationships made it possible for them to think about the future and gave them a sense of self-respect.

Linda Biehl calls Nepi and Khali her sons, first-born and second-born. I had the opportunity to interview Linda while doing my research in Cape Town and observed an interaction she had with Nepi. I had just spent an hour with this remarkable woman, and as we came out of her office at the Amy Biehl Foundation, her secretary asked her if she could work in another appointment that afternoon. She told her secretary that she could meet with that person before three o'clock but not to make any appointments after that. She indicated that she was taking Nepi shopping for a car seat for his newborn daughter. She looked at me with great concern in her eyes and said, "I'm so worried that Nepi's daughter have a proper car seat. You know young people these days just don't have the concern about car safety." As I was leaving, Nepi came out of the work-room, and to emphasize this point she said to him, "Nepi, don't schedule any appointments after three o'clock today. You and I are going car seat shopping for that new daughter of yours!" It was an amazing thing to hear from the woman who had lost her own precious daughter at the hands of this young man.

Of the six political perpetrators interviewed for this study, only one did not experience a feeling of being accepted back into the community after receiving forgiveness. In my final conversation with him in Pollsmoor Prison, Khaya poignantly shared,

> The past is always haunting me. I feel I am not supposed to be here. People think I am a violent person, that I am not a trustful person. I heard them say they forgave me. I think they were sincere, but they wanted justice still. In their voices I could hear this. (interview, September 27, 2002)

Conclusion

The findings in this study support the idea that empathy helps facilitate the interpersonal environment conducive to offering and receiving forgiveness. It was found that perceptions about perpetrators—based on their attitude, personal presentation, and outward appearance—were not always indicative of what they were actually experiencing within. The use of detachment and arrogance by perpetrators, often interpreted as lack of remorse or insensitivity to the victim, may actually be defense mechanisms protecting them from fear, shame, and humiliation.

The findings of this study support the idea that violence harms both the victim and the perpetrator. Although the harm is not always apparent, it was found that the psychological wounds expressed by perpetrators included the feeling of being poisoned by the experience, the feeling of being weighed down by the memory of the atrocity, and the feeling of pain whenever the event was remembered.

The findings of this study also support the idea that the offering of unconditional forgiveness, or forgiveness as a gift, increases the ability of the perpetrator to self-forgive. Self-forgiveness came only as perpetrators received forgiveness from the person or persons they had harmed.

The findings of this study support the idea that forgiveness is an important interpersonal experience by which perpetrators may be able to move beyond the immobilizing effects of their transgressions toward a future. Without the gift of unconditional forgiveness, the perpetrator, and perhaps even the victim, may remain confined to the injury from which neither may ever recover.

Because of the methodology used in this study, the conclusions cannot necessarily be generalized to apply to all perpetrators and victims. However, this study's findings do indicate a need to continue seeking understanding of the role of empathy and forgiveness in bringing inter-personal healing to perpetrators and victims. If the importance of these human acts continues to be a significant area of study in interpersonal healing and the alleviation of human suffering, it will be necessary to implement tangible and practical applications for promoting the occurrence of empathy and forgiveness.

Finally, the study implies that in an environment where human beings practice the principles of servant-leadership, empathy, forgiveness, and healing, there is hope for redemption in the hearts of some of the most hardened persons, the most unrepentant perpetrators, and hope for the restoration of community. This finding alone is perhaps the most important implication of this study. Such a revelation of hope may be the most useful finding for future researchers interested in studying this phenomenon, and for all those who suffer and have yet to make the decision to seek and receive forgiveness. This hope is centrally found in expressions of lasting and unconditional forgiveness, not bound by the remorse or denial of the perpetrator. Such forgiveness, unconditional and persevering, is integral to the soulfulness found in those who have been greatly harmed but have chosen a way of life attuned to the nature of legitimate power and greatness: a life lived for others. Even in the face of grave evil, this study revealed a resilience of human spirit I found uncompromising and filled with mercy. At the outset of my research I was unsure, even questioning the heart of humanity. I can now say a life for others, a servant-led life, exists, heals the world, restores us to one another, and gracefully makes us whole.

Epilogue

It has been twenty-six years since South Africa's first democratic election, and it has been eighteen years since I interviewed the men in this study. In looking at their lives since then, I found that five of the six continue to practice the principles of servant-leadership so beautifully modeled for them in the forgiveness they received from their victims and in the restorative justice process of the Truth and Reconciliation Commission. Only one man, Khaya, has not continued to develop in the same way that the other five have. I interviewed Khaya in Pollsmoor Prison, where he was awaiting trial for his alleged involvement in the robbery of an armored car in Cape Town. He told me that he wished that he could have gone on with his schooling and that he would have liked to have become an attorney, but life in the township was harsh and brutal—not much better for him or his family now than during the apartheid years. Although he had asked for forgiveness and was granted it by several church members and family members of victims who had died in the Saint James Church massacre, he did not feel that he had truly been forgiven. Nepi and Khali both work at the Amy Biehl Foundation in Cape Town in direct relationship with Linda Biehl. An unrelenting love has overcome the stolid denial and hardness that accompanied the early years after Amy's death. Today, Nepi and Khali, men of Africa who killed Amy Biehl, call Amy's mother their mother, and she calls them her sons. Together they work to improve the quality of life for families and children living in the townships.

In 2003 Letlapa, the Azanian People's Liberation Army commander who ordered the attack on the Heidelberg Tavern that resulted in the death of Ginn Fourie's daughter Lyndi, extended an invitation to Ginn to come to a reconciliation ceremony with him in a township outside of Johannesburg. Ginn accepted the invitation, and in a moving address publicly acknowledged Letlapa's request and extended forgiveness to him. During the ceremony in Letlapa's village, Letlapa and Ginn were given special names in his home language. The names symbolize a unique greeting, so that each time the two meet they can greet one another in this way: one asks of the other, "Where are you?," and the response is, "I am with you."

Today Ginn and Letlapa speak together internationally in honor of forgiveness, and since the reconciliation ceremony they have created the Lyndi Fourie Foundation, which helps political perpetrators and amnesty recipients receive personal counseling and vocational training in order to develop marketable skills to support themselves and their families.

In yet another act of servant-leadership, Ginn Fourie helped Stone, the man who killed her daughter, obtain a commercial-size chainsaw and contracts with the city of Cape Town to cut wood and clear brush. The chainsaw and the contracts enabled Stone, in turn, to be able to hire five additional men to assist him with the brush and wood clearing projects. Prior to this Stone had had no work, no future, and no hope of supporting his family. With Ginn's help, Stone became a businessman, capable of helping other men support their families as well.

Brian Mitchell, the police captain who ordered the attack on the house in the village of Trust Feed Village in which eleven innocent people were killed also continues living the principles of servant-leadership. Brian makes presentations around South Africa and internationally to bring attention to the plight of the Zulu people of Trust Feed. He is committed to restoring the community that he helped destroy during the apartheid struggle. In the attack, Brian's actions resulted in the death of innocent people, among them women and children. When the people of Trust Feed brought him back for a day of reconciliation and forgiveness, inviting him to live in the village, he felt his soul transformed. "I was dead until that day," he said. "And after that day I lived." Today he continues to work raising funds to construct a community center, hand in hand with those whose family members he had killed.

The lives of these men were redeemed through the restorative justice process of the Truth and Reconciliation Commission as they were once again reunited with the community of people they had deeply injured. Greenleaf's (1977) genuine test of servant-leadership is compellingly illustrated in the way these men have made deliberate choices to serve. Only a short time ago these men were denounced and vilified for their roles in the devastation of human lives and property. Political amnesty and interpersonal forgiveness gave them a future and another opportunity to live meaningful lives. In turn, the people they serve also have the opportunity to grow as persons and "become healthier, wiser, freer, more autonomous, and more likely themselves to become servants" (pp. 13–14).

References

Amnesty International / Human Rights Watch Briefing Paper. (2003). Truth and justice: Unfinished business in South Africa. Retrieved from http://www.hrw.org/ backgrounder/africa/truthandjustice.htm

Arendt, H. (2000). *The human condition (2nd ed.).* Chicago: University of Chicago Press.

Borris, E. R. (2003). The healing power of forgiveness. Occasional Paper Number 10, Institute for Multi-Track Diplomacy, Arlington, VA.

Bowman, R. F. (2005). Teacher as servant leader. *The Clearing House, 78*(6), 257–260.

Burton, M. (1998). Looking back, moving forward: Re-visiting conflicts, striving towards peace. Unpublished paper given at the conference "Dealing with the Past: Reconciliation Processes and Peace Building," June 8–9, 1998, Belfast, Northern Ireland.

Byrne, C. C. (2004). Benefit or burden: Victims' reflections on TRC participation. *Journal of Peace Psychology, 10*(3), 237–256.

Enright, R. D. (1991). The moral development of forgiveness. In W. M. Kurtines and J. L. Gewirtz (Eds.), *Handbook of moral behavior and development: Volume 1: Theory* (pp. 123–152). New York, NY: Psychology Press.

Erikson, E. (1963). *Childhood and society* (2nd ed.). New York, NY: W. W. Norton.

Ferch, S. (2005). Servant-Leadership, forgiveness, and social justice. *The International Journal of Servant-Leadership, 1*(1), 97–111.

Foster, D. (2000). The Truth and Reconciliation Commission and understanding perpetrators. *South African Journal of Psychology, 30*(1), 2–9.

Foster, D., Davis, D., & Sandler, D. (1987). *Detention and torture in South Africa: Psychological, legal, and historical studies.* Cape Town: David Phillip.

Fourie, G. (2000). The psychology of perpetrators of political violence in South Africa: A personal experience. *Ethnicity and Health, 5*(3/4), 283–289.

Gilligan, J. (1996). *Violence: Our deadly epidemic and its causes.* New York, NY: Grosset/Putnam.

Gobodo-Madikizela, P. (2002). Remorse, forgiveness, and rehumanization: Stories from South Africa. *Journal of Humanistic Psychology, 42*(1), 7–32.

Gobodo-Madikizela, P. (2004). *A human being died that night.* Boston, MA: Houghton Mifflin Company.

Greenleaf, R. (1977). *Servant leadership: A journey into the nature of legitimate power and greatness.* New York, NY: Paulist Press.

Holloway, R. (2002). *On forgiveness: How can we forgive the unforgivable?* Edinburgh: Cannongate Books.

Howatson-Jones, I. L. (2004). The servant leader. *Nursing Management, 11*(3), 20–25.

Kressel, N. J. (1996). *Mass hate.* New York, NY: Plenum Press.

Krog, A. (1998). *Country of my skull: Guilt, sorrow, and the limits of forgiveness in the new South Africa.* New York, NY: Three Rivers Press.

Laub, J. A. (1999). *Assessing the servant organization: Development of the Servant Organizational Leadership Assessment (SOEA) instrument* (Unpublished doctoral dissertation). Florida Atlantic University.

Lax, A. *A culture of reconciliation in Africa: The South African Truth and Reconciliation Commission: Transformative justice, the restoration of dignity, and reconciliation.* Unpublished paper.

Myers, D. (1999). *Social psychology* (6th ed.). Boston, MA: McGraw-Hill College.

Nicholas, L. J. (2000). Expert witness testimony in the criminal trial of Eugene de Kock: A critique of the posttraumatic stress disorder (PTSD) defense. *South African Journal of Psychology, 30*(1), 33–36.

Orr, W. (1998). The Truth and Reconciliation Commission. *Continuing Medical Education, 16,* 142–143.

Sendjaya, S., & Sarros, J. C. (2002). Servant leadership: Its origin, development, and application in organizations. *Journal of Leadership & Organizational Studies, 9*(2), 57–65.

Smith, B. N., Montagno, R. V., & Kuzmenko, T. N. (2004). Transformational and servant leadership: Content and contextual comparisons. *Journal of Leadership & Organizational Studies, 10*(4), 80–92.

Sparks, A. (1994). *Tomorrow is another country: The inside story of South Africa's negotiated revolution.* Johannesburg, South Africa: Struik Book Distributors.

Spears, L. C. (Ed). (1998). *Insights on leadership: Service, stewardship, spirit, and servant-leadership.* New York, NY: John Wiley and Sons.

Spears, L. C. (2005). The understanding and practice of servant-leadership. *The International Journal of Servant-Leadership, 1*(1), 29–45.

Spears, L. C., & Lawrence, M. (2004). *Practicing servant-leadership: Succeeding through trust, bravery, and forgiveness.* San Francisco, CA: Jossey-Bass.

Staub, E. (1989). *The roots of evil.* Cambridge, England: Cambridge University Press.

Tatum, J. B. (1995). Meditations on servant-leadership. In L. C. Spears (Ed.), *Reflections on leadership* (pp. 308–312). New York, NY: John Wiley and Sons.

Terrell, M. N. (2004). Making truth fit: The Truth and Reconciliation Commission, its misunderstood gift, and its underanalyzed legacy. Retrieved from http://www.stanford.edu/~jbaugh/saw/ManonTruthReconcil.html

Tutu, D. M. (1999). *No future without forgiveness.* New York, NY: Doubleday.

Villa-Vicencio, C., & Verwoerd, W. (2000). *Looking back, reaching forward: Reflections on the Truth and Reconciliation Commission of South Africa.* Cape Town: University of Cape Town Press.

Chapter 3

Enlightened Leadership in a Changing, Troubled World

GEORGE PATRICK MURPHY

One of the more positive responses flowing from the global economic, ethical, political, and spiritual crises that have challenged social architecture over the past thirty years has been the gradual emergence of a new leadership paradigm. The servant-leadership movement has gone mainstream. It now represents a powerful alternative guiding leadership philosophy embraced by an increasing number of leaders from within the for-profit, nonprofit, governmental, and professional arenas. I believe that the fundamental benefits inherent in the theory and practice of servant-leadership represent an exciting opportunity for leaders to develop and enhance their leadership efficacy as they seek to enable the people and organizations they serve to survive and flourish, even in the face of challenging, rapidly changing times. The concepts inherent in the philosophy and theory of servant-leadership are easy enough to grasp on an intellectual basis. However, personally integrating its key tenets and successfully leading the institutional, organizational, and cultural shifts required to adopt them requires extensive interior assessment, time, effort, creativity, and foresight on the part of enlightened individuals who fully embrace the spirit of selfless contribution to a good beyond their own self-interest. The journey to becoming an authentic servant-leader promises to be a richly transformative and rewarding endeavor for those possessing the insight, courage, and stamina to chart new courses of action for themselves and those whom they have the privilege of leading.

Servant-Leadership as a Guiding Philosophical Principle

The founding father of the servant-leadership movement, Robert K. Greenleaf, provided the scholarly foundation for understanding this rapidly advancing contemporary leadership theory. A visionary, Greenleaf (2002) captured the essence of the underpinning philosophy of the servant-leader when he wrote more than thirty years ago,

> The servant leader is servant first. . . . It begins with the natural feeling that one wants to serve, to serve *first*. Then conscious choice brings one to aspire to lead. . . . The difference manifests itself in the care taken by the servant-first to make sure that other people's highest-priority needs are being served. The best test . . . is: Do those served grow as persons? Do they, *while being served,* become healthier, wiser, freer, more autonomous, more likely themselves to become servants? (p. 27; emphasis in original)

Ramsey (2006) further captured the spirit of servant-leadership when she quoted Laub, who explained,

> Servant leadership is an understanding and practice of leadership that places the good of those led over the self-interest of the leader. Servant leadership promotes the valuing and development of people, the building of community, the practice of authenticity, the providing of leadership for the good of those led, and the sharing of power and status for the common good of each individual. (as cited in Ramsey, 2006, p. 113)

Ramsey elaborated further, writing,

> The broadening view of servant-leadership embeds holistic leadership practices not only in the corporate boardroom, but in social and political interactions that rely upon, even demand, the need for people who are dedicated to making the world a better place for all to live. (p. 113)

Since the 1980s, the philosophy of servant-leadership has gained widespread and growing acceptance. It has merited advocacy from mainstream leadership studies leaders, noted scholars, popular writers, and distinguished practitioners. Warren Bennis, Stephen Covey, Peter Senge, Margaret Wheatley, Parker Palmer, Larry Spears, and Max De Pree, to name a few, have all endorsed and promoted the philosophy of servant-leadership. All cite the visionary acumen of Robert Greenleaf and reflect the power of incorporating the tenets of this leadership theory into modern-day leadership practice within for-profit, not-for-profit, institutional, governmental, and organizational contexts. Clearly, the philosophy and practice have caught on and are gaining momentum. Not only does servant-leadership have wings, but also its proponents and organizational "converts" are rapidly emerging as front-runners in their respective fields. Within the world of business, an increasing number of enterprises have "adopted servant-leadership as part of their corporate philosophy or as a foundation for their mission statement" (Spears, 2004, p. 17).

The servant-leadership movement did not burst on the scene as a quick-fix leadership theory "flavor of the month." By definition and design, its personal and organizational inculcation involves fundamental change in the hearts, minds, and souls of its adherents. Making such deep and profound change is time-intensive hard work, not for the faint of heart. Changing beliefs, attitudes, behaviors, and management practices is a transformative process; for that reason, effecting such change requires a new vision coupled with energetic championing and inspiration. In short, it requires the inspired leadership of self and others.

Highly successful enterprises such as the Toro Company, Synovus Financial, Zeno Group, the Vanguard Group, Costco, Men's Wearhouse, Southwest Airlines, Starbucks, TD Industries, and ServiceMaster have (or until recently, had) visionary, principle-driven leaders and like-minded leadership team members who are (or were) staunch advocates of advancing the philosophy and practice of servant-leadership (although not all of them use the term) as their guiding operating platform for culture building and operating their thriving businesses. Likewise, a growing number of successful, best-in-class, smaller, less-visible enterprises have leaders who practice the tenets of servant-leadership in their business organizations.

The traits exhibited by these leaders match those in Larry Spears's (2004) summation, gleaned from Greenleaf's works, of the ten key characteristics of servant-leaders. Spears cites listening, empathy, healing, persuasion, awareness, foresight, conceptualization, commitment to the growth of people, stewardship, and building community as common traits exhibited by efficacious servant-leaders (Spears, 2004, pp. 13–18).

Based on my studies of servant-leadership and my own experience as a business and not-for-profit leader, I would add forgiving, restoring, and focusing relentlessly on customer and clientele needs to Spears's list of characteristics required to be an authentic and effective servant-leader. Such a list can be invaluable in supporting a leader's attempts to build a holistic self and organization.

Servant-leadership, with its inherent empowering, inclusive, collaborative, and liberating elements, is an approach whose time has arrived. It appears to me to be the prevailing leadership theory that best responds to the complex and rapidly changing business environments in which we must navigate today. The fact that the aforementioned leading servant-leadership-oriented companies are emerging as business segment "winners" confirms my personal choice to adopt the servant-leadership model as the guiding leadership philosophy and culture-building cornerstone of the organizations for which I serve as a leader and mentor.

Servant-leadership not only "feels right"—that is, is consistent and compatible with my values, ethics, guiding principles, and leadership style—it also substantiates my belief that if companies do not adopt it, they will be vulnerable to competitive intrusions from progressive organizations that have done so. Additionally, they will have foregone a potentially significant opportunity to establish a significant competitive advantage and to establish healthy, thriving organizational cultures of integrity. But before a company can be run on servant-leadership principles, its leaders must passionately embrace the relevant thinking and serve as pioneers in championing service-first practices.

Self-Examination, Reflection, and Determination: The First Steps toward Becoming a "Leader for Others"

A prerequisite to becoming an authentic and enlightened leader seeking to "serve first" is a cultivated, deep self-awareness. Business leaders of purpose, conviction, courage, and compassion are at peace with themselves and with those they serve. Self-examined leaders know who they are and which principles cannot be abandoned. Such leaders have engaged in internal wrestling regarding personal meaning, ethics, and purpose. These leaders appreciate their positive attributes. Conversely, honest, thorough, and sometimes painful self-assessment unveils these leaders' shortcomings. Once they are aware of their strengths and weaknesses, they can nurture the former and mitigate the latter. Not until leaders have engaged in such self-analysis and conducted a deep and comprehensive moral assessment are they able to be of optimal service to those led.

I believe that an individual's first step in becoming an authentic and trustworthy servant-leader is to achieve personal clarity regarding doing the right things for the right reasons. Leaders must conduct constant self-assessment regarding their innermost thoughts, biases, and feelings while endeavoring to become the best leaders possible.

After an intense level of moral, soul-searching assessment, a self-examined individual (and leader) may hypothetically query in advance some of our projected responses to even the most challenging dilemmas and circumstances. These self-assessments and reflections may help us respond with personal integrity to situations and circumstances that later confront us. Some of these theoretical questions might be: What extremes would we go to ensure our very survival? What would we be willing to risk to preserve our integrity in regard to that which we intimately and passionately value (for example self-dignity, preservation of life, freedom, justice, and the pursuit of happiness)? To what degree would we be willing to endure pain, transgressions, suffering, oppression, and loss of self-respect with regard to the aforementioned noble values? What external forces and environments would cause us to abandon our previously held values and principles? How deep would our personal moral resolve be to remain fair, honest, respectful, responsible, loving, and compassionate if we found ourselves in the horrid conditions and circumstances so eloquently articulated by Wiesenthal (1976), Wiesel (2006), Frankl (2006), and other survivors of the atrocities of the Holocaust? When do we have a personally defined moral responsibility to stand up and resist the recognized oppression perpetrated against individuals, communities, and races? Do we choose to forgive our transgressors *as* we forgive those who trespass against us? Do we lead and choose to follow processes enabling unconditional restorative justice (as did Nelson Mandela), unconditional restorative justice (as practiced by the South African Truth and Reconciliation Commission), retributive justice (seen in the Nuremberg trials of Germany), or retaliatory justice (as propagated by the mafia and gangs)? What is our premeditated stance against wrongdoers who have violated our rights, either individually or as a community? Do we seek first that which is good in ourselves and others, or do we look for the bad? Do we seek to contribute to the well-being and benefit of others, or are we driven by our self-interest? In times of severe adversity and loss, do we retain our faith and trust in a higher power, or do we sever our spiritual relationships and lose our trust and faith in others?

We cannot help but wonder how we would respond if we were placed in such circumstances. Hypothetical self-assessment and reflection, spurred by education and exposure, help us test the clarity, depth, and intensity of our professed value and ethical systems. This type of self-analysis, though potentially painful, may give us intense and provocative insight into who we *really* are, thereby informing our self-knowledge. The juxtapositions give us insight into our true heart and, as Rabbi Moishe put it when speaking to Wiesel (2006), into the "God within me" (p. 5). The self-prediction of our responses, following a self-review of our professed principles, values, and ethics, can also help us clarify our personal perspectives on the topics of forgiveness, restoration, and justice. Although ideally we will never have to experience atrocities or horrific scenes such as those experienced by victims of the Holocaust, or the evils of apartheid that gripped South Africa, or the oppression so prevalent in the Arab Spring, insights gained through such interior assessment can help an individual define and shape who he or she is, as a person and as a leader. As we challenge ourselves to formulate responses to our personal inquiries and seek to answer questions such as those listed above, and to project corresponding responses, we move a step closer to understanding our own meaning and purpose in life. Do we view ourselves as good and worthy of the love of God and others, or as unworthy, perhaps even as bad persons in need of forgiveness, restoration, and perhaps redemption to become whole again? As we assess where we are on life's mysterious path, do we project the qualities of a decent or an indecent person? As Frankl (2006) wrote, "There are two races of men in this world, but only these two—the 'race' of the decent man and the 'race' of the indecent man. They are found everywhere; they penetrate into all groups of society" (p. 86).

Throughout our lives, we have wonderful opportunities to learn and to experience personal growth flowing from our current and past encounters with the good and evil forces that confront us or are initiated from within. Our struggles, suffering, exposure to atrocities, and bouts with darkness all provide opportunities for self-discovery, healing, beneficial change, hope, and rebirth (Ferch, 2012). Conversely, engagements and personal encounters with truth, love, justice, forgiveness, compassion, beauty, and joy also penetrate our human existence and serve to enlighten us and give us reason and purpose to live a full and rich life of meaning steeped in authentic service to others (Ferch, 2012). I believe that in the final reckoning, who we are, assuming we desire to become whole, contributing, spiritual, and "others first" people, is greatly influenced by how we choose to deal with the darkness of evil and the light of goodness as they are, inevitably, cast upon us. Do we succumb to the harsh and sometimes repugnant forces that have shackled us and held us captive within the depths of our inner prison, or do we seek to escape and pursue new beginnings and vistas as we toil to regain our wholeness and well-being as we vigorously set out on a long climb toward the transcendental?

A study of servant-leadership provides a wonderful backdrop that enables us to gain an informed perspective and to learn from the individuals and organizations, communities and nations, that have experienced the harshest depths of evil, as well as the freedoms and discoveries emanating from the heights of goodness. As we learn and apply our knowledge, we open ourselves to new expansive and examined possibilities in the formulation of our individual choices and responses to the forces of good and evil. Although our behaviors and actions may be influenced by circumstances beyond our control, I believe our choice of responses and attitudes remains within our control. This is the gift of free will and freedom of choice bestowed upon us by our creator. Perhaps, as Wiesel postulated, God tolerates evil because it paves a potential path to an even greater level of goodness.

In this chapter, I will look back on the worst confrontation with a dark force I experienced in my thirty-five years in business as a manager and leader. The setting is a large business organization. After providing the personal and organizational systems' contextual background, I recount how I viewed the challenges though the lens of the value system and ethics I subscribed to at that time in my life. I then examine how, in the face of conflict inherent in the examined problem, I sought to maintain my personal integrity and to preserve the dignity of the people I was privileged to lead in an environment fraught with uncertainty, mistrust, anger, and fear, by describing my responses and corresponding actions. I evaluate my life-giving responses (and lapses), reflecting the light of the new learning and insights gained thus far through study of servant-leadership. I share my self-critique while addressing the self-posed questions: Did I do enough? What more could I have done with the benefit of my recent discoveries and subsequent life learning? I also examine recent examples of processes used in asking for and receiving forgiveness based on what I have studied in the doctoral program in leadership studies at Gonzaga University. Finally, I summarize my thoughts and offer a recommendation, hopeful that I contribute to a sense of hope and optimism that, in me, stems from a belief in the overarching strength of the force of goodness to overpower evil.

Personal Contextual Background for Organizational Problem Understanding

As I commenced and advanced in my business career, an exercise I did in a graduate school class at the University of Southern California several decades ago proved invaluable. We were asked to define our life goals: personal, professional, and spiritual. After identifying our guiding life principles and core values, we were asked to write a fictional obituary and to note, in a sentence or two, how we wanted to be remembered after we were gone. My remembrance statement was: "He lived his life and conducted his business with integrity." The aspirational values I selected were fairness, honesty, respect for others, responsibility for my actions, and always showing compassion and love for others. A strong work ethic, creativity, competitiveness, collaboration, and contribution were listed as my operative values. Some of my selected guiding life and professional principles were to treat everyone respectfully, be inclusive, be humble, and lead by example. On the spiritual front, I selected the three overarching goals of loving God with the entirety of my mind, body, and spirit; loving my neighbor as myself; and when harm to others is unavoidable, mitigating it to the extent possible.

As I discovered later, living and behaving in accordance with these values and principles severely tested my resolve and resilience as I dealt with the organizational business problem described in the following paragraphs. These ideals also proved to be the trough from which I would drink in order to maintain my equilibrium during the chaotic and difficult times ahead.

At the time I made my decision to pursue a business career, I had two lingering concerns. First, I was worried that I might not be able to maintain my values and live within the constructs of my principles, given the highly charged and often cutthroat world of big business; second, I wondered whether my recently developed and coveted people-first leadership style would be compatible with the realities of the proverbial mandate to "make the numbers at all costs" so pervasive in corporate cultures.

I had decided that working for a leading Fortune 100 company would be the career path that would best allow me to play to my strengths. Successfully doing so would provide my wife and me with the optimum opportunity to raise our eventual family in agreeable environments while providing the lifestyle and professional achievements we desired. Also playing heavily into my early career decision was my aspiration to enjoy and excel at a job I could become passionate about. I also set out to prove to myself and to others that "good guys" could not only survive but also flourish in the highly competitive and politicized world of big business. (At the time, I defined a "good guy" as a person notable for the way in which he or she accepted responsibility, exhibited good character, treated others with respect and compassion, and conducted business with integrity. In my mind, good guys also seemed to have a lot of fun and to enjoy full and active lives.)

The company I chose was the quality and innovative leader within its industry. Additionally, it represented what I believed to be a perfect personal fit in terms of my long-term career aspirations, while holding highly desirable enterprise values and having created a very positive, ethical culture. It also had an excellent reputation for having the best people and leadership in the sector. In addition, its growth prospects for the division for which I was recruited were excellent.

The enterprise clearly met the criteria I had identified while seeking the "the best possible company for me." It would enable me to pursue my passion for business and to realize my dream of a long career of contribution and distinction, while fulfilling my need to make enough money to meet my long-term financial objectives.

Business Problem Contextual Background

After early career success, I advanced quickly, and the company seemed to take a special interest in me as a person while rewarding me with a series of rapid promotions and the continuing designation of being a "high-potential" associate. The company (particularly our commercial division) and I prospered and flourished for my first eighteen years of employment.

A benefit of being designated a "high-potential performer" at the company's world headquarters was that the senior leadership served as volunteer mentors. In my case, both the CEO and the worldwide leader of my division acted as my mentors and role models. Both of these gentlemen were great teachers and promoters of personal growth and development—true servant-leaders. Looking back now, with the benefit of studying and understanding the philosophical underpinnings, key tenets, and characteristics of true servant "others first" leadership, and using Larry Spears's (2004) ten characteristics of an authentic servant-leader as an evaluative standard, I would rate these executives as business servant-leaders of integrity. They consistently "talked the talk and walked the walk" exemplified in true servant-leadership (Spears, 2004, p. 17). In addition, they were extremely competent, competitive, hardworking, and ethical businessmen who were quick to smile. I was honored to call them friends.

The CEO was forced to retire by the board of directors after serving more than twenty years; during the last ten of those years, he also served as chairman of the board of directors. The salient reasons cited by the board, when announcing the decision to force retirement, centered on the CEO's documented deficiencies in not leading a reversal of the two-year cascading financial performance trend, his inability to "right-size" the company via the failed execution of multiple "restructuring" efforts, and his failure to deliver the targeted return-on-investment ratios associated with a multibillion-dollar capital expenditure program designed to expand the capacity of one of the corporation's highly profitable but underperforming divisions. The board members had decided it was time to bring in a proven, restructuring type of CEO. They recruited and chose a highly publicized, ruthlessly successful restructuring specialist CEO to "save" the company. Wall Street responded immediately and favorably. Our stock price quickly began to rise. Clearly, the board had made the right decision from the perspective of shareholders.

For weeks following the tenured CEO's "retirement," a sense of anger, loss, denial, and uncertainty about the future seemed to preoccupy the minds of all 33,000 global employees. These feelings and emotions were particularly manifested among the more than 1,600 dedicated loyalists (including me) who were located at the worldwide headquarters.

On a sunny day in late April, following weeks of hearing nothing from our new CEO (although we had all been visited and challenged by his outside consulting group, who were "assisting" with his "reorganization work and evaluation of personnel"), the entire executive headquarters staff was summoned to the cafeteria for a mandatory thirty-minute meeting with our new leader. At the appointed hour, the new chairman-CEO entered from the back of the room, surrounded by what looked like a contingency of Secret Service agents and four sharply dressed senior executive types. He walked swiftly and confidently to a podium. Turning to face the crowd and without taking off his sunglasses, he boomed, red-faced,

> You cowards should be ashamed of yourselves . . . how could you continue to work for such a weak, ineffective group of corporate leaders who ran this once fine company into the ground? If you had any guts or smarts, you would have left this dismal place a long time ago. . . . I have just fired the whole worthless lot of them. Effective immediately, these fine gentlemen [motioning to the four executive types] will be running the show.

We learned later that the sole exception to the firing barrage was the worldwide leader of my division, the most profitable and fastest-growing business unit in the company's portfolio of holdings.

In the days that followed, all remaining senior executives were asked to present their plans, budgets, and projected head counts. In my case, I was leading (while serving as the North American, Commercial Division, vice president of sales and channel development) the National Sales and Customer Service Group, which was responsible for close to a billion dollars of profitable revenue. This team was widely recognized as the best in the commercial industry. I had been recently "interrogated," without notice, by a group of four sales and marketing "experts" from the new CEO's "hired gun" consultancy. I was grilled and tested from 8 a.m. until 5 p.m. that dismal day. At the conclusion of the interviews, I was told to "cease all hiring and await further direction."

After two weeks, I was revisited by the consultant experts. They informed me that I had been selected to stay in my role, that my already aggressive financial forecasts and plans had been slightly modified upward, and that my already sparse operating budget was being reduced dramatically. I was also warned that I was expected by the CEO to make the numbers at an accelerated pace and with a 20 percent reduction in head count. I was told, confidentially, that the company was being "right-sized" from 33,000 people to a number below 20,000. Also confided was that the headquarters staff would be reduced from 1,600 to 485, and that I had been selected to implement the yet-to-be-developed "downsizing" plan for the entire USA Commercial Division Sales and Marketing USA Group—affecting hundreds of dedicated associates. I was devastated on hearing the "good news" and receiving their "congratulations." How could I ever implement a plan that was sure to decimate and slowly lead to the demise of the company, division, and team that I cherished and had been an integral part of building? How could I carry out my assigned task while maintaining my personal integrity, while upholding my afore-mentioned values and living into my core principles? That challenge, and the surrounding challenge of having to create a process of retention and termination that passed "legal muster," was a daunting proposition. The degree of difficulty in terms of meeting our new leader's expectations was exponentially multiplied by the directive to execute my plan within three weeks—or "suffer the consequences." In the days and weeks that followed, I struggled, agonized, and lost a lot of sleep worrying about the job elimination and termination plan for which I was now accountable.

Value- and Principle-Driven Response to the Downsizing Problem

How could I maintain my valued integrity while leading the design and execution of the massive division downsizing initiative? This was a huge moral and ethical dilemma. From my perspective, the mandated downsizing was arbitrary, cold-blooded, and unjustified. It did not reflect the reality that our division had for years exceeded our plan expectations and had grown at a pace that more than justified the capital outlays the corporation had bestowed on us. I decided that, given my leadership role and my values, I had a moral and ethical responsibility to aggressively challenge and confront the new corporate leadership team and the hired-gun consultants with a logical, data-supported presentation that justified our division's being granted an exemption, or at least a significant reduction in the size and scope of the reduction numbers. The consultants quietly listened to my exemption request. At the conclusion of my presentation, they stated that they had already taken these factors into consideration when setting the reductions and that the figures were not negotiable. The 20 percent head count reduction would remain in effect. They went on to remind me how lucky I was. Other divisions that performed less well were facing up to a 40 percent personnel reduction mandate. I was once again devastated. The CEO also told me that if I did not feel up to the task, he would bring in someone who would deliver the intended results. I picked up my materials and slowly, almost blindly, walked down the long hallway back to my office. The initial battle to "save" my beloved division had been waged. I had lost a fight I had no chance of winning.

After a night of reflection (clouded by moments of anger, spite, and self-pity, along with thoughts of resignation), I decided that it would be irresponsible of me to abandon my team and the great people who had been so dedicated to the company and supportive of me personally over the years. I owed it to them, and to myself, to do all that I could to preserve the goodness of our division's legacy. This became my driving professional purpose. That night, I concluded that the right thing to do was to remain in my role. Staying with the company was the first, most essential choice I had to make as I prepared to once again face the "Slasher CEO" force of evil. I committed to myself that, once again, I would seek to prove that the "good guys" could rise above it all and emerge victorious in the long term. I decided to use my gained knowledge of how things were really done at the headquarters and in the marketplace to do everything in my power to preserve the nucleus of what had made us so special as an organization. "Survive and thrive" became my inner, and soon my external, message. I would rally my team with a vision of hope and a tangible strategy that showed that a "good life after the war" was our destiny.

The first plank in the plan was to retain our corporate "top performer" status. The rest flowed from there. I reasoned that great results, achieved in spite of the siege, would be our salvation. Meeting the inflated business performance targets would greatly enhance our collective chances of survival. Doing so would also allow us to emerge in a future position of strength, regardless of the corporate environment we found ourselves in. I was reminded of the old adage "What does not kill you makes you stronger." The words took on new meaning that night and in the ensuing months. With these thoughts swirling and flowing, I noticed that creative thoughts began to surface (although slowly at first), and I began to see new possibilities once again. My attitude and mood also began to improve as my newly defined purpose became clearer and served as a guide for my ensuing actions.

Over the following days, I calculated, after conducting a little research on the CEO and his self-appointed position as the dean of the "Restructuring CEO Academy," that once the restructuring had taken place, he and his "merry men" would grab their spoils and move on to the next unsuspecting enterprise whose board had decided that what was needed was a quick restructuring "fix." It seemed to me that this was how the guy got his "high." He was good at it, and he was personally banking tens of millions of dollars in short order. I reasoned that if we could band together and protect each other, we would outlive the CEO and survive to rise again in glory. I made a commitment to myself: I would design a plan and execution strategy that would not only deliver the numbers but would do so in a way that reflected my (our) values and be carried out within the context of my centered principles. This commitment set the stage for my team's work in executing the mandated downsizing with as much compassion and empathy as possible under the circumstances. We would treat those being affected with respect, trying to minimize the negative impact on each individual and his or her family. We would also do everything in our collective power to ensure that each individual came out of the downsizing process in the most advantageous position possible.

The first step in orchestrating the restructuring plan was to define a new organizational structure that ideally would support the deliverance of the short-term earnings objectives while ensuring the viability of our newly minted longer-term strategic plan. Once this task was complete, we could legally begin the selection and rehiring process that provided the human resources (within the allowable head count allocation numbers) needed to deliver the forecasts.

My team did masterful work in helping me shape and finalize a winning, legally approved plan in less than two weeks. Concurrent with this work I and my very capable personal assistant undertook a clandestine effort that began the distasteful outplacement process in the first move toward what we knew would be an immediate downsizing of our organization.

I knew we would have to orchestrate outplacement encounters at four regional and twenty-six district office locations. Working independently, and with the help of the district and regional administrative assistants, we booked the hotels and made the other logistical arrangements to facilitate individual outplacement service engagements with the yet-to-be-contracted professional firms who specialized in such work. I reminded myself at the time that we were firmly committed to orchestrating what would become known as the "Black Friday" event with as much fairness and compassion as possible. We would seek to preserve the dignity and self-respect of the affected individuals, in spite of the speed with which we were required to act given the arbitrary three-week deadline for completing the "right-sizing" effort.

With the help of a skillful and empathetic corporate human resources manager, we made arrangements to hire the best corporate outplacement firms across the country. Direction was given to prepare "exit packages" that included full benefits and salary continuance for up to six months for every associate who would be affected. Since we had not yet completed the selection and hiring process to staff the new organization's structure and did not know who would be retained or who would be downsized, exit packages had to be generated for everyone in the division in anticipation of the potential that the individualized packages might be needed to facilitate the anticipated termination encounters on "Black Friday." This was a herculean task for our HR department, but they, agreeing that we should display the highest level of compassion possible, did yeoman's work to support this effort.

I also insisted that no "mass firing" tactics be deployed. Every affected individual would be engaged by a company supervisor and a professional outsource service-provider skilled at helping people process the trauma of being "let go." These folks were also skilled at developing individual, need-based job searches. We signed up for the platinum-level outplacement services for every eventual victim of the "right-sizing" process. This strategy would ensure that each individual received as much assistance as possible as we helped folks find a new employment home. To increase the care and respect offered when leading the termination sessions, I reminded all involved with carrying out the "right-sizing" activities that it could easily have been us on the receiving end of the termination engagement table.

During this planning phase, I also had a divine inspiration that could potentially serve to reduce our 20 percent reduction number to 10 percent. We could "transfer" our existing dedicated food-service sales and marketing personnel to an outside independent sales and marketing firm that specialized in providing services to the food-service industry. I next quietly negotiated a deal with the president of this national firm that would provide for the immediate hiring of the displaced associates—en masse. The salary and benefit package offered would replicate the one they currently enjoyed. The scope and nature of the work would remain largely unchanged. Retained company management would provide the specifications dictating the ongoing priorities and performance expectations for this group. The net effect on the displaced employees was that they would be terminated and then immediately rehired by the outsourcing firm at the same pay level, with approximately the same core benefits, that they were receiving at the time of the "right-sizing." Their work responsibilities would remain essentially the same. All that materially changed was the name on their paycheck. These folks would also be told that the door would possibly be reopened for them to rejoin our company's team as future opportunities arose.

This was my creative response to the big challenge as I sought to minimize the often traumatizing and emotionally demoralizing impacts of being "fired." By successfully executing this plan, we were eventually able to achieve 50 percent of our head-count-reduction objective while minimizing some of the potential harm done to the folks involved. Another positive aspect of this approach was that our valued customers in the food-service sector would not be negatively affected by the inevitable diminishing of the service and representation levels that would result from the downsizing. We pulled this "salvation" strategy off with only minor problems, much to the delight of all involved. The "good guys" had registered their first minor victory, and nobody on the corporate leadership team knew that there had even been a skirmish. Confidence within the team was building.

There were some potential personal risks inherent in this plan, given the CEO's explicit direction to refrain from hiring outside consultants, accompanied by the threat of firing, on the spot, any manager who violated this directive, and the almost maniacal pleasure "the Rifleman" seemed to take in pulling the "firing" trigger. I could have been terminated for insubordination. From my viewpoint, the CEO operated without conscience, compassion, or regard for anything that transcended his huge ego and overt need for financial gain, power, public notoriety, and Wall Street adulation. He got immediate action through the use of intimidation, coercion, and unilateral decision making. "The Rifleman," as his lieutenants called him, spread terror, stress, and anxiety wherever he ventured; his leadership style was all "command and control." I decided to proceed with my plan in spite of the risk of being fired. I did so knowing that the potential benefits of the outsourcing decision overshadowed the risks. I also correctly assumed that the risk of being "caught" would be minimized as long as we met the head count and earnings numbers. I reasoned with myself that the CEO's radar would not reach the executional detail level of this plan. Fortunately, this was a good read on the situation. My plan went undetected.

We ended up making both the head count reduction and the financial growth objectives. I executed the downsizing successfully without compromising my core values. After a year of survival and good earnings performance, I was offered a promotion to become the division vice president of the Asia Pacific region and relocate to the company's Hong

Kong regional headquarters. My group's North American "top performer" status was maintained and strengthened. I therefore jumped at the opportunity to take on an exciting new business challenge and at the chance to escape the prison-type atmosphere that had engulfed the worldwide headquarters. It had gotten so bad that the CEO had actually received death threats and hired a full-time bodyguard to be next to him at all times while at the office.

Eventually, the company was sold to a leading strategic buyer for more than $9 billion. "The Dean of Restructuring" earned more than $125 million in buyout incentives and accelerated option grants. Our division was cited as being the "diamond" that drove the strategic buyer's acquisition desires. Our new owners valued what we had done in the marketplace and recognized that it was our great people who had enabled our sustained success. They paid billions for this goodwill.

My family and I had moved to Hong Kong (the company's Asia Pacific headquarters) months earlier. I was asked to remain with the "new" company and to serve as the Asia region vice president with accountability for the commercial business division and for creating the integration plans and future strategies that would ensure a bright future for the region and its customers and people. My beloved Commercial Group had found a new nurturing home within the new enterprise. Our "survive and thrive" vision had been realized without compromising integrity. Nonetheless, I felt an unhealthy amount of anger as a result of the callous actions and coldhearted tactics of the Rifleman and his henchmen while executing the downsizing plan and during the sale of the company.

Forgiveness Applications

Before studying servant-leadership, I thought little about the benefits of a forgiveness process as a key component of one's personal or leadership philosophy or practice. The bitterness I felt toward the CEO and his ruthless tactics seemed just and reasonable. I found myself telling "despicable Rifleman" stories whenever the opportunity presented itself. Doing so only kept those wounds open and was unhealthy for me. I could feel the anger and anxiety return each time I publicly responded to the question, what was it like working for the notorious hatchet CEO? I often told my story with a sense of vengeance motivated by a strong need to seek revenge and retaliation.

Recently, after studying and learning about Nelson Mandela's brand of personal unconditional forgiveness, including his process designed to mend old wounds, as well as the application of restorative justice practiced by the Truth and Reconciliation Commission under Desmond Tutu's (1997, 2004) leadership in South Africa, I became intrigued by the often untapped power of asking and granting forgiveness and its healing properties and restorative benefits. For the past two years I have consciously chosen to regularly seek opportunities to practice forgiveness and to avail myself of the well-being associated with freeing myself from retaliatory revenge-seeking and then moving on to a more serene state of being.

My new insights have taught me that forgiveness and its supportive processes offer a great potential for unleashing personal healing and growth and for making me a better person and servant-type leader who possesses "the confidence and footing . . . to cross the chasm of personal growth to arrive at a life devoted to helping fulfill the highest priority needs of those being served" (Ferch, 2012, p. 46). I learned that incorporating an authentic forgiveness process into our personal and communal lives holds the potential for liberation and rebirth. It holds the promise of lessening the burden of carrying the destructive feelings of fear, hatred, anger, revenge, embarrassment, guilt, isolation, despair, self-pity, and depression. It opens the door to conflict resolution. It opens the door to the restoration of fellowship, peace, and harmony. It has become apparent to me that if I am to avail myself of the power and corresponding benefits promised by the acts of seeking and giving forgiveness, I must have a personal process for sensitizing myself to the need to invoke the power of forgiveness. My created process includes the following actions:

- Recognizing that my actions, comments, and behaviors may cause more harm, injustice, and damage to an individual than I may believe or intend.

- Recognizing that the act of seeking legitimate forgiveness often takes courage, time, and energy, and is hard work—there are no quick fixes.

- Recognizing that if I feel that I have in some way caused harm to another, I should immediately and humbly admit and acknowledge my wrongdoing or offense and apologize for the *specific* act and request forgiveness. I should let the harmed consider my request, and if that person shares feelings, patiently listen and not become defensive or combative. The harmed person may need to know that I fully understand the depth and breadth of the pain I have caused before she or he grants forgiveness. I should avoid trying to justify my actions or omissions that I deem to be in need of forgiveness.

- Recognizing that the harmed may or may not find it in his or her heart to immediately forgive, and that it may take time to do so as the person engages in a personal healing process. If it's appropriate, I should acknowledge this to the harmed person and be patient.

- Offering to make amends, restitution, or reparations in an effort to make the offended person whole again. If forgiveness is granted, I should express my appreciation and welcome the prospects of a mended relationship and the potential for a new and fresh beginning.

- Understanding that once forgiveness has been granted, I need to begin the conscious effort to free myself of the burden of worry, fear, and anxiety for my harmful acts. To continue to carry the burden of guilt and remorse is an impediment to my own healing and growth. This does not mean that I should forget my transgression, however. Remembering serves as a powerful reminder that I desire to never repeat the wrong action or offense.

- Recognizing, if I am the one who has been harmed, that until I forgive in my heart and mind, I may carry the unhealthy burden of anger, hate, contempt, revenge seeking, and anxiety, and therefore reminding myself daily to pray for the strength to forgive. A good reminder is the sage teacher who, when asked how often we should forgive one who has harmed us, replied, "Seventy times seven."

- Recognizing that I hold what could be an abusive power over those who have harmed me. By not forgiving, I may continue to inhibit their healing and potentially cause them lasting harm. By forgiving, I open the door to restoring and rebuilding a loving and cherished relationship full of new possibilities for mutual growth after healing.

- Being empathetic and sympathetic with my transgressors. I do not know, and cannot know, all that the other person has experienced in life, nor do I know his or her genetic makeup or family history and dynamics. All of these factors may have contributed to the commission of the offensive actions.

- Remembering that only God is perfect. As mortals, we will all find ourselves in a position of needing to seek forgiveness for our actions or evil thoughts and intentions. How would we hope to be received by another as we approached asking for forgiveness for the same or a similar offense? As they say in twelve-step programs, "Progress, not perfection, is the goal."

I have learned that forgiveness requires a deliberate and sincere effort if the benefits described above are to be enjoyed. I have also discovered that being deliberate in incorporating forgiveness into my leadership repertoire has enabled me to be a more effective facilitator and resource in promoting a spirit of openness, reconciliation, and harmony within the organizations I serve.

Personal Example Asking for Forgiveness: Application of "The Process"

I recently had a chance to ask forgiveness in a business setting where I serve as chairman of the board. The CEO of this enterprise and I were spending three days together in one-on-one, all-day strategy and plan development sessions. We really enjoy each other's company and have a lot of mutual respect for each other, but this was the first time we'd had the opportunity to work together in a creative session. At the end of the first day together, we were both emotionally and physically drained. We had a very spirited discussion that turned into a somewhat heated exchange. In my closing "argument" I needlessly "shattered" his position on a proposed business direction. It was a topic in an area in which I have a lot of knowledge and practical experience. He had very little experience with the subject being discussed, but he had recently spent a lot of time and energy developing what he'd thought was a great plan.

At the end of my tirade he conceded that he would have to go back to the drawing board. I had "won"; he had "lost." I could tell that he felt deflated and defeated as a result. He immediately became silent and removed. A short time later, I drove him back to his hotel; he sat dejected and said very little during the ride. He simply said, "Thanks for the day and the ride" after we had arrived at his hotel. As I drove home, I reflected on our earlier exchange. I concluded that I had been insensitive and needlessly aggressive in our debate. I had wounded him with my passionate "attack" on his position. I had not given him the respect he had earned and deserved. I felt very uncomfortable with the thought that I might have damaged our emerging business and mentoring relationship. I also recognized that I might have negatively influenced our chances of having open and free-flowing exchanges over the next two days. My actions had jeopardized the potential quality of the outcomes we were anticipating would flow from our three days together.

I decided to apply my new process of asking for forgiveness. On returning home, I drafted a personal email in which I thoughtfully identified what I believed to be the things I had done that might have caused him harm and that might have damaged our relationship going forward—particularly my overly aggressive attack on his position and my lack of sensitivity to his feelings. I closed by asking his forgiveness for my actions and asked that he try to not worry too much about the matter that night, adding that I had some additional reconciling thoughts that we could talk about the next day. I also told him that since it was late and we both were tired, he need not respond to my email; we could talk when we were together the next day.

When I picked him up early the next morning, the bounce had returned to his step. He greeted me with his usual warm smile and firm handshake. He told me how much he appreciated receiving my email and that he was really looking forward to the day ahead. The new process had delivered the hopeful benefits of restoration and produced a fresh start.

More recently, I have had two other forgiveness process applications in other work-related situations, including one in which I was able to accept a public apology and immediately grant a public "absolution" by downplaying the impact of the offending incident and commenting that we could all learn from the situation and move on in a positive manner. So far, the process indeed works for me!

I have decided that I will apply the process principles to rid myself of the burden of carrying the aforementioned feelings of anger, revenge,

and ill will that I have harbored against "the Rifleman" for many years.
That work has just begun, but I already feel a sense of release and freedom
as a result of acknowledging the need to grant forgiveness (in my heart),
in an attempt to heal this very old yet lingering wound. I look forward
to experiencing the process as it once again "works its magic," and to the
emotional healing that will surely follow. I also acknowledge that this may
be a complex process application of my forgiveness model and may include
getting the counsel of a trusted mentor as I seek resolution. I find that
knowing I have the opportunity to free myself of needlessly carrying the
unhealthy burden of anger and ill will, directed at an individual who has
long since been removed from my life, is a liberating and exciting prospect.

Advantages of Servant-Leadership as a Guiding Philosophy

As mentioned earlier in this chapter, there is an ever-expanding body of
scholarly research and relevant case studies that validate the positive, often
dramatic performance outcomes being enjoyed by organizations that have
embraced the spirit and practice of servant-leadership in their mission,
future vision, and organizational culture. Enlightened leaders who have the
gift of foresight and possess strong conceptualization skills have increasingly
recognized that successfully incorporating the tenets of servant-leadership
into their personal leadership philosophy and their organization's social
hierarchy may foster cultures of integrity and achievement while building
sustainable competitive advantage.

The servant-leadership movement is not without its skeptics and
detractors. Often heard are the doubting voices of those who have not
thoroughly studied, understood, or otherwise experienced the multiple
benefits accruing to leaders and organizations that have adopted servant-
leadership as an overarching way of life and as a guiding philosophy. I had
an experience recently, during a live-time discussion, that confirmed some
of the prevailing perceptions as articulated by a group of successful senior
scholars and professionals. The fields of law, business, healthcare, education,
and not-for-profits were represented at the gathering. The setting was the
inaugural executive advisory board meeting of the fledgling Center for
Transformative Ethical Leadership, convened in 2013.

As a founding director and lead author of the proposed vision,
mission, and promise documents for the center, I had expressed my belief

that servant-leadership, as an accepted and rapidly growing theory and practice in organizations around the globe, could be "a wonderful framework, philosophy, and cornerstone platform to be incorporated into our eventual curriculum, symposium, seminar, and distance-learning offerings." I further spoke of the self-assessment and interior discovery work that a true servant must process, which enables that servant-leader to help others to grow, to become healthier, more discerning, collaborative, and self-governing, thereby inspiring them to be more likely to make greater contributions to "the cause" and produce positive outcomes sought by the people they serve.

Finally, I noted that

> a person who has done the self-assessment work may emerge with a vision of greater contribution and a commitment to meeting the needs of others, as opposed to primarily seeking to satisfy his or her own egocentric drive for increased power, control, popularity, prestige, and wealth.

Some of the board members' responses to my presentation, as I remember them, follow:

- "People in organizations today are under tremendous pressure to survive and meet financial commitments. Servant-leadership seems to be too 'touchy-feely' and vague to give people what they need."

- "As a state-funded, public institution, we have to be careful not to appear to be preaching specific religious practices."

- "I am not too sure this servant-leadership stuff fits into what we are trying to accomplish with our mission and vision."

- "We will be trying to reach a lot of lawyers—they won't necessarily relate to servant-leadership."

- "Shouldn't we be focused more on transformative leadership theory?"

- "I think we should focus more on professional ethics."

I did not have time to offer countering thoughts or provide more insights into the theory, art, and practice espoused by the servant-leadership movement. I have, however, been thinking about how to better position the philosophy, theory, and practice of servant-leadership. My background in general management has taught me that if people are to remain interested in a new proposition, they must first "see" the advantages of investing the exploratory time and effort before they can understand that there is something in it for them. They must be intrigued by the offering, learn about the potential benefits, and relate to how it helps them meet existing needs. They want to know the advantages that will accrue to them if they "buy in." Sometimes positioning the advantages first captures their imagination, opening the door for further engaged dialogue. In hindsight, that is what I should have done in my presentation to the executive advisory board. Therefore, I have chosen to list the top benefits I believe accrue to leaders and organizations steeped in the philosophy of servant-leadership:

- Vibrant and flourishing cultures. Such cultures attract, retain, and develop the most talented, ethical, and committed people—the number-one asset of any successful organization, institution, or enterprise.

- Sustainable competitive advantage and better organizational outcomes. The company is likely to see increased associate morale, esprit de corps, communication, productivity, collaboration, participation, creativity, responsibility, and accountability.

- A culture of contribution. Everyone in the organization is inspired to make a personal optimal positive contribution to meet the needs of the organization, its people, and its stakeholders, clientele, and patrons, creating delight for all.

- Personal and organizational health and well-being: The organization harnesses the power of individual and organizational healing, optimism, relationships, and achievements while facilitating improved mental, physical, and spiritual wellness.

- An "as one" spirit. Such a spirit inspires alignment and movement as a unified community in pursuit of a common vision, mission, and promise to achieve commonly held outcomes while being guided by collectively held values and principles.

Once the potential outcomes accruing from the practice of servant-leadership are understood and appreciated, leaders and associates are more likely to wonder how they might avail themselves and their organization of these benefits. After all, what leader or organizational stakeholder would not want to enjoy the personal and organizational benefits flowing from successfully creating a culture of service and contribution?

In summary, the practice of servant-leadership represents an opportunity for everyone associated with an organization to experience positive engagements and relationships, a high level of achievement, and self-fulfillment. Servant-leadership affords the potential for a pervasive, deep, and enduring level of happiness through its adherents' contributory efforts to develop and assist others and to build and to participate in organizations that prosper and flourish.

A center or institute that is focused on research and education on the topic of servant-leadership and to which respected scholars and servant-leader-type practitioners contribute could help the theory and practice of servant-leadership to grow significantly. Cultures of integrity, ethical behaviors, and prosperity would proliferate. The above benefits can and must be further developed, elaborated on, substantiated, and refined to support the creation of such a center, which will allow many of us to experience the benefits of living more authentic and meaningful lives while concurrently helping us to strengthen and sustain healthier, more resilient, and more prosperous organizations.

References

Ferch, S. (2012). *Forgiveness and power in the age of atrocity: Servant-leadership as a way of life.* Lanham, MD: Lexington Books.

Frankl, V. (2006). *Man's search for meaning: An introduction to logotherapy.* New York, NY: Vintage Books. (Original work published 1946).

Greenleaf, R. (2002). *Servant leadership: A journey into the nature of legitimate power and greatness* (25th anniv. ed.). New York, NY: Paulist Press.

Ramsey, M. (2006). Servant leadership and unconditional forgiveness: The lives of six South African perpetrators. *International Journal of Servant-Leadership* 2, 113–139.

Spears, L. C. (2004). The understanding and practice of servant-leadership. In L. C. Spears & M. Lawrence (Eds.), *Practicing servant leadership* (pp. 9–24). San Francisco, CA: Jossey-Bass.

Tutu, D. (1997). *No future without forgiveness.* New York, NY: Doubleday.

Tutu, D. (2004). *God has a dream: A vision of hope for our time.* New York, NY: Random House.

Wiesel, E. (2006). *Night* (Rev. ed.). New York, NY: Hill and Wang. (Originally published 1960).

Wiesenthal, S. (1976). *The sunflower*. New York, NY: Schocken.

Chapter 4

Justice and Forgiveness

Self-Responsibility and Human Dignity in the Midst of Conflict

Rakiya Farah

Amartya Sen (2006) notes, "The world in which we live is not only unjust, it is, arguably, extraordinarily unjust" (p. 237). We live in an imperfect world. Of that, there is no doubt. One of the defining features of the last century has been the sheer extent of social disintegration, economic turmoil, and human violence made more potent by technological advancement. It is no surprise, then, that the role of leadership has been placed under increasing scrutiny as the world seeks new ways to address its problems.

The question of justice in an imperfect and conflict-ridden world is a fundamental one for servant-leadership practitioners, who, according to Robert Greenleaf (2002), are concerned with "remaking the world" (p. 318), first by attending to the inner self, and then by radiating the fullness of that self out into the world. Greenleaf's characterization of that process as a kind of "inner radiance" (p. 308) is as beautiful as it is wise, for a self that can resist the assaults of the world is a self that can shine its light onto the world.

Justice theorist John Rawls (1973) articulated the primacy and priority of justice, describing it as the "fundamental character of a well-ordered human association" (p. 5) and "the most important virtue of institutions" (p. 6). In a less abstract vein, Greenleaf (2002) observed the development of institutions into the role of caring for and serving people, giving institutions a major role to play in improving society:

If a better society is to be built, one that is more just and more loving, one that provides greater creative opportunity for its people, then the most open course is to *raise both the capacity to serve and the very performance as servant* of existing major institutions by new regenerative forces operating within them. (p. 62)

Greenleaf's identification of institutions as servants, caregivers, and vehicles of meaning, and not simply as machines of production in pursuit of profit, or community-less distributors of social goods, is important for questions of justice, which are inescapably tied to our judgments about civic virtue and the common good (Sandel, 2011). By placing the ideal of love within his conception of a good society, Greenleaf draws us more deeply into the heart of justice. For King (1986), too, love is our salvation, the antidote to the violence and injustice of our age. Significantly, the notion of regeneration suggests an organic and unbounded movement toward wholeness. Servant-leadership, with its commitment to human wholeness and flourishing, lends itself to restorative processes that build community. As such, it is a potent antidote to the relational poverty, oppression, and lack of meaning that characterizes so many of today's organizations.

Organizational Conflict

In reflecting on the idea of injustice in the workplace, I am struck by the extent to which relational poverty provides fertile ground for us to harm one another. The organization I previously worked for is a multinational communications consultancy headquartered in the United Kingdom, with offices worldwide. I worked for the Middle East division of the organization in its main office in Qatar. Producing written material in the Arabic language was a critically important part of our work. Due to cost cutting, the top management became unwilling to hire a specialist translator. As a result of this, as well as the lack of objective job and role requirements, responsibility for the translation of written materials fell to the Dubai office. A consultant and a newly promoted associate director would service requests from all four offices in the Middle East, overseen by a general manager.

The Dubai office routinely responded to translation requests with irritation and disrespect. They complained about the number of requests coming through, or the lack of notice in receiving them. In response to a translation request I made, the associate director and general manager were condescending and disrespectful. They angrily refused to translate the document according to the deadline and blamed my office for overloading them. When my manager failed to intervene, I rose to their anger, responding rashly and somewhat sarcastically. While my manager considered their behavior unreasonable and privately praised my response, the e-mail exchange was not constructive and served only to entrench the interoffice animosity and resentment. This conflict damaged working relationships and undermined employee satisfaction and morale.

It is worth nothing that the conflict was part of a more generalized organizational malaise fueled, in part, by a lack of human resources. People were stretched and under pressure. Communication between offices and colleagues was minimal, and most employees below the management level had never met one another. This begs the question, to what extent is meaningful relationship possible in circumstances that tend toward negativity, distrust, and alienation?

Self-Responsibility in the Midst of Conflict

Organizations can be places of psychological and emotional pain—there is stress, anxiety, and fear. When conflict arises, there can be interpersonal injury. Although the above example was a relatively minor conflict, it generated considerable negativity and ill feeling. I initially felt justified in my response. I felt that I had been composed and responded abruptly only when pushed to the brink and in the face of aggression. However, according to Greenleaf, the servant "views any problem in the world as *in here,* inside oneself, not *out there*" (as cited in Senge, 1995, p. 240). In the light of this statement, self-responsibility requires an honest examination of one's personal role in contributing to conflict, and to its potential resolution.

Reyes (n.d.) said, "I take total responsibility for everything that happens to me and what I create. . . . I have sovereignty and self-determination over what I say and how I interact. I choose consciously to interact with love and compassion." Instead of this model of authentic freedom and loving intentionality, I sought to give my colleagues in Dubai a taste of their own medicine, as it were, and I simply reacted. This desire to return violence with violence is a retributive response to pain and suffering, and reflects a popular focus on desert (Miller, 1992) when considering questions of justice. This contrasts with the needs focus of restoration. Significantly, Miller (2003) posits a relationship between the nature of social relations within a given group—solidaristic community, instrumental associations, citizenship—and the justice response it elicits. Certainly, when people are not mutually invested, when relations are seen predominantly as a means to an end, when self-interest is the primary motivation, people will tend to seek retribution over restoration. In the case at hand, the deficient relational environment and instrumental nature of social relations within the group led to a negative, retributive climate.

The punitive approach entails the redistribution of harm, not its containment or diminishment, and not its resolution into meaning (Frankl, 2000). Yet it is a testament to the power of forgiveness that meaning can be extracted from even the gravest harms. One only has to consider Sylvia Fraser (2007), whose book *My Father's House* tells the story of the horrendous incest she suffered at the hands of her father. Even so, her journey of forgiveness led her to proclaim one day, "I have burst into an infinite world full of wonder" (p. 253). What a delicately poignant reminder of the luminosity in the human condition, which emerges even from the deepest abyss if we are willing to illuminate it.

The experience of wonder and possibility, represented by the metaphor of *seeing the unicorn* (Greenleaf, 2002), is the key to our responsibleness and the will to be an agent of change in the world. The alternative is negativity, which is an obstacle to interrelationship (Ferch, 2010). Indeed, it takes tremendous optimism to believe that a commitment to embracing others with love and compassion—often despite a disinclination to do so—can have a positive impact. In the organizational problem at hand, a large part of me wanted to respond differently in the situation. I even wondered whether in discerning the deeper issues behind the behavior of my colleagues in Dubai, and bringing these hidden areas to light, I might lead them to respond positively to me. But ultimately, I did not have faith in my ability to influence in this way, and I missed an opportunity to respond hopefully to the situation. Inevitably, in an environment devoid of meaning, apathy can result (Frankl, 2000). Therefore, it is incumbent on the leader to nurture his or her "interior resilience" (Ferch, n.d.) in the midst of conflict, through hope, courage, and faith in our ability to be reconciled with one another.

It is an uncommon thing for a person take full and unequivocal responsibility for his or her actions. Although I suspected that pressure and a sense of injustice were driving my colleagues' behavior, I chose not to let this understanding infuse my interactions with acceptance, empathy, and warmth. Instead, my local office colleagues and I complained, blamed, and rationalized our own behavior in the light of theirs. This was a failure not just of self-responsibility but also of humility, which requires that one refrain from self-justification and denial (Tutu, 1999). Being humble was difficult because I felt attacked. I also felt slightly humiliated at being spoken to with disrespect in an e-mail seen by my peers and my manager. Faced with hostility and disrespect, my ego was triggered, hindering a more constructive, life-giving response. This is an example of the role of shame and the ego in obstructing the creation of an environment conducive to humility and the forgiveness process (Ramsey, 2006). The wisdom of the servant-led environment is brought into sharp relief here. Two of its key principles—*first among equals* and *servant first*—focus our attention on the other and on the community, so that the rigid, protective, self-interested stance is undermined in favor of appropriate vulnerability, humility, and service.

Human Dignity and Relatedness

For Greenleaf, it is essential to base organizational life on "interrelatedness" (Senge, 1995, p. 240), which is deeply personal, as opposed to "thingness" (p. 240), which is impersonal. In other words, the most irreducible thing about our organizations is the fact of our connectedness as people, not the fact that we happen to be pursuing common organizational goals. The former view of organizations is grounded in the Kantian notion of the dignity and inherent worth of persons. It provides an anchor in the midst of conflict. Certainly, it is far more difficult to act recklessly or to deliberately harm others when there is a deep sense of our common dignity and humanity.

In the problem outlined, interrelatedness was missing. We were locked into the "community-less environment" (Greenleaf, 2002, p. 52) that Greenleaf warns us about. The fact that I did not have a relationship with my Dubai colleagues beyond the mechanical and impersonal form of e-mail communication made it impossible for us to feel connected to one another, whereas connectedness and empathy are integral to justice (Braithwaite, 2006). This deficiency created inevitable "misunderstandings and poor interactive behaviors" (Ferch, 2001, p. 119). Insofar as these were uncaring behaviors devoid of love, they undermined the dignity of everyone involved.

For Freire (2006), Greenleaf's "thingness" is objectification, which is akin to dehumanization. He stated, "The oppressed have been destroyed precisely because their situation has reduced them to things. In order to regain their humanity they must cease to be things and fight as men and women" (p. 68). Similarly, when we are denied relatedness in the workplace, we are dehumanized, because we are being asked to function as less than our whole selves. McCollum (1995) outlines the effect on organizations of what Henry Mintzberg called "machine bureaucracy" (p. 241). A style of organizing that is particularly common in the public relations industry, this kind of bureaucracy is highly mechanical with sharp hierarchical divisions, creating an extremely alienating experience for employees. At its most extreme and inhuman, "it succeeds in eliminating from official business love, hatred, and all purely personal, irrational and emotional elements which escape calculation" (Lazar, n.d., p. 3). The fact that I had always remained silent when the associate director and general manager were difficult and unhelpful, simply because they were closer to the top of the hierarchy, was evidence of this bureaucracy. Feeling my personal autonomy and dignity assaulted fueled my resentment. Equally, I suspect that my translation requests subverted the traditional hierarchical and patriarchal style of management, generating resistance.

Forgiveness

Leaders who wait for people to behave properly before responding in life-giving ways cannot hope to heal, restore, or reconcile. Tutu (1999) states, "Jesus did not wait until those who were nailing him to the cross had asked for forgiveness" (p. 272). Instead, Jesus led the way, using forgiveness not as a response but as an initiating tool to transcend harm and transform relationships. Seen this way, forgiveness is an extension of self-responsibility in that it starts with the self and then turns out toward the world (Greenleaf, 2002).

Many years ago, I asked my mother for forgiveness for my years of hostility and bitterness toward her after she divorced my father. What motivated me was the feeling that I was responsible, and that healing and wholeness needed to begin with me. Previously, I had felt that I could not love and embrace my mother until she recognized and confessed to the hurt she had caused me. This meant that I was locked into my role as both an oppressor and a victim—an oppressor because I consciously sought to punish my mother, and a victim because I was unable to transcend my anger, though I often tried. In keeping with Tutu's (1999) contention that "our unforgiveness undoes us" (p. 156), my quality of life was diminished, as evidenced in my self-destructive behavior.

It was after an intrapersonal experience of divine grace and forgiveness that I felt the need to ask my mother to forgive me. Forgiveness has been described as a bridge (Ramsey, 2006; Tutu, 1999) between a past that constrains us and a future that liberates us. What I needed more than anything was to be freed from a painful, debilitating past. Yet the process was not entirely self-centered. Though it began with me, it was essentially about our relationship. Reyes (n.d.) said that our role as servant-leaders is to "bring out the best in people" and to "optimize their humanness and sense of personhood." I felt the truth of this statement very acutely in the interpersonal context. It no longer mattered who was right and who was wrong. My overwhelming desire was to be accountable for my actions. Through my accountability, I hoped to validate my mother's worth—her dignity—and restore the love between us. In practical terms, this led me to forego the desire to settle the score. I put my scorecard down and asked her forgiveness, taking full and unequivocal responsibility for my role in contributing to *her* pain. This initiating act was the essence of forgiveness as gift, as love (Braithwaite, 2006; Ramsey, 2006), because it was without condition. Her response, in accepting my love, brought us back into relationship.

I experienced this process as both liberating and empowering because I regained a sense of self-efficacy and hope in the future of our relationship. Through forgiveness, I was also able to see beyond my mother's actions to her simple dignity and personhood. I expressed my gratitude for my mother and for the person she was. "You matter," is what I meant to convey. "And you matter to me." I recall feeling intensely vulnerable in front of her, yet still safe. This event freed me from the guilt and shame that I had carried with me for so long. My loving potential as a person, which had been so elusive, I could now grasp. Although I cannot speak for my mother, the emotion we shared suggests that she also had a great burden lifted. Today, our relationship is freer and more affectionate, understanding, mature, and loving. This experience supports Braithwaite's (2006) call for a more intelligent form of justice, one that is capable of "flipping vicious circles of hurt begetting hurt into virtuous circles of healing begetting healing" (p. 403). In keeping with MLK's notion of loving one's oppressor for mutual salvation, Freire's (2006) articulation of mutual humanization, and

Tutu's (1999) will to love through forgiveness, my mother and I emerged lifted, cleansed, and free to be different people.

There are a number of insights to be drawn from this experience. First, forgiveness is a transformative tool that promotes healing and reconciliation. This is because being forgiven frees us from past behavior "so that we can be different people, choosing and acting differently in the future" (Wiesenthal, 1998, p. 184). As such, it is deeply restorative—not retrospectively but prospectively. This kind of justice and forgiveness does not simply undo harm; it raises us up to "the richness and fullness of life for which we have been created" (Tutu, 1999, pp. 155–156). This is a higher vision of what it means to be human, and I dare say the only vision worth striving for.

Secondly, the series of tit-for-tat e-mails my colleagues and I exchanged was part of a cycle of "reprisal and counterreprisal" (Tutu, 1999, p. 260) that needed to be broken through forgiveness, both as an attitudinal stance and as a behavior. This would have enabled those involved to move beyond negative thoughts, feelings, and behavior. In the same way that my relationship with my mother is today infused with tenderness and compassion made more profound by the memory of pain, we can experience a similar restoration through our capacity to forgive and heal workplace harm. By practicing love in community (Greenleaf, 2002), we can build just, lasting, and meaningful relationships where these have not existed. This is a truly life-giving response to the daily reality of pain and suffering.

Dialogue

Discussing her experience of employee resistance when spearheading organizational change, McGee-Cooper (n.d.) said that we need to reframe what people are saying in order to understand what they are feeling and experiencing. This stance then enables a two-way relationship that is transformative. What if I had sought to really listen and identify the fears and frustrations driving my colleagues' behavior? These likely included budgetary and resourcing frustrations, alienation and disaffection, a feeling of being overworked, and interoffice competitiveness. Bringing these deeper issues out into the open, rather than simply reacting to the surface behavior, reduces projection and creates a space for honest and constructive dialogue.

Dialogue is essential in the midst of conflict. All too often, we are engaged in communication, which is purely functional, instead of dialogue, which builds community and "gives rise to the forces that unhinge the way we harm each other, opening us toward a more accepting and empathic understanding of one another" (Ferch, 2005, p. 107). As an illustration of the distinction, one might observe the way in which "How are you?" has become little more than a platitude in professional settings, instead of serving its original purpose as an invitation to mutual understanding and relationship. With regard to conflict, viewing a person with love and understanding means that one is invested in an outcome that honors that person, so that the win-lose mind-set of interpersonal conflict gives way to a *community-full* win-win mind-set.

Taking my organization as a microcosm of the corporate world, a new corporate spirit is surely needed in order to support conversation and better ways of relatedness. In very practical terms, Morris (n.d.) advocates a "positive framework of ideas" according to which people know how to deal with differences and conflict. Such a framework was present in Townsend & Bottum, an organization credited by Frick (1995) for its servant-leadership culture. According to Spears (n.d.), this culture was fostered through a set of core values, including "nurturing the positive in people" (p. 274). The attitudinal and behavioral stances associated with this value included being nonvengeful, controlling anger, practicing forgiveness, not harboring grudges, and seeing the positive in people. From this position, one interprets others' actions in the best possible light, and one is "present and vigilant to that person's truth" (Reyes, n.d.), respecting their autonomy and individual voice.

Morris (n.d.) goes on to state that such a culture is formed by informal workplace conversations and observations. Put differently, the key to building a more just and loving corporate culture is relational conversation, in which we are fully present to one another. Based on the idea that communication should deepen a relationship and not just resolve conflict, relational conversation is employed in the therapeutic setting to "increase relational fortitude and promote a consistent level of intentional and loving connection" (Ferch, 2001, p. 118). Underpinning such conversation is a foundation of justice and forgiveness as a means to resolve conflict, so that authentic relationship can emerge. This is more than just exchanging ideas; it is sharing meaning (Senge, 1995, p. 226).

It is possible to build this sense of connectedness and empathetic understanding within organizations. With this foundation in place, we can create truly life-giving and life-enriching organizations in which power and love, justice and mercy, are brought into balance.

Conclusion

The idea of proportionality and desert is a misnomer in the world of servant-leadership because it lacks moral imagination. Let's talk, instead, about transformation. Restorative justice is transformative, in that it is capable of restoring the dignity and humanity of the person, addressing the need for meaning, and revitalizing our collective future. With the insights and reflections of this chapter, I have sought to highlight the value of pursuing deeper and more meaningful relationships within organizations. Relational conversation, underpinned by a foundation of justice and forgiveness, demonstrates mutual commitment and mutual respect. It is thus an appropriate tool for building relatedness and shared meaning as the basis for a caring, compassionate and life-giving organization.

Faced with the daily reality of conflict, pain, and suffering, leaders need to cultivate a vision of human possibility that is solid and without bounds. Palmer (2004) expresses this imperative with this thought: "As I stand in the tragic gap between reality and possibility, this small, tight fist of a thing called my heart can break open into greater capacity to hold more of my own and the world's suffering and joy, despair and hope" (p. 178). This greater capacity is the key to interior resilience in the midst of conflict. It entails an openness, vulnerability, and courage of the heart. It requires a leader who dares to venture more deeply into the center of a problem, setting the stage for others to avoid the "fight or flight" urge, and to stay. Forgiveness and reconciliation require that we stay and that we commit to one another, that we commit to being responsible.

In the words of Kahlil Gibran (1977), "The erect and the fallen are but one man standing in twilight between the night of his pigmy-self and the day of his god-self" (p. xii). Such an insight calls into question our urge to punish and alienate the other, and calls us, instead, to be sources of light in the midst of darkness.

References

Braithwaite, J. (2006). Doing justice intelligently in civil society. *Journal of Social Issues, 62*(2), 393–409. doi:10.1111/j.1540-4560.2006.00456.x

Ferch, S. R. (2001). Relational conversation: Meaningful communication as a therapeutic intervention. Counseling and Values. Retrieved from http://www.highbeam.com/doc/1G1-69750628.html

Ferch, S. R. (2005). *Servant-leadership, forgiveness, and social justice. The International Jouranl of Servant-Leadership, 1*(1), 97–113.

Ferch, S. R. (2010). *Introduction to module 2.* [Audio file]. Retrieved from Gonzaga University course notes.

Ferch, S. R. (n.d.). Servant-leadership and the interior of the leader: Facing violence with courage and forgiveness. Part I. Retrieved from Gonzaga University course notes.

Frankl, V. (2000). *Man's search for meaning.* New York, NY: Basic Books.

Fraser, S. (2007). *My father's house: Memoir of incest and healing.* London, England: Virago Press.

Freire, P. (2006). *Pedagogy of the oppressed.* New York, NY: Continuum.

Frick, D. M. (1995). Pyramids, circles, and gardens: Stories of implementing servant-leadership. In L. C. Spears (Ed.), *Reflections on leadership* (pp. 257–281). New York, NY: John Wiley and Sons.

Gibran, K. (1977). *The prophet.* Hertfordshire, England: Wordsworth Editions.

Greenleaf, R. K. (2002). *Servant leadership: A journey into the nature of legitimate power and greatness.* New York, NY: Paulist Press.

King, M. L., Jr. (1986). *A testament of hope: The essential writings of Martin Luther King, Jr.* San Francisco, CA: HarperCollins.

Lazar, D. (n.d.). *Max Weber on bureaucracy.* Retrieved from http://docs.google.com

McCollum, J. (1995). Chaos, complexity, and servant-leadership. In L. C. Spears (Ed.), *Reflections on leadership* (pp. 241–256). New York, NY: John Wiley and Sons.

McGee-Cooper, A. (n.d.). *Resistance.* [Video file]. Retrieved from Gonzaga University course notes.

Miller, D. (1992). Distributive justice: What the people think. *Ethics, 102*(3), 555–593. doi:10.1086/293425

Miller, D. (2003). *Principles of social justice.* Cambridge, MA: Harvard University Press.

Morris, T. (n.d.). Conflict. [Video file]. Retrieved from Gonzaga University course notes.

Palmer, P. J. (2004). *A hidden wholeness.* San Francisco, CA: Jossey-Bass.

Ramsey, M. (2006). Servant-leadership and unconditional forgiveness: The lives of six south African perpetrators. *The International Journal of Servant-Leadership, 2*(1), 113–139.

Rawls, J. (1973). *A theory of justice.* Cambridge, MA: Harvard University Press.

Reyes, R. (n.d.). *Conflict.* [Video file]. Retrieved from Gonzaga University course notes.

Sandel, M. J. (2011). Justice: What's the right thing to do? *Boston University Law Review, 91*(4), 1303–1310.

Sen, A. (2006). What do we want from a theory of justice? *Journal of Philosophy, 103*(5), 215–238.

Senge, P. M. (1995). Robert Greenleaf's legacy: A new foundation for twenty-first century institutions. In L. C. Spears (Ed.), *Reflections on leadership* (pp. 217–240). New York, NY: John Wiley and Sons.

Spears, L. C. (n.d.). *Conflict*. [Video file]. Retrieved from Gonzaga University course notes.

Tutu, D. (1999). *No future without forgiveness.* New York, NY: Doubleday.

Wiesenthal, S. (1998). *The sunflower: On the possibilities and limits of forgiveness.* New York, NY: Schocken Books.

Chapter 5

Servant-Leadership Applied to Balance World Inequalities and Enhance Global Forgiveness and Restoration

Christian B. Cabezas

Many years have passed since the end of World War II, a war that stemmed from hate, unhealthy ambition, and a sense of superiority from within different cultures, and in which millions of lives were lost. Some, including a number that were survivors of that war, have documented and described the horrors and atrocities that were committed. Wiesenthal (1998) raised the dilemma of the possibility of forgiveness of the perpetrators of the massacres committed in this war. Nelson Mandela and Desmond Tutu (1999), with their experience in South Africa and the Truth and Reconciliation Commission, have shown the world that it is possible to forgive even the most hardened perpetrators of evil acts, but have also pointed out the imperative need to find truth before forgiveness and restoration can be obtained.

The history of both world wars has been widely shared through generations and cultures, and currently there is a general collective sense of remorse and fear of repeating such mistakes that makes us believe that we are far from suffering similar wars. In fact, violence continues to haunt us in recurrent cycles, forcing us to experience the devastating effects of people's agency, which is producing similar consequences: the loss of millions of human lives, again caused by unhealthy ambition and a sense of superiority within cultures. On a global level, economic and social inequalities increase every year with fatal consequences. Globalization, with its utopian promise of the opportunity for development in every country, seems to have only further accentuated inequalities and economic crises

99

in developing countries. Yates (2004/2006) suggested that, contrary to information promulgated by international financial organizations, inequality among countries is growing every year. He mentioned as an example that in the United States, life expectancy for women is about eighty years, and in Switzerland it is eighty-two, but in Afghanistan it is forty-six, and in Sierra Leone it is thirty-nine. Infant mortality per 1,000 births is 3.98 in Norway but 101 in Ethiopia.

This chapter will explore the current tragedies that developing countries face as victims of postcolonialism. It will also look at the imperative need humans have to find and communicate truth to achieve justice, so as to forgive and break the oppressive cycle that currently enforces inequalities. These inequalities, which are supported by ill-formed human agency, lead to the loss of an enormous quantity of innocent lives every year. It is our obligation as human beings to hold ourselves accountable for injustices that are currently being perpetrated, and to enforce restoration. Some decades ago, Greenleaf, referring to servant-leadership as the new form of leadership needed to heal societies, stated,

> The servant-leader is servant first . . . it begins with the natural feeling that one wants to serve, to serve first . . . that person is sharply different from one who is leader first, perhaps because of the need to assuage an unusual power drive or to acquire material possessions. (Greenleaf, 1977/2002, p. 27)

Currently, the world seems to need more of this type of leader—one who is not solely concerned with making their nation an empire that economically and politically dominates other nations but rather one who shares in the responsibility of global development. As Ferch (2012) stated, "The servant-leader transcends himself or herself to become the steward of others, capable of raising up future generations, and confident in building community" (p. 155). There is an urgent need for leaders from both developed and developing countries to work together and share accountability in regard to solving global inequalities that affect the majority of people in the world.

Unequal Relationships in the Global Scenario

Bulbeck (1998/2006) stated, "The third world is a category produced and reproduced by capitalist imperialism, referred to in oppositions between industrialized north and developing south, or core and periphery" (p. 38). This assumed distinction between countries depending on their economic growth has also influenced the manner in which their citizens treat each other. Dominant cultures have assumed a hierarchical position of power and influence over those considered weaker. The defining difference between these cultures resides in the accumulation of capital. Yates (2004/2006) defended the idea that the inequality among countries is endemic to the effect of capitalism. He stated, "Capitalism is an economic system in which the nonhuman means of production are owned by a small minority of all persons. Wealth inequality in a market economy must, again as a consequence of the nature of the system, generate income inequality" (p. 337). He also suggested that capitalist economies espouse egalitarian values, but that the consequences of their normal operations are extraordinarily inegalitarian, and this contradiction is apparent in relationships among nations. Referring to the same issue, Mies (1993/2006) proposed that the economic, social, and ecological costs of constant growth in the industrialized countries have been and are being shifted to the colonized countries in the South. She stressed that there is a catching-up myth enforced by the colonizers. According to Mies, "The very progress of the colonizers is based on the existence and the exploitation of those colonies" (p. 153). She also suggested that the poverty of underdeveloped nations is not a result of natural lagging behind but is rather a direct consequence of the development of rich industrial countries that exploit the so-called periphery in Africa, South America, and Asia.

Williams (1980/2006) analyzed the interaction of imperialist nations with weaker ones. According to him, "Superior economic power subjects an inferior political economy to its own preferences" (p. 83). He suggested that this unbalanced relationship existed between Great Britain and Argentina between 1870 and 1914, in former years between the United States and many countries in the Western Hemisphere (such as Canada, Cuba, and Panama), and between all industrial powers and what has become known as the third world.

Today, people from different cultures have automatically assumed a dominant/dominated role in the global scenario without wondering about or challenging this unequal relationship or how they achieved that role. Analyzing history along the path that consolidated this relationship, it is possible to infer that their positions have been defined based on previous abuses committed against people in dominated cultures as well as on environmental destruction. Kloby (2004/2006) stated,

One of the major reasons for the development problems that
exist in much of the world today is the destruction of indigenous social relationships and productive economic practices, as
well as the evolution of various patterns of relationships that
were established during the era of colonialism. (p. 99)

It is clear that colonialism has left important traces in the world's
interactions that have molded unfair and unequal relationships between
countries and their people. For instance, although a long time has passed
since Latin American countries' colonization and exploitation by European
empires, this unfair interaction persists, and Latin America maintains its
passive role today. As Galeano (1997/2006) pointed out,

It continues to exist at the service of other's needs as a source
and reserve of oil and iron, of copper and meat, of fruit and
coffee, the raw materials and foods destined for rich countries
which profit more from consuming them than Latin America
does from producing them. (p. 127)

Considering this unfair interaction, it is misleading and even deceiv-
ing to talk about free trade between these nations. Galeano (1997/2006,
p. 129) also put a lot of emphasis on the economic and cultural richness
that was sacked from Latin American countries during colonization, which
has also affected their current condition. He put forth the example of
Bolivia, which, while being one of the world's most poverty-stricken
countries, could boast of having nourished the wealth of the wealthiest.
He also mentioned Mexico, stating that the economic surplus drained
from it in the form of silver and gold exports between 1760 and 1809
has been estimated at some five billion present-day dollars. In Bolivia, in
Cerro Chico, Potosi, alone, eight million lives were lost over the course
of three centuries. Galeano (1997/2006) explained, "The Indians, including
women and children, were torn from their agricultural communities and
driven to the Cerro. Of every ten who went up in the freezing wilderness, seven never returned" (p. 136). According to him, the massacre of
Indians that began with Columbus never stopped. It continued in the
following centuries in all of the Latin American countries, as well as in
the indigenous territories of the United States.

Rothenberg (2006) defended the idea that the inequalities of wealth
and power that orchestrate relations between countries in the world today

cannot be understood unless we place them in the context of colonization and its consequences for development. She also stated that "the challenge that faced the English and other European empire builders and U.S. imperialism somewhat later, was to find a way to justify this process" (p. 77). Rothenberg also underlined the rationale that the dominating nations have used to justify their imperialistic actions. According to her, on the one hand, they emphasized the importance of color, maintaining that those who were not white were inferior; on the other, they justified their actions by citing Christianity and the need to either convert or destroy heathens, who were portrayed as agents of the devil. According to Mies (1993/2006), in the colonization process (both former and current), not only the colonizers but the colonized as well must accept the lifestyle of those on top as the only model of the good life. According to the process of the acceptance of these values, the lifestyle and standard of living of those on top are invariably accompanied by a devaluation of an individual's own culture, work, technology, and lifestyle, and often philosophy of life and social institutions as well. Regarding this very subject, Mies (1993/2006) stated, "In the beginning this devaluation is often violently enforced by the colonizers and then reinforced by propaganda, educational programs, a change of laws, and economic dependency, for example through the debt trap" (p. 151).

The new forms of domination are more subtle and sophisticated. They are practiced directly not by developed countries but by third parties that represent their interests, such as the international financial organizations. Yates (2004/2006) showed that, contrary to what is promulgated by these international financial organizations, who are mainly influenced by developed countries, inequality among countries is growing every year. According to Black (2006), in Latin America and in the Caribbean, Africa, and much of Asia during the second half of the 1980s, foreign aid and new loans and investments did not begin to compensate for the debt service payments from those areas into the coffers of first world banks. Joseph Stiglitz (2002/2006)—a Columbia professor, Nobel Prize recipient in economics in 2001, former chief economist, and senior vice president of the World Bank from 1997 to 2000—critically expressed how globalization was promulgated by developed countries as a solution for developing nations. When referring to developing nations, Stiglitz (2002/2006) wrote, "These countries were told by the West that the new economic system would bring them unprecedented prosperity. Instead, it brought unprecedented poverty[,] in many respects, for most people"

(p. 421). He also suggested that Western countries have pushed poor countries to eliminate trade barriers but have kept their own barriers. This paradox prevents developing countries from exporting their agricultural products, thus depriving them of desperately needed export income. This in turn reinforces economic underdevelopment.

Black (2006) also noted that income poverty is found in combination with other deprivations, since the poor are less able to defend their rights to services, to personal security, or even to things that we used to believe were free, such as relatively unpolluted air and water. For instance, Black (2006) pointed out that the water supply per capita in developing countries in the late 1990s was only one-third of what it had been in 1970, and that 40 percent of the population in those countries lacked proper sanitation. He also mentioned that in these countries, seventeen million people die each year from curable infections and parasite diseases. HIV/AIDS kills another twenty-three million—fourteen million of those in sub-Saharan Africa, where half the population lacks access to medical services (Black, 2006, p. 328).

According to Rodney (1972/2006), in recent times, economists have recognized in colonial and postcolonial Africa a pattern that has been termed "growth without development" (p. 119), though it has been denied for centuries. The pattern consists of finding a developing country that has many enterprises and exporting all of the profit abroad, and as a result, the economy becomes more and more dependent on the metropolis. Rodney (1972/2006) also stated that "there was growth of the so-called enclave import-export sector, but the only things which developed were dependency and underdevelopment" (p. 119). Majavu (2006) explained that international financial institutions' debt trap also strongly affected African countries. According to him, every year African countries spend about $15 billion repaying debts to the IMF and World Bank and their creditors. Servicing these debts diverts money from spending on essential things such as health care and providing citizens with clean water, and education. Majavu (2006) stated that African countries pay $1.51 in debt services for every $1 they receive in aid (p. 507).

The underdevelopment caused by colonialism was also perpetuated in the educational systems. According to Rodney (1972/2006) the main purpose of the colonial school system was to train Africans to help man the local administration at the lowest ranks and to staff the private capitalist firms owned by Europeans. He stated, "It was not an educational system designed to give young people confidence and pride as members of African societies, but one which sought to instill a sense of deference towards all that was European and capitalist" (p. 122). According to Rodney, "In Africa, both the formal school system and the informal value system of colonialism destroyed social solidarity and promoted the worst form of alienated individualism without social responsibility" (p. 125).

Sachs (2006) underlined the impossibility of developing countries providing better health services and attention to their citizens because they are obligated to use most of their budgets to pay debts to other governments, the IMF, and the World Bank. They are immersed in the paradox of not advancing because they have to pay the debts accrued to "advance" and "develop." El Saadawi (1997/2006) also noted that international institutions such as the IMF and the World Bank implanted the so-called development policies that perpetuate poverty and an increasing flow of money and riches from South to North. For example, "From 1984 to 1990 the application of structural adjustment policies in the South led to the transfer of $178 billion from the South to the commercial banks in the North" (El Saadawi, 1997/2006, p. 401).

Even though these international financial institutions were created to support development and avoid economic crisis, they have led to deteriorating conditions in developing countries, securing the prevalence of power of Western developed countries at the expense of developing countries. Unfortunately, the ones who suffer the consequences are those with the lowest social status in developing countries. Farmer (2003/2006) referred to structural violence as the tragic condition in which people from developing countries have to live as a result of their governments' poor political and economic decisions, which were influenced by the interests of developed countries. Farmer also pointed out that not only are the poor more likely to suffer, but their suffering is less likely to be noticed. He insisted that we have a responsibility to identify the forces conspiring to promote suffering.

In a related issue, Booker and Minter (2001/2006) defined "global apartheid" as

> an international system of minority rule whose attributes include: differential access to basic human rights; wealth and power structured by race and place; structural racism, embodied in global economic progress, political institutions and cultural

assumptions; and the international practice of doubled standards
that assume inferior rights to be appropriate for certain others,
defined by location, origin, race or gender. (p. 518)

They also noted that some priority steps toward changing global
apartheid are clear and immediate, such as addressing the AIDS pandemic
through adequate funding for treatment and prevention, canceling illegit-
imate debt, stopping the imposition of catastrophic economic policies on
poor countries, and halting trade rules that value corporate profit over
human life. They concluded, "Genuine globalization requires that global
democracy replace global apartheid" (Booker & Minter, 2001/2006, p. 522).

Developed Countries' Lack of Awareness and Perceptual Biases Affecting Equality

Social scientists have argued that individualism is more prevalent in
industrialized Western societies than in other societies, particularly those
more traditional societies within developing countries (Wibbeke, 2009).
Individualism formation has been explained by its origins in Protestantism
and the process of civic emancipation in Western societies that resulted
in social and civic structures that elicited the role of individual choice,
personal freedom, and self-actualization (Inglehart, 1997). Studies measuring
cultural dimensions have found that the United States is one of the most
individualistic cultures in the world (Chhokar, Brodbeck, & House, 2008).
Concerning perception and attribution style, individualism assumes that
judgment, reasoning, and causal inference are generally oriented toward the
person rather than the situation or social context. In contrast, definitions
of *collectivism* suggest that social context, situational constraints, and social
roles figure prominently in personal perception and causal reasoning (Choi,
Nisbett, & Norenzayan, 1999).

Others support the idea that individualistic societies place more
emphasis on personal attributions than on situations, in contrast to collectivistic societies. This difference causes attribution errors that affect the fair
judgment of individuals, and consequently perpetuates injustices. Morris
and Peng (1994) tested the hypothesis that dispositionalism in attribution
for behavior is more widespread in individualistic than in collectivistic
cultures. In their study they found that English-language newspapers were

more dispositional and Chinese-language newspapers were more situational in explanations of the same crimes (mass murders). The same authors found in a survey that Chinese respondents differed in their assessments of personal dispositions and situational factors as causes of recent murders and in counterfactual judgments about how the murders might have been averted by changed situations. In addition, as these authors predicted, American reporters showed a pattern of "ultimate attribution error," which is defined as "the tendency to underestimate the impact of situational factors and to overestimate the role of dispositional factors in controlling behavior" (Pettigrew, 1979). In this study, American reporters attributed the causes of the crimes more to personal dispositions and less to situational factors for the out-group (Chinese) than for the in-group (American), while Chinese reporters did not differentiate. These findings suggest that Americans (an individualistic culture) are more influenced by attribution error than are members of a collectivistic culture. Furthermore, they are even more influenced by this error when the target of the evaluation is a member of another culture, who in most cases might be a member of a minority group.

Another perceptual bias attributed more to people in the United States is "selective processing," which occurs when ambiguous acts are given a more negative interpretation (e.g., aggressive) when performed by a minority target (of stereotypical attributes) but are given a more positive interpretation (e.g., playful) when performed by a white target. In an experiment involving jury decision making (Bodenhausen, 1988), the defendant's ethnicity was subtly revealed either before or after the other case evidence had been processed. The analysis of the results revealed that the stereotyped defendant (a member of a minority) was seen as more likely to be guilty than the nonstereotyped one (a white person) only when the stereotype (revealing the ethnicity) was activated before the evidence was considered.

Other studies referring to perceptual biases have assessed the assumption that people in individualistic cultures experience more of these perceptual errors than people from collectivistic cultures. For instance, in a series of experiments, Gelfand et al. (2002) predicted that self-serving biases of fairness would be more prevalent in individualistic cultures, such as the United States, in which the self is served by focusing on making one's positive attributes "stand out" and by showing oneself to be better than others (an unrealistic assumption). Three studies that used different methodologies (free recall, scenarios, and a laboratory experiment) supported this notion. All of them found differences between participants from individualistic and collectivistic cultures, with significant effects.

Perceptual bias and the consequent cultural unawareness, which affects many people from developed countries and is impeding the halt of the inequality cycle, could be produced by cultural contexts. At the top of the list of the American privileges, Schwalbe (2002/2006) put

> not having to bother unless one chooses, to learn about other countries; and not having to bother, unless one chooses, to learn about how U.S. foreign policies affect people in other countries. A corollary privilege is to imagine that if people in other countries study us, it's merely out of admiration for our way of life. (p. 604)

Schwalbe (2002/2006) also stated that this obliviousness can be very harmful. He noted, "We then lose a mirror with which to view ourselves. Combined with power the result can be worse than innocent ignorance. It can be smug self-delusion, belief in the myth of one's own superiority, and a presumed right to dictate morality" (p. 604).

When analyzing the reasons why there is currently no visible solution to these evident inequalities, it is clear that developed countries lack awareness of developing countries' conditions. It would be unfair to blame the citizens of developed countries for the harmful decisions their governments sometimes make that enforce inequalities in the world. However, we have a shared responsibility as human beings to be aware of disparities that affect other citizens. One of the identified characteristics of the servant-leader is awareness. Ferch (2012) stated, "Servant-leaders notice their own faults, [and] promote reconciliation not only in the family but across races, cultures, and creeds" (p. 160).

Since this unawareness seems to be prevalent in the dominant individualistic cultures of nations that hold global power, it appears to be a little pessimistic to think that this unawareness cycle could end by their own initiative. Why would people who hold positional power spontaneously decide to gain knowledge of the less privileged and share their power with the powerless? I decided to respond to this question from a qualitative and personal point of view by sharing personal experiences that are directly related to the problem of inequality among cultures and the possibility of restoration.

Personal Experiences of Unequal Treatment
and Possible Restoration

In the global scenario, the economic policies and international financial organizations of developed countries affect developing countries' conditions by perpetrating inequalities. On a more personal level, inequalities are enforced by developed countries' citizens' perceived sense of superiority, which causes them to unconsciously commit acts of discrimination against citizens of developing countries. Cultural ignorance plays a strong role in perceptual biases against people from developing countries. Continuing on this personal level, I can describe what I experienced as a member of a minority from a developing country while visiting a developed country when I was a graduate student in the United States some years ago. As the only international student coming from a developing country, I felt that I was treated differently. The experience that affected me the most was when I was challenged by a professor who publicly mentioned that I was inferior because of my Latin American origin. He was the professor of the most difficult class in my master's program, and one that many students failed. He constantly asked me questions about things we had not reviewed in class or been assigned to read, with the sole intent of publicly ridiculing me for not knowing the answers. When I was not able to respond, he said that it was because I was from a "poor undeveloped country." Because I had received a scholarship to study in that program, I had the obligation to pass all of my courses with a high grade. I recall that when as a part of that course I had to present a research paper to an important audience from different universities, the professor became very disappointed when he realized that I had done an excellent job and that the audience had congratulated me. He publicly stated that he disagreed with the audience's evaluation. During that class, I studied and worked harder than I ever had in my life, mainly out of my fear of failure. I felt very lucky that this professor did not grade the tests himself and had teaching assistants who completed that task for him. I obtained outstanding grades on all the tests. I was able to overcome that enormous challenge, and I obtained an A in that class. I doubt that I would have gotten that grade if the professor had been the one who graded the tests, because I understand that his biased perception about my performance and his unfair judgment about my intellectual inferiority were due to my country of origin.

I remember that under all the pressure I felt during that semester, I could not sleep well at night, and also that my dignity as a human being was hurt. When I finished the program and graduated, I realized that this particular experience had made me grow. However, I realized that this professor in his position of power would negatively affect other students from developing countries. I sent him an email explaining how I felt during his class and also stating that I already forgave him for treating me unfairly. I did not receive an answer. Taking into consideration the words of Tutu (1999), it is possible for me to not consider this person as evil but instead to understand his behavior within the possible context that made him react in that specific way. Tutu suggested that we "had to distinguish between the deed and the perpetrator, between the sinner and the sin, to hate and condemn the sin while being filled with compassion for the sinner" (p. 83).

Another personal experience that touched my life was when I was treated differently by my future in-laws when I first met them. When I initially met my wife (an American), we both felt that we had an enormous personal connection that made us want to be together despite the difficulties that we could face for being from different cultures. We started with a long-distance relationship, with visits every time we could afford to pay for tickets to travel between countries. Our relationship progressed and became more serious. Her parents manifested to her that they were against us having a relationship because of my country of origin. On my first visit with them, I wanted to calm them down by telling and showing them how serious I was about my commitment to the relationship. Unfortunately, they did not care about this and openly expressed to me that they were against our relationship based on my culture and race. They told me that they knew that all Latin Americans are lazy, alcoholic, and physically abusive toward their partners. I felt humiliated because I felt discriminated against on the basis of my origin.

After some years, my girlfriend and I got married, and my relationship with my parents-in-law improved on the surface. However, deep inside I still held resentment about the things they had said. I realized that I had not healed, and needed restoration in our relationship. They had never apologized for what they had said. On the occasions when we met again, I realized that I could not be myself or openly demonstrate affection even when they treated me with respect. I had some wounds that needed to be healed, not through time but through real forgiveness. I also realized that we were only ignoring and denying what had happened, so the issue was unresolved.

Serveral years ago I started a doctoral program in leadership studies at Gonzaga University and had the great opportunity to familiarize myself with the concepts of servant-leadership and restorative justice. One of the courses that most affected me was called "Leadership, Restorative Justice, and Forgiveness." During this course we learned the difference between retributive and restorative justice. In retributive justice people look for retribution for damages by punishing the perpetrators, but this does not usually heal wounds. The perpetrators receive punishments that generally do not help them improve as human beings. In restorative justice, however, people do not seek revenge. Instead, they can heal their wounds and grow mutually with the perpetrators of the damages. With this different type of justice, restoration and reconciliation are obtained as a result of human understanding and healing between individuals. Tutu (1999) described the success of reconciliation by saying that it is achieved "when we will know that we are indeed members of one family, bound together in a delicate network of interdependence" (p. 274).

From the learning I gained in this specific course at Gonzaga, I was inspired to obtain restorative justice in my own personal situation. I realized that after being hurt, I was expecting some type of retributive justice that was probably never going to come. I also realized that I had unresolved issues and that my own level of self-awareness had been affected by my past. However, learning about servant-leadership and restorative justice opened up new possibilities to obtain something far more valuable, which is to heal and be healed. Ferch (2012) stated, "Just as the servant-leader is servant first, the servant-leader asks forgiveness first and does not wait for the other to take the initial steps towards reconciliation" (p. 139).

This personal experience of learning about forgiveness and reconciliation was also an excellent way to prove to myself that people from developed countries could change their perceptual biases and support equality between cultures. They only needed to be accompanied in this process. We need to be accountable for our own pain and recovery together. Greenleaf (1977/2002) stated, "Love is an indefinable term . . . its manifestations are both subtle and infinite. But it begins . . . with one absolute condition: unlimited liability. As soon as one's liability for another is qualified to any degree, love is diminished by that much" (p. 52).

With a new optimistic desire to heal and be healed, I decided to talk to my parents-in-law. First, I wanted to ask for their forgiveness for my coldness toward them. I also wanted to offer them my own forgiveness for what they had said and done. Their initial reaction was total denial mixed with an attempt to minimalize the conflict. Their response was that they did not remember the things that I was affirming they had said, and they expressed that they had always accepted me for who I was. I did not want them to avoid this issue because I felt that in that case real forgiveness could not be really granted, since truth was not acknowledged. As I reminded them again of their initial attitude and their words, they finally admitted to them. They affirmed that they had been influenced by their cultural unawareness and that they were sorry that their words and attitude had hurt me. I forgave them for their initial unfair treatment. I was greatly surprised that they finally admitted that they were wrong and that they were also glad that it was I who brought up this topic because they were too ashamed to do it. They also told me that they admired me for my bravery for talking openly about this, and they felt very lucky to have me as their son-in-law, a member of the family. This healing event came at the most appropriate time, as my wife and I are expecting our first child. This new member of our family will come into the world in a different generation, based on equality, forgiveness, and mutual respect between our cultures. We will make sure that this happens with the help of our parents.

Servant-Leadership among Cultures and the Possibility of Forgiveness and Equality in a Global Scenario

The personal experience described above might not provide clear evidence of a world that is changing rapidly in a positive way toward achieving equality among all people. However, this experience demonstrated that with restorative justice and the application of some servant-leader characteristics identified by Spears (1998), such as listening, empathy, healing, awareness, stewardship, commitment to the growth of others, and building community, it is possible to achieve real change in societies. As Greenleaf (1977/2002) stated,

> All that is needed to rebuild community as a viable life form for large numbers of people is for enough servant-leaders to show the way, not by mass movements, but by each servant-leader demonstrating his or her unlimited liability for a quite specific community-related group. (p. 53)

From this personal experience I can see that people from dominant cultures are probably not able to understand their perceptual errors when judging people from dominated cultures if there is no responsible accompaniment by the latter. People from developing countries cannot remain silent or passive. We must accompany people from developed countries in the responsibility of healing our societies. Ferch (2012) stated, "Power then is not only the power to forgive, but the power to evoke in others the tenacity to respond to darkness with light, to respond to evil with good, and to respond to hatred with love" (p. 45). People who suffer from cultural ignorance and commit injustices based on their perceptual biases cannot be left alone to solve these problems by themselves. They need to be understood, their limitations need to be considered, and they need to be guided to overcome their lack of awareness.

Martin Luther King Jr. defended the idea that people from minorities who were discriminated against had to love their oppressors to change their condition. Ferch quoted him, "When we love the oppressor, we bring about not only our own salvation, but the salvation of the oppressor" (as cited in Ferch, 2012, p. 13). In practice, it is very hard for people who suffer different types of abuses to express love to the people who are perpetrating the abuses, but it is the only way to break the dominating/dominated interaction and obtain a common healing. There is a lot to do to achieve equality in the world, especially because some abuses between cultures have resulted in inner hate and misunderstanding. However, we should start this healing process immediately in our own personal cases by recognizing our suffering and facing our accountability in the world's healing process. Ferch (2012) stated, "In facing ourselves, especially in the darkness of our experiences of unavoidable suffering, love can touch even our deepest wounds" (p. 177). If we adopt this practice of mutual forgiveness in our personal lives, it is probable that together, being from different cultures, we can heal the soul of the world. People from developing countries should not look for retributive justice after having experienced abuses from dominant cultures.

On a global level, representatives from our different nations, with our different realities, can learn and practice real forgiveness and restorative justice and become servant-leaders who contribute to change the currently unequal conditions that affect everyone in the world. As Ferch (2012) stated, "True leadership heals the heart of the world" (p. 194). Global inequalities are not going to be changed only by poor or rich nations. This is a challenge in which both developed and undeveloped countries need to engage together. That is the only way to sustainable global coexistence among countries. It is imperative that we start working toward breaking the oppressive cycle that affects most of the world's population. We, people from developed and undeveloped countries alike, need to start holding ourselves accountable for our shared future and begin the healing process together immediately.

References

Black, J. K. (2006). Inequality in the global village. In P. Rothenberg (Ed.), *Beyond borders: Thinking critically about global issues* (pp. 323–330). New York, NY: Worth. (Original work published 1999).

Bodenhausen, G. V. (1988). Stereotypic biases in social decision making and memory: Testing process models of stereotype use. *Journal of Personality & Social Psychology, 55*, 726–737.

Booker, S., & Minter, W. (2006). Global apartheid: AIDS and murder by patent. In P. Rothenberg (Ed.), *Beyond borders: Thinking critically about global issues* (pp. 517–522). New York, NY: Worth. (Original work published 2001).

Bulbeck, C. (2006). Fracturing binarisms: First and third worlds. In P. Rothenberg (Ed.), *Beyond borders: Thinking critically about global issues* (pp. 37–40). New York, NY: Worth. (Original work published 1998).

Chhokar, J. S., Brodbeck, F. C., & House, R. J. (Eds.). (2008). *Culture and leadership, across the world: The GLOBE book of in depth studies of 25 societies.* New York, NY: Lawrence Erlbaum Associates.

Choi, I., Nisbett, R. E., & Norenzayan, A. (1999). Causal attribution across cultures: Variation and universality. *Psychological Bulletin, 125*, 47–63.

El Saadawi, N. (2006). Women and the poor: The challenge of global justice. In P. Rothenberg (Ed.), *Beyond borders: Thinking critically about global issues* (pp. 400–408). New York, NY: Worth. (Original work published 1997).

Farmer, P. (2006). Suffering and structural violence. In P. Rothenberg (Ed.), *Beyond borders: Thinking critically about global issues* (pp. 368–393). New York, NY: Worth. (Original work published 2003).

Ferch, S. R. (2012). *Forgiveness and power in the age of atrocity.* New York, NY: Lexington Books

Galeano, J. (2006). Open veins of Latin America. In P. Rothenberg (Ed.), *Beyond borders: Thinking critically about global issues* (pp. 127–141). New York, NY: Worth. (Original work published 1997).

Gelfand, M. J., Higgins, M., Nishii, L. H., Raver, J. L., Dominguez, A., Murakami, F., Yamaguchi, S., & Toyama, M. (2002). Culture and egocentric perceptions of fairness in conflict and negotiation. *Journal of Applied Psychology, 87*, 833–845.

Greenleaf, R. K. (2002). *Servant leadership: A journey into the nature of legitimate power and greatness* (25th anniversary ed.). L. C. Spears (Ed.). New York, NY: Paulist Press. (Original work published 1977).

Inglehart, R. (1997). *Modernization and postmodernization.* Princeton, NJ: Princeton University Press.

Kloby, J. (2006). The legacy of colonialism. In P. Rothenberg (Ed.), *Beyond borders: Thinking critically about global issues* (pp. 99–106). New York, NY: Worth. (Original work published 2004).

Majavu, M. (2006). Debt, reforms, and social services in Africa. In P. Rothenberg (Ed.), *Beyond borders: Thinking critically about global issues* (pp. 507–509). New York, NY: Worth. (Original work published 2004).

Mies, M. (2006). The myth of catching up development. In P. Rothenberg (Ed.), *Beyond borders: Thinking critically about global issues* (pp. 150–157). New York, NY: Worth. (Original work published 1993).

Morris, M. W., & Peng, K. (1994). Culture and cause: American and Chinese attributions for social and physical events. *Journal of Personality & Social Psychology, 67,* 949–971.

Pettigrew, T. F. (1979). The ultimate attribution error: Extending Allport's cognitive analysis of prejudice. *Personality and Social Psychology Bulletin, 5,* 461–476.

Rodney, W. (2006). How Europe underdeveloped Africa. In P. Rothenberg (Ed.), *Beyond borders: Thinking critically about global issues* (pp. 107–125). New York, NY: Worth. (Original work published 1972).

Rothenberg, P. S. (Ed.). (2006). *Beyond borders: Thinking critically about global issues.* New York, NY: Worth.

Sachs, J. (2006). Macroeconomics of health: No health available at $7.50 per person per year. In P. Rothenberg (Ed.), *Beyond borders: Thinking critically about global issues* (pp. 364–367). New York, NY: Worth.

Schwalbe, M. (2006). The cost of American privilege. In P. Rothenberg (Ed.), *Beyond borders: Thinking critically about global issues* (pp. 603–605). New York, NY: Worth. (Original work published 2002).

Spears, L. C. (1998). *Insights on leadership: Service, stewardship, spirit, and servant-leadership.* New York, NY: John Wiley and Sons.

Stiglitz, J. (2006). Globalization and its discontents: The promise of global institutions. In P. Rothenberg (Ed.), *Beyond borders: Thinking critically about global issues* (pp. 419–431). New York, NY: Worth. (Original work published 2002).

Tutu, D. (1999). *No Future without forgiveness.* New York, NY: Doubleday.

Wibbeke, E. S. (2009). *Global business leadership.* Burlington, MA: Elsevier.

Wiesel, E. (2006). *Night.* New York, NY: Hill and Wang.

Wiesenthal, S. (1998). *The sunflower.* New York, NY: Schocken Books.

Williams, W. A. (2006). Empire as a way of life. In P. Rothenberg (Ed.), *Beyond borders: Thinking critically about global issues* (pp. 81–88). New York, NY: Worth. (Original work published 1980).

Yates, M. (2006). Poverty and inequality in the global economy. In P. Rothenberg (Ed.), *Beyond borders: Thinking critically about global issues* (pp. 330–339). New York, NY: Worth. (Original work published 2004).

PART II

SERVANT-LEADERSHIP, FORGIVENESS, AND SOCIAL ISSUES

Chapter 6

Servant-Leadership, Forgiveness, and Social Justice

Shann Ray Ferch

One of the defining characteristics of human nature is the ability to discern one's own faults, to be broken as the result of such faults, and in response, to seek a meaningful change. Socially, both forgiveness and the disciplined process of reconciliation draw us into a crucible from which we can emerge more refined, more willing to see the heart of another, and more able to create just and lasting relationships. Such relationships—robust, durable, enjoyable, and courageous—form what is best in people, in families, and in the workplace. The will to seek forgiveness, to forgive, and to pursue reconciliation may be a significant part of developing the kind of wisdom, health, autonomy, and freedom espoused by Robert Greenleaf in his idea of the servant-leader, an idea whose time has arrived, an idea that is destined to remain on the vanguard of leadership theory, research, and practice.

In reflecting on the uncommon and profound depth of Greenleaf's theory, I am reminded of the hollow existence experienced by so many, a thought captured by Thoreau's well-known societal indictment that most people "lead lives of quiet desperation." It is a difficult truth, one that runs subtly beneath the surface of our lives, our organizations, and our communities. More specifically, I am reminded of my grandfather. Upon his death from alcoholism some years ago, I remember feeling disappointed about the lack of time I had had with him, the lack of good time spent in conversation, of good experiences shared. He died having lost the basic respect of others, a man without an honored leadership position in his own family, a person no one went to for wisdom or sanctuary. In his later years, filled with despondency and self-pity, he was largely alone. Though he had once been strong and vital, few family members were close to him when he died. At one time he had been a true Montanan, of unique joy and individual strength, a man who loved to walk the hills with his family after the spring runoff in search of arrowheads. But his joy for life was eclipsed by his condition before death. He had become morose and often very depressed—a depression that hailed from the sanctions the family had placed on him, disallowing him to obtain alcohol for the last years of his life. In the end, it seemed he had given up.

"What happened to him?" I asked my father.

"He stopped dreaming his dreams," my dad replied.

In making this statement my father echoed a truth forwarded by Greenleaf in 1977: "For something great to happen, there must be a great dream. Behind every great achievement is a dreamer of great dreams" (p. 16).

Servant-Leadership

The idea of the leader as servant is rooted in the far-reaching ideal that people have inherent worth—not only a dignity to be strived for but also, beneath this striving, a dignity irrevocably connected to the reality of being human. Philosophically, if one believes in the dignity of the person, then the ideas of servant-leadership and the experience of leading or being led from a servant perspective not only make sense but contain the elegance, precision, and willpower necessary for human development.

The nature of change in the contemporary climate is both complex and swift. Notably, the intensity of such movement has brought with it the exposure of major character flaws in local, national, and international leadership personas, thus increasing the urgent need for a more purposeful, more lasting response in society. Presently, leaders who are able to build community without sacrificing productivity, and who are able to embrace diverse potential rather than adhering to traditional, more hierarchical approaches, are inspiring a growing movement in business, the social services, education, and religion (Northouse, 2001). The more traditional model of leadership, often heavily based on hierarchical structure and a designated chain of command geared toward increased efficiency, has resulted not only in the moral decline of the relational environment but also in a pervasive malaise common to the psyche of the contemporary working person. The practices of servant-leadership foster a deeper, more personal sense of vision and inclusiveness, and produce responses to the failures of leadership found in traditional models. On the rise in scholarly literature, studies in forgiveness and restorative justice form one expression of the present need for responses to failures of leadership. Such studies validate the capacity for moral fortitude, point to greater efficiency and productivity, and maintain a healthy sense of hope and meaning in organizations.

Seeking Responses to the Failures of Contemporary Leadership

A common experience of being led from the traditional model is one of dominance or control, while the experience of being servant-led is one of freedom. In the words of Greenleaf (1977), those who are servant-led become "healthier, wiser, freer, more autonomous" and "more likely themselves to become servants" (pp. 13–14). A true sense of forgiveness—not a false forgiveness that overlooks the harm caused by others but a true forgiveness inherently bound to the ideas of integrity and justice—can move us toward the kind of robust and resilient relationships that build the foundation of legitimate power, both personally and professionally. It is in legitimate power, a form of power Greenleaf expressed from a servant-first mentality, that we experience the human capacity for love and greatness.

Throughout society, in the culture of families, groups, communities, and corporations, the call for effective leadership is increasing (Gardner, 1990). The old leadership model in which leaders directed others toward increased productivity at the expense of personal meaning often concentrated on correcting problems and maintaining the status quo (Bass, 1960; Burns, 1978; Harrison, 1997). Change itself is taking place at such a rapid pace that people often find themselves caught in a storm of stress (Senge, 1990). Moving forward, incorporating the wisdom of past models, and moving beyond the industrial mind-set to one that is more relational, we face the increasing need for leaders who through their integrity inspire us to seek a better vision of what it means to be human (Goleman, 1995; Heifetz, 1994; Kouzes & Posner, 1987). In response, Greenleaf (1977) proposed that we need leaders who understand the nature of humanity and who can foster a deep sense of community. Such leaders embrace diversity rather than insisting on uniformity. They understand what it means to develop the freedom, health, wisdom, and autonomy of others. They understand forgiveness and are able to develop just restoration, rather than push for legality and retribution (Harris, 1999). The ideas of servant-leadership, uniquely positioned in contemporary leadership theory and practice, can be seen in movements that have brought dead organizations to new life, and reconciliation and healing to nations deeply wounded by human atrocities (Greenleaf, 1977; Spears, 1998; Tutu, 1999).

My first recollections of trying to understand servant-leadership were in connection with significant others who gave me a vision of the dignity of life. Often these were people who stepped out of their world into mine and drew me into the larger concept of living to which they had attuned their lives. This concept, something central to their own identity, inevitably had to do with internal, relational, and societal movements that have noticeably transformed humanity—movements such as quietness, discernment, courage, forgiveness, and love. Even without an intentional understanding of Greenleaf's ideas, each of the people who influenced me, women and men, were servant-leaders. Each had a sense of fearlessness regarding self-discovery, accompanied by a disciplined, creative approach to relational meaning that became an antidote to the "terrifying emptiness" (Smith, 1957, p. 78) that is too often our collective experience of one another.

Before being influenced toward a greater understanding of what it might mean to be a servant and a leader, early on I was almost entirely given to images of bravery or ambition. I lived consumed by hopes of advancement and adulation. Much of my early professional development was spent envisioning others adoring me: me as the sports champion, me on top of the world, me the big money maker, the professional man, the leader of mighty corporations. And before this, as a high school athlete, I lived needy for the praise of others, often carrying about a vague wish that by some chance others would suddenly devote themselves to telling stories of my excellence.

Conveniently, in the world I conceived, my faults were protected; I didn't want anyone to notice my faults or point them out, and I spent most of my energy trying to please others so they would have no reason to be disappointed in me, even as I lived a life that was both unaware of and unconcerned with the personal well-being of others. If someone poked a hole in my façade, as did happen on occasion, my deflation was immediate and complete, and people discovered that inside I was defensive and rigid, a fragile person. I had little idea of what it might mean to be true to myself or someone else.

I grew up in Montana, a state where basketball was valued as highly as family or work, and Jonathan Takes Enemy, a Crow Indian who played for Hardin High School, was the best basketball player in the state. He led a school with a years-long losing tradition into the state spotlight, carrying the team and the community on his shoulders all the way to the state tournament, where he averaged 41 points per game. He created legends that twenty years later are still spoken of in state basketball circles, and he did so with a fierceness that made me both fear and respect him. On the court, nothing was outside the realm of his skill: the jump shot, the drive, the sweeping left-handed finger roll, the deep fade-away jumper. He could deliver what we all dreamed of, and with a venom that said *Don't get in my way.*

I was a year younger than Jonathan, playing for an all-white school in Livingston. When our teams met in the divisional tournament, he and the Hardin Bulldogs delivered us a crushing 17-point defeat. At the close of the third quarter, with the clock winding down and his team comfortably ahead, Takes Enemy pulled up from a step in front of half court and shot a straight, clean jump shot. Though the shot was taken from more than 20 feet beyond the three-point line, his form remained pure. The audacity and power of it, the exquisite beauty, hushed the crowd. A common knowledge came to everyone: few people can even throw a basketball that far with any accuracy, let alone take a legitimate shot with good form. Takes Enemy landed, and as the ball was in flight, he turned, no longer watching, and began to walk back toward his team bench. The buzzer sounded, he put his fist in the air, and the shot swished into the net. The crowd erupted.

In his will to even take such a shot, let alone make it, I was reminded of the surety and brilliance of so many Native American heroes in Montana who had painted the basketball landscape of my boyhood. Stanford Rides Horse, Juneau Plenty Hawk, and Paul Deputy of St. Labre. Elvis Old Bull of Lodge Grass. Marty Roundface, Tim Falls Down, and Marc Spotted Bear of Plenty Coups. Joe Pretty Paint and Takes Enemy of Hardin. Many of these young men died as a result of the violence that surrounded the alcohol and drug traffic on the reservations, but their image on the court inspired me toward the kind of boldness that gives artistry and freedom to any endeavor. Such boldness is akin to passion. For these young men, and for me at that time, the passion was basketball.

But rather than creating in me my own intrepid nature, seeing Takes Enemy only emphasized how little I knew of courage, not just on the basketball court but in life as well. Takes Enemy breathed a confidence I lacked, had a leadership potential that lived and moved. Greenleaf (1977) wrote, "A mark of leaders, an attribute that puts them in a position to show the way for others, is that they are better than most at pointing the direction" (p. 15). Takes Enemy was the embodiment of this quality. He and his team seemed to work as one, and they were able to play with fluidity and joy and breathtaking abandon. I began to look for this leadership style as an athlete and as a person. The search led me to people who led not through dominance but through freedom of movement, and such people led me toward the experience of humility, forgiveness, and relational justice. One of the most potent of these experiences came from the mentoring I received from my future wife's father.

My wife, Jennifer, and I were in our twenties, not yet married. I was at the dinner table with her and her family when Jennifer's father made a short, sharp-edged comment to her mother. At the time he was the president of a large multinational corporation based in Washington State. Thinking back, I hardly noticed the comment, probably because of the nature and intensity of the ways I had previously experienced conflict. To me, most conflicts revealed a simmering anger or a resentment that went underground, plaguing the relationship and taking a long time to disperse. I did not give Jennifer's father's comment a second thought until some time after the meal, when he approached me as I was relaxing on the couch. He had just finished speaking with his wife over to one side of the kitchen when he approached.

"I want to ask your forgiveness for being rude to my wife," he said.

I could not imagine what he was talking about. I felt uncomfortable, and tried to get out of this awkward conversation as soon as I could.

"You don't have to ask me," I said.

But from there, my tension only increased. I had not often been in situations in which things were handled in such an equitable way. My work experience had been that the person in power (typically, but not always, the male) dominated the conflict, so that the external power remained in the dominant one's hands, while internally everyone else (those not in power) suffered bitterness, disappointment, and a despairing, nearly hopeless feeling regarding the good of the relationship. Later, in my family and work relationships, I found that when I lived from my own inordinate sense of power, I too, like those I had overpowered, would have a sick feeling internally for having won my position through coercion or force rather than through the work of a just and mutual resolution. In any case, in the situation with Jennifer's father, I felt tense and wanted to quickly end the moment by saving face for both of us. "You don't have to ask me," I said.

"I don't ask forgiveness for your benefit," he answered. "I ask in order to honor the relationship I share with my wife. In our family, if one person hurts another, we not only ask forgiveness of the person who has been hurt, but also of anyone else who was present in order to restore the dignity of the one we've hurt." Later I found the same practice was common in the culture he had created in the corporation he led.

From this relatively brief experience, I gained respect for myself and began to see the possibilities of a family and work culture free of perpetual binds and rifts, and free of the entrenched criticalness that usually accompanies such relationships. My own life was like a fortress compared with the open lifestyle Jennifer's father espoused. I began to understand that much of my protected-ness, defensiveness, and unwillingness to reveal myself might continue to serve as a fortification in future conflicts but would not lead me to more whole ways of experiencing the world. I also began to see that the work of a servant-leader requires the ability to humble oneself, and a desire to honor relationships with others as sacred. In Greenleaf's (1977) work, this takes the form of listening and understanding. Only the one who is a servant is able to approach people by first listening and trying to understand rather than by trying to problem-solve or "lead." Just as "true listening builds strength in other people" (p. 17), it follows that a lack of listening weakens people. In the following section a story by Tolstoy illumines this idea.

Tolstoy on the Essence of Listening and Understanding

Traditional leadership models often create an environment in which leaders take action without taking accountability for the emotional or spiritual well-being of themselves or those they lead. This can result in an elitist mentality in which leaders assume a false sense of direction. In this way, leaders (even those who are well meaning) who do not make themselves accountable to the deeper issues of leadership end up diminishing themselves and others by approaching the work environment as a leader first rather than as a servant first. In Tolstoy's story "The Three Hermits," the bishop is such a leader: a person with good intentions but blind to the dignity latent in those he seeks to lead.

In the story, the bishop was traveling on a merchant ship when he overheard a man speaking of three hermits who had lived for years on a nearby island, devoting themselves to prayer. The crew members did not believe the man, saying it was just a legend, an old wives' tale. But the man persisted. He related how some years before, he had been shipwrecked off the island in question, taken in by the hermits, and sheltered and fed by them while they rebuilt his boat. He told the crew that the hermits were devout men of prayer, the most saintly men he had ever met. Overhearing this, the bishop demanded that the captain take him to the island. It was out of the way, and the captain was reluctant, but the bishop was determined, and offered to pay the captain for his trouble. The captain relented, and in the early morning, while the ship anchored offshore, the bishop was let off on the hermits' island. The hermits emerged, walking slowly toward the visitor. They were old and grizzled, with long beards. Having been away from civilization so long, they spoke little and appeared meek and afraid. The bishop asked them how they'd been praying. The tallest one seemed to be the spokesman.

"Very simply, my lord," he said. "Three are we. Three are Thee. Have mercy on us."

"I must teach you how to pray, then," said the bishop.

"Thank you, my lord," the three hermits replied, and the bishop proceeded to require them to memorize the Lord's Prayer. It was long, hard work; the hermits were out of practice. Throughout the day they fretted at how difficult it was for them to memorize, and they feared they would disappoint the bishop. In fact, it was nearly night before the three could recite to the bishop the prayer he'd taught them, but finally the last of them had it, and then the bishop flagged the small boat to take him back to the ship. He felt he had served his purpose that day, served God, and enlightened the three men.

When the ship set sail the bishop was on deck, high up in the fore of the ship, near the captain, looking back at the ship's wake and the path of the moon. They sailed for some time but he did not feel like sleeping. He felt satisfied. The work had been hard work, but good work, and necessary. Just then he saw a silver sphere far back on the dark of the water moving toward the ship at a tremendous pace. The bishop was afraid. The entire crew was on deck now, watching it, trying to make out what it might be. Eventually the sphere seemed to split into three. Then the bishop clearly saw three lights, three men, long beards flowing in the wind—it was the hermits, moving over the water with great speed.

They approached the ship and floated up to where the bishop was seated, stopping in front of him just beyond the railing. They had pained looks on their faces.

"What is it?" cried the bishop.

"Father, Father," pleaded the taller one, "forgive us. We've forgotten the prayer you taught us. Please teach us again."

Hearing this, the bishop immediately fell on his face. "Go your way," he said. "Pray as you have prayed. God is with you. Have mercy on me."

Servant-Leadership, Forgiveness, and Social Justice

Gadamer (1993) in philosophy, and Freire (1990) in education, speak of the importance of dialogue in understanding the world and initiating change across broad human scientific, societal, and interpersonal levels. Greenleaf (1977) speaks of the absolute necessity of trust, a form of love in which people are free of rejection. He stated, "The servant always accepts and empathizes, never rejects. The servant as leader always empathizes, always accepts the person, but sometimes refuses to accept some of the person's effort or performance as good enough" (p. 21). In meaningful dialogue the servant as leader submits to a higher perspective, one that can be pivotal to the development of the self in relation to others. Greenleaf addressed this when he stated that the real motive for healing is to heal oneself, not to change others, implying that the true motive for serving is to serve oneself, for one's own betterment. In this light one seeks to heal or seeks to serve not necessarily for others but for the greater good of oneself and, by extension, the greater good of the community. Such healing may best take place in a community that initiates and sustains meaningful dialogue.

Meaningful dialogue gives rise to the forces that unhinge the way we harm each other, opening us up to a more accepting and empathic understanding of one another. Greenleaf, in forwarding an ideal of love in community, places servant-leadership firmly in the contemporary landscape of the family, the workplace, and the global pursuit of social justice. In this landscape, the retributive justice in mediating familial and professional conflicts represented by the legal system is replaced by the idea of a community of forgivers, people with the foresight and vision to build a just and lasting reconciliation, people interested in the deeper restoration that is the result of a disciplined and unflinching look at the wrongs we do to one another.

Forgiveness studies in the social sciences have gathered an immense following in the last two decades through research that is beginning to connect the will to forgive with reductions in depression, anger, heart problems, and immune-deficiency levels (for excellent reviews of the will to forgive in individuals, marriages, and families, see McCullough, Sandage, &Worthington, 1997 and McCullough & Worthington, 1994). New bridges are forming between the social sciences and the study of leadership, pointing organizations toward the acceptance and empathy Greenleaf envisioned. This involves the development of leaders who are able to understand the way people diminish one another, leaders who are able to instill in the organization a culture of acceptance, empathy, and relational justice. From this perspective, the servant-leader creates an environment in which forgiveness can be asked and granted, and does so by example. Two people who come together to reconcile, who choose to forgive and be forgiven, can experience a cleansing in which embittered rigidity becomes transformative openness (Valle & Halling, 1989). The leader can exemplify this process, and in settings of strong relational trust, the process can become embedded in the life of the organization. An early look at forgiveness in leadership settings detailing an intentional, specific approach to forgiveness work, was published in the *Journal of Leadership Studies* (Ferch & Mitchell, 2001).

In the contemporary global landscape, the traditional route of retributive justice is shown in the response to World Wars I and II, and reaches its apex in the international spectacle of the Nuremberg trials. Though retributive justice seeks a just response to wrongs committed, it usually does so through punitive or violent means (e.g., imprisonment, death, and so on). Retributive justice, especially in its most undisciplined or wanton forms, tends to beget more alienation between people, oppression, atrocities, and spiritual poverty. Restorative justice, as promoted by leaders such as Martin Luther King Jr. during the civil rights movement and Nelson Mandela and Archbishop Desmond Tutu in response to the atrocities of apartheid in South Africa, has sought a different answer to the harms of humanity.

Martin Luther King Jr. an exquisite servant-leader on the international scene, stated that the oppressor will never willingly give up his or her power—a statement of clarity that explains why we are often drawn toward violence in an attempt to overthrow the oppressor or silence in an attempt to escape the oppression: the fight-or-flight response. King, a pupil of Gandhi, advocated neither violence nor silence. He furthered his discernment regarding the unwillingness of the oppressor with the following revolutionary idea, akin to Greenleaf's idea of the servant-leader's response to injustice: rather than hate or distance ourselves from the oppressor, we should love the oppressor (King, 1986). King believed that when we love the oppressor we bring about not only our own salvation but also the salvation of the one who harms us.

Nelson Mandela, the first democratically elected president of South Africa, was another extraordinary contemporary servant-leader. From a country suffering bloodshed and hate, he and those around him effectively built a country of hope. He held to a vision of South Africa involving reconciliation, in which black and white Africans could live and rule together without retribution or violence. He spent more than twenty-seven years as a political prisoner, eighteen imprisoned at Robben Island, yet Mandela refused to be vengeful either personally or politically. Notably, on his release he refused to gain power through suppression of dissent, and his refusal to deny the humanity of those who imprisoned him or those who confessed to the most heinous of human right abuses drew the people of his country toward the monumental task of forgiving in the face of grave injustices, forgiving even atrocities that demonstrated the brutality of the human condition at its worst (Mandela, 1994).

Mandela, Tutu, and other democratically elected officials designed the Truth and Reconciliation Commission in response to the atrocities committed during the apartheid years. They felt that retribution, whether legal or punitive, would result only in widespread violence, a violence that had plagued many African countries emerging from colonialization. The commission held a specific and drastic vision, and because of the deep respect the majority of South Africans felt for these leaders, the country implemented a plan of forgiveness and reconciliation, of restorative justice, unlike any the global political community had ever seen. Rather than seek out those who committed crimes against humanity, bring them to justice, and punish them, the commission asked for honesty. The commission asked people to honestly admit what they had done, where and when and how they had harmed, abducted, tortured, and killed others. The result of telling the truth was that the perpetrators would receive amnesty; they would go free. At the same time, the commission asked the people of South Africa to respond with forgiveness. The commission made this vision of truth and reconciliation an act of law with the hope that it would give people a chance to hear of lost and dead family members, friends, and loved ones, and a chance to truly grieve the harms the nation had suffered.

Tutu, as chairman of the Truth and Reconciliation Commission, clearly stated:

> The Act says that the thing you're striving after should be "ubuntu" rather than revenge. It comes from the root (of a Zulu-Xhosa word), which means "a person." So it is the essence of being a person. And in our experience, in our understanding, a person is a person through other persons. You can't be a solitary human being. We're all linked. We have this communal sense, and because of this deep sense of community, the harmony of the group is a prime attribute. (Harris, 1999, p. 26)

Some years after the Truth and Reconciliation Commission hearings, South Africa remains largely free of bloodshed. The country's legacy, which is unique among the political, governmental, and military communities of the world, has begun to be defined by forgiveness and reconciliation rather than by force, retribution, or violence.

I do not think it far afield to say that most Americans have not read the works of one of our own, Martin Luther King Jr. let alone the works of leaders such as Mandela and Tutu. We often generate an egocentrism that insulates us, even from the kind of international servant-leadership ideas that are presently changing the world. Greenleaf (1977) made an unrelated but poignantly fitting statement while attending an international symposium in 1976: "Our African friend has said that we Americans are arrogant. It hurts—but I accept the charge" (p. 307). In acceptance, empathy; in empathy, listening; and in listening, understanding. Such understanding may turn our self-absorption toward real care for others and in turn make us wiser, healthier, and better able ourselves to become servants, better able ourselves to lead.

Conclusion

The hope for forgiveness and reconciliation is not without its critics. We shed our naivete when we realize that human evil exists despite our best efforts to forgive and reconcile. The echo of King's words remains—the oppressor will never willingly give up power. Even so, the deeper echo of King's words resounds even more strongly: when we love the oppressor, we bring about not only our own salvation but the salvation of the oppressor. In these words we find solace regarding our own failures, inequities, injustices, character flaws, and great harms. Members of our own families can live with an enduring sense of loving and being loved. Women and men in our communities can be true women and true men, not displaced, not diminished. And in our workplaces we can work with joy, a sense of calling, and the personal meaning that accompanies good work. These things are possible, for it is in the servant-leader, in his or her movement toward healing the self, toward truly serving, that a response to the failures of leadership emerges. On the horizon of this landscape, a landscape that is as personal and spiritual as it is political and global, we see ourselves free of what binds us, and we walk in such a way that others are drawn forward so that they, too, may be free.

References

Bass, B. M. (1960). *Leadership, psychology, and organizational behavior.* New York, NY: Harper and Brothers.

Burns, J. M. (1978). *Leadership.* New York, NY: Harper and Row.

Ferch, S., & Mitchell, M. (2001) Intentional forgiveness in relational leadership: A technique for enhancing effective leadership. *Journal of Leadership Studies, 4,* 70–83.

Freire, P. (1990). *Pedagogy of the oppressed.* New York, NY: Continuum.

Gadamer, H. G. (1993). *Truth and method* (J. Weinsheimer & D. G. Marshal, Eds.). (2nd rev. ed.). New York, NY: Continuum.

Gardner, J. W. (1990). *On leadership.* New York, NY: The Free Press.

Goleman, D. (1995). *Emotional intelligence.* New York, NY: Bantam.

Greenleaf, R. K. (1977). *Servant-Leadership: A journey into the nature of legitimate power and greatness.* Mahwah, NJ: Paulist Press.

Harris, M. K. (1999). A call for transformational leadership for corrections. *Corrections Management Quarterly, 3,* 24–31.

Harrison, R. (1997). Why your firm needs emotional intelligence. *People Management, 3*(1), 41.

Heifetz, R. A. (1994). *Leadership without easy answers.* Cambridge, MA: Belknap Press of Harvard University Press.

King, M. L., Jr. (1986). *A testament of hope.* San Francisco, CA: HarperCollins.

Kouzes, J. M., & Posner, B. Z. (1987). *The leadership challenge: How to get extraordinary things done in organizations.* San Francisco, CA: Jossey-Bass.

Mandela, N. R. (1994). *Long walk to freedom.* Boston, MA: Little, Brown and Company.

McCullough, M. E., Sandage, S. J., & Worthington, E. L., Jr. (1997). *To forgive is human*. Downers Grove, IL: InterVarsity.

McCullough, M. E., & Worthington, E. L. (1994). Encouraging clients to forgive people who have hurt them: Review, critique, and research prospectus. *Journal of Psychology and Theology, 33*, 3–20.

Northouse, P. G. (2001). *Leadership: Theory and practice*. (2nd ed.). Thousand Oaks, CA: Sage Publications.

Senge, P. M. (1990). *The fifth discipline: The art and practice of the learning organization*. New York, NY: Doubleday.

Smith, R. (1957). Pity the childless couple. *American Mercury, 84*, 76–78.

Spears, L. C. (Ed.). (1998). *Insights on leadership: Service, stewardship, spirit, and servant-leadership*. New York, NY: John Wiley & Sons.

Tutu, D. M. (1999). *No future without forgiveness*. New York, NY: Doubleday.

Valle, R. S., & Halling, S. (Eds.). (1989). *Existential-phenomenological perspectives in psychology: Exploring the breadth of human experience*. New York, NY: Plenum Press.

Chapter 7

Forgiveness and Reconciliation as an Organizational Leadership Competency within Transitional Justice Instruments

Andrew Campbell

The sociocultural and ethnic trauma experienced by victims of human rights violations affect not only postreconstruction activities but also stable governance initiatives as transitional leaders foster national reconciliation in a postconflict environment. Scholars note that demands on transitional leaders range from macroeconomic stabilization and generation of employment to the reduction of corruption and sustainability of markets; at the same time, physical and territorial security call for accountability and justice for perpetrators under the rule of law in the aftermath of human rights violations committed during conflict (Oola, 2015; Sammi, 2010; Saunders, 2011). Yet if forgiveness and reconciliation are not included as a key ingredient, long-term peace and stability are uncertainties.

The argument is that an important component for practitioners facilitating transitional justice mechanisms should be forgiveness and reconciliation (Jirsa, 2004; Sammi, 2010; Tutu, 2000). This is because forgiveness, if practiced in combination with mechanisms of transitional justice such as judicial accountability, truth telling, governance, and reparations, carries great potential for building peace (Oola, 2015). In addition, the inclusion of forgiveness and reconciliation is a critical relational component of leadership competency for any organizational leader in today's highly competitive environment (Abbasi, Rehman, & Bibi, 2010; Bass & Bass,

2008; Senge, 1990). According to Kymenlaasko (2012, p. 432), forgiveness is an important leadership competency because it is a way for individuals to repair damaged workplace relationships and overcome debilitating thoughts and emotions resulting from interpersonal injury. In essence, forgiveness and reconciliation are critical competencies for both practitioners and organizational leaders executing transitional justice instruments.

The problem is that forgiveness and reconciliation are relatively new and uncharted as individual leadership competencies within the transitional justice and organizational leadership fields (Aquino et al., 2008; Palanski, 2012). The reason for this is that tenets of forgiveness and reconciliation are controversial and complex within a transitional justice and organizational context (Borris, 2003; Ferch, 2012; Jirsa, 2004; Kymenlaasko, 2012; Palanski, 2012). As a result, the leader's role regarding the long-term impact of forgiveness and reconciliation on an organization is empirically untested (Kymenlaasko, 2012; Llewellyn & Philpot, 2014). That said, internal and external organizational conflict adversely affects working relationships and team cohesion as well as a constructive organizational climate. Given different leadership styles, organizational leaders with the acumen to model a leadership approach constructively resolves interpersonal discourse through restorative justice processes and drives individual, organizational, and social change (Kidder, 2007). Therefore, the author postulates that servant-leaders create an organizational climate for social change through forgiveness as well as creating a pathway for reconciliation. In other words, the aim of this chapter is to provide an introduction to forgiveness and reconciliation as key components of leaders' ability to resolve organizational and global challenges and sustain harmony.

This chapter will provide four significant contributions of the leadership and transitional justice disciplines. First is a definition and conceptual understanding of forgiveness and reconciliation within transitional justice and leadership disciplines. Second is the creation of a body of knowledge that introduces forgiveness and reconciliation as an organizational leadership competency for practitioners within a transitional justice context. Third is the initiation of a dialogue generating new knowledge of the critical roles that world religions play in facilitating forgiveness and reconciliation within peacebuilding activities. And the final contribution is laying a theoretical foundation on which servant-leaders can develop the competencies necessary for forgiveness and reconciliation to occur within peacebuilding organizations.

Forgiveness

Definition of Forgiveness

A review of the literature reveals that definitions of forgiveness are similar among transitional justice and organizational leadership scholar-practitioners. Transitional justice scholars define *forgiveness* as a "willingness to abandon one's right to resentment, negative judgment and indifferent behavior toward one who unjustly hurt us, while fostering the undeserved qualities of compassion, generosity, and even love towards him or her" (Saunders, 2011, p. 122).

Organizational leadership scholars define *forgiveness* as "a matter of a willed change of heart and the successful result of an active endeavor to replace bad thoughts such as bitterness and anger with compassion and affection" (Petersen, 2007, p. 62). In *Forgiveness: A Sampling of Research Results*, Bullock (2008) defines *forgiveness* as "a process (or the result of a process) that involves a change in emotion and attitude regarding an offender. Most scholars view this as an intentional and voluntary process, driven by a deliberate decision to forgive" (p. 5). According to Yergler (2005), an operational definition of *forgiveness* "is the act of releasing another from the guilt, shame, or deserved retribution they have merited through their own intentional or unintentional actions directed at another which have resulted in hurt, anger, animosity and relational polarization" (para. 10). In essence, as a victim forgives and reconciles with a perpetrator that inflicted emotional hurt, physical harm, and sociopolitical injury, the victim releases the emotional power the perpetrator has over the victim.

Forgiveness is a difficult and long-term process of deciding not only to repair the emotional tags associated within an abusive organizational climate but also to release past anger, hostility, and bitterness over workplace interpersonal emotional and psychological injury (Church, 2010). In short, scholars note that forgiveness is an organizational leadership competency for leaders in both private and public learning organizations (Bass & Bass, 2008; Jirsa, 2004; Palanski, 2012; Senge, 1990).

Conceptualization of Forgiveness

Forgiveness is an internal process of individual courage that cognitively, emotionally, and spiritually transforms the meaning of the traumatic event as well as promotes the release of rooted transgression by the perpetrator, wiping the slate clean and restoring a cooperative relationship (Church, 2010; Doorn, 2008; Hunter, 2007; Simon & Simon, 1990). However, victims are often unable or unwilling to forgive the perpetrator or release the person from the offense. In particular, Stone (2002) states that

> learning to practice forgiveness begins with learning how to forgive ourselves—the person we are usually the hardest on; it is only through demonstrating forgiveness towards ourselves that we can teach it to others and begin to create a more forgiving culture. (p. 282)

In fact, Kymenlaasko (2012) argues that an individual leader's ability to accept responsibility and forgive an individual for their personal failures, as well as demonstrate forgiveness by making amends for inadvertent hurtful feelings toward others, creates a positive organizational climate. At the same time, Kymenlaasko (2012) notes that an "organizational culture that does not promote forgiveness will engage in negative and destructive politics. Employees will be afraid to speak out, hiding their true feelings" (p. 435). Thus, as leaders display dishonesty, cursing, organizational power politics, and manipulative command and control measures, a toxic organizational climate is created that not only damages internal relationships but also incurs a spillover effect that adversely affects external relationships with stakeholders (Ferch, 2012; Kymenlaasko, 2012).

In a transitional justice context, the seminal work of Ellis Cose's (2004) *Bone to Pick: Of Forgiveness, Reconciliation, Reparation, and Revenge* suggests that nonstate actors and leaders of

> rogue states are, by definition, beyond civilized constraints. And at times they must be met with something significantly more compelling than an understanding heart. The need for justice, the call for war, the hunger for revenge: all are as old as mankind, and no less enduring. (p. 3)

Needless to say, victims often find it hard to let go, forgive, and move on from experiences associated with a traumatic event. Therefore, scholars question the relevance and utility of forgiveness in the aftermath of gross human rights violations, as well as its role within the Rome Statute that governs the international criminal court (Ferch, 2012; Hazan,

2006; Mobekk, 2005; Tutu, 2000), particularly in the current landscape of global social justice where retributive justice to redress wrongs through the legal justice system is the norm (Ferch, 2012).

In the article "Is There a Place for Forgiveness in the Justice System?" Worthington (2013) notes that the traditional justice system is cold, with little room for individuals or social healing. In addition, Inazu (2009) posits that amnesty is a legal forgiveness concept that exercises the state's coercive power to pardon the perpetrator from punishment for a criminal act without consent from the victim. He continues the argument that "legal forgiveness satisfies legal justice. It does not and cannot erase the personal debt between the wrongdoer and the victim" (Inazu, 2009, p. 13). Indeed, Worthington (2013) points out that "forgiveness does not affect what the justice system does. Justice is social. Forgiveness is internal" (para. 2). He continues by postulating that practitioners believe there is a place for forgiveness in today's jurisprudence through a restorative justice process. In other words, scholar-practitioners agree that forgiveness plays a significant role in transforming organizations, restoring relationships, and rebuilding trust between parties in an effort to strengthen organizational performance (Doorn, 2008; Ferch, 2012; Palanski, 2012).

As previously discussed, forgiveness is an anchor within a restorative justice process. The process of forgiveness involves recognizing that "we cannot change the event itself, but we can change the meaning we give to the event" (Borris, 2003, p. 9). Thus, the issue is that victims are often unable or unwilling to let go of the emotional tags associated with their hurt, resentment, bitterness, vengefulness, and hatred toward the perpetrator. Victims can decide to forgive and release the emotional tags. However, the fact is that those victims find it very difficult to let go, forgive, and move on from experiences associated with personal grievances, such as ethnic cleansing, rape, torture, and beheadings. The reason it is important for practitioners in transitional justice organizations to develop leadership competencies is that these experts facilitate and lead victims through the emotional and intellectual process of forgiveness as a means of freeing both parties from the emotional tags connected with the pain, guilt, and bitterness (Armour & Umbreit, 2004; Borris, 2003; Brudholm & Rosoux, 2009; Cose, 2004; Llewellyn & Philpot, 2014; Tutu, 2000). In essence, developing a comprehensive leadership program that strengthens individual leadership attributes and competencies such as empathy, emotional intelligence, accountability, humility, and compassion is critical for current and future transitional justice practitioners who intend to lead victims through the forgiveness process in today's multicultural organizational environment.

Recent research shows that forgiveness can bring peace and stability to communities and foster economic development (Oola, 2015). In the context of transitional justice organizations, practitioners who are responsible for implementing the constructs of individual and collective forgiveness play a key role in transitioning a society toward peace and security in the aftermath of conflict. For example, Oola (2015) surveyed 640 people in Uganda who had suffered serious violence or injustice, and 68 percent of respondents reported having forgiven the perpetrator. Similarly, 86 percent of all respondents agreed that "it is good for victims to practice forgiveness in the aftermath of violence" (p. 16). As a result, there has been a movement within the transitional justice discipline for retributive justice elements to include components of restorative justice that create opportunities to facilitate the psychosocial healing process through forgiveness and reconciliation (Cashman, 2014; Fehr & Gelfand, 2012; Petersen, 2007; Tutu, 2000).

The Complexity of Forgiveness

As previously discussed, research by transitional justice and organizational leadership scholar-practitioners revealed that the complexity of forgiveness derives from a unilateral action by the victim to restore interpersonal relations (Doorn, 2008), but most scholars also believe that forgiveness is a social matter governed by institutions (Jirsa, 2004; Saunders, 2011). Therefore, forgiveness supports the organizational culture development as transitional justice scholar-practitioners assist victims to psychosocially heal the suffering caused by emotional and physical events rather than to cling to resentment, bitterness, and revenge. However, scholars note that forgiveness-related constructs form a bilateral relationship that requires the victim's willingness to release the emotional attachment to the traumatic event as well as the offender's willingness to acknowledge the harm, sincerely apologize and ask forgiveness, and make restitution (Armour & Umbreit, 2004; Ferch, 2012; Worthington, 2013). This bilateral relationship creates an organizational culture in which forgiveness requires individual courage to let go of seeking revenge and bitterness as well as to accept the risk of trusting that perpetrators will not reengage in wrongdoing.

In highly political and stressful environments, organizations experience interpersonal conflict and performance mistakes that affect organizational objectives (Senge, 1990). When personality conflicts arise between leaders and followers, it creates not only disrespect, disloyalty, and organizational tension but also an organizational climate of bitterness, resentment, and anger (Riggio, Chaleff, & Lipman-Blumen, 2008). The *Workplace Bullying Institute* assessed abusive conduct within American workplaces, and empirical evidence suggests that 67 percent of employees within the United States experience emotional and psychological violence in the workplace (Namie, 2014). According to the *Workplace Bullying Institute*, Opperman (2008) described abusive conduct as bullying that

> is usually seen as acts or verbal comments that could "mentally" hurt or isolate a person in the workplace. Sometimes, bullying can involve negative physical contact as well. Bullying usually involves repeated incidents or a pattern of behavior that is intended to intimidate, offend, degrade or humiliate a particular person or group of people. It has also been described as the assertion of power through aggression. (para. 12)

Thus, as leaders are organizationally abusive through dishonesty, cursing, organizational power politics, or manipulative command and control measures, a toxic organizational climate is created that damages team cohesiveness, collaboration, and innovation (Ferch, 2012; Kymenlaasko, 2012). In fact, Kymenlaasko (2012) posits that an "organizational culture that does not promote forgiveness will engage in negative and destructive politics. Employees will be afraid to speak out, hiding their true feelings" (p. 435). As a result, victims are often unable or unwilling to forgive the perpetrator or release the person from the offense.

Scholars argue that to restore a relationship and forego the demand of retribution, forgiveness may be attained through individualistic attitudinal decision making, spiritual influences, and cultural traditions (Armour & Umbreit, 2004; Borris, 2003; Petersen, 2007; Simon & Simon, 1990; Worthington, 2013). For that reason, Borris (2003) argues forgiveness is "a voluntary act in which a person makes a decision, a choice about how he or she will deal with an event concerning the past" (p. 8). According to Petersen (2007), "Forgiveness is a matter of a willed change of heart and the successful result of an active endeavor to replace bad thoughts of such bitterness and anger with compassion and affection" (p. 62). As noted, scholars argue that forgiveness is a slow and difficult internal process of individual courage that cognitively, emotionally, and spiritually transforms the meaning of the traumatic event as well as emotionally relieves the perpetrators, allowing them to wipe the slate clean and restore a cooperative relationship (Church, 2010; Doorn, 2008; Hunter, 2007; Simon & Simon, 1990).

Emotional and psychological components associated with the traumatic event include painful thoughts of, feelings toward, and beliefs about the offender (Borris, 2003). The psychosocial act of forgiveness not only emotionally frees both parties from the guilt and pain produced by the traumatic event but also collectively fosters local and national reconciliation beyond the institutionalized requirements of human rights law (Doorn, 2008; Ferch, 2012; Scott, 2010; Tutu, 2000). This suggests that victims may cognitively and intellectually understand the decision to forgive but are often unable or unwilling to let go of the emotional tags associated with the hurt, resentment, bitterness, vengefulness, and hatred toward the perpetrator. As previously argued, forgiveness is the victim's practice of letting go of the emotional tags associated with traumatic experiences, but it does not mean excusing, overlooking, forgetting, condoning, or trivializing the harm committed by the perpetrator. Research by Borris (2003) reveals that part of the forgiveness process is recognizing that "we cannot change the event itself, but we can change the meaning we give to the event" (p. 9).

The result of unforgivingness is an organizational culture of low productivity, passive-aggressive behavior, and low morale (Kymenlaasko, 2012). Conversely, an organizational culture of "forgiveness is an essential element of attaining a more nurturing and fulfilling work climate" (Kymenlaasko, 2012, p. 437). The literature addresses true forgiveness as a gift granted only by the victim to the offender and after the victim has come to terms with the past and emotionally eliminated the desire for revenge (Borris, 2003; Church, 2010; Cose, 2004; Inazu, 2009; Llewellyn & Philpot, 2014). Basically, forgiveness transforms a pathway for transitional justice practitioners in order to facilitate social and national healing through reconciliation (Brudholm & Rosoux, 2009; Kymenlaasko, 2012; Palanski, 2012). In other words, the preponderance of literature reveals that the complexity of forgiveness is a social interaction among individuals designed to resolve intrapersonal and interpersonal conflicts the goal of peaceful coexistence within organizations and nations (Ferch, 2012; Hunter, 2007; Judge, Piccolo, & Kosalka, 2009; Kirkpatrick & Locke, 1991; Kymenlaasko, 2012; Palanski, 2012).

Reconciliation

DEFINITION OF RECONCILIATION

Within the context of leadership and other fields, there is less reconcilia-tion research than for organizational forgiveness (Palanski, 2012). As with forgiveness research, the challenge is that there is limited empirical research on reconciliation, and it is problematic within any context (Palanski, 2012). The reason for this is that reconciliation is dependent on the willingness and emotional development of the victim. According to Jirsa (2004), "Concepts of resentment and forgiveness are individual and personal in a way that justice (i.e., legal guilt and responsibility) is not" (p. 12).

Nevertheless, analysis of the literature identified common themes in defining reconciliation within an organizational and transitional justice context. For instance, Tripp, Bies, and Aquino (2007) define *organizational reconciliation* as "an effort by the victim to extend acts of goodwill toward the offender in the hope of restoring the relationship" (p. 22). Similarly, Yarn and Jones (2009) suggest that "reconciliation refers to the establishment of cooperative relations between persons, either individuals or groups, who have been at variance without regard to whether they have had a prior cooperative relationship" (p. 65). According to an article by Souto (2009), "Reconciliation and Transitional Justice: How to Deal with the Past and Build the Future," the United Nations Peacekeeping support operations define *reconciliation* as "a social process within which people deal with the past, acknowledge past atrocities and suffering, and at the same time change destructive attitudes and behaviour into constructive relationships toward sustainable peace. It includes a whole society" (p. 3). Daly (2000) posits reconciliation as a means "to defer the right to retribution to the extent that retribution would obstruct peace" (p. 87). Lerche (2000) defines *reconciliation* as a "process of developing a mutual conciliatory accommo-dation between antagonistic or formerly antagonistic persons or groups. It often refers to a relatively amicable relationship, typically established after a rupture in the relationship involving one-sided or mutual infliction of extreme injury" (para. 3).

The issue, as Doorn (2008) argues, is that "forgiveness is possible without reconciliation. Reconciliation, however, is not possible without forgiveness" (p. 390). Hence, the trend toward restorative justice involves transitional justice practitioners who develop the relational intelligence to understand the interpersonal dynamics between victim and perpetrator as well as to cultivate an environment that fosters social change through forgiveness and reconciliation after a period of conflict (Cashman, 2014; Kidder, 2007). In essence, the process of forgiveness as a leadership competency is focused on individual healing, whereas the process of reconciliation centers on restoring the relationship between victim and perpetrator, which then makes it possible for social healing as well as governance stabilization and economic reconstruction (Doorn, 2008; Worthington, 2013). In other words, the literature revealed that reconciliation is an important element in fostering and promoting restoration of interpersonal relationships within a toxic organizational climate as well as socioethnic groups in a postconflict environment (Doorn, 2008; Souto, 2009).

CONCEPTUALIZATION OF RECONCILIATION

Researchers note that forgiveness and reconciliation are important relational elements not only in leading today's organizational workplace but also as a central tenet in the execution of transitional justice instruments (Doorn, 2008; Ferch, 2012; Palanski, 2012). Reconciliation is important in a transitional justice context for organizational, communal, and societal healing from human rights abuses (Lerche, 2000; Souto, 2009; Yarn & Jones, 2009). However, scholars note that forgiveness and reconciliation have a complex interdependent relationship (Brudholm & Rosoux, 2009; Doorn, 2008; Ferch, 2012; Llewellyn & Philpot, 2014). For example, victims may conditionally forgive perpetrators once they are held accountable, have acknowledged their wrongdoing, revealed the truth surrounding the traumatic event, and expressed remorse (Hunter, 2007). Nevertheless, forgiveness is an individual issue, as victims psychosocially heal from emotional tags associated with and experienced in a human rights abuse event even when perpetrators fail to acknowledge what they have done, show remorse, or be held accountable (Hunter, 2007). Conversely, forgiveness sets the social condition for the process of reconciliation to restore and heal not only interpersonal relationships but also constructively rebalance the political, legal, and economic injustices toward preventing the prospect of renewed conflict (Doorn, 2008). For that reason, Doorn (2008) argues that "forgiveness is possible without reconciliation. Reconciliation, however, is not possible without forgiveness" (p. 390). In other words, the process of forgiveness is focused on individual healing, whereas the process of reconciliation restores the victim–perpetrator relationship toward sustainable societal healing that makes it possible for governance stabilization and economic reconstruction (Doorn, 2008; Worthington, 2013).

The decomposition of reconciliation reflects two levels of analysis. First, scholars argue that the conceptualization of reconciliation at the micro level is not only an individual leadership competency but also an interpersonal endeavor between oneself and another individual (Doorn, 2008; Ferch, 2012; Jirsa, 2004; Scott, 2010; Simon & Simon, 1990). Specifically, effective leaders with an organizational learning mind-set accept the possibility of failure and transform the organizational climate away from emotional resentment, bitterness, and anger toward openness, transparency, and trust that over time enables risk taking and innovation in organizational decision making and performance outcomes (Kymenlaasko, 2012; Maltby et al., 2008; Palanski, 2012; Petersen, 2007). For reconciliation to take hold, victims, emotionally, must believe that the reoccurrence of traumatic incidents will cease as trust is rebuilt between parties. In a transitional justice context, one could argue that the choices, actions, and decisions of transitional leaders have a long-term impact on the sustainability of peace and security in a postconflict environment.

The macro-level analysis within the conceptualization of reconciliation occurs at the organizational, intergroup, communal, national, and international levels with the aim of collectively redressing the physical, emotional, and spiritual wounds committed by abusive leaders (Doorn, 2008; Ferch, 2012; Senge, 1990; Simon & Simon, 1990). Transitional justice scholar-practitioners conceptually posit that reconciliation contributes to societal healing through restorative justice mechanisms and is more effective in sustaining confidence building than retributive justice models of justice.

Restorative justice models conceptually bring together perpetrators, victims, and communal leaders in order to promote healing and reconciliation in response to human rights violations (Sirleaf, 2013). That said, restorative justice through forgiveness and reconciliation is a form of justice that bridges the system of jurisprudence and restoration of social healing (Armour & Umbreit, 2004; Worthington, 2013). Thus, Llewellyn and Philpot (2014) argue that "restorative justice and reconciliation are relational concepts of justice" (p. 16). Armour and Umbreit (2004) state that

> restorative justice seeks to elevate the crime victims and community members, hold offenders directly accountable to the people they have violated, and restore the emotional and material losses of victims by providing a range of opportunities

for dialogue, negotiation, and problem solving that can lead
to a greater sense of community safety, conflict resolution and
healing for all involved. (p. 1)

According to Fehr and Gelfand (2012), "Restorative justice values
can provide a strong foundation for forgiveness climate by emphasizing
the importance of bringing all parties into the conflict resolution process"
(p. 670). Given the fact that restorative justice plays an integral role in
facilitating forgiveness and societal reconciliation, it also creates a therapeutic
effect that builds a common narrative toward national reconciliation in a
postconflict environment (Ferch, 2012; Hazan, 2006; Llewellyn & Philpot,
2014). Basically, drawing people, organizations, and nations toward healing
requires bold leadership in order to integrate restorative justice models
within the larger social order as political and civil society leaders apply
pressure on judicial actors to employ retributive justice models as a means
to sustain peacebuilding frameworks (Ferch, 2012; Llewellyn & Philpot,
2014; Petersen, 2007; Sirleaf, 2013).

Forgiveness Religious Themes

There is a growing body of knowledge recognizing the influential role
that monotheistic beliefs play in shaping social justice paradigms. Research
has revealed that forgiveness is thematically intertwined not only with
many of the world's religions but also with components of organizational
leadership and transitional justice instruments (Hunter, 2007; Llewellyn
& Philpott, 2014). Scholars postulate that forgiveness and reconciliation
within "religions has maintained a central place in the struggle for social
justice" (Ngunjiri, 2010, p. 762). According to Siddiqi (2013), "Justice, law
and order are necessary for the maintenance of a social order, but there
is also a need for forgiveness to heal the wounds and to restore good
relations between the people" (para, 18). That said, forgiveness and reconciliation are central pillars of restorative justice as victims psychosocially
heal from mass atrocities.

Retributive justice ignores the victims' emotional component in
levying punishment against a perpetrator who committed a human rights
violation. However, restorative justice enables psychosocial healing by not
only punishing the offender but also facilitating individual forgiveness and
communal reconciliation in an effort to reintegrate the offender back

into society (Worthington, 2013). According to Fehr and Gelfand (2012), "Retributive justice focuses on keeping victims and offenders apart while carrying out punishment via [a] third party; restorative justice focuses on bringing victims, offenders, and community together for the ultimate goal of healing" (p. 669). In other words, restorative justice measures go beyond retributive justice as a social justice mechanism in enabling victims to psychosocially heal from mass atrocities and other human rights violations.

Forgiveness is a central tenet within the frameworks of restorative justice and the resolution of organizational conflict (Fehr & Gelfand, 2012). It is therefore important to distinguish among the different theological connections, as forgiveness is generally articulated within Hindu, Islamic, Judaic, and Christian traditions (see table 7.1). For instance, atonement is a central tenet in the Hindu tradition, and forgiveness is not only available through compassion for the hurt caused by the offender but also universally held as part of the essence of an individual's personality (Hunter, 2007). The Islamic tradition believes that forgiveness consists of human and divine elements, as human rights violations are an infliction against both God and human relations (Siddiqi, 2013).

In the Judaic tradition, forgiveness requires an act of contrition by the perpetrator toward the victim and that the victim accept the request for forgiveness, followed by prayer and fasting. However, the offender asking for forgiveness and the victim refusing to forgive out of spite or seeking vengeance as a condition of forgiveness restricts spiritual development and relationship with God (Sipe & Frick, 2009). "Christianity developed a body of doctrine about forgiveness based on Jewish ideas, although there are diverse interpretive traditions" (Hunter, 2007, pp. 35–36). As a central component within the Christian tradition, forgiveness comprises a confession of sin, repentance of wrongdoing, and reflection of God's unconditional and absolute love (Hunter, 2007; Mittelstadt & Sutton, 2010). Romans 4:7–8 (New International Version) states, "Blessed are those whose inequities are forgiven, and whose sins are covered; blessed is the one against whom the Lord will not reckon sin." In this situation, the perpetrator acknowledges the act of murder as sin, confesses the sin, and asks for forgiveness not only from the victim but also God. In the Christian faith, Jesus is willing and able to forgive every sin, and it is arrogant to think that any of our sins are too great for God to cover. Basically, though our faith is weak, our conscience is sensitive, and our memory haunts us. God's word declares that sins confessed are sins forgiven. Table 7.1 illustrates forgiveness within various religious writings.

Table 7.1. Religious Themes of Forgiveness

Religion	Reference	Religious Scriptures	Principles
Hindu	Mahabarata Udyoga Parva Section 33	"There is only one defect in forgiving persons, and not another; that defect is that people take a forgiving person to be weak. That defect, however, should not be taken into consideration, for forgiveness is a great power. Forgiveness is a virtue of the weak, and an ornament of the strong. Forgiveness subdueth (all) in this world; what is there that forgiveness cannot achieve? What can a wicked person do unto him who carrieth the sabre of forgiveness in his hand? Fire falling on a grassless ground is extinguished of itself. And unforgiving individual defileth himself with many enormities. Righteousness is the one highest good; and forgiveness is the one supreme peace; knowledge is one supreme contentment; and benevolence, one sole happiness. Verily, those six qualities should never be forsaken by men, namely, truth, charity, diligence, benevolence, forgiveness and patience."	• Law of Karma holds the perpetrator accountable • Let it go or continue to suffer • Quality of believer • Moral virtue • Psychologically based • Karma based • Spiritual well-being (Hunter, 2007)
Islam/ Muslim	Sat An-Nur (The Light) 24:22	"Let not those among you who are endued with grace and amplitude of means resolve by oath against helping their kinsmen, those in want and those who migrated in the path of God. Let them forgive and overlook. Do you not wish that God should also forgive you? Indeed God is Oft-Forgiving, Most Merciful."	• God's choice to forgive and punish • High societal value • Human basis for relationships (Siddiqi, 2013)

Religion	Reference	Religious Scriptures	Principles
Judaism	2 Chronicles 7:14	"If my people who call my name and humble themselves, pray seek my face, and turn from their wicked ways, then I will hear from heaven, and will forgive their sin and heal their land." • Selich—offender acknowledge and apologize • Mechilah—restore the relationship • Kapparah—atonement accomplished at Yom Kippurim "Nevertheless, because by this deed you have utterly scorned the Lord, the child that is born to you shall die."	• Interpersonal relationship between God and man • Repetence • Genuinely seek forgiveness • Sin has no consequences (Sipe & Frick, 2009)
	2 Samuel 12:14		
Christianity	Matthew 6:14–15	"For if you forgive men when they sin against you, your heavenly father will also forgive you. But if you do do not forgive men their sins, your Father will not forgive your sins." "I will remember their sins and their lawless deeds no more. Where there is forgiveness of these, there is no longer any offering for sin."	• Starts with intrapersonal request and willingness • Link through Jesus Christ to God's forgiveness • Granted by God unconditionally (Sipe & Frick, 2009)
	Hebrews 10:17–18		

Source: Campbell, 2017.

It is worth noting that Bishop (1968) postulates that justice and retribution are centrally grounded within Islamic and Judaic belief systems. According to Bishop (1968), "Forgiveness was conditional—you are under obligation only if you have been or know you will be forgiven too. You are under no obligation to forgive those who do not forgive you" (p. 5).

Yet victims who demand vengeance and retribution for past wrongdoings are unable not only to emotionally recover from what happened but also to let go and release the emotional tag associated with the pain without a religious belief.

When forgiveness is requested and unilaterally and bilaterally granted, the perpetrators must recognize that they do not deserve it but also cannot demand it. Christian doctrine postulates that although perpetrators cannot demand forgiveness, perpetrators can be confident in receiving forgiveness, because God's grace is loving and wanting to restore us to himself. Thus, the appeal to forgive a person who caused physical and emotional harms must be for God's love and mercy, not for God's justice. Further analysis reflects a theme common among religions that without a spiritual component, individuals are incapable of psychosocial healing from the bitterness, anger, and resentment of past wrongs within an organization or from a human rights violation (Mittelstadt & Sutton, 2010). Therefore, common religious themes show that accompanying forgiveness are moral virtues, benevolence, reliance on a leader's spiritual relationship to address interpersonal and intrapersonal sins, and he accountability of the perpetrator. "Do not take revenge, my friends, but leave room for God's wrath, for it is written: It is mine to avenge; I will repay says the Lord . . . do not be overcome by evil, but overcome evil with good" (Romans 12:19–21n).

Organizational bullying, human rights violations, and political violence by leaders are acts of evil toward another person. That said, a review of the literature concludes that forgiveness is an integral ingredient of individual psychosocial healing, facilitates restoration of individual and community healing, and necessitates spiritual strength as societies heal from human rights atrocities in a postconflict environment.

Leadership

The leadership style of the person in charge of an organization influences not only the culture but also the relational climate as transitional justice practitioners assist victims to psychosocially heal from mass atrocities in a postconflict environment. One of the significant challenges is that leaders fail to deal with organizational conflict in a constructive manner. Organizational leadership scholars note that a leader transforms conflict from a force that can be destructive and divisive into one that is healing and connecting. Since we human beings urgently need to make conflict work for us rather than against us, those who can lead through conflict hold the key. (Gerzon, 2006, p. 50)

It is noteworthy that in achieving organizational goals and objectives, managers and leaders tend to focus on productivity at the expense of the interpersonal dimension (Bolman & Deal, 2008). In the interpersonal dimension, across the full spectrum of societal and organizational levels, conflicts arise when leaders confuse perception with reality (Ferch, 2012; Gerzon, 2006; Tutu, 2000). Research shows that organizational leaders view interpersonal conflict through the lens of personal perceptions, values, and beliefs, and conclude that they must be true. The challenge is that leaders interpret a particular situation based on an observation, the biased opinions of others, or an interpretation of the situation rather than facts, and it is difficult to alter that perception (Mendenhall et al., 2013). Hence, an organizational leader who interprets a situation through their own lens tends to create a reality based on a belief structure that frames not only the perception but the response measures as well.

Another challenge is that one's belief and emotional tags in the interpretation of events seem real, leading to the mistake of concluding that one's perceptions are real. Studies show that 92 percent of organizational conflict is derived from interpersonal misperceptions (Gerzon, 2006). Bass and Bass (2008) postulate that organizational dysfunction, organizational bullying, and societal conflict are created when leaders react to events based on perceptions. As a result, certain characteristic judgments and beliefs are assigned that influence the leader's perceptions as well as decision making toward persons involved in an organizational conflict. Nevertheless, Bolman and Deal (2008) and Gerzon (2006) postulate that in a multicultural environment, the effectiveness of leaders who mediate ethnic and social conflict within transitional justice organizations is determined by clarifying intentions and avoiding misperceptions.

Leadership scholars argue that misperceptions created from a lack of reflective dialogue, understanding, listening, and empathy result in organizational conflict (Ferch, 2012; Gerzon, 2006). Therefore, a leader who creates an organizational climate that restores the balance of relationships away from perception management toward forgiveness "can lead offenders to interpret conflict episodes as events that necessitate reconciliation and thus, motivate them to apologize to their victims" (Fehr & Gelfand, 2012, p. 669). In essence, a leader who invests the time, energy, and resources in understanding the mental maps of individuals and listens to different interpretations of operational goals and beliefs constructively mediates organizational conflict free from misperceptions and emotional interference of irrational thought.

In contrast, organizational leaders who resolve conflict through misperceptions and power politics produce a lack of forgiveness as well as low organizational performance. In the same way, organizational leaders of transitional justice who focus on accomplishing the operational end states of peacebuilding activities at the expense of investing the resources toward understanding the sociocultural and political dimensions damage not only the postconflict transitional ecosystem but also the legitimacy of sustainable peacebuilding programs (Bolman & Deal, 2008; Ferch, 2012). For example, transitional justice practitioners claim there is a lack of a coordinated strategic peacebuilding framework among the 140 nongovernmental organizations that implement projects along the Horn of Africa (Tsadik, 2014). According to Tsadik (2014), "it's not enough to add yet another well-meaning project, workshop, dialogue to the peacebuilding mix without a greater understanding of what is already ongoing, and how to relate one's contribution to other initiatives and actors out there" (para. 5). Tsadik (2014) notes that there is a perception among constituents that internal politics within transitional justice organizations to garner donor resources plays a greater role than the impact or effectiveness of service delivery in executing peacebuilding instruments across the Horn of Africa.

Scholars suggest that organizational forgiveness doesn't necessitate releasing the perpetrator of responsibility for abusive actions. Rather, the victim steps down from the position of judgment, anger, and resentment into one of entrusting the situation to emotional support systems. An organization culture of unforgivingness leads to intergroup conflict, bitterness, and resentment (Namie, 2014; Palanski, 2012). Bolman and Deal (2008) argue that

> organizations depend on the environment for resources they
> need to survive, [and] they are inevitably enmeshed with
> external constituents whose expectations or demands must be

heeded . . . [and] often speak with loud but conflicting voices, adding to the challenge of managerial work. (p. 235)

That said, individual and organizational communications must change and expose misperceptions and hidden agendas through restorative measures by generating an atmosphere of multiagency trust, collaboration, consensus building, and transparent dialogue. This is because integrating forgiveness within an organizational culture not only frees the victim as well as the perpetrator to see others more clearly but also sustains restorative measures toward reconciliation (Kidder, 2007). As a result, the ecosystem of transitional justice organizations serves the interests of organizational and cultural healing and reconciliation rather than the internal organizational self-interests of survival (Ferch, 2012; Gerzon, 2006). In the end, if the process of forgiveness and healing is to succeed, leader engagement that creates an organizational culture of interpersonal healing and forgiveness not only heals the emotional and relational hurts people experience within an organization but also increases retention, increases productivity, and shapes a more cohesive and effective organization (Bolman & Deal, 2008).

Much of the literature suggests that while the execution of transitional justice instruments spans multicultural boundaries, most leadership scholars believe that organizations are cultures with distinctive beliefs, values, and customs (Bolman & Deal, 2008; Ferch, 2012). Research by Glynn and DeFordy (2010) states that "leaders are assumed to have a repertoire of leadership attributes and behavioral styles from which they can draw, adapting these as needed to the demands of the specific task situation or the particular followers they lead" (p. 123). Therefore, scholars postulate that at individual, team, and organizational levels there are relevant leadership competencies that transitional justice practitioners can develop in creating a forgiveness and reconciliation culture within organizations executing transitional justice instruments. To illustrate, research published in *Culture, Leadership, and Organizations: The GLOBE Study of 62 Societies* by House et al. (2004) identified a universal set of global leadership competencies, such as win–win problem solving, integrity, accountability, political savvy, team building, encouraging, communication, and visioning, that shape an organizational culture of forgiveness and reconciliation. In essence, the transitional justice leader who fails to lead an organizational culture of forgiveness and reconciliation hampers the relational effectiveness of individual, organizational, community, and global conflict resolution measures toward peace and stability.

In today's global environment, scholars argue that transitional justice practitioners serve the public in exercising conflict resolution measures as well as leading forgiveness and reconciliation activities toward peace and stability within a sphere of influence at the local, national, and global levels (Ferch, 2012). However, organizational leaders who govern the activities of transitional justice instruments not only manage the process of forgiveness and reconciliation within restorative justice in the face of mass atrocities but also mediate interpersonal, intrapersonal, and situational offenses in the workplace (Ferch, 2012; Palanski, 2012; Sanchez & Rognvik, 2012). Scholars posit that servant-leaders create a culture of forgiveness and reconciliation from internal as well as external workplace offenses (Barbuto & Millard, 2012; Barnabas & Clifford, 2012; Ferch, 2012). Yergler (2005) agrees, stating that a "servant leader must incorporate forgiveness as a leadership competency if the benefactors of that leadership are to experience true transformation" (para. 3). Basically, the quality of transitional justice organizations rests on a mixture of leadership attributes that reach beyond an individual's personal interests to the interests of an organization (Bass & Bass, 2008; Smith, 2005; Yergler, 2005).

Themes that emerged from the literature showed that servant-leadership practices and values are culturally transparent and globally similar. Scholars note that servant-leaders are not only concerned and sensitive toward others within a societal and organizational context but also support leaders' intercultural and religious values and beliefs (Winston & Ryan, 2008). Much of the literature suggests that Jewish values and beliefs found in the Talmud support servant-leadership in the form of kindness, humility, integrity, forgiveness, and temperance (Winston & Ryan, 2008). Similarly, the Hindu tradition in the Bhagavad Gita characterizes servant-leadership as compassion, the exercise of authority with discretion, giving others the benefit of the doubt, and leading with generosity (Winston & Ryan, 2008). Winston and Ryan (2008) state that "servant leaders focus more on humility and less on self and focus more on the needs of others and the higher-order values of duty and social responsibility than on the needs of self" (p. 216). That said, from a review of the literature, a number of essential ingredients of servant-leadership competencies emerged as requisites to fostering a climate of organizational forgiveness and reconciliation.

Table 7.2 compares leaders who display unforgivingness and forgiveness on an organizational level, and also addresses the servant-leadership

Table 7.2. Organizational Leader Impact of Forgiveness

Organization Level	Lack of Forgiveness	Forgiveness Culture	Servant-Leadership	Leadership Competence
Individual	• Self-doubt • Anger • Withdrawal • Poor health • Guilt • Fear • Depression • Low self-esteem (Stone, 2002) • Revenge • Aggression • Avoidance • Passive/ • Aggressive behavior (Fehr & Gelfand, 2012)	• Happiness • Presence • Personal responsibility • Peace of mind • Authenticity • Choice • Openness (Stone, 2002) • Benevolence • Compassion • Understanding • Restorative justice (Fehr & Gelfand, 2012)	• Compassion • Individual transformation • Selflessness • Powerful catalyst • Center of organizational forgiveness (Yergler, 2005) • Healing • Listening • Self-awareness • Empathy • Benevolence • Decisiveness (Smith, 2005)	• Self-awareness • Integrity • Encouragement • Confidence builder • Tolerance • Leading oneself • Intercultural intelligence • Emotional intelligence (House et al., 2004) • Resilience • Technical competence • Resourcefulness (Mendenhall et al., 2013)
Dyad	• Conflict • Blame • Avoidance • Mistrust	• Partnership • Collaboration • Trust • Open communication	• Persuasion • Credibility • Empowerment (Smith, 2005)	• Collaboration • Leading others • Negotiation • Accountability

continued on next page

Table 7.2. Continued.

Organization Level	Lack of Forgiveness	Forgiveness Culture	Servant-Leadership	Leadership Competence
Dyad (con't.)	• Punishment • Frustration • Anger • Defensiveness (Stone, 2002) • Rejection • Revenge (Fehr & Gelfand, 2012)	• Supportiveness • Information sharing • Compassion • Respect (Stone, 2002) • Restorative justice (Fehr & Gelfand, 2012)		• Conflict management (Van Velsor, McCauley, & Ruderman, 2010) • Conflict management • Emotional intelligence • Relational intelligence (Mendenhall et al., 2013)
Team	• Internal competition • Manipulation • Negative politics • Stress • Frustration • Distance • Fault finding (Stone, 2002)	• Mutually supportive • Interconnection • Direction • Sense of belonging • Cooperation • Clarity of roles (Stone, 2002) • Restorative justice (Fehr & Gelfand, 2012)	• Altruism • Steward of resources • Relationship builder • Power sharing • Balance interests • Influence (Bass & Bass, 2008)	• Conflict resolution • Networking • Problem solver (Diacoff, 2012) • Team builder • Problem solver • Negotiation (Mendenhall et al., 2013)

Organization			
• Secrecy • Mistrust • High turnover • Low allegiance • Political posturing • Confusion (Stone, 2002) • Uncooperation • Avoidance • Dysfunction • Competition • Organizational sabotage (Fehr & Gelfand, 2012)	• Open authentic culture • Empowerment • Pride in organization • Meaningful work • Values in action (Stone, 2002) • Optimism • Trust • Integrity • Restorative justice approach to conflict • Cultural values • Empathy • Emotional maturity • Altruism • Self-transcendent values (Fehr & Gelfand, 2012)	• Commitment to the growth of people • Building community • Strategic foresight (Smith, 2005) • Building community • Listening • Empathy • Foresight • Persuasion • Stewardship • Healing • Power sharing in decision making • People over production (Ferch, 2012; Smith, 2005)	• Lead others • Lead the organization • Think strategically • Balance conflict demands • Initiate and implement change • Change agent • Cross-cultural relational skills • Systems thinking/plan • Intercultural intelligence • Organizational strategic foresight • Social intelligence (Diacoff, 2012; Van Velsor et al., 2010)

Source: Campbell, 2017.

competencies needed to foster an organizational culture of forgiveness and reconciliation in the case of workplace offenses.

The analysis revealed that individual unforgivingness produces not only frustration leading to anger, mistrust, and revenge in victims but also organizational and societal mistrust, secrecy, and dysfunction. Yergler (2005) states that unforgivingness "gives rise to acts of injustice, retribution, sabotage, indifference and isolationism" (para. 4). As a result, individual unforgivingness adversely affects a leader's social and relational ability to build horizontally, vertically, and across cooperative relationships; provide team building; and promote a culture of high organizational performance. That said, it is "egregious when a leader fails to offer forgiveness to those under his or her charge who wronged the leader" (Yergler, 2005, para. 1). Conversely, individual forgiveness builds restorative organizational justice and trust, and provides space for leaders to influence a climate of respect, cooperation, and constructive organizational conflict resolution. By fostering a climate of organizational forgiveness and reconciliation, leaders create a supportive environment I which individual growth toward emotional, relational, and spiritual maturity not only strengthens the organizational human capital development but also increases organizational performance.

Servant-Leadership

Transitional justice measures have a deterrent effect that potentially alters the behavior of key stakeholders. After an extensive literature review this researcher proposes that the most appropriate theoretical leadership framework facilitating individual and organizational forgiveness, as well as reconciliation, is servant-leadership. Scholars postulate that an additive pillar within servant-leadership constructs must incorporate organizational forgiveness as a component of leadership competency frameworks (Ferch, 2012; Doraiswamy, 2012; Spears, 2010). This is because transactional leadership focuses on the social exchange of individual leadership, and transformational leadership centers on developing followers into leaders, but servant-leadership advocates leaders who transcend individual interests to serve in the best interest of the organization (Avolio, 2010; Avolio & Gardner, 2005; Bass & Bass, 2008). Therefore, Doraiswamy (2012) and Spears (2010) argue that servant-leaders characteristically possess the sense-making capacity that fosters an awareness of interpersonal growth development and organizational healing in those who are led. Contextually speaking, the transformative nature of servant-leaders who experience the restorative and releasing power of forgiveness within an organizational and transitional justice environment makes these leaders better equipped to understand and facilitate social and relational conflict resolution. That said, servant-leaders shape an organizational climate that creates a safe place not only for individuals to heal interpersonal relationships within an organizational context but also extends reconciliation to the larger societal community.

Much of the literature points out that while servant-leaders subordinate personal interests to serve others, emerging scholars view forgiveness as an important component of relational power, persuasion, and trust (Doraiswamy, 2012; Ferch, 2012; Spears, 2010). Servant-leaders of transitional justice organizations that have forgiveness as an organizational culture possess the social and emotional intelligence to negotiate and mediate socioethnic, religious, and political ideological differences and move toward peace and reconciliation. Faced with organizations in which transitional justice practitioners who experience human rights violations may develop unresolved personal issues, thereby producing organizational issues of anger toward the perpetrator, servant-leaders play a critical role within the forgiveness process by displaying empathy and listening, employing a trust-based relationship, and exhibiting spiritual compassion (Doraiswamy, 2012; Ferch, 2012; Spears, 2010). As a result, the integration of forgiveness as an individual competency within the transitional justice discipline produces a learning environment that develops a high-performing organization to sustain social change toward peace and stability (Mendenhall et al., 2013; Van Velsor, McCauley, & Ruderman, 2010).

Critics may argue that there is no role for forgiveness or reconciliation within an organizational leadership and transitional justice discipline. However, history demonstrates that the backdrop of personal suffering played an integral role in not only developing leaders who practice political nonviolent engagement but also in recovering societal injustices. For example, after twenty-seven years of prison, Nelson Mandela provided leadership by coalescing differing political parties and ideologies, sharing leadership among socioethnic lines, bestowing values of resilience, and through forgiveness and reconciliation uniting a country for future generations (Tutu, 2000). In essence, Mandela demonstrated the leadership characteristics of humility, resilience, accountability, and spirituality that enabled him to lead South Africa in developing a national policy of forgiveness and reconciliation as a means to heal societal injustice (Ferch, 2012; Tutu, 2000; Worthington, 2013).

Conclusion and Further Research

This chapter has introduced forgiveness and reconciliation as playing an integral role within the evolving field of organizational leadership and transitional justice. The incorporation of forgiveness and reconciliation within the disciplines of organizational leadership and transitional justice is a paradigm shift. Hence, given the fact that transitional justice is a strategic enabler of statecraft in a postconflict environment, introducing into the mix the role of forgiveness as a competency development not only enables mechanisms for individual growth but also strengthens the capability of practitioners to shape and implement transitional justice mechanisms at multiple levels within an organization. Therefore, with limited understanding or application of forgiveness within organizational leadership concepts, as well as the transitional justice formula, this chapter postulates that servant-leadership is the most appropriate theoretical leadership construct. Nonetheless, introducing forgiveness as a path toward reconciliation for individual, organizational, and national healing begins a conversation about transitional justice actors as critical players for peace and stability on the global stage. In doing so, this perspective advances several contributions for further transitional justice and leadership theory development and research.

First, the review suggests the need for research that examines the relationship among transitional justice, organizational leadership concepts, and forgiveness with regard to peacebuilding activities. For example, researchers who empirically assess the impact and application of integrating religious edicts with forgiveness and organizational leadership within a transitional justice context contribute not only to the understanding and value of forgiveness in implementing transitional justice mechanisms but also to how servant-leaders influence organizational culture in a complex and politically uncertain environment. Second, it is possible that servant-leaders creating a learning environment in which forgiveness plays an operational role may increase operational performance and shape the context of transitional justice organizations. Third, future research is needed to empirically examine the validity and role of forgiveness as an organizational leadership competency within an organization executing transitional justice instruments. Finally, it would be beneficial to conduct research on whether and how forgiveness as an individual and collective competency shapes local, organizational, communal, national, and international reconciliation measures.

In sum, this chapter introduced the definition and conceptualization of forgiveness and reconciliation as organizational leadership competencies within the transitional justice discipline. Noteworthy is the fact that tenets of forgiveness and reconciliation are resident within the world's primary religions, only practiced differently. Thus, with limited theoretical understanding of forgiveness and reconciliation and its role within conflict resolution, this chapter offered servant-leadership as a leadership competency within transitional justice and other organizations. Therefore, there is a watershed opportunity for leadership scholar-practitioners to show that integrating forgiveness as a leadership competency has a significant role in sustaining organizational conflict resolution and global peacebuilding measures.

References

Abbasi, A. S., Rehman, K., & Bibi, A. (2010). Islamic leadership model an accountability perspective. *World Applied Science Journal, 9*(3), 230–238. Retrieved from http://www.ciitlahore.edu.pk/Papers/539-8589027206976587208.pdf

Aquino, K., Bennett, R., Kim, T., Lim, V., & Shapiro, D. (2008, April). Workplace offense and victims' reactions: The effects of victim-offender (dis) similarity, offense-type and cultural differences. *Journal of Organizational Behavior, 29*(3), 415–433. Retrieved from http://dx.doi.org/10.1002/job.519

Armour, M. P., & Umbreit, M. S. (2004, February 18). The paradox of forgiveness in restorative justice. *Center for Restorative Justice and Peacemaking,* 1–14. Retrieved from http://fetzer.org/sites/default/files/images/Parodox_of_Forgiveness_in_RJ.pdf

Avolio, B. (2010). Pursuing authentic leadership development. In N. Nohria & R. Khurana (Eds.), *Handbook of leadership theory and practice* (pp. 739–768). Boston, MA: Harvard Business Press.

Avolio, B. J., & Gardner, W. L. (2005). Authentic leadership development: Getting to the root of positive forms of leadership. *The Leadership Quarterly, 16,* 315–338. Retrieved from http://dx.doi.org/10.1016/j.leaqua.2005.03.001

Barbuto, J. E., & Millard, M. L. (2012). Wisdom development of leaders: A constructive developmental perspective. *International Journal of Leadership Studies, 7*(2), 233–245. Retrieved from https://www.regent.edu/acad/global/publications/ijls/new/vol7iss2/IJLS_Vol7Iss2.pdf

Barnabas, A., & Clifford, P. S. (2012). Mahatma Gandhi—An Indian model of servant leadership. *International Journal of Leadership Studies, 7*(2), 132–150. Retrieved from https://www.regent.edu/acad/global/publications/ijls/new/vol7iss2/IJLS_Vol7Iss2.pdf

Bass, B. M., & Bass, R. (2008). *The handbook of leadership: Theory, research, and managerial applications* (4th ed.). New York, NY: Free Press.

Bishop, D. (1968). Forgiveness in religious thought. *Studies in Comparative Religion, 2*(1), 1–5. Retrieved from http://www.studiesincomparativereligion.com/public/articles/Forgiveness_in_Religious_Thought-by_Donald_H_Bishop.aspx

Bolman, L. G., & Deal, T. E. (2008). *Reframing organizations: Artistry, choice, and leadership* (4th ed.). San Francisco, CA: Jossey-Bass.

Borris, E. R. (2003). The healing power of forgiveness. *Institute for Multi-Track Diplomacy, Occasional Paper Number 10*, 4–26. Retrieved from http://imtd.imtdeast.org/papers/OP-10.pdf

Brudholm, T., & Rosoux, V. (2009). The unforgiving reflections on the resistance to forgiveness after atrocity. *Law and Contemporary Problems, 72*(33), 33–49. Retrieved from http://www.law.duke.edu/journals/lcp

Bullock, M. (2008). Forgiveness—definitions and overview. In N. Anderson & M. Bullock (Eds.), *Forgiveness: A sampling of research results* (pp. 4–7). Washington, DC: Office of International Affairs.

Campbell, A. (2017). Forgiveness and reconciliation as an organizational leadership competency within transitional justice instruments. *The International Journal of Servant-Leadership, 11*(1), 139–186.

Cashman, G. (2014). *What causes war? An introduction to theories of international conflict* (2nd ed.). Lanham, MD: Rowman and Littlefield.

Church, M. (2010). *Love-based leadership: Transform your life with meaning and abundance.* Bloomington, IN: Balboa Press.

Cose, E. (2004). *Bone to pick: Of forgiveness, reconciliation, reparation, and revenge.* New York, NY: Washington Square Press.

Daly, E. (2000). Transformative Justice: Charting a path to reconciliation. *International Legal Perspectives, 12*, 73–183. Retrieved from http://center.theparentscircle.org/images/dc6b8763212c4002b3587f5ce0573c26.pdf

Diacoff, S. S. (2012, September 5). Expanding the lawyer's toolkit of skills and competencies: Synthesizing leadership, professionalism, emotional intelligence, conflict resolution and comprehensive law. *Santa Clara Review, 52*(3), 795–874. Retrieved from http://digitalcommons.law.scu.edu/cgi/viewcontent.cgi?article=2716&context=lawreview

Doraiswamy, I. R. (2012, May). Servant or leader? Who will stand up please? *International Journal of Business and Social Science, 3*(9), 178–182. Retrieved from http://ijfssnet.com/journals/vol_3_nov_9_may_2012/21.pdf

Doorn, N. (2008). Forgiveness and reconciliation in transitional justice practices. *Ethical Perspectives, 15*(3), 381–398. Retrieved from http://dx.doi.org/10.2143/ep.15.3.2033157

Fehr, R., & Gelfand, M. J. (2012). The forgiving organization: A multilevel model of forgiveness at work. *Academy of Management Review, 37*(4), 664–688. Retrieved from http://dx.doi.org/10.5465/amr.2010.0497

Ferch, S. R. (2012). *Forgiveness and power in the age of atrocity.* Plymouth, England: Lexington Books.

Gerzon, M. (2006). *Leading through conflict: How successful leaders transform differences into opportunities.* Boston, MA: Harvard Business School.

Glynn, M. A., & DeFordy, R. (2010). Leadership through an organizational behavior lens: A look at the last half-century research. In N. Nohria & R. Khurana (Eds.), *Handbook of leadership theory and practice* (pp. 119–158). Boston, MA: Harvard Business School.

Hazan, P. (2006, March). Measuring the impact of punishment and forgiveness: A framework for evaluating transitional justice. *International Review of the Red Cross, 88*(861), 19–47. Retrieved from http://dx.doi.org/http://dx.doi.org/10.1017/S1816383106000038

House, R. J., Hanges, P. J., Javidan, M., Dorfman, P. W., & Gupta, V. (2004). *Culture, leadership, and organizations: The globe study of 62 societies.* Thousand Oaks, CA: Sage Publications.

Hunter, A. (2007). Forgiveness: Hindu and western perspectives. *Journal of Hindu-Christian Studies, 20*(11), 35–42. Retrieved from http://dx.doi.org/10.7825/2164-6279.1386

Inazu, J. D. (2009). *No future without (personal) forgiveness: Re-examining the role of forgiveness in transitional justice* [Legal]. Retrieved from 10 Hum Rts. Rev. 309, http://scholarship.law.duke.edu/cgi/viewcontent.cgi?article=2740&context=faculty_scholarship

Jirsa, J. (2004). *Forgiveness and revenge: Where is justice?* In A. Cashin & J. Jirsa (Eds.), *Thinking together* (pp. 1–28). Paper presented at the IWM Junior Fellows' Conference, Winter 2003. Retrieved from http://www.iwm.at/wp-content/uploads/jc-16-05.pdf

Judge, T. A., Piccolo, R. F., & Kosalka, T. (2009). The bright and dark sides of leader traits: A review and theoretical extension of the leader trait paradigm. *The Leadership Quarterly, 20,* 855–875. Retrieved from http://dx.doi.org/10.1016/j.jeaqua.2009.09.004

Kidder, D. (2007). Restorative justice: Not "rights" but right way to heal relationships at work. *International Journal of Conflict Management, 18*(1), 4–22. Retrieved from http://dx.doi.org/10.1108/10444060710759291

Kirkpatrick, S. A., & Locke, E. A. (1991). Leadership: Do traits matter? *Academy of Management Executive, 5*(2), 48–60. Retrieved from http://sbuweb.tcu.edu/jmathis/Org_Mgmt_Materials/Leadership%20-%20Do%20Traits%20Matgter.pdf

Kymenlaasko, I. V. (2012). Forgiveness as a leadership tool. *Global Conference on Business and Finance Proceedings, 7*(1), 432–445. Retrieved from www.forgivenessandhealth.com

Lerche, C. (2000). Peacebuilding through reconciliation. *The International Journal of Peace Studies, 5*(2). Retrieved from http://www.gmu.edu/programs/icar/ijps/vol5_2/lerche.htm

Llewellyn, J., & Philpott, D. (2014). Restorative justice and reconciliation: Twin frameworks for peacebuilding. In J. J. Llewellyn & D. Philpott (Eds.), *Restorative justice, reconciliation, and peacebuilding* (pp. 14–36). Oxford, England: Oxford University.

Maltby, J., Wood, A. W., Day, L., Kon, T. W., Colley, A., & Linley, P. A. (2008). Personality predictors of levels of forgiveness two and a half years after the transgression. *Journal of Research in Personality, 42,* 1088–1094. Retrieved from http://dx.doi.org/10.1016/j.jrp.2007.12.008

Mendenhall, M. E., Osland, J. S., Bird, A., Oddou, G. R., Maznevski, M. L., Stevens, M. J., & Stahl, G. K. (2013). *Global leadership: Research, practice, and development* (2nd ed.). New York, NY: Routledge.

Mittelstadt, M., & Sutton, G. (2010). *Forgiveness, reconciliation, and restoration: Multidisciplinary studies from a Pentecostal perspective.* Eugene, OR: Wipf and Stock Publisher.

Mobekk, E. (2005). Transitional justice in post-conflict societies—Approaches to reconciliation. In A. Ebnother & P. Fluri (Eds.), *After intervention: Public security management in post-conflict societies—From intervention to sustainable local ownership* (pp. 261–292). Retrieved from http://www.isn.ethz.ch/Digital-Library/Publications/Detail/?ots591=0c54e3b3-1e9c-be1e-2c24-a6a8c7060233&lng=en&id=101631

Namie, G. (2014). 2014 WBI U.S. workplace bullying survey. *Workplace Bullying Institute,* 1–19. Retrieved from http://www.workplacebullying.org/multi/pdf/WBI-2014-US-Survey.pdf

Ngunjiri, F. W. (2010). Lessons in spiritual leadership from Kenyan women. *Journal of Education Administration, 48*(6), 755–768. Retrieved from http://dx.doi.org/10.1108/09578231011079601

Oola, S. (2015). Forgiveness: Unveiling an asset in peacebuilding [Special issue]. *Refugee Law Center.* Retrieved from http://refugeelawproject.org/files/others/Forgiveness_research_report.pdf

Opperman, S. (2008, 3 December). Workplace bullying: Psychological violence? Retrieved from http://www.workplacebullying.org/2009/05/04/workplace-bullying-psychological-violence/

Palanski, M. E. (2012). Forgiveness and reconciliation in the workplace: A multilevel perspective and research agenda. *Journal of Business Ethics, 109,* 275–287. Retrieved from http://dx.doi.org/10.1007/s10551-011-1125-1

Petersen, R. L. (2007). Forgiveness and religion: A schematic approach. *ARA Journal, 31,* 61–64. Retrieved from http://www.bostontheological.org/assets/files/peacebuilding/petersen_religion_forgiveness.pdf

Riggio, R. F., Chaleff, I., & Lipman-Blumen, J. (2008). *The art of followership: How great followers create great leaders and organizations.* San Francisco, CA: Jossey-Bass.

Sammi, C. (2010). *Who wants to forgive and forget? Transitional justice preferences in post-war Burundi* (Master's thesis, Yale University). Retrieved from http://www.nyaapor.org/pdfs/samii_forgive_forget101206.pdf

Sanchez, E., & Rognvik, S. (2012). *Building just societies: Reconciliation in transitional settings.* Retrieved from Workshop Report Accra, Ghana: http://www. un.org/en/peacebuilding/pbso/pdf/Reconciliation%20workshop%20report% 20WEB.pdf

Saunders, R. (2011). Questionable associations: The role of forgiveness in transitional justice. *The International Journal of Transitional Justice, 5,* 119–141. Retrieved from http://dx.doi.org/10.1093/ijtj/ijr003

Scott, J. (2010). Atoning, reconciling, and forgiving: Interdisciplinary investigations of justice. *Reviews in Cultural Theory, 1*(2), 18–30. Retrieved from http://www. reviewsinculture.com/media/reviews/31-RCT122010ScottRadzikQuinn McGonegal.pdf

Senge, P. M. (1990). *The fifth discipline: The art and practice of the learning organization.* New York, NY: Doubleday.

Siddiqi, M. H. (2013). The power of forgiveness: An Islamic perspective. Retrieved from http://www.onislam.net/english/reading-islam/understanding-islam/ ethics-and-values/451497-the-power-of-forgiveness-an-islamic-perspective. html?Values=

Simon, S. B., & Simon, S. (1990). *Forgiveness: How to make peace with your past and get on with your life.* New York, NY: Warner Books.

Sipe, J. W., & Frick, D. M. (2009). *Seven pillars of servant leadership: Practicing the wisdom of leading by serving.* Mahwah, NJ: Paulist Press.

Sirleaf, R. (2013). *2013 Restorative justice action plan for the criminal justice system.* Retrieved from https://www.gov.uk/government/uploads/system/uploads/ attachment_data/file/259782/restorative-justice-action-plan-2013.pdf

Smith, C. (2005, December). *The leadership theory of Robert K Greenleaf.* Retrieved from https://www.essr.net/~jafundo/mestrado_material_itgjkhnld/IV/Lideran %C3%A7as/Lideran%C3%A7a%20servidora_Greenleaf.pdf

Souto, V. S. (2009). *Reconciliation and transitional justice: How to deal with the past and build the future.* Retrieved from Peace Operations Training Institute, http:// cdn.peaceopstraining.org/theses/souto.pdf

Spears, L. C. (2010). Character and servant leadership: Ten characteristics of effective, caring leaders. *Journal of Virtues and Leadership, 1*(1), 25–30. Retrieved from http://www.regent.edu/acad/global/publications/jvl/vol1_iss1/Spears_Final. pdf

Stone, M. (2002). Forgiveness in the workplace. *Industrial and Commercial Training, 34*(7), 278–286. Retrieved from http://dx.doi.org/10.1108/00197850210447282

Tripp, T. M., Bies, R. J., & Aquino, K. (2007, March). A vigilante model of justice: Revenge, reconciliation, forgiveness, and avoidance. *Social Justice Research, 20,* 10–34. Retrieved from http://dx.doi.org/10.1007/s11211-007-0030-3

Tsadik, H. (2014). Why the Horn of Africa needs more strategic peacebuilding. Retrieved from http://life-peace.org/why-the-horn-of-africa-needs-more-strategic-peacebuilding/

Tutu, D. (2000). *No future without forgiveness.* New York, NY: Random House Press.

Van Velsor, E., McCauley, C. D., & Ruderman, M. N. (2010). *Handbook of leadership development* (3rd ed.). San Francisco, CA: Jossey-Bass.

Winston, B. E., & Ryan, B. (2008). Servant leadership as a humane orientation: Using the GLOBE study construct of humane orientation to show that servant leadership is more global than western. *International Journal of Leadership Studies, 3*(2), 212–222. Retrieved from http://www.regentuniversity.org/acad/global/publications/ijls/new/vol3iss2/IJLS_V3Is2_Winston_Ryan.pdf

Worthington, E. L. (2013). Forgiveness and justice. *The Power of Forgiveness*, 1–3. Retrieved from http://www.thepoweroffforgiveness.com/pdf/Worthingoton.pdf

Yarn, D. H., & Jones, G. T. (2009). A biological approach to understanding resistance to apology, forgiveness, and reconciliation in group conflict. *Law and Contemporary Problems, 72,* 63–81. Retrieved from http://web.b.ebscohost.com/ehost/pdfviewer/pdfviewer?sid=48aff8c1-3a4e-49f5-b90f-fcaf7126b6b4%40sessionmgr111&vid=32&hid=118

Yergler, J. D. (2005). Servant leadership, justice and forgiveness. *Creative Leadership*. Retrieved from http://www.refresher.com/Archives/!jdyservant.html

Chapter 8

Living Justice and Forgiveness in an Organization during a Religious Crisis

A Proposition

Maduabuchi Leo Muoneme

In this chapter, I will integrate aspects of the histories of my family, nation, local environment, and organization for the purpose of creating a backdrop and historical stage for solving a problem. The chapter will be interwoven with true stories. The organization in question is my high school alma mater, Federal Government College Jos (FGC Jos), in the Plateau State, North Central Nigeria. In the milieu of a national history, I will paint a family memoir of how I arrived at Jos and eventually became part of the organization, and will subsequently describe the macrocontext in which my organization was infected by a crisis.

This macrocontext will be followed by an interpretation of the crisis. I choose to engage history and my macroenvironment because of the need for leaders to develop foresight: *understanding the past, engaging the future, and recognizing blind spots* (DeGraaf et al., 2004, p. 152). Greenleaf (1977/2002) viewed foresight as a central ethic of leadership; the refusal of a leader to see is seen as an ethical failure. Foresight means looking at present events with the analytical lens of projections made in the past and looking toward the future (Greenleaf, 1977/2002).

After discussing the hermeneutics of the crisis, I will proffer a life-giving response. In my organization, during the phase of resolution, the scenario and propositions for solution will become hypothetical, since my leadership of the organization will be a suppositional leadership. The life-giving response will have an immediate response and a long-term-vision response. Toward the culmination of the chapter, I will make use of an intermission to render an appropriate interior vignette sandwiched between the servant-leadership pattern of school administration and school allegory. This act of intermitting serves as a respite but is also a convex lens to guide the reader toward a convergence of the ideas of restorative justice and servant-leadership.

In addition to shedding light on the problem with restorative justice, I will view the conflict through an analytical and optimistic lens, and then, adopting the philosophy of servant-leadership, will proffer ways in which the crisis can be transformed into a watershed moment at the school. Before I begin, I want to quickly present a broad-stroke portrait of servant-leadership.

The servant-leader idea developed through Robert Greenleaf's experience in and discernment regarding business, education, and theology-oriented institutions (Greenleaf, 1977/2002). In organizations directed by servant-leaders, the members become healthier, wiser, freer, and more self-governing (Greenleaf, 1977/2002). They become motivated to serve others. Servant-leaders consciously choose to serve first, followed by the aspiration to lead (Greenleaf, 1977/2002). Wheatley (1998) believes it is the nature of our existence to desire to serve others (p. 349). Servants should be leaders, and leaders should be servants. Servant-leaders trust the humanness of those they lead, and help followers to understand themselves (Wheatley, 1998). Through intentness in listening, servant-leaders dispose themselves to receive insights to create the right roadmap for an organization (Greenleaf, 1977/2002). Provision of direction is a key aspect of servant-leadership (Spears, 1998).

Historical Background: Family Arrival at Jos

Leonard was a handsome young chemistry student at the University of Ibadan in Nigeria in 1966. Cecilia was a beautiful young student at the Queen of the Rosary College in Onitsha, Nigeria, in 1966. They did not know each other. Then the rumbling explosion of the Nigerian Civil War changed the trajectory of their histories. Before the civil war broke out, there had been anti-Igbo pogroms in northern Nigeria. This caused many Igbos living in northern and western Nigeria to leave their homes, livelihoods, educations, and occupations and return to their villages, towns, and cities in southeastern Nigeria. Leonard left his university education and returned to his hometown of Nanka, in Anambra State, which at that time was part of Biafra. Cecilia also left her high school education and fled to Nanka. Biafra was the name for the southeastern part of Nigeria that wanted to secede from Nigeria because of persecution in the north.

The Biafran government wanted Leonard to use his knowledge of chemistry to manufacture explosives and bombs for the Biafran Army. But as a young man Leonard had made up his mind never to use his knowledge of science to destroy human life. He declined, since he was essentially a pacifist. Then an attempt was made to conscript Leonard into the Biafran Army, but he managed to escape and instead opted to join the International Red Cross. As the civil war raged on, Leonard met Cecilia, who was also working for the Red Cross. They were both Catholic, and they both served in Caritas (a charity-based organization), where they cooked food for the war's victims. In the midst of the war, they fell in love and performed a traditional marriage ceremony, followed by a wedding in a Catholic Church on October 25, 1969. Three months after their wedding, the civil war stopped. After the war, Leonard returned to Ibadan to continue his university education. Since he had not studied chemistry for three years because of the civil war, he switched to botany. After graduation, he received a federal government appointment as a high school biology and science teacher. He was asked to go to Jos, in North Central Nigeria. At Jos, Leonard and Cecilia raised five children: Leo, Ben, Ngozi, Ugo, and Joe. Their first child, Leo (the author of this chapter), was born on July 17, 1970, and their last child, Joe, was born on March 10, 1978. Leonard and Cecilia arrived at Jos with me and Ben in 1973.

The military head of state of Nigeria, General Yakabu Gowan, had a vision of national unity, peace, and reconciliation after the civil war. One of the means by which he hoped to attain this vision was through *pro unitate* (for unity) schools. These schools, called federal government colleges, were scattered throughout the country. They were meant to be model schools, with staff and students of mixed ethnic groupings in Nigeria. It was in one of these schools, Federal Government College Jos, that my parents first served. I grew up in Jos and attended FGC Jos for high school (class of 1986). Federal Government College Ilorin in western Nigeria was another unity school where my parents served.

Jos is not a large city like Lagos, Kano, or Port Harcourt. However, as a serene, friendly, and cosmopolitan city, Jos used to attract residents and visitors from various parts of Nigeria and beyond. Jos is 4,000 feet above sea level. The city's beautiful landscape of rocks, valleys, and plains communicates peace to its dwellers. Growing up, I experienced peace in the land of the beautiful people and splendid volcanic rocks of Jos. Three of my closest friends at FGC Jos were Muslims. Tribalism and religious bigotry were not part of the experience of my generation of classmates in Jos. Even the Nigerian Civil War, which was fought over a geographic division rather than a religious schism, was not part of the experience of my classmates. We simply grew up knowing that there had been a terrible war at some point in our national history.

The Socioreligious Landscape in Which My Organization Is in Trouble

Today, the peace in Jos has been overthrown. Things have changed drastically. Jos is now a militarized city, segregated along religious lines. The first major conflict in Jos occurred in 2001 and was volcanic, because no one could have predicted it happening in the Nigerian city of peace. Jos had always been an oasis of peace in Nigeria; its motto is "Home of Peace and Tourism" (Kaigama, 2012, p. 12). In March 2001, some villages in the Plateau State began to experience serious armed crisis that eventually climaxed in the capital city of Jos on September 7, 2001 (Kaigama, 2012). A serene city was transformed into a panic-stricken territory. With this alteration, the "Home of Peace and Tourism" became an empty slogan, as peace and tourism started to fade away. The year 2001 was the year of my priestly ordination. That year I was assigned to serve in a Jesuit high school and parish in Lagos, and my parents, after having served in different locations in Nigeria, retired in a home in Jos.

When the 2001 crisis erupted, there were reprisals between Christians and Muslims. Some youths from another section of Jos seeking vengeance came to the area where my parents and my two youngest brothers were living, Rock Haven, and wanted to cause problems. Security was sparse and scattered, raising the level of fear in the community. Nobody wanted to risk their safety, so everyone stayed indoors. My younger brothers, who had never witnessed such turmoil before, tried to create a shield for my parents. The advancing youths descended on the home of a neighboring Muslim family and set it ablaze. Fortunately, the family was absent. My mum, risking her life, courageously ran out of our family compound with a crucifix and begged the youths to stop.

After my mum pleaded with them, the youths changed their minds and immediately began fetching water to douse the fire. During this crisis, the only law on the land was reprisal. It was in the midst of this chaos that the law of retaliation entered FGC Jos, my alma mater. Federal Government College Jos is a co-ed boarding school, and students from different parts of the country live and study together there. Thankfully, no student was hurt during the 2001 crisis.

The crisis erupted like a volcano in other parts of the Plateau State in 2002, 2003, 2004, and 2006 (Kaigama, 2012). In 2008, there was another violent eruption in Jos. The crisis was so serious there that some Catholic monks were attacked in an Augustinian monastery. I visited Jos for Christmas 2008. That year, the popular Christmas Mass vigils were suspended in the parishes because of the curfew. The Nigerian military were all over the place to enforce peace. I remember two soldiers visiting my family home on Christmas Day. After we served them Christmas meals, I engaged them in conversation. One was a Christian, and the other was a Muslim. I was impressed with the integration and unity in the Nigerian army and wished it were the same in the populace of Jos. It is poignant that a military organization served as a model of integration in modern Nigerian society.

Over the years, and with each violent crisis, Jos is experiencing segregation at an exponential rate. Christians and Muslims have been realigning themselves based on geographic territories. After the crisis in 2008 my siblings and I had to arrange for my parents to leave Jos. It was the last straw. Though my parents were living at a family property in an area of relative peace, we felt it was needless for them to be living in fear at their age. They now live in Abuja. One of my brothers, Ugo, still lives in Jos. He works for an electric power company. After one of the crises, I visited his office and was happy to see that he and his office staff, a Muslim engineer, remained close friends in spite of the conflict and tension. My brother's wife is a medical doctor and consequently has witnessed the influx of victims of the bloody conflicts, both Christian and Muslim, to Jos University Teaching Hospital. With each outbreak of violence, many people are killed, and many residents of Jos are displaced (Orji, 2011). Christians and Muslims are both victims and perpetrators in this conflict (Human Rights Watch, 2001). Jos, which I always equated with peace, is so tense and volatile that people sleep with one eye open. On Fridays, tensions reach their climax, because all preceding crisis occurred on Fridays (the Muslim day of prayer). The Catholic Archbishop of Jos said, "The other day a man was being chased by bees, and when he was running for cover everybody started running to nowhere and for no reason in particular" (Kaigama, 2012, p. 159). Muslims and Christians in the market ran helter-skelter thinking another crisis had broken out.

This is the situation that my organization, FGC Jos, is immersed in. During the 2001 crisis, a mosque in the school was burned by some students who wanted to avenge the burning of churches in the city. We assume that the arsonists were Christian students, but there is no evidence, since the mosque fire was set secretly. As a result of the crisis, a serious rift was created in the school organization. The student body in FGC Jos remains ethnically as well as religiously mixed, so it is similar in that respect to my time as a student there in the 1980s. The academic and nonacademic staff is a mix of Christians and Muslims.

There is tension at the school, and in the context of this chapter I want to present some hypothetical servant-leadership ideas for change. In this hypothetical context, I have the burden of leadership as principal of FGC Jos during the crisis. I need to establish short-term and long-term goals to harmoniously resolve this crisis at the school level, yet remain aware that the school is not insulated or isolated from the socioreligious and political reality of the Jos metropolis. Ultimately, the goal is to achieve forgiveness, peace, and justice.

Critical Interpretation of the Setback

In organizations, problems are sometimes difficult to discuss in isolation from the dynamic of the macroculture. National or ethnic issues (the perspective of the macroculture), organizational issues, occupational issues (the perspective of the subculture), and microsystem issues are all linked (Schein, 2010, p. 5). It is in this light that I analyze my organization's macrocontext in order to deepen my understanding of the challenges and possibilities within the organization. The metaphor for the micro- and the macrocontexts is a tree within a forest. It is one thing to analyze a tree standing alone; it is another thing to analyze a tree as part of the forest ecosystem. The things we observe inside organizations are reflections of the "national culture, and the interplay of subcultures[,] because they often reflect the primary occupational cultures of the organization members" (Schein, 2010, p. 55). The new democratic dispensation in Nigeria is a paradox of sorts. Nigerians want democracy, and democracy has created a watershed in the nation's political history, with mounting social violence in some parts of the country (Lewis, 2003). While some organizations are reaping the dividends of democracy, my organization, a high school, was caught in the middle of political tensions that spilled over into a religious conflict.

As a hypothetical leader of this conflict-affected school located within the hotbed of a conflict-affected city, I am taking the responsibility of doing a critical analysis of the problem by looking into its root cause. As a pedagogical technique, I will engage myself as a hypothetical leader who wants to create a culture of deep listening and profound respect for human life by building bridges of goodwill and collapsing walls of bigotry. One goal of this pedagogic procedure endeavors to model and demonstrate a soulful and cogent resolution to the predicament. Using my imagination, I contemplate the scenario of the school climate and respond to the question of what a servant-leader would do, if he or she were there.

In my organization's crisis, a problem at the macrolevel infected our school environment. The demographic makeup of FGC Jos is culturally diverse in a similar manner to the city of Jos. There is no recent demographic data based on religion in Jos (Orji, 2011, p. 475). However, ethnic groups in Jos are categorized as indigenous (original inhabitants) and nonindigenous (settlers). This categorization is in line with the 1979 and 1999 constitution of Nigeria (Orji, 2011). The "indigenous" population controls the political governance of Jos. This is not unusual, since in other states of Nigeria, the indigenous populations also control the political governance.

The settlers in Jos include different ethnic groups, such as Hausa, Yoruba, Igbos, Tiv, and Urhobo. These are excluded from politics. However, the Hausa settlers (also known as the Jasawa) in Jos argue that by virtue of their Nigerian citizenship, they ought to participate in politics regardless of where their ancestors come from (Orji, 2011, p. 475). In contrast, the Yorubas, Igbos, Tivs, and Urhobos, who have lived in Jos as long as the Hausas, do not see participation in Jos metropolis politics as their inherent right (Orji, 2011). While these other settlers (Yorubas, Igbos, Tivs, Urhobos) and "indigenous" populations of Jos are predominantly Christian, the Hausa settlers are predominantly Muslim. For the Hausas, the process of struggling for political inclusion sometimes leads groups to resort to violence (Orji, 2011). Orji (2011) said, "The contest between the 'indigenous' communities and the Jasawa over political control of Jos is the underlying issue behind the Jos conflict" (p. 476).

Governor Adams Oshiomhole of Edo State (central southern Nigeria) has called for the abolition of the indigeneship clause (Ejembi, 2013). Such a move will give every Nigerian the ability to contest elections wherever he or she may be residing. Oshiomhole, who has lived most of his life in Kaduna State (northern Nigeria) cannot contest elections in Kaduna. He had to return to his state of origin. He said, "I had no choice about where I was born, but I chose where to live" (Ejembi, 2013). As the Nigerian nation is contemplating constitutional amendment, Oshiomhole thinks that the concept of indigeneship in Nigeria's public policy should be completely abolished (Ejembi, 2013).

Orji (2011) also identified an economic factor in the Jos conflict. With the devastation of the private sector in Nigeria and the slow rate of economic growth, many Nigerians quickly turned to the government sector for access to social, economic, and political opportunities (Orji, 2011). Jos is located in North Central Nigeria, and northern Nigeria generally has a Hausa-Fulani political hegemony (Orji, 2011). Consequently, it is very easy for Hausa-Fulani people in the north to access government at the highest level. Because those in Jos cannot do this, frustration and deep-seated feelings of political or power deficits build up. This leads one to discern that the Jos crisis is a political crisis with religious colorations. Furthermore, omnipresent corruption, unemployment, and poverty also help to fuel the conflicts in Nigeria.

There is, nevertheless, also a religious dimension to the conflict (Orji, 2011). The protagonists of the Jos crisis are the Jasawa (predominantly Muslims) and the indigenous (predominantly Christians). The indigenous population is made up of Berom, Aftzere, and Anaguta, to mention but a few. Educated Christians and Muslims have interpreted the Jos conflict as a case of political manipulation of religion (Orji, 2011). Hence, we can extrapolate that the root cause is political, while the dominant manifestation is religious (Orji, 2011).

The burning of the mosque at FGC Jos can be seen as a manifestation of the nonreligious disputes of the city of Jos. Sometimes simple land disputes between an indigene Christian and a nonindigene Muslim can spill over into a religious crisis. All it takes is for a symbol of faith to be attacked. Thus, some manifestations of the political crises of Jos are attacks on churches and mosques. An attack on a religious symbol sets off a chain reaction by evoking strong emotions and provoking members of the affected religious affiliation to seek revenge. Therefore, in the case of Jos, when a church is attacked to spite the Christian indigenes, the Christian settlers also get provoked and join the indigenes to defend their centers of worship. Once reprisal takes place, it leads to a vicious cycle of violence. "Honor of ethnicity" and "honor of religion" are both being defended (Orji, 2011, p. 478).

In addition to the religious dimension, there is also a policy dimension to the Jos crisis (Orji, 2011). Without a state policy to initiate and implement effective peace-building measures at the local government levels and district levels, it will be difficult to bring the crisis under control. Jos is heavily militarized, and the military presence is merely enforcing peace. Despite the military presence, there are still ongoing reprisals and armed conflicts in the rural parts of the Plateau State. Orji (2011), quoting Human Rights Watch, said that the former president, Olusegun Obasanjo, indicted the former governor of the Plateau State, Joshua Dariye, after the May 2004 violence for failing to create a policy of peace:

> As of today, there is nothing on [the] ground and no evidence to show that the state Governor has [the] interest, desire, commitment, credibility, and capacity to promote reconciliation, rehabilitation, forgiveness, peace, harmony and stability. If anything, some of his utterances, his lackadaisical attitude and seeming uneven-handedness over the salient and contending issues[,] present him as not just part of the problem, but also as an instigator and a threat to peace. (p. 478)

In 2007, a new governor, Jonah Jang, was elected to lead the Plateau State. In addition to the political crisis he inherited, he is also challenged with terrorism in the state. The *Boko Haram* (an extremist minority Muslim group) has taken advantage of the Jos crisis to bomb Christian churches during Sunday masses and services. Recently, *Boko Haram* has been causing general mayhem in northern Nigeria. With this added dimension, the complexity of the Jos crisis rises to an exponential level. There is extreme fear and mistrust among the people of Jos. There is also a ripple effect. When Christian settlers from other states in Nigeria are attacked in Jos or in parts of northern Nigeria, Muslims in southern Nigeria become targets of reprisals in those predominantly Christian states. In addition, there is a legal dimension to the crisis. There is a movement in northern

Nigeria for the expansion of *shari'a* (the Islamic system of law). Most of the northern states have adopted the *shari'a* system of law. The first state to do so was Zamfara in 1999. Plateau State does not have *shari'a,* and many Christians will galvanize against it.

This macrocontext has a bearing on my organization, both in the past (2001) and today. As a hypothetical leader in FGC Jos, I will articulate my life-giving response to this crisis in the next section of this chapter. The anecdotes in my response below will be embellished with fiction, not facts. To reiterate, at the time of the Jos crisis, I was in Lagos, but in this chapter, I will envisage myself as a leader at FGC Jos saddled with creating light out of the darkness of this predicament. I will also approach this allegory from multiple viewpoints, seeking to honor all major religions, which have a fundamental respect for life. It is only the extremist elements of the different religions that deviate from this fundamental vocation to revere life.

Life-Giving Response to the Problem

Pattern of School Administration

Servant-leadership is the proposed system of administration in this organization. Greenleaf regarded the institution as servant, and the principal leader as first among equals (Greenleaf, 1977/2002). In this model, the leaders remain "first," but they collaborate with competent peers. This deviates from the traditional model of a chief atop a hierarchical pyramid (Greenleaf, 1977/2002). The servant-leadership model is "a balanced team of equals under the leadership of a true servant who serves as *primus inter pares,* first among equals" (Greenleaf, 1977/2002, p. 253). Greenleaf emphasized that in a serving institution, all—not most or almost all— who embrace its philosophy "are lifted up to nobler stature and greater effectiveness than they are likely to achieve on their own or with a less demanding discipline" (Greenleaf, 1977/2002, p. 252).

A servant-leader will prefer to use his or her moral authority instead of formal authority or positional power. Formal authority and positional power do not promote authentic openness and trust, and should be used only as a last resort (Covey, 2002). A leader that employs moral authority exerts greater influence in an organization through persuasion, empathy, and trustworthiness (Covey, 2002). The principles of servant-leadership are universally applicable (Covey, 2002). Servant-leaders are humble, reverent, teachable, respectful, determined, and caring (Covey, 2002). Moral authority is achieved through servant-leadership, and two key pillars of moral authority are sacrifice and humility (Covey, 2002). Leaders who practice the principle of sacrifice are able to live with humility and courage, and they are able to apologize and to forgive others (Covey, 2002). Echoes of the servant-leadership model described above will be reflected in the imagined setting and imagined summit below. But before setting the stage for the school parable, in the intermission that follows I will paint a vignette of the power and wisdom of nonviolence and the folly and blindness of hostility.

INTERNAL VIGNETTE: AN END OF TWO VILLAGES

Two thousand years ago, two villages named Masara and Doya existed in peace and harmony, separated by a large river called the River Gwam. On both sides of the river were two beautiful farming communities that enjoyed green vegetation and abundant fish for many decades. One year there was a great famine, and the width of the River Gwam began to narrow and draw the women of both villages closer and closer until their buckets began to hit each other in dissonance as they struggled to fetch the scarce water. One day, in the commotion by the river, a woman from Doya lost all the water from her bucket. In frustration, she pushed the woman from Masara who had caused the accidental loss of water into the shallow river. The women from Masara retaliated and overpowered the Doyan woman, slapped her, and inflicted many injuries on her. The bruised woman and her own colleagues hurried back to their village to report what had happened to the chief of Doya and his council of elders.

While the council of elders of Doya was holding a meeting on what action to take regarding the victimized woman, the military youths of Doya, electrified with provocation over what had happened to one of their women, took their military weapons and started advancing to the River Gwam to challenge the people of Masara. When the youths of Masara saw the Doyan youths advancing with a war song, the youths of Masara began to say to themselves, "Who the hell do the Doyan youths think they are?" Consequently, the Masara military youths quickly prepared their weapons and began marching toward the River Gwam with their own war songs. As both military sides drew closer to the narrow river, there was frenzy in the atmosphere. It was going to be a ferocious mother of all wars. The military youths from Doya apparently had superior might, and they were calculating the right minute to launch their weapons.

The chief of Doya heard that a fierce battle was imminent. He hurriedly left his palace and, ignoring his entourage, began running toward the river, barefooted and without his royal garments. When he got to the river, the war songs had reached a deafening pitch. The frenzy had reached the point of no return. The chief of Doya ran to the bank of the shallow river and stood between his Doyan youths and the youths of Masara. Then, to the astonishment of both sides, he knelt down and, facing his Doyan youths, gestured with both hands in a vertical oscillating motion and begged his military youths to drop their weapons of destruction. After this frantic attempt to dissuade them from triggering a war, the youths stopped chanting their war songs and began dropping their weapons one after the other. In reciprocation, the youths of Masara began to do the same until there was complete silence. The chief now stood and exhorted both warring sides to be farsighted and foresighted. He told them to look across the river and behind them and observe the vistas. When the military youths looked at the horizon, they saw wailing children clinching to their terrified mothers. The chief of Doya then eloquently and loudly proclaimed to both sides:

> If you ignite a battle, you will spill blood on our lands and on our waters. You will die like fools! River Gwam will be polluted! The remaining fish will perish! Our mothers and children from both communities will have no future but a painful and slow-motion death. We must learn to live together in peace in time of plenty and in time of scarcity. Yes, there is famine on our land, but there is such a thing as sharing. Our hands are meant for service of each other and not for combat with each other. Let us stop raising hackles and return to our respective villages.

Before the chief of Doya could finish his appeal, the youths of both sides had been swiftly transformed by the streaming words of nonviolence that gushed from the chief's mouth. It was as if the ice water of ceasefire had been poured over the warriors. The next day, the women and the youths of both villages reconciled and resolved their differences. A water service distribution committee was created. This committee was composed of members of the Doya community and members of the Masara community. With sacrifice and the discipline of adapting to austerity measures, everyone began to discover oases of peace in the growing wildernesses of the River Gwam.

Unexpectedly, the heavens opened, and heavy rains began to pour into the river and onto the land. The banks of the River Gwam began to expand, and the space between the people of Doya and the people of Masara started widening, but the citizens of the two villages had developed strong bonds of peace and interdependence during their time of learning to share in scarcity. Though the river had expanded, and yams (*doya*), maize (*masara*), and fish were now abundant on the extensive green banks of the river, the two village communities built a bridge across the River Gwam. It was the end of the two villages, and the beginning of a united community founded on the perpetual pillars of reconciliation, peace, love, and service. To this day, this community continues to blossom in a fountain of freedom.

School Allegory and Imagined Setting

It is 11:30 p.m. The dust raised by the Jos crisis is gradually settling because of the presence of military troops and the imposed curfew, but the burnt mosque in FGC Jos is still smoldering. I have already informed the police station, and so there is a police presence in the school compound. Students have returned to their hostels. The staff members living in the school compound have returned to their homes. I called an emergency meeting of the academic vice principal, a Muslim, and administrative vice principal, a Christian. Also invited to this meeting at the school's conference room are the school's Muslim imam, Protestant chaplain, and Catholic chaplain. A few other teaching staff and nonteaching staff (mixture of Christians and Muslims) are present. The chaplains and the Imam each give a short invocation before we commence. In each prayer there is an expression of gratitude to the Almighty Creator that no member of our school community was injured or killed. Everybody at this meeting is shaken by the recent tragic events in Jos, and by the pandemonium and tension in the school compound caused by the burning of a mosque.

As I envision it, there is complete silence in the conference room after the prayer. We try not to break that silence, and everyone listens to his or her inner voice. After some minutes of silence, I look at the imam. He understands my vulnerability and knows that I am deeply hurt and shaken. He speaks, and his voice soothes my aggrieved emotions. He reiterates his gratitude that no member of our school community was hurt. At this point we still do not know exactly which student or students started the fire. I muster courage and speak. I thank everyone for coming and express my sorrow for what has happened. I assure the Muslim imam and the group that we will take personal responsibility for seeing that the school rebuilds a new mosque in the near future.

Rather than talking, I want to hear the emotions and words of my administrative colleagues, imam, chaplains, and staff. The school's secretary takes notes as everyone offers advice on how to move forward. With lessons of leadership from Greenleaf (1977/2002), I want everyone to help generate a new and cogent meaning and a superior wisdom. The more ideas that are put forward, the more we are all able to have "*a sense for the unknowable* and be able to *foresee the unforeseeable*" (p. 35). At the end of this emergency meeting, which goes past midnight, these are our resolutions:

Resolutions

- We will all return to our respective homes and have some rest.

- Classes will be cancelled tomorrow, and we will call a school assembly (including every staff and student) by 7:30 a.m.

- During the assembly, the imam and the Christian chaplains will lead a morning prayer for peace.

- The principal will remind the Christians and Muslims of the love and harmony that we have been enjoying at the school.

- The sacrilege of the mosque will be condemned.

- The principal will announce that the mosque will be rebuilt.

- The school secretary will be on phone most of the day to answer phone calls from parents in different parts of the country in order to let them know that things are under control.

- Since we still do not know who the arsonist is, we will denounce the evil act and ask everyone to examine his or her conscience.

- The principal will ask the Muslims and the group for forgiveness on behalf of the unknown arsonists.

- A brief lecture on the political roots of the crisis will be given to the students after lunch. Everybody will be made to understand that any participant in the crisis is a stooge of ill-meaning politicians (who hardly get hurt during these conflicts).

- There will also be a workshop on the philosophy of nonviolence and the healing power of love and the pathology of hate. Concepts from Mahatma Gandhi and Martin Luther King Jr. will be used in the workshop.

- We will reconvene in the near future to deliberate on long-term resolutions.

The Morning Assembly after the Incident

We decide to use the restorative justice philosophical approach to repair the harm caused to the school community, and especially to our Muslim students and staff. The chaplains and the imam lead us through a peace and unity covenant in which we agree to walk hand in hand and avoid any form of segregation in the classrooms, hostels, dining hall, library, labs, or sports fields. We aim to reach an agreement to remain a model of unity and love to the citizens of Jos, and to agree to a commitment to peace. The covenant opens with a candle-lighting ceremony to be performed by the imam on behalf of the Muslims, and the Protestant and Catholic chaplains on behalf of the Christians. In restorative justice, rituals help transform an environment into an ennobling space (Bender & Armour, 2007). The candle-lighting ceremony helps dispel the darkness of hate and violence. Experiencing a spiritual bond that shows we are connected to something bigger than ourselves inspires us to hold hands throughout the chaplains' and imam's invocations.

The spiritual dimension of restorative justice becomes a focus in the reading of the Bible and the Quran. Scriptural and Quranic readings remind us of the reverence for life. Bender and Amour (2007) defined *spirituality* as reverence for life. Workshops occurring throughout the day provide opportunities for group dialogue. After creating an atmosphere for reconciliation, as principal, I speak to the entire school population, asking for forgiveness for the fact that this assault on one of the school's religious centers happened under my leadership. The events that happen in organizations cannot be completely insulated from effective or inept organizational leadership. The incident could have been forestalled if there had been greater foresight on my part.

With heartfelt sorrow for what happened, I begin:

> On behalf of the college, and as principal of this college, I am sorry for this unfortunate incident in one of the worship centers of our school, and I want to ask the forgiveness of the entire school community, especially my Muslim staff and students, for what happened yesterday. It is a sacrilege against our Creator and Heavenly Father, who gave life to each us and who wants us to live together.

With this earnest apology, an environment is created in which forgiveness can be asked and granted by others (Ferch, 2004). True humility and the sincere asking for forgiveness can draw people to a leader and evoke in them the desire to be responsible (Ferch, 2012). I demand a change of heart and behavior in the persons who set fire to the mosque. I also ask that no one be witch-hunted and that we enhance our school environment of trust. This environment is meant to prompt the culprits to come to me or to the school chaplains. Stressing the capacity for good that God has planted in each of us can help everyone commit to tapping into that capacity. We humans have a wonderful capacity for good in spite of the evil in the world (Tutu, 1997).

LONG-TERM MEASURES

We propose that the school administration and staff plan and organize a fundraising luncheon including the entire school body, parents, and alumni. The purpose of the luncheon is to help rectify the injustice that was done by the burning of the mosque. The proceeds of the luncheon will go toward the efficient reconstruction of the mosque. This renaissance of solidarity will make a statement about the reign of peace in our school organization. Restorative justice encourages a sense of inclusion as well as a recognition of our common humanity (Bender & Armour, 2007). The luncheon will give our school community that sense of inclusion and recognition of our common dignity as persons regardless of our religious faiths, and hope will be reborn.

The fundraising will help the offenders learn about the impact of the crime they committed and induce appropriate guilt in them. Muslim and Christian key speakers will be invited and during the luncheon will speak about the principle of harmonious living. At the end of the day, we wish to have created a tighter common bond of human solidarity. The essential message will be that if the right hand is affected, we will be concerned, and if the left hand is affected, we will be equally concerned. The goal will be to empower the victims, create healing, offer compassion, and advocate forgiveness on the part of everyone (Bender & Armour, 2007).

This crisis will become a *kairos* moment for all of us to turn toward deeper love, compassion, forgiveness, and union. It will offer the opportunity for conversion, and for respect for the dignity of the life of every person on earth. With lessons learned from Tutu (1997), we will endeavor to avoid the extremes of the Nuremberg trials by not witch-hunting the arsonists. Neither will we sweep the offense under the carpet and offer blanket amnesty to the unknown offenders. Rather, our employing the methods of the Truth and Reconciliation Committee of South Africa will create a favorable atmosphere for the perpetrators to repent, come forward to the school authorities, and confess their actions. If we surmise that the lives of the culprits will be endangered outside the school walls, then their identities will be revealed to only a few school officials. The intention is not to humiliate or hurt the arsonists. As with South Africa's Truth and Reconciliation Committee, the idea is to forgive the offenders and invite them back into the community (Ferch, 2011).

Another long-term measure will be the intensified "dialogue of life." Kaigama (2012) advocated a dialogue of life in which Christians and Muslims sincerely open up to share and accept each other at deeper levels. This dialogue includes the customary sharing of gifts between Christians and Muslims at Christmas and Sallah (Kaigama, 2012). This practice, which is already occurring among our Christian and Muslim staff, will become encouraged at a deeper level. As part of dialogue for life, religious tolerance can be embedded in our school curriculum. Narratives of the peaceful coexistence of Christians and Muslims (as exemplified among the Yoruba ethnic group in western Nigeria) will be shared during school assemblies from time to time. Social harmony in the school will also be promoted through the spirit of *ubuntu*. *Ubuntu* is an African cultural belief in collectivity that is indispensable to the creation and acceptance of truth and reconciliation (Androff, 2010). Tutu (1997) affirmed that a person with the spirit of *ubuntu* feels that he or she "belongs in a greater whole and is diminished when others are humiliated or diminished" (p. 31).

In the African idiom, a human being is a human being through the lens of the other (Ferch, 2012; Tutu, 1997). *Ubuntu* spirit is present in servant-leaders and those they lead. Ferch (2012) expressed it:

> The servant-leader not only sees us whole . . . not diminished, not destroyed . . . the servant-leader lives in such a way that we become whole, and in so doing, we bring wholeness, or a sense of that which is holy, to the world. (p. 99)

It is in the spirit of *ubuntu* that the school will pursue restorative justice. What is holy to the world must respect the dignity of the human person created in God's image. Restorative justice is not about punishment but about a redress of imbalances, the repair of broken relationships, or the rehabilitation of the culprits and the wounded (Tutu, 1997). Films such as *Anne Frank* (2001), *Gandhi* (1982), and *Martin Luther King Jr.—I Have a Dream* (2005), as well as other inspirational films about the philosophy of nonviolence, can be shown to the school community during movie weekends in order to train the students, staff, and administrators to eschew any form of bigotry or hatred.

Crises at family, organizational, and local levels often escalate because no one is listening. Training in deep listening skills will be a key element in a communication workshop for staff and students of the school community. We will also extend this model of deep listening beyond the walls of the school. Listening is one of the characteristics of servant-leadership. Spears (2004), a close disciple of Greenleaf, came up with the following ten tenets as keys to the development of servant-leadership: listening, empathy, healing, awareness, persuasion, conceptualization, foresight, stewardship, commitment to the growth of people, and building community. As I mentioned previously, foresight is a central ethic of leadership (Greenleaf, 1977/2002). Leaders fail ethically if they refuse to foresee time and space horizons (Greenleaf, 1977/2002). The "lead" that leaders have is foresight, and if this lead is missing, leaders lose their ability to lead an organization (Greenleaf, 1977/2002, p. 40). Leaders with foresight are able to immerse themselves in current events while keeping sight of the lessons of history and projections of the future (Greenleaf, 1977/2002). In addition to a communication workshop, there will be leadership-training opportunities for the staff and students to learn in detail about foresight and the other nine characteristics of servant-leadership.

Crippen (2004), who considers servant-leadership a paradigm for educational leadership, suggested that the ten characteristics of servant-leadership identified by Spears are in hierarchical order. Here I will briefly highlight each characteristic in Spears's ranking. The internal action of listening requires the commitment to listen to ourselves and to others. Empathetic understanding of others generates trust (Crippen, 2004). The potential for healing in servant-leadership can help our staff and students heal themselves and each other. Awareness assists everyone in our school in appreciating issues of ethics and values. The spirit of persuasion engenders moral authority rather than positional power. Through conceptualization, I believe we will be able to dream great dreams for a peaceful coexistence between Christians and Muslims. With foresight, everyone will be able to visualize the long-term consequences of our decisions (Gunnarsson & Blohm, 2011). Stewardship reminds every staff and student that, as a member the institution, he or she plays a significant role in "caring for the wellbeing of the institution and serving the needs of others in the institution" (Crippen, 2004, p. 14). Any person committed to the growth of people engenders the will to nurture others (Crippen, 2004). The last characteristic, building community, can rouse students and staff to create a home and sense of belonging for everyone.

As a hypothetical servant-leader in this organization, I would seek to galvanize the school staff, alumni, chaplains, and imam to take it as our deontological duty to collectively pay a visit to the governor, senators, and representatives of our state. In this context, it is important for the state and nation to fully democratize their polities and eschew the negative use of religion in political and legal systems. Asking the state government to take progressive measures to desegregate the city of Jos is an important goal. The state can then introduce opportunities for a dialogue of life between Christians and Muslims in civil service. A revision of the state's educational curriculum is in order so that topics such as religious tolerance, nonviolence, restorative justice, and forgiveness are embedded in the curriculum. If children begin to learn retributive justice (especially from their parents), the future of Jos will remain buried in a systemic circle of violence. Efforts to forestall this type of future gives life to our children. A state government that establishes more industries to curb the unemployment and poverty that fuel conflicts is a government that liberates its people.

Finally, in order for Jos to have an environment in which forgiveness can be sought, the establishment of a truth and reconciliation committee can help hold everyone (Christians and Muslims) accountable for what they have done, with restoration, not retribution, as the foundation. This committee, made up of respectable Christian and Muslim leaders, is to be modeled after the South African Truth and Reconciliation Committee.

References

Androff, D. K. (2010). Truth and Reconciliation Commissions (TRCs): An international human rights intervention and its connection to social work. *British Journal of Social Work, 40,* 1960–1977.

Bender, K., & Armour, M. (2007). The spiritual components of restorative justice. *Victims & Offenders, 2*(3), 251–267.

Chacour, E., & Hazard, D. (1984). *Blood brothers.* Grand Rapids, MI: Chosen Books.

Covey, S. (2002). Foreword. In L. C. Spears (Ed.), *Servant-leadership: A journey into the nature of legitimate power and greatness* (pp. 1–13). New York, NY: Paulist Press.

Crippen, C. (2004). Servant-leadership as an effective model for educational leadership and management: First to serve, then to lead. *Management in Education, 118*(5), 11–16.

DeGraaf, D., Tilley, C., & Neal L. (2004). Servant-leadership characteristics in organizational life. In L. C. Spears & M. Lawrence (Eds.), *Practicing servant-leadership* (pp. 133–166). Indianapolis, IN: Jossey-Bass.

Ejembi, S. (2013). Abolish indigeneship clause—Oshiomhole. Retrieved from http://ihuanedo.ning.com/profiles/blogs/abolish-indigeneship-clause-oshiomhole

Ferch, S. R. (2004). Servant-leadership, forgiveness, and social justice. In L. C. Spears & M. Lawrence (Eds.), *Practicing servant-leadership* (pp. 225–240). Indianapolis, IN: Jossey-Bass.

Ferch, S. R. (2011). Servant-leadership and the interior of the leader: Facing violence with courage and forgiveness. In S. R. Ferch & L. C. Spears (Eds.), *The spirit of servant-leadership* (pp. 21–49). New York, NY: Paulist Press.

Ferch, S. R. (2012). *Forgiveness and power in the age of atrocity.* Lanham, MD: Lexington Books.

Greenleaf, R. K. (2002). *Servant leadership: A journey into the nature of legitimate power and greatness* (25th anniversary ed.). L. C. Spears (Ed.). New York, NY: Paulist Press. (Original work published 1977).

Gunnarsson, J., & Blohm, O. (2011). The welcoming servant-leader: The art of creating hostmanship. In S. R. Ferch & L. C. Spears (Eds.), *The spirit of servant-leadership* (pp. 68–85). New York, NY: Paulist Press.

Human Rights Watch. (2001, Dec. 18). Jos: A city torn apart. Retrieved from https://www.hrw.org/report/2001/12/18/jos/city-torn-apart

Kaigama, A. K. (2012). *Peace, not war: A decade of interventions in the plateau state crises (2001–2011)*. Jos, Nigeria: Hamtul Press.

Lewis, P. M. (2003). Nigeria: Elections in a fragile regime. *Journal of Democracy, 14*(3), 131–144.

Orji, N. (2011). Faith-based aid to people affected by conflict in Jos, Nigeria: An analysis of the role of Christian and Muslim organizations. *Journal of Refugee Studies, 24*(3), 473–492.

Schein, E. H. (2010). *Organizational culture and leadership* (4th ed.). San Francisco, CA: Jossey-Bass.

Spears, L. C. (2004, Fall). Practicing servant-leadership. *Leader to Leader, 34*, 7–11.

Spears, L. C. (Ed.). (1998). *Insights on leadership: Service, stewardship, spirit, and servant-leadership.* New York, NY: John Wiley and Sons.

Tutu, D. M. (1997). *No future without forgiveness.* New York, NY: Image Doubleday.

Wheatley, M. J. (1998). What is our work? In L. C. Spears. (Ed.), *Insights on leadership: Service, stewardship, spirit, and servant-leadership* (pp. 340–351). New York, NY: John Wiley and Sons.

Chapter 9

Toward a Servant-Led Response Rooted in Forgiveness and Restorative Justice in the Catholic Clergy Sexual Abuse Scandal and Cover-Up

DUNG Q. TRAN

A Story of Clergy Abuse and Asking for Forgiveness

A chill in the air, fog smearing his windows, Tom Blanchette drove west of Boston to Lexington. He had an appointment with Father Joseph Birmingham. It had been 25 years since Birmingham's going-away party in Sudbury, where they last spoke. "How could I ever explain to anybody that I had lain naked in Father B.'s bed over a hundred times? I didn't know how to explain these experiences. All I knew was I didn't like it. But I saw him every Saturday and Sunday, because I worked in the church rectory; I saw him at least one night a week for catechism classes, and at least one night a week he was at our house for dinner. Every time we were alone he pursued sexual activity. For two years I would say we had sex two or three times a week, sometimes two or three times a day."

Until he was in his twenties, Tom had never mentioned a word of this history. One morning as Tom and an old friend were reminiscing about their teenage years, Father Birmingham's name came up. The friend grew angry and said, "That bastard . . . he queered me." Tom then polled his brothers and learned that Father B. had solicited sex from them too. Within a week, Tom and his mother had compiled a list of 25 victims.

As Tom entered his thirties, he decided that something was seriously wrong. All these years he had not been able to develop a lasting relationship with a woman—at the age of forty he remained doggedly single. Even a stable place to live was too much of a commitment for him. He moved at least once a year. The bite of alcohol snuck up on him. He joined Alcoholics Anonymous and began his 12 steps. The fifth required him to sit down with people in his life and forthrightly detail where he had done them wrong. He knew he had to find Birmingham. Reached on the phone, Birmingham agreed to a visit and on this frigid early winter day Tom headed to see him with some trepidation. When Tom arrived, Father Birmingham was open and encouraging, which impressed Tom. "I've had some experiences in my life and I've realized that some of the difficulties were a result of the relationship that I had with you," Tom began. "I played sports in high school, got good grades, and went to college for a year, but then decided to enlist in the army. I went to the military academy for a year, but decided against a military career. I then landed at Boston College and graduated there. I then went to work for a friend from high school and ended up selling tires for a few years. All those years, I never attended Mass. After my father died in 1981, I started being a little introspective and had a spiritual awakening. I started to attend a little Episcopal church in Akron, Ohio, which was beneficial for me. I felt a disregard for the Catholic Church." He paused and continued. "You know," Tom said dexterously, "what you did to me and my brothers and all those other boys in Sudbury was wrong. You had no right to do it. And I don't think anybody has ever told you that before."

"Now let me tell you my story," the priest said. "I've endured a difficult life myself. I was an only child and both of my parents have died. I've had a lot of personal difficulties and recently some medical ones. I seem to be troubled with a lung disorder that defies diagnosis. I've been removed from ministry for sexually abusing boys. I'm not allowed to say Mass. I'm sort of under house arrest here. I can't leave the grounds unless accompanied by two adults. I can't have any contact with kids. I'm seeing a psychiatrist in Boston."

Tom then interjected, "The real reason I've come is to make amends to those I have harmed. Now, I know I didn't do outright harm to you. But I've come to ask you to forgive me for the hatred and resentment I've felt toward you for the past twenty-five years." Infuriated, Birmingham rose from his seat and bellowed, "Why are you asking me for forgiveness?"

Overcome with tears, Tom said, "Because the Bible tells me to love my enemies and to pray for those that persecute me." Slowly Birmingham slid back into his chair and began to weep as well.

Months later, Tom heard that Father Birmingham was dying and was overwhelmed by a desire to see him again. Tom arrived at the hospital and found a man propped up in a chair, breathing ponderously through a mask. His hair was gone and his sight was half lost to whatever consumed him. Entering the silent room, Tom knelt next to Birmingham's chair and took his hand. He then prayed silently for a few minutes. Tom then said, "Father, it is Tommy Blanchette from Sudbury. I've come to visit you, Father. Is it okay if I pray for you?" Birmingham nodded. Tom closed his eyes. "Father, in the name of Jesus Christ I ask you to heal Father Birmingham in the body, the mind, and the spirit. Father, forgive him his sins through the shed blood of Jesus Christ, that he too might have eternal life." Birmingham closed his eyes and seemed to be asleep. Tom then gathered his hollow frame up in his arms and carried him to his bed. He smoothed a blanket over Birmingham and through the stream of his own tears he wished Father Birmingham a good night. That would be the final encounter between Tom and Father B., as Birmingham passed away just a few hours later.

Introduction

Numerous commentators, across several decades, have chronicled the Catholic Church's clergy sexual abuse crisis and cover-up (Ballano, 2019; Berry, 1994/2000; Chinnici, 2010; D'Antonio, 2013; Doyle, Sipe, & Wall, 2005; Formicola, 2014; Frawley-O'Dea, 2007; Goode, McGee, & O'Boyle, 2003; Investigative Staff of the *Boston Globe*, 2002; Keenan, 2012; Plante & McChesney, 2011; Wills, 2000). According to Sr. Carol Keehan, former president and chief executive officer of the Catholic Health Association, who in 2010 was identified by *TIME* magazine as one of the 100 most influential people in the world, characterized the sexual abuse saga as "an unprecedented crisis of historic proportions" (as cited in Fox, 2019, para. 2). For Italian theological historian Faggioli (2017), the sexual abuse scandal and cover-up is the most devastating crisis "since the Protestant Reformation, with still near-daily reminders of its scope, the fumbling nature of the institutional response, and the pain done to the victims and their families" (para. 1).

The scandal is a complex situation involving personal, relational, and social systems (Dokecki, 2004). The cover-up and vehement denials by ecclesiastical church leaders (Flynn, 2003) led devout yet disgruntled Catholics to "pursue a more coordinated strategy of activism" (Shirky, 2008, p. 144) by forming various groups that actively advocated for and against the leaders of the Catholic Church. Activist groups such as Voice of the Faithful (Bruce, 2011) and various pundits have urged Catholic Church officials to consider operating and functioning in a more transparent manner (Buckley, 2005; Cafardi, 2008; Reese, 1996; Sipe, 1995; Swidler, 1996, 2007). According to Horowitz (2019), scrutiny of the Catholic Church has continued to escalate "as some of its top prelates, including cardinals in the United States and Australia, have been publicly disgraced as abusers" (para. 7). Additionally, "As attorneys general across the United States have opened investigations into the church" (para. 7), many US bishops and religious orders, such as the Jesuits, have published lists of credibly accused clergy going back many decades.

In response to the pain, anger, and confusion, more concrete measures have been enacted to safeguard vulnerable populations and reduce the risk of future clergy abuse (Cafardi, 2008; Francis, 2019; United States Conference of Catholic Bishops, 2003). Many survivors-victims have been able to receive monetary compensation from the Church for their suffering. Countless bishops, including Popes Benedict XVI and Francis, have met with survivors-victims and listened to their stories of sexual abuse. These acts of empathy, listening, and healing led bishops to seek forgiveness from survivors-victims. Asking for forgiveness is an important first step toward healing for the abuse survivor-victim, for the priest abuser, and for the Catholic Church at large. The opening vignette testifies to the horizon of the possible (Ferch, 2008) that can emerge when efforts are made to reflectively discern our interior movements. This deepening and broadening of a person's character can result in the deepening and broadening of the character of others, a hallmark of servant-leadership (Sipe & Frick, 2015).

With all of this in mind, the purpose of this chapter is threefold: (1) to examine the sexual abuse crisis and the ways in which Catholic Church leaders and survivors-victims in the United States have responded to this scandal; (2) to analyze the US Church hierarchy's response in light of the servant-leadership characteristics of listening, empathy, and healing; and (3) to explore how the role of asking for forgiveness between survivor-victim and perpetrator can lead toward restorative justice and wholeness.

A History of the *Reported* Scandal
in the United States (1983–Present)

The US Catholic Church's contemporary abuse scandal originated in Henry, Louisiana, when molestation allegations were brought against Father Gilbert Gauthe in 1983 (Cafardi, 2008; Frawley-O'Dea, 2007; Investigative Staff of the *Boston Globe*, 2002; Jenkins, 1996; O'Reilly & Chalmers, 2014; Plante, 1999; Wills, 2000). The Gauthe case contained all of the factors that became routinely associated with the clergy abuse crisis. In her review of more than 100 newspaper articles related to the scandal, clinical psychologist Frawley-O'Dea (2007) concluded that the clergy abuse scandal was characterized by a "deadeningly repetitive paradigm of perpetration and cover-up" (p. 1).

Between 1950 and the early 1990s, a priest was generally assigned to a parish or other pastoral setting. Usually charismatic and full of enthusiasm, he focused his energies on activities with adolescent youth (Frawley-O'Dea & Goldner, 2007). Over time, he cultivated friendships with young people, primarily boys between 11 and 15 years of age. Some of the boys came from broken homes and lacked the guidance of a father figure, while others came from established and loving families (Frawley-O'Dea, 2007). All of the adolescents were raised to respect and trust priests, as they were spiritual and holy men. Eventually, the priest would introduce sex into his relationship with a young person.

At some point, a survivor-victim's parent, parishioner, fellow priest, or the survivor-victim himself would complain to the pastor, diocesan representative, or local bishop about the inappropriate sexual behavior. When an allegation was made, there were several probable outcomes. Years ago, the whistle-blower would be rebuked for trying to "bring scandal to the Church," a Catholic cliché implying an offense considered to be far graver than anything the priest might have done (Cozzens, 2004; Cafardi, 2008; Kennedy, 2002; Sipe, 1995; Wills, 2000). In this situation, the scolded accuser was sent home and, as whispers of the accusations circulated throughout the rumor mill of the parish or organization, was likely ostracized by both clergy and fellow parishioners (Bruni & Burkett, 1993/2002; Frawley-O'Dea, 2007).

Back at the rectory, chancery, or provincial house, the pastor, bishop, or religious superior would confront the priest, and in a number of cases, the accused priest acknowledged the veracity of the abuse claims (Frawley-O'Dea & Goldner, 2007). After confessing his wrongdoing, the priest would vow never to sin again. As decades went by, it became routine for priests to be sent for psychological evaluation and/or treatment. After being treated, the reformed priest turned up in another pastoral setting, where no one was informed about his prior alleged or acknowledged problems. Oftentimes, the priest abused again, and the cycle was repeated (Cafardi, 2008).

As the years went on and bishops came under increasing public pressure to do more about sexual abuse, another scenario emerged when a priest was accused of past or present abuse. By the mid-1980s and into the early 1990s, once a complaint was deemed serious, the victim was assured that the priest would be removed from any ministry involving children (Berry, 1994/2000; Cozzens, 2004). The Church would offer to pay for the survivor-victim's counseling expenditures. As accusers became more aggressive in their demands for restitution, sometimes drawing on legal counsel to help them, classified monetary settlements were reached. Although the Catholic Church has been excoriated for negotiating confidential legal settlements, it was often the victims who desired that their abuse and monetary payouts remain private (Frawley-O'Dea, 2007).

Once again, it was standard procedure for the sexually abusive priest to be sent away for further psychological evaluation and treatment. The effectiveness and credibility of the treatment programs and discharge plans varied widely (Bruni & Burkett, 1993/2002). According to psychologists Frawley-O'Dea and Goldner (2007), "Recommendations about fitness for ministry did not always represent the priest's psychosexual organization well or his propensity to reoffend" (p. xiii). When priests were reassigned, "the receiving clergy and community typically were not informed about the priest's background and therefore there was no particular supervision of his activities" (Frawley-O'Dea, 2007, p. 4).

Although the model presented varied widely, this was "more or less the characteristic pattern of sexual abuse and the response to it enacted by Catholic Church leaders for decades" (Frawley-O'Dea, 2007, p. 5). From the Father Gauthe case in 1983 onward, the Church's handling of the sexual abuse of children by priests became more publicized. It escalated into an American crisis in 2002 when news of the Boston archdiocese's intentional concealment efforts made national headlines (Investigative Staff of the *Boston Globe*, 2002; Muller & Kenney, 2004; Shirky, 2008).

Sipe (1990) contended that "between 1983 and 1987, an average of one case per week of past or present sexual abuse by a priest was reported nationwide" (p. 12). Beginning in 1987, the Catholic hierarchy began formally addressing the burgeoning abuse crisis. Many members of the clergy blamed victims and the media (Frawley-O'Dea, 2007). Archbishop emeritus of Boston, Cardinal Bernard Law, publicly criticized the media coverage as unfair, and from the pulpit noted, "By all means we call down God's power on the media, especially the *Boston Globe*" (Shirky, 2008, p. 147; Investigative Staff of the *Boston Globe*, 2002, p. 7).

In 1992, the United States Conference of Catholic Bishops established what came to be known as the "Five Principles" (Cafardi, 2008; United States Conference of Catholic Bishops, 1996). These principles urged "greater openness about abuse allegations, prompt response to allegations, removal of accused offenders from ministry for referral for evaluation and treatment, compliance with civil law, and reaching out to victims and their families" (Frawley-O'Dea & Goldner, 2007, p. xiv). After 1992, many bishops took steps to strengthen their response toward new sexual abuse allegations by establishing advisory boards that included lay people to help bishops evaluate abuse reports (United States Conference of Catholic Bishops, 1996). In 1993, the United States Conference of Catholic Bishops formed an Ad Hoc Committee on Sexual Abuse. The committee was charged with developing "diocesan guidelines for responding to accused and/or guilty clergy—as well as to victims and their families—and to help bishops better screen candidates for priesthood" (Frawley-O'Dea & Goldner, 2007, p. xv). For the rest of the 1990s, bishops continued to formally respond to the complaints about priests.

In 2002, the sexual abuse crisis reached a new critical stage in Boston, where "by the end of 2002, at least 500 people had come forward with claims [that] they were abused by Boston-area clergy" (Investigative Staff of the *Boston Globe*, 2002, p. 100). The exposure of serial sexual abuse and the subsequent cover-ups shattered the sacred respect traditionally lavished on priests and bishops by the laity (Fleming, Fleming, & Matousek, 2007). The spiritual leaders of a Church "dedicated to promoting Christian values had desecrated those values. It was as if firefighters had become arsonists, or doctors had intentionally spread disease" (Muller & Kenney, 2004, p. 1).

These actions were a betrayal of an implicit trust that the laity and institutional Church had bestowed on priests and bishops. Muller and Kenney (2004) noted "that many had lost the sense of security the Church had provided. People were questioning whether they had been too trusting" (p. 21). Frawley-O'Dea and Goldner (2007) observed that "lay people who at one time would have done what they were told by priests and bishops stood up to the clergy and demanded accountability for the crimes of a priest and the complicity of his ecclesiastical superiors" (p. xiii). Media publishers and editors, once deferential to the Church, stayed on the story and made it national news (Shirky, 2008). The relationship between the laity and the Church would be forever changed.

The story of Father John Geoghan's serial abuse of children over three decades and the Boston archdiocese's intentional concealment efforts swept the national news headlines. Boston became a watershed event as innumerable revelations of priestly sexual abuse of minors and administrative cover-up throughout the US Catholic Church saturated national media outlets. By late April 2002, "176 priests from twenty-eight states and the District of Columbia had resigned or been removed in cases of sexual abuse" (Frawley-O'Dea, 2007, p. xv). The year 2002 also saw the resignation of several bishops as a result of the scandal (Investigative Staff of the *Boston Globe*, 2002; Shirky, 2008). The crisis had reached such a disastrous zenith that Pope John Paul II took the extraordinary step of summoning the American cardinals to the Vatican to discuss the sexual abuse crisis (Blaney, 2009). As a result of the media firestorm, both the United States Conference of Catholic Bishops and the Conference of Major Superiors of Men used their summer meetings to apologize to survivors-victims and to pass stronger measures to keep sexually abusive priests away from children (Conference of Major Superiors of Men, 2002; United States Conference of Catholic Bishops, 2003).

As Catholic leaders were attempting to reform and regroup, lay people began to organize in an attempt to defend and reform a church they loved so dearly (Muller & Kenney, 2004). Diocesan finances began to shrink as lay groups such as Voice of the Faithful organized to exert financial and pastoral reform power in the Boston archdiocese (Bruce, 2011; Shirky, 2008). More traditional Catholics also organized in an effort to defend the Church, forming groups with names such as Faithful Voice. Dissatisfied clergy also banded together to support each other through the formation of a unified voice in the controversy (Frawley-O'Dea, 2007).

By the end of 2002, the landscape of the American Catholic Church was drastically altered. Boston's archbishop, Cardinal Bernard Law, ultimately acquiesced to public opinion and submitted his resignation to Pope John Paul II. The Boston archdiocese and countless other local Catholic Churches across America were now embroiled in protracted legal negotiations over financial settlements for survivors-victims. As of August 2018, it was written, "lawsuits by abuse victims have so far forced dioceses and religious orders in the United States to pay settlements totaling more than \$3 billion" (Gjelten, 2018, para. 1). The financial settlements have been an important first step toward healing for survivor-victims, their families, priest perpetrators, and the Catholic Church at large.

However, these payouts have significantly affected the Church's fiscal ability to sustain its services, and in many instances have bankrupted a diocese. As of January 2019, the following 21 (arch)dioceses or religious orders in United States territories have filed for bankruptcy protection in chapter 11:

Agana, Guam (2019)
Winona-Rochester, Minnesota (2018)
Santa Fe, New Mexico (2018)
Crosier Fathers and Brothers (2017)
Great Falls-Billings, Montana (2017)
New Ulm, Minnesota (2017)
Duluth, Minnesota (2015)
St. Paul-Minneapolis, Minnesota (2015)
Stockton, California (2014)
Helena, Montana (2014)
Gallup, New Mexico (2014)
Christian Brothers of New York (2011)
Milwaukee, Wisconsin (2011)
Oregon Province of the Society of Jesus (2009)
Wilmington, Delaware (2008)
Fairbanks, Alaska (2008)
San Diego, California (2007)
Davenport, Iowa (2006)
Spokane, Washington (2004)
Tucson, Arizona (2004)
Portland, Oregon (2004). (Eugenio, 2019; Reilly, 2018)

As legal scholar Reilly (2018) noted in her "analysis of the legacy of the Catholic cases for bankruptcy law" (p. 1),

the price of bankruptcy relief has been an intense public scrutiny of previously private matters, including the external consequences of inter-hierarchical relationships prescribed in canon law. The bankruptcy cases have made it clear that Catholic religious organizations are economic actors in the secular world. Decisions made within the Catholic hierarchy of authority under canon law for internal religious purposes have profound external consequences, not only on creditors outside the Church, but also on the faithful within it. (p. 44)

Since the spring of 2018, the consequences on external and internal Church stakeholders has escalated dramatically due to a series of alarming developments involving Pope Francis's management of the abuse scandal that have dominated international news headlines. The first was the mass resignation of Chilean bishops, one of whom Francis initially defended against allegations of abuse cover-up (Sherwood, 2018). The second was the release of scathing letters from Italian Archbishop Carlo Maria Viganò, a former papal ambassador to the United States, alleging that Vatican leaders, including Popes Benedict XVI and Francis, were aware of the sexual misconduct allegations against former Cardinal Theodore McCarrick, archbishop emeritus of Washington, DC, and Newark, New Jersey (Harlan, Pitrelli, & Boorstein, 2018). Once a trusted adviser of Francis, McCarrick has resigned from the College of Cardinals, been permanently suspended from public ministry for substantiated accusations of sexual misconduct with minors, and dismissed from the priesthood (D'Emilio, Winfield, & Thomas, 2019).

Compounding the latest phase of the crisis was the publication of a Pennsylvania grand jury report detailing the abuse of 1,000 children by 300 priests and the systematic cover-up by Church leaders (Goodstein & Otterman, 2018). Given these disconcerting developments, a recent Pew Survey revealed that confidence in Francis's leadership had plummeted. As of September 2018, only 31 percent of US Catholics rated Francis's management of the abuse scandal as good or excellent, which decreased 14 percentage points from earlier in 2018, and was down 24 points from a peak of 55 percent in June 2015 (Pew Research Center, 2018).

Needless to say, this scandal-plagued period weakened both Pope Francis and the Catholic Church's credibility, public image, and moral authority on the world stage. Time will tell what lessons the institutional Catholic Church will learn from this ghastly episode of spiritual betrayal. Hopefully, further steps toward acknowledged wrongdoing, transparency, wholeness, and restoration to "combat these crimes that betray the trust of the faithful" (Francis, 2019, para. 3) can be taken by survivor-victims, Catholic clergy, and the Church at large.

Servant-Leadership and the Catholic Church:
A Life-Affirming Vision

The mission and vision of the Catholic Christian Church and Robert Greenleaf's philosophy of servant-leadership have a tremendous amount in common. As a lifelong student of organizations, Greenleaf (1996) had an enduring interest in Roman Catholicism given its status "as the largest, most influential non-governmental institution in the world" (p. 142). While Greenleaf (1977/2002) regarded the US Catholic Church as "our largest single force for good" (p. 248), he also held that US Catholicism

> fails to realize its potential for good in society as a whole because, I believe, it is seen as predominantly a negative force. The issues on which the Church is in opposition, such as birth control, abortion, euthanasia, divorce, and communism, are specific and defined, and the actions of the Church are vigorous and sustained. . . . One must oppose those things one believes to be wrong, but one cannot lead from a predominantly negative posture. (p. 248)

Perhaps this unprecedented historical moment of challenge for the Catholic Church is an opportunity for a more positive approach to spiritual and organizational renewal. This could begin with a return to the life-affirming ideals that undergird Catholic-Christianity and servant-leadership.

For Greenleaf (1996),

> The idea of servant is deep in our Judeo-Christian heritage. *Servant* (along with *serve* and *service*) appears in the Bible more than thirteen hundred times. . . . Part of the human dilemma is that the meaning of *serve*, in practical behavioral terms for both persons and institutions, is never completely clear. Thus one who would be servant is a life-long seeker, groping for light but never finding ultimate clarity. One constantly probes and listens, both to the promptings from one's own inner resources and to the communications of those who are also seeking. Then one cautiously experiments, questions, and listens again. Thus the servant-seeker is constantly growing in self-assurance through experience, but never having the solace of certainty. (p. 201)

At its best, the life-affirming enterprise that is the Catholic Church is a vocation of loving evangelization that welcomes all people and instills in them habits of reflection in order to serve as a beacon of grace to fashion a more humane and just world (Paul VI, 1975). The evangelizing mission of the Catholic Church resonates with Greenleaf's contention that servant-leaders endeavor to build a more caring society (Greenleaf, 1977/2002). He also encouraged those in leadership positions to assume more personal responsibility and accountability, with the goal of building a more life-giving world. Greenleaf (1977/2002) offered a new mode of leadership that featured more caring on the part of the leader:

> A new moral principle is emerging which holds that the only authority deserving one's allegiance is that which [is] freely and knowingly granted by the led to the leader in response to, and proportion to, the clearly evident servant structure of the leader. Those who choose to follow this principle will not casually accept the authority of existing institutions. Rather, they will freely respond to only individuals who are chosen as leaders because they are proven and trusted as servants. To the extent that this principle prevails in the future, the only viable institutions will be those that are predominantly servant-led. (pp. 23–24)

Greenleaf (1977/2002) contended that a desire to lead had to be preceded by a fundamental desire to serve. He noted, "The servant-leader is a servant first . . . it begins with a natural feeling that one wants to serve, to serve first. Then the conscious choice brings one to aspire to lead" (p. 27). In choosing to lead, Greenleaf believed that servant-leaders needed proper motivation to lead. He appealed for leaders to "make sure that the other people's highest priority needs are being served" (p. 27). Leadership fixated on acquiring wealth, satiating ego, or wielding abusive power would only objectify and marginalize followers, leaving them feeling unappreciated. As Spears (2015) stated, "At its core, servant leadership is a long term, transformational approach to life and work—in essence, a way of being—that has the potential for creating positive change throughout our society" (p. 9).

Similarly, the Catholic Church exists to inculcate an enthusiasm for the Catholic faith that inspires people to share that life-affirming truth with others so as to renew the world. For the United States Conference of Catholic Bishops (1990),

The mission of evangelization is entrusted by Christ to his Church to be carried out in all her forms of ministry, witness, and service. By evangelizing, the Church seeks to bring about in all Catholics such an enthusiasm for their faith that, in living their faith in Jesus and strengthened by the sacraments, most especially the celebration of the Eucharist, they freely share that faith with others to transform the world. (p. 1)

The Catholic Church's emphasis on freedom, enthusiasm, and transformation resonates deeply with Greenleaf's reimagination of leadership power. He held that power should be exercised by the leader only to provide opportunities, individual autonomy, and alternatives for followers (Van Kuik, 1998). Power is shared, not abused for personal gain (Clark, 2010). Power from servant-leaders results in followers' commitment to organizational goals (Westre, 2003). Leadership committed to service "implies that power is shared with followers and used to cultivate their autonomy rather than coerce or manipulate them" (Van Kuik, 1998, p. 34).

After many years of thoughtful analysis of Greenleaf's original writings, Spears (2004) "extracted a set of ten characteristics of the servant-leader that [he] viewed as being of critical importance" (p. 13). These characteristics are listening, empathy, healing, awareness, persuasion, conceptualization, foresight, stewardship, commitment to the growth of people, and building community (Spears, 1995). For the sake of brevity, this chapter will focus on only three characteristics. The following section will explore the characteristics of listening, empathy, and healing as identified by Spears (2004) in light of the vignette of asking for forgiveness between abuse victim Tom Blanchette and his abuser, Father Joseph Birmingham.

Toward Forgiveness and Restorative Justice through Listening, Empathy, and Healing

As previously noted, the mission of the Catholic Church includes the spiritual formation and cultivation of people who are willing to place their gifts and abilities at the service of the common good. By virtue of its biblical and spiritual tradition, the Catholic Church is a servant-led organization charged with forming the next generation of servant-leaders. Despite these genuine and altruistic intentions, what if a leader is not living up to Greenleaf's ideals of servant-leadership? What if the formal spiritual leaders of the servant-led organization are not passing Greenleaf's "best test?" What if priests, who by virtue of their ordained ministry are servant-leaders, are wielding their power in a way that is mentally, spiritually, emotionally, psychologically, or sexually abusive? What if their superiors ignore cries for life-affirming leadership, leaving the traditionally docile laity exhausted, angry, frustrated, and hopeless? What can be done? How is this overcome?

To start answering some of these questions, it is imperative to examine the sexual abuse and forgiveness-asking vignette involving Tom Blanchette and Father Birmingham, as well as the abuse crisis as a whole through the servant-leadership characteristics of listening, empathy, and healing espoused by Greenleaf (1977/2002) and codified by Spears (2004). Exploring these characteristics will pave the way for a more holistic understanding of forgiveness and restorative justice.

LISTENING

Leaders ought to maintain a deep commitment to listening intently to others. Servant-leaders identify the will of a group and aid in the clarification of that will. Listening also requires attentiveness to the interior movements within. The practices of listening and regular reflection are essential to the growth of the servant-leader (Spears, 2004). Greenleaf (1977/2002) stated, "I have a bias about this which suggests that only a true natural servant automatically responds to any problem by listening first" (p. 17). He added that "true listening builds strength in other people" (p. 17).

Strength building through listening is critical for abuse survivors-victims, their families, and the entire Catholic community. But instead of pastorally listening, as they should have learned to do through formation and tradition, Catholic leaders were preoccupied with preventing "scandal" (Cafardi, 2008; Frawley-O'Dea, 2007). The prevalence of priestly pedophilia and ephebophilia, along with the subsequent cover-up by priest superiors, was devastating for the entire Catholic Church. The abuse of minors could have been avoided. Exacerbating the laity's frustration was the benign response of Catholic bishops who ignored the relentless cries for leadership and a listening ear.

I was deeply moved by the postabuse meeting between Tom Blanchette and Father Birmingham. Particularly striking was how both survivor-victim and abuser shared their 25 years' worth of difficulties. Tom and Father Birmingham were connected by their former sexual relationship and by the subsequent consequences and relational difficulties that ensued. This common ground built on intensely personal sharing kindled in Tom, the victim, a desire to seek the forgiveness of his abuser. I found this to be immensely poetic and profound. Philosopher North (1998) noted that "from the injured party's point of view, forgiveness will have the effect of preventing the wrong from continuing to damage one's self-esteem and one's psyche, so bringing to an end the distortion and corruption of one's relations with others" (p. 18).

In an effort to minimize the damage experienced by victims, the US bishops devoted a significant portion of their 2002 summer meeting agenda to listening to the abuse testimony of victims (United States Conference of Catholic Bishops, 2003). This crucial moment in American Catholicism initiated a wave of meetings between bishops and abuse victims (Cafardi, 2008). Oftentimes, these meetings were a requirement of the legal settlements between victims and the Church (Frawley-O'Dea, 2007). Since 2002, numerous bishops, cardinals, and popes have personally met with survivors-victims of priestly sexual abuse.

Most recently, Pope Francis met privately with Chilean survivors of clergy abuse. He listened to their stories, prayed with them, and invited them to the Vatican. This action, coupled with the pope's strong rhetoric denouncing priestly sexual abuse as evil and sinful, was an important example of servant-leadership. The pope's act of listening to the stories of abuse epitomizes the idea that servant-leadership "is rooted in the far-reaching ideal that people have inherent worth, a dignity not only to be strived for, but beneath this striving a dignity irrevocably connected to the reality of being human" (Ferch, 2012, p. 18).

Empathy

Greenleaf (1977/2002) advocated for leaders to both hear the message conveyed and attempt to understand the message from another's perspective. Spears (2015) wrote,

> People need to be accepted and recognized for their special and unique spirits. One assumes the good intentions of co-workers and does not reject them as people, even while refusing to accept their performance. The most successful servant-leaders are those who have become skilled empathetic leaders. (p. 10)

Greenleaf (1977/2002) maintained that leaders who demonstrated empathy would kindle more trust among followers. He opined,

> People grow taller when those who lead empathize and when they are accepted for what they are, even though their performance may be judged critically in terms of what they are capable of doing. Leaders who empathize and who fully accept those who go with them on this basis are more likely to be trusted. (p. 35)

When the salacious details of abuse and cover-up dominated the national news in 2002, the general public felt betrayed and became less trusting of Catholic clergy and the hierarchy at large (Fleming, Fleming, & Matousek, 2007; Investigative Staff of the *Boston Globe*, 2002). The constant cries for assistance and help by survivors-victims, their loved ones, and other priests had for so long fallen on deaf ears (Shirky, 2008; Sipe, 1995). Bishops, in a sense, rejected the good intentions of their subordinates, the laity. They were more concerned with preventing Church scandal and maintaining the status quo (Cafardi, 2008; Frawley-O'Dea, 2007).

Now, as many of the abuse cases are being legally settled, and concrete measures aimed at safeguarding children and preventing further abuse are being taken, the lay faithful are slowly beginning to trust the Catholic Church again (Flynn, 2003). As more and more efforts are made to support victims and reform the institutional Church, perhaps future generations will once again be able to implicitly trust the Catholic Church as a whole.

As previously mentioned, cultivating trust demands that the leader empathize with and accept others for who they are (Spears, 2015). Not only does empathy cultivate trust, it is "a consistent predictor of forgiveness" (Belicki, Rourke, & McCarthy, 2008, p. 166). In a study in which participants were asked to imagine scenarios of being infected with HIV or losing a loved one to a car accident caused by a drunk driver, it was observed "that empathic concern was positively related to reaching out to the offender in compassionate ways" (Williams et al., 2005). This sense of empathic concern was certainly felt by Tom Blanchette when he received the news that Father Birmingham was dying of cancer. Even though at their first meeting Tom had sought out Birmingham for his own personal healing, confronting his abuser allowed Tom to share his difficulties and listen to the struggles of his abuser. This dialogue connected the two with their humanity, a humanity that allowed Tom (the survivor-victim) to seek forgiveness of Father Birmingham (his abuser), and a humanity that elicited a strong feeling of compassion toward the dying child abuser that compelled Tom to visit and pray for him. In those acts, Tom Blanchette realized "the essence of being a person" (Tutu, 1999, p. 26). In that moment, Blanchette embodied Tutu's (1999) invitation to a forgiveness response: "In our experience, in our understanding, a person is a person through other persons. You can't be a solitary human being. We're all linked" (p. 26).

Healing

Like Tutu (1999) and King (1993), Blanchette was "obeying the imperative of his faith" (p. 93) by loving his oppressor. The forgiveness response of Tom Blanchette was a profound moment of transformation and healing. With regard to healing, Spears (2015) wrote,

> Learning to heal is a powerful force for transformation and integration. One of the great strengths of servant-leadership is the potential for healing oneself and others. Many people have broken spirits and have suffered from a variety of emotional hurts. Although this is part of being human, servant-leaders recognize that they have an opportunity to make whole those with whom they come in contact. (p. 10)

Related to healing, Greenleaf (1977/2002) pondered, "Do those being served grow as [a] person; do they, while being served, become healthier, wiser, freer, more autonomous, more likely themselves to become servants? And, what is the effect on the least privileged in society; will they benefit, or at least, not be further deprived" (p. 27)? For Greenleaf, the behaviors and actions of followers are the ultimate judge of whether a leader embodies the essence of servant-leadership. As Covey (1998) claimed, "I believe that the overwhelming majority of people in this country, with the right kind of servant-leadership at all levels, most importantly at the family level, could heal our country" (p. xviii).

In the midst of this great tragedy and atrocity is an opportunity for institutional and personal healing in the Catholic Church. The story of Tom Blanchette asking Father Joseph Birmingham for forgiveness poignantly illustrates that institutional healing begins with personal actions undergirded by the servant-led desire to seek forgiveness. In Father Birmingham's last hours of life, Tom's desire to be physically and prayerfully present was the servant-leader's recognition of the desire to make both himself and Father Birmingham whole.

Toward Restorative Justice in the Sexual Abuse Scandals

Restorative justice is a process and relational model of justice that "involve[s], to the extent possible, those who have a stake in a specific offense and to collectively identify and address harms, needs, and obligations, in order to heal and put things as right as possible" (Zehr, 2002, p. 37). Restorative justice focuses on restoring the survivor-victim. Typically, restorative justice "occurs after a person has admitted to or has been convicted of a crime. Instead of sentencing, the convicted person is directed to meet with the victim and the victim's supporters and work out mutually agreed-upon outcomes" (Worthington Jr., 2006, p. 248). In addition, these outcomes can involve some form of restitution to the survivor-victim, "apologies might be given, and impact statements are listened to and often responded to by the offender so the offender learns of the personal effects his or her crime has had on victims" (p. 248).

The poetic narrative featuring Tom Blanchette and Father Joseph Birmingham, as well as the stories of Popes Benedict XVI, Francis, and other bishops meeting with abuse victims, exemplifies the inherent holistic and relational value of the restorative justice model. It is my fervent prayer that survivors-victims, priestly perpetrators, Catholic leaders, and their supporters continue along this path of healing. May this journey be marked with empathic listening and an authentic recognition that "my humanity is caught up, is inextricably bound up, in yours and that we belong in a bundle of life" (Tutu, 1999, p. 31).

Concluding Reflection

As evidenced above, organizational and personal introspection and asking for forgiveness are crucial practices and processes for realizing our potential and becoming more fully alive. Reflectively asking for forgiveness is an opportunity to become healthier, wiser, freer, and more autonomous as a servant-leader (Greenleaf, 1977/2002). The discernment of both gifts and faults is pivotal for personal growth and development. The recognition of strengths allows us to recognize the beauty in ourselves and in the world. Conversely, accepting our shortcomings is an opportunity to seek meaningful change (Ferch, 2004). Forgiveness and reconciliation with the "other" offers the potential to "emerge more refined, more willing to see the heart of another, and more able to create just and lasting relationships" (Ferch, 2012, p. 17). As Tutu (1999) noted, "Thus, to forgive is indeed the best form of self-interest since anger, resentment, and revenge are corrosive of the summum bonum, the greatest good, communal harmony that enhances the humanity and personhood in the community" (p. 35). In Ferch's (2005) view, "The will to seek forgiveness, the will to forgive, and the will to pursue reconciliation may be a significant part of developing the kind of wisdom, health, autonomy, and freedom espoused in Robert Greenleaf in his idea of the servant-leader" (p. 97). For Harold Kushner (1998),

> To be forgiven is to feel the weight of the past lifted from our shoulders, to feel the stain of past wrongdoing washed away. To be forgiven is to feel free to step into the future unburdened by the precedent of who we have been and what we have done in previous times. (pp. 184–185)

In short, "each of us is more than the worst thing we've ever done" (Stevenson, 2014, p. 290).

Ultimately, the project of discerning one's faults and seeking forgiveness for those faults is a monumental task. Yet, as the vignette of Tom Blanchette and Father Joseph Birmingham indicates, the simple yet challenging act of asking for and seeking forgiveness can enlarge the heart of both victim and perpetrator. The image of Tom Blanchette carrying the fragile frame of his dying priestly abuser to his hospital bed is a powerful one. In that moment, Blanchette became more than the survivor-victim-recipient of the clergy sexual abuse narrative; he embodied the narrative's continuation to the extent that he was transformed by it (Voiss, 2015).

This chapter began with the task of examining the landscape of the clergy abuse scandal in the United States through the lens of forgiveness and its connection to servant-leadership, as embodied in the episode of asking for forgiveness involving Tom Blanchette and Father Joseph Birmingham. I remain hopeful that similar encounters of reconciliation, healing, and peace between survivors-victims and perpetrators will continue to occur. I pray that asking for and granting forgiveness will make possible the transforming of the scars of sexual abuse into the "kind of liberty and responsibility attuned to the central essence of servant-leadership—a leadership that evokes in others greater health, autonomy, freedom, and wisdom, as well as the deepened will to serve the most important needs of humanity" (Ferch, 2010, p. 77).

Note

The story of Tom Blanchette and Father Joseph Birmingham is excerpted from France (2004) and Investigative Staff of *the Boston Globe* (2002).

References

Ballano, V. O. (2019). *Sociological perspectives on clerical sexual abuse in the Catholic hierarchy: An exploratory structural analysis of social disorganization.* New York, NY: Springer.

Belicki, K., Rourke, J., & McCarthy, M. (2008). Potential dangers of empathy and related conundrums. In W. Malcolm, N. DeCourville, & K. Belicki (Eds.), *Women's reflections on the complexities of forgiveness* (pp. 165–186). New York, NY: Routledge.

Berry, J. (1994/2000). *Lead us not into temptation: Catholic priests and the sexual abuse of children.* New York, NY: Doubleday.

Blaney, J. R. (2009). The Vatican's response to the sexual abuse crisis in America: An image restoration study. In J. R. Blaney & J. P. Zompetti (Eds.), *The rhetoric of Pope John Paul II* (pp. 199–210). Lanham, MD: Lexington.

Bruce, T. C. (2011). *Faithful revolution: How voice of the faithful is changing the church.* New York, NY: Oxford University Press.

Bruni, F., & Burkett, E. (1993/2002). *A gospel of shame: Children, sexual abuse, and the Catholic Church.* New York, NY: Harper Collins.

Buckley, P. (2005). *A sexual life, a spiritual life: A painful journey to inner peace.* Dublin: Liffey Press.

Cafardi, N. P. (2008). *Before Dallas: The U.S. Bishop's response to clergy sexual abuse of children.* Mahwah, NJ: Paulist Press.

Chinnici, J. P. (2010). *When values collide: The Catholic Church, sexual abuse, and the challenges of leadership.* Maryknoll, NY: Orbis.

Clark, R. (2010). *The better way: The church of agape in emerging Corinth.* Eugene, OR: Resource Publications.

Conference of Major Superiors of Men. (2002). Improving pastoral care and accountability in response to the tragedy of sexual abuse. Retrieved from http://cmsm.org~justice-statements/statement-sexual-abuse.shtml

Covey, S. R. (1998). Servant-leadership from the inside out. In L. C. Spears (Ed.), *Insights on leadership: Service, stewardship, spirit, and servant-leadership* (pp. xi–xvii). New York, NY: John Wiley and Sons.

Cozzens, D. (2004). *Sacred silence: Denial and the crisis in the church.* Collegeville, MN: Liturgical Press.

D'Antonio, M. (2013). *Mortal sins: Sex, crime, and the era of Catholic scandal.* New York, NY: Thomas Dunne.

D'Emilio, F., Winfield, N., & Thomas, T. (2019, February 16). *Vatican defrocks former U.S. cardinal McCarrick for sex abuse. Fox News.* Retrieved from https://www.foxnews.com/us/vatican-defrocks-former-us-cardinal-mccarrick-for-sex-abuse

Dokecki, P. R. (2004). *The clergy sexual abuse crisis: Reform and renewal in the Catholic community.* Washington, DC: Georgetown University Press.

Doyle, T. P., Sipe, R. A. W., & Wall, P. J. (2005). *Sex, priests, and secret codes: The Catholic Church's 2000-year paper trail of sexual abuse.* Santa Monica, CA: Volt.

Eugenio, H. (2019, January 15). Guam archdiocese files for bankruptcy to pay off clergy sex abuse claims. *USA Today.* Retrieved from https://www.usatoday.com/story/news/nation/2019/01/15/archdiocese-agana-files-bankruptcy-pay-clergy-sex-abuse-claims/2587462002/

Faggioli, M. (2017, December 20). A report with ramifications: Australia's findings on clerical sex abuse. *Commonweal.* Retrieved from https://www.commonwealmagazine.org/report-ramifications

Ferch, S. R. (2004). Servant-leadership, forgiveness and social justice. In L. C. Spears & M. Lawrence (Eds.), *Practicing servant-leadership: Succeeding through trust, bravery, and forgiveness* (pp. 225–240). San Francisco, CA: Jossey-Bass.

Ferch, S. R. (2005). Servant-leadership, forgiveness and social justice. *The International Journal of Servant Leadership, 1*(1), 97–114.

Ferch, S. R. (2008). Servant leadership and love: The horizon of possible. *The International Journal of Servant Leadership, 4*(1), 15–18.

Ferch, S. R. (2010). Consciousness, forgiveness and gratitude. In D. van Dierendonck & K. Patterson (Eds.), *Servant-leadership: Developments in theory and research.* New York, NY: Palgrave-Macmillan.

Ferch, S. R. (2012). *Forgiveness and power in the age of atrocity: Servant-leadership as a way of life.* Lanham, MD: Lexington Books.

Fleming, P., Lauber-Fleming S., & Matousek, M. T. (2007). *Broken trust: Stories of pain, hope, and healing from clerical abuse survivors and abusers.* New York, NY: Crossroad.

Flynn, E. P. (2003). *Catholics at a crossroads: Coverup, crisis, and cure.* New York, NY: Paraview Press.

Formicola, J. R. (2014). *Clerical sexual abuse: How the crisis changed U.S. Catholic Church-State relations.* New York, NY: Palgrave Macmillan.

Fox, T. C. (2019, May 28). Avoid simplistic solutions to church problems, Sr. Carol Keehan tells graduates. *National Catholic Reporter.* Retrieved from https://www.ncronline.org/news/people/avoid-simplistic-solutions-church-problems-sr-carol-keehan-tells-graduates

France, D. (2004). *Our fathers: The secret life of the Catholic Church in an age of scandal.* New York, NY: Broadway Books.

Francis. (2019, May 7). Vos estis lux mundi. Apostolic letter. Retrieved from http://w2.vatican.va/content/francesco/en/motu_proprio/documents/papa-frances-co-motu-proprio-20190507_vos-estis-lux-mundi.html

Frawley-O'Dea, M. G. (2007). *Perversion of power: Sexual abuse in the Catholic Church.* Nashville, TN: Vanderbilt University Press.

Frawley-O'Dea, M. G., & Goldner, V. (Eds.). (2007). *Predatory priests, silenced victims: The sexual abuse crisis and the Catholic Church.* Mahwah, NJ: The Analytic Press.

Gjelten, T. (2018, August 18). The clergy abuse crisis has cost the Catholic Church $3 billion. *NPR.* Retrieved from https://www.npr.org/2018/08/18/639698062/the-clergy-abuse-crisis-has-cost-the-catholic-church-3-billion

Goode, H., McGee, H. & O'Boyle, C. (Eds.). (2003). *Time to listen: Confronting child sexual abuse by Catholic clergy in Ireland.* Dublin: The Liffey Press.

Goodstein, L., & Otterman, S. (2018, August 14). Catholic priests abused 1,000 children in Pennsylvania, report says. *New York Times.* Retrieved from https://www.nytimes.com/2018/08/14/us/catholic-church-sex-abuse-pennsylvania.html?module=inline

Greenleaf, R. K. (1996). *Seeker and servant.* San Francisco, CA: Jossey-Bass.

Greenleaf, R. K. (2002). *Servant-leadership: A journey into the nature of legitimate power and greatness* (25th Anniversary ed.). Mahwah, NJ: Paulist Press. (Original work published 1977).

Harlan, C., Pitrelli, S., & Boorstein, M. (2018, August 26). Former Vatican ambassador says Popes Francis, Benedict knew of sexual misconduct allegations against McCarrick for years. *Washington Post.*

Horowitz, J. (2019, May 9). Pope issues first rules for Catholic Church worldwide to report sex abuse. *New York Times.* Retrieved from https://www.nytimes.com/2019/05/09/world/europe/pope-francis-abuse-catholic-church.html

Investigative Staff of the *Boston Globe.* (2002). *Betrayal: The crisis in the Catholic Church.* Boston, MA: Little, Brown.

Jenkins, P. (1996). *Pedophiles and priests: Anatomy of a contemporary crisis.* New York, NY: Oxford University Press.

Keenan, M. (2012). *Child sexual abuse and the Catholic Church: Gender, power, and organizational culture.* New York, NY: Oxford University Press.

Kennedy, E. (2002). *The unhealed wound: The church and human sexuality.* New York, NY: St. Martin's Griffin.

King, C. S. (1993). *My life with Martin Luther King, Jr.* (Rev. ed.). New York, NY: Puffin Books.

Kushner, H. S. (1998). In H. J. Cargas & B. V. Fetterman (Eds.), *The sunflower: On the possibilities and limits of forgiveness* (pp. 183–185). New York: Schocken.

Muller, J. E., & Kenney, C. (2004). *Keep the faith, change the church.* Boston, MA: Rodale.

North, J. (1998). The "ideal" of forgiveness. In R. D. Enright & J. North (Eds.), *Exploring forgiveness* (pp. 15–34). Madison: University of Wisconsin Press.

O'Reilly, J. T., & Chalmers, M. S. P. (2014). *The clergy sex abuse crisis and the legal responses.* New York, NY: Oxford University Press.

Paul VI. (1975). *Evangelli nuntiandi: Apostolic exhortation of his holiness, Pope Paul VJ.* Vatican City: Libreria Editrice Vaticana.

Pew Research Center. (2018, October 2). Confidence in Pope Francis down sharply in U.S. Retrieved from https://www.pewforum.org/2018/10/02/confidence-in-pope-francis-down-sharply-in-u-s/

Plante, T. G. (Ed.). (1999). *Bless me father for I have sinned: Perspectives on sexual abuse committed by roman Catholic priests.* Westport, CT: Praeger.

Plante, T. G., & McChesney, K. L. (Eds.). (2011). *Sexual abuse in the Catholic Church: A decade of crisis, 2002–2012.* Santa Barbara, CA: Praeger.

Reese, T. (1996). *Inside the Vatican: The politics and organization of the Catholic Church.* Cambridge, MA: Harvard University Press.

Reilly, M. T. (2018). Catholic dioceses in bankruptcy. Retrieved from https://elibrary.law.psu.edu/cgi/viewcontent.cgi?article=1104&context=bankruptcy

Sherwood, H. (2018, May 18). All Chilean bishops offer their resignation over sexual abuse cover-up. *Guardian.* Retrieved from https://www.theguardian.com/world/2018/may/18/chilean-bishops-offer-their-resignation-over-sexual-abuse-cover-up

Shirky, C. (2008). *Here comes everybody: The power of organizing without organizations.* New York, NY: Penguin.

Sims, B. J. (1997). *Servanthood: Leadership for the third millennium.* Cambridge, MA: Cowley.

Sipe, A. W. R. (1990). *A secret world: Sexuality and the search for celibacy.* New York, NY: Brunner/Mazel.

Sipe, A. W. R. (1995). *Sex, priests, and power: Anatomy of a crisis.* New York, NY: Brunner/Mazel.

Sipe, J. W., & Frick, D. M. (2015). *Seven pillars of servant leadership: Practicing the wisdom of leading by serving* (2nd ed.). Mahwah, NJ: Paulist.

Spears, L. C. (Ed.). (1995). *Reflections on leadership: How Robert K. Greenleaf's theory of servant leadership influenced today's top management thinkers.* New York, NY: John Wiley and Sons.

Spears, L. C. (Ed.). (2004). *Practicing servant leadership: Succeeding through trust, bravery, and forgiveness.* San Francisco, CA: Jossey-Bass.

Spears, L. C. (2015). Introduction to servant-leadership. In S. R. Ferch, L. C. Spears, M. McFarland, & M. R. Carey (Eds.), *Conversations on servant-leadership: Insights on human courage in life and work* (pp. 1–18). Albany, NY: SUNY Press.

Stevenson, B. (2014). *Just mercy: A story of justice and redemption.* New York, NY: Spiel & Grau.

Swidler, L. (1996). *Toward a Catholic constitution.* New York, NY: Crossroad.

Swidler, L. (2007). *Making the church our own: How we can reform the Catholic Church from the ground up.* New York, NY: Sheed and Ward.

Tutu, D. (1999). *No future without forgiveness.* New York, NY: Doubleday.

United States Conference of Catholic Bishops. (1990). *Go and make disciples: A national plan and strategy for Catholic evangelization in the United States.* Washington, DC: United States Conference of Catholic Bishops.

United States Conference of Catholic Bishops. (1996). *Bishop's ad hoc committee on sexual abuse (Vol. 3).* Washington, DC: United States Conference of Catholic Bishops.

United States Conference of Catholic Bishops. (2003). *Promise to protect, pledge to heal: Charter for the protection of children and young people.* Washington, DC: United States Conference of Catholic Bishops.

Van Kuik, A. (1998). *The meaning of servant leadership.* Unpublished doctoral dissertation. University of Manitoba, Canada.

Voiss, J. K. (2015). *Rethinking Christian forgiveness: Theological, philosophical, and psychological explorations.* Collegeville, MN: Michael Glazier.

Westre, K. R. (2003). *Servant-leadership in sport.* Unpublished doctoral dissertation. Gonzaga University, Spokane, WA.

Wiesenthal, S. (1997). *The sunflower: On the possibilities and limits of forgiveness* (Rev. and exp. ed.) New York, NY: Schocken.

Williams, C. V., DeMunck, K., Belicki, K., & DeCourville, N. (2005, June). *The role of empathy and apology in the forgiveness of friends vs. strangers.* Paper presented at the annual meeting of the Canadian Psychological Association, Montreal, Quebec, Canada.

Wills, G. (2000). *Papal sin: Structures of deceit.* New York, NY: Doubleday.

Worthington Jr., E. L. (2006). *Forgiveness and reconciliation: Theory and application.* New York, NY: Routledge.

Zehr, H. (2002). *The little book of restorative justice.* Intercourse, PA: Good Books.

Chapter 10

Fascism and Forgiveness

ELENI PRILLAMAN

Leadership is a term often used in education and in the workplace. But the concept of servant-leadership "is often forgotten, and its principles are directly applicable to those who wish to lead" (Tarr, 1995, p. 79). According to Robert Greenleaf, "servant-leadership begins with the natural feeling that one wants to serve, to serve first. Then conscious choice brings one to aspire to lead" (Spears, 1995, p. 4). When I thought about the word *leader*, there were several other words that came to mind. Words such as *powerful, assertive,* and *manager.* These are the words traditionally found in a résumé or on an employment application, or that applicants use to describe themselves during an interview. But these words do not describe the servant-leader. "The servant-leader is a listener, is task-oriented, has a strategic sense, is eager to understand, to empathize and to collaborate, and does not escape becoming the target of many challenges and tests" (Tarr, 1995, p. 81). Although it can be difficult to empathize with others when their situations seem unfamiliar, a servant-leader finds a way to understand, to serve others. And when a strategic plan is overturned by something unexpected, it may be easy to claim ignorance, but a servant-leader cannot escape challenges or tests, even if she tries to. For this reason, Tarr (1995) claims that "servant-leadership falls into the category of one of those 'impossible things'" (p. 79). I believe servant-leadership derives from a feeling, something with which the servant-leader is born. It is an instinct to serve and lead others, even those she does not know or understand. This is the beauty of servant-leadership.

For some, such as myself, this instinct has to be awakened. It took me a while to realize that servant-leadership had always existed in my life. It had been exemplified in many of my teachers, priests, family members, friends, and even in me. But it was not until my graduate studies that I came to understand the concept of servant-leadership. According to Rieser (1995), servant leadership "serve[s] both you and me. Not just you or me. Us. . . . [It is] the key to my relationship with myself, with other humans, and perhaps with creation" (p. 49). Servant-leadership has taught me how to serve others and myself, and in doing so, I learned how to accept others and myself. "The great power of the servant-leader idea is that it releases us by giving us permission to serve others" (Rieser, 1995, p. 56). This is what servant-leadership did in my life. It released me. Through servant-leadership, I was empowered and able to confront a haunting experience from my past.

In my early teenage years, I became an "employee" for the first time. My brother and I were active in sports and joined a basketball camp for the summer. When we completed the camp, I was offered the opportunity to serve as one of the assistant coaches in the fall. Since then, I have worked at a hospital cafeteria, in a stable, and for major corporations in the entertainment industry. Now I am fortunate to work in education, and I believe it is where God wants me to be. People often ask me about my experiences working in entertainment, but my most memorable job was at the hospital cafeteria. I was sixteen years old and a sheltered teenager. Up until that point I had known only how to be Greek—I went to a Greek school and a Greek Church, had Greek family and friends, and had had no boyfriends. My parents had enrolled me at an all-female liberal arts Catholic high school. We wore uniforms, and my mother picked me up after school every day.

My mother and father have always been exceptional parents and great mentors. Thus, when I decided that I was in need of a job that offered more hours and more pay, I turned to them for help. My mother worked at a hospital and arranged an interview for me with human resources. I had hoped they would find a place for me at the hospital, and they did. I was offered the opportunity to work the tray line at the hospital's cafeteria. I contemplated the position for about a day. I remembered walking downstairs to the cafeteria with my mother during her breaks. There was always the aroma of fresh coffee, and there was a kind cashier. These warm thoughts guided me toward accepting the position.

At the end of my first day, I remember thinking that I never again wanted to wear scrubs or a hairnet. I was assigned to work the fried food station on the tray line, while others worked in the milk, bread, soup, coffee, and dessert sections. All of us were needed in order for the tray line to function effectively. When a tray had been delivered to every patient, on every floor, the tray line stopped. Then I would tidy up my station as quickly as possible so I could take a short break before cleanup duty. I usually had about ten minutes to eat a snack or chug some fountain soda. Then it was back to the cafeteria and to our assignments on the cleanup line. Each tray would come back to the line, and depending on where I was assigned, I would have to strip trays of coffee cups, plates, or silverware. The leftover food was thrown into the garbage disposal. Many of the trays would return soaked in vomit or blood. Some would still have needles on them. I used to pretend my easily torn latex gloves were protective armor. By the end of my first week, I was regretting my decision to take the job. The cafeteria was always cold, and it resembled what I imagined a slaughterhouse would look like. My coworkers did not help make work more tolerable, either. Everyone was miserable. People often arrived at work inebriated, and they frequently used profanity. This was the first time I had African American and Hispanic coworkers. In fact, this was the most interaction I had ever had with people of other races and cultures. I remember feeling timid and fearful of them, but I did not know why. A couple of months passed, and I continued working at the cafeteria. From a young age, my parents had instilled a strong work ethic in me. Once I had committed to something, it was rare for me to quit. The hours felt like days, the days like weeks. I officially dreaded going to work. Then something unexpected happened at the cafeteria. A new supervisor was hired.

Tim was shy and often hid under his baseball cap. He seemed to be no more than a couple years older than I was, and I found him attractive. He was always fair-minded, unlike his predecessor, who used to assign the most coveted jobs to her closest friends. Most of the employees were much older than Tim and me. Perhaps this is why it seemed like I had nothing in common with them. Each time I arrived at work I would greet Tim with a hello. I thought it was the courteous way to treat your supervisor. Then we began to talk more, and before I knew it, we were spending our breaks together. Sometimes I would sit outside with him while he smoked a cigarette. Other times we would have a snack inside.

Our coworkers began to question our friendship, but Tim never commented on anything that they said. He rarely spoke to any of the other employees unless it was necessary.

One night I was on floors. This meant that when everyone was finished with their work, I had to spray down all of the cafeteria floors in preparation for the breakfast tray line the next morning. Tim could not leave until all of the employees were gone, so he helped me. He also offered to drive me home, since I lived only a couple blocks away from the hospital. My mother was waiting in the driveway when I arrived. Tim introduced himself to my mother and was very respectful toward her. My mother was impressed by Tim. She agreed to let him drive me home whenever I needed a ride. Tim began calling me at home and inviting me out on the weekends. It seemed like our friendship had quickly escalated to a relationship. My parents were very strict and did not allow me to date. But I had access to a family vehicle and agreed to meet Tim at his friend's house one night. When I entered the home I was taken aback by all of the people. I recognized some girls from my high school. One of them sat next to me in French class. She always wore white laces in her shoes. When I asked her why she had changed her original laces, she said it was to represent white power. When I told my mother about the girl in French class, she had said, "Don't be rude, but don't be too friendly either." At that moment I was reminded that I had lied to my mother, and I was alarmed at being in the same home as the girl with the white laces. My conscience started to feel heavy, and I explained to Tim that I felt ill. He walked me to my car and gave me a peck on the cheek. I never spoke to him about why I really felt ill that night.

A few days later I learned that two of my friends had been assaulted at a party. When they had arrived at the party, they had noticed a Confederate flag hanging on the wall, the band Skrewdriver was playing on a radio, and the people there had swastika tattoos on their arms and legs. My friends immediately sensed danger and rushed out of the apartment. Beer bottles were thrown at their heads as they raced down the stairs and out the front door. One of my friends fell to the ground, and he was kicked repeatedly. Eventually, my friends got away, and thankfully they were well enough to share their experiences with me. When I asked why they had been attacked, they explained that they had unknowingly gone to a party hosted by one of the town's greatest white power advocates. They told me his name. Tim's name.

Innumerable thoughts swirled around in my head. I was in denial and wondering how common it was for people to share the same name.

Determined to find out for myself, I made plans to visit Tim's apartment over the weekend. I went alone, and as I walked up the flights of stairs, I thought about my friends running down them while darting beer bottles. I knocked on his door, and he welcomed me inside. Ironically, he had been watching *Eye for an Eye*, a somber film about retributive justice. Then I saw it—the flag, the CDs, and the swastika tattoo on his leg accompanied by a tribute to the SS. I was in the apartment. I searched for a reason to leave, but regardless of how sick I felt, I knew that excuse had been exhausted. I spent one hour with Tim in his racist, white-power-infested apartment and told him I had to be home before curfew. He walked me to my car, and I drove home feeling restless. That night, I called Tim to confront him about his lifestyle and to blame him for what had happened to my friends. He admitted that everything my friends told me was true, but he denied having any part in it. As Tutu (1999) wrote, "Those accused of horrendous deeds almost always try to find ways out of even admitting that they were indeed capable of such deeds. They adopt the denial mode and take refuge in feigned ignorance" (p. 269). Tim apologized for allowing the incident to occur. He expressed his feelings toward me and assured me that if he had known they were my friends he would have stopped it. This comment did not sit well with me. How could I forgive someone who willingly allowed another person to be assaulted in front of his own eyes? The only wrong Tim saw in the situation was that my friends were harmed. I could not understand how this was the same person who was fair-minded in the workplace and who cared about me.

Our conversation intensified as we talked about Tim's childhood, his beliefs, why he was so angry toward other races, and the horrible things he had done. I learned that the scar I had seen on his head was from a lead pipe—and a fight he had picked with some Hispanic men in his neighborhood. I learned that the reason he never spoke to our coworkers was because he hated them. He went on to inform me that Hitler had been an intelligent person, deserving of respect and recognition. I was furious but kept Tim on the phone long enough to ask him to consider the millions of innocent people who were tortured and killed during World War II. Then I heard a click. The conversation had ended.

The next day, I sat in my backyard, soaking up the sun and listening to music, and could not help but think about the conversation I had had with Tim. I wondered if I was in trouble. What about my family? Would I find crosses burning in our front yard? I heard the phone ring inside the house, and my mother called me in to answer it. It was Tim. He apologized, and said he would change. I begged him to change, but

I could not accept Tim's apology. Tutu (1999) believes that "it is and has always been God's intention that we should live in friendship and harmony," but I did not know how to continue a friendship with Tim (p. 263). I had never had a problem forgiving my friends, but what Tim had done, and who he was, was greater than anything I could comprehend. A few weeks later, Tim quit working at the cafeteria, and I never spoke to him again. But Tim became a recurring presence in my mind.

During my graduate studies, I enrolled in a course on servant-leadership, justice, and forgiveness. I read Holocaust literature and watched *The Diary of Anne Frank.* And I began to think about Tim. I wondered if he truly had changed. After conducting a brief Internet search, I discovered that Tim was the leader of a racist skinhead organization. I instantly felt saddened and resentful toward him. I thought about my family, who had died in World War II, the genocide of the Jews, and of Elie Wiesel. When Wiesel (2003) was finally liberated from the Nazis, his "first act as a free man was to throw himself onto the provisions. Not of revenge" (p. 99). How could Wiesel face the atrocities of the war and not seek revenge on the Nazis, while I sought revenge on my German?

Tim had not changed, and I blamed myself. I could not help but wonder whether the outcome would have been different had I forgiven Tim years ago. If I had accepted Tim's apology for his past, maybe he would have changed his future. He might have treated others differently. He might not be serving as the leader of an internationally recognized racist organization. When my mother had arranged that meeting for me with human resources, I had hoped I would get hired for a job. I had no idea I would come face to face with racism.

As a result, I was left with a challenge. Something inside me wanted to contact Tim and offer my forgiveness.

> Forgiveness does not mean condoning what has been done. In the act of forgiveness we are declaring our faith in the future of a relationship and in the capacity of the wrongdoer to make a new beginning on a course that will be different from the one that caused wrong. (Tutu, 1999, pp. 271–273)

But I was scared of what repercussions could come from this powerful and freeing transformation. And I was scared of Tim.

Racist organizations are notorious for violence and hate crimes. Thus, there was a monumental amount of risk associated with contacting Tim. *Risk* is defined as "exposure to the chance of injury or loss; danger, hazard, peril" (Bethel, 1995, p. 135). Contacting Tim would be perilous, but "risk taking is integral to both leadership and living" (Bethel, 1995, p. 135). Tutu (1999) wrote, "When you embark on the business of asking for and granting forgiveness, you are taking a risk" (p. 269). And Bethel (1995) said, "Risk taking becomes your servant when it is part of a plan—part of a powerful picture of the changes, a vision of the future" (p. 135). It "can fuel enthusiasm and expansion, which leads to doing even more" (p. 145). The risk I felt then was reminiscent of what I had felt years ago, when I went to Tim's apartment, confronted him for his actions, and challenged his beliefs. What I realized was that I had always wanted to forgive Tim. But forgiveness is a key characteristic of the servant-leader, and the servant-leader inside me had not been awakened.

Once the servant-leader within is awakened, "it can expand human potential. It offers the individual a means to personal growth—spiritually, professionally, emotionally, and intellectually" (Spears, 1995, pp. 11–12). Leadership is important in education and in the workplace, but I believe it applies to all aspects of life. And servant-leadership involves living life in a way that will positively benefit others. "It is a long term, transformational approach to life and work, in essence, a way of being that has the potential to create positive change throughout our society" (p. 4). By forgiving others, we empower ourselves and positively influence our society. I want to offer Tim my forgiveness in the hope of releasing myself from the past and "raising the quality of life throughout society" in the future (p. 12). This hope is what caused me to share my story.

Previously, the fear and anger I harbored from my experiences with Tim had justified my reasons for avoiding him. And in order to prevent endangering my family or myself, I will not contact Tim. But eventually, when I do see Tim again, I will not avoid him. I will respect him for the fair-minded and caring way he had always treated me. And I will offer him my forgiveness. There is no future without forgiveness. I am optimistic that forgiveness can heal my negative feelings. I can only hope it will heal Tim too.

References

Bethel, S. M. (1995). Servant-leadership and corporate risk taking: When risk taking makes a difference. In L. C. Spears (Ed.), *Reflections on leadership* (pp. 135–148). New York, NY: John Wiley & Sons.

Rieser, C. (1995). Claiming servant-leadership as your heritage. In L. C. Spears (Ed.), *Reflections on leadership* (pp. 49–60). New York, NY: John Wiley & Sons.

Spears, L. C. (1995). Introduction: Servant-leadership and the Greenleaf legacy. In L. C. Spears (Ed.), *Reflections on leadership* (pp. 1–16). New York, NY: John Wiley & Sons.

Tarr, D. L. (1995). The strategic toughness of servant-leadership. In L. C. Spears (Ed.), *Reflections on leadership* (pp. 79–86). New York, NY: John Wiley & Sons.

Tutu, D. (1999). *No future without forgiveness.* New York, NY: Random House.

Wiesel, E. (2003). *Night.* Saint Paul: EMC/Paradigm.

Chapter 11

Amazing Grace

Seeking Grace and Forgiveness in Law Enforcement

LENA PACE

Amazing Grace

Amazing Grace, how sweet the sound,
That saved a wretch like me.
I once was lost, but now am found
Was blind but now I see . . .
T'was Grace that brought us safe thus far,
And Grace will lead us home.

On the thirteenth day of May each year, thousands of people gather in Judiciary Square in Washington, DC. As the sun draws low in the sky, buses begin to arrive, police escorts' lights and sirens announcing the survivors. Family after family disembarks, stepping down in front of the reflecting pool of the National Law Enforcement Officers Memorial. They are handed red roses and are escorted to their seats by an officer in dress uniform. Around their necks hang their identities—name; status as coworker, wife, husband, friend, survivor of a fallen officer; and date their officer was killed in the line of duty. Surrounding them as they step forward, the memorial wall wraps around the square, garbed in wreaths, notes, pictures drawn by the children of the fallen, agency patches, and people crying as they touch the engraved name of their loved one. Later, once everyone is seated and darkness has fallen, the crowd is silent as the first notes of a well-known hymn pierce the night air, echoing off stone. "Amazing Grace," a woman or man or bagpipe sings out, "how sweet the sound."

On August 9, 2002, when I had recently graduated from the Federal Law Enforcement Training Center, I received a phone call from my park superintendent, informing me that my friend and academy classmate, Kristopher William Eggle, had been murdered in the line of duty. Chasing drug smugglers who'd driven across the Mexican border, Kris had been ambushed and shot below his body armor with an AK-47. His murderer was almost immediately shot and killed by other officers. Kris knew he was dying, dropped his duty belt, and tried to stop the bleeding before crumpling to the ground. His best friend was the first on scene. Kris bled out before the ambulance reached him.

In 2003, I was a survivor at the memorial. Since that year, I have attended National Police Week almost every May. My experiences each year stay with me, both burden and motivation. I have met many survivors, some of whom travel to the memorial every year. This year, I met a man who told me about his son, who had been killed almost ten years ago. The man handed me his business card that identified him as a "Survivor" and listed his son's agency, rank, name, and end of watch.[1] His identity had become inextricably linked to the death of his son.

The death of my friend Kris is very much tied to my professional identity. And because law enforcement is a career that necessarily permeates one's personal life, it is also tied to my personal identity. Like the man with the business card, I am a survivor. And, like him, I have carried with me a great deal of anger and bitterness, not only toward the man who shot my friend, but toward every person who would harm a police officer, leave a child without a mother, or a wife without a husband. It is that anger that has carried me forward in my career as a spokeswoman for officer safety, and for the professionalization of law enforcement in my agency, and as a leader who puts people first. But perhaps anger is not the best motivation, for what good can come of something so dark?

Greenleaf (1977/2002) says that a servant-leader must "view any problem in the world as in here, inside oneself, not out there" (p. 57), and as such, I begin to look inside myself and at the cultural norms and assumptions I have accepted in my life and my career in order to discover how to overcome this anger and instead build positive, healthy community. Ferch (2012) quotes Brian Mitchell, a police officer who experienced

South Africa's apartheid years: "As a policeman . . . you only see the bad side of life. You are involved in that evil side of life" (p. 40). As a leader in a law enforcement agency, I have experienced both the darkness that life has to offer and the joy and fulfillment that comes from a life dedicated to service to society. Greenleaf (1977/2002), who coined the term *servant-leadership*, says that in order to lead, leaders must first become aware of the truth of their situation, and that while awareness might not bring a person comfort, it will allow them to be awakened in order to better see things as they are. Through this process, I hope to become more aware of the truth of law enforcement in society today, and of my own ability as a police officer to both forgive and serve.

It is telling, I think, that the song "Amazing Grace" has become a central feature of police funerals, as the lyrics speak of the power of forgiveness, of our own humanity and shortcomings, and of the capacity of grace to help us overcome life's challenges. There is power in grace, and grace can help us overcome the personal and national consequences of the anger, bitterness, and resentment that lingers after a peace officer is killed in the line of duty. There is a brokenness in law enforcement today, and a need for a change, for police agencies to adopt a servant-leadership approach to organization and community relationships. In this chapter I explore the role of forgiveness—both asking for and granting forgiveness—as a way of healing and moving forward, both for the family members of the fallen and for the law enforcement profession as a whole as it carries the pain of these murders over the years. I suggest that we can create positive outcomes from the great deal of passion and energy that are created when a community comes together over such a tragedy. Ultimately, I believe that through such coming together and healing, law enforcement officer killings might be reduced on a nationwide basis.

Collective Responsibility

A famous Norman Rockwell painting, *The Runaway*, depicts a uniformed state trooper leaning over to help a young boy in a soda shop, an iconic ode to the reason I and my brothers and sisters in law enforcement chose this profession: to serve. The painting hangs in police stations around the country, and even graces the wall in my own office, a reminder of our mission, which is to help people. In today's society, I believe that this image of the police officer as savior is often forgotten, and that the relationship between many police agencies and the communities they serve are in need of repair.

In the United States, on average, a peace officer is killed in the line of duty every 54 hours (Officer Down Memorial Page, 2012). These peace officers walk a "thin blue line" between the people of this nation and those who would hurt them, swearing their lives in the service of others, knowing that on any given day they may be called names, spit on, stabbed, shot at, or even killed. In the culture of today, they will be ridiculed and hated, as is evidenced by popular music that pokes fun at law enforcement, video games that grant points for killing cops, and the media that smears the names of good officers who are forced to kill in defense of self or others. I have lived my adult life knowing that many hate me, my profession, and what I stand for. Even those who say that they support law enforcement will often attack the credibility of an officer who issues them a ticket for speeding, will sing along to the lyrics of a song about killing the police, or, more commonly, will remain silent as an officer, dedicated to a life of service, is killed every other day.

It bears mentioning, of course, that not every police officer is honorable, and that officers may at times betray the trust of those they are sworn to protect. American police history is rife with stories of the violation of civil liberties, of racism and excessive force. In a recent meeting with two representatives of the gay community within my jurisdiction, I was told stories from their youth of being singled out by police because of their sexual orientation. While the officers within my agency today had not participated in those specific acts, the pain of these men remained fresh, and I empathized with their ongoing mistrust of law enforcement. By sitting down with these men for an hour on their patio, listening to their stories, and offering open and honest dialogue, we began to heal the rift between us. Because their trust had been violated, it was incumbent upon me to be the one to reach out.

Wiesenthal (1998) speaks to the nature of collective responsibility for crimes against persons, in reference to the atrocities committed during the Holocaust. "No German can shrug off the responsibility," he writes. "As a member of a guilty nation he cannot simply walk away like a passenger leaving a tramcar" (p. 93). By the same token, Tutu (1999) theorizes that when a nation forgets or ignores such evils, it in effect victimizes the injured parties a second time by not acknowledging their pain. He writes that we must "look the beast in the eye" in order to move forward into the future (p. 28). Yet in the United States, more often than not, it seems to be accepted unquestioningly that officers will be killed, an unfortunate result of the dangerous jobs they do. Tutu suggests that apartheid was allowed to continue in South Africa for so long because so many people turned a blind eye, accepting the comfort of the status quo and failing to examine the assumptions by which they lived.

Patrick (2005) writes, "The protection of the lives and safety of those who enforce the law is the responsibility of the society that gives them the mission and reaps the benefit of that service" (p. 45). Balic (1998) argues that "those who might appear uninvolved in the actual crimes, but who tolerate acts of torture, humiliation, and murder, are certainly also guilty. Looking away may be a comfortable but ultimately disastrous path, the effects of which are incalculable" (p. 110). It is time for the citizens of the United States to stand behind those who choose to serve and protect them. And as a first step in this process, those of us who serve and protect must step forward and offer love and forgiveness to our communities.

Law Enforcement in America

National Police Week offers an opportunity not only for survivors to gather and heal but also for the law enforcement community to come together, brothers and sisters united in the same cause: to serve and protect. Martin Luther advocated a strong connection between life and work, and Thompson (2000) supports the same today. Luther believed that vocation should be raised to "an unprecedented level of importance in the life of the individual," imbued with "meaning and purpose" (p. 17). The law enforcement profession offers—even requires—this high level of dedication to work, in large part because of the immense responsibility these officers have to protect society and its citizens (Grossman & Christensen, 2008). With great responsibility comes the potential for great power, and it is the acceptance of this responsibility that sets law enforcement and the military apart from the majority of society. This separation, however, need not be oppositional.

The law enforcement profession is tasked with enforcing society's widely accepted moral rules. Wall (2008) argues that such rules are "necessary for an orderly social existence" and asks, "What would society be like if there were no rules against lying, stealing, breaking promises, and killing each other?" (p. 27). In a lecture delivered at the US Naval Academy, William J. Bennett argued that military (and, by extension, police) action is about honor, and "about defending those noble and worthy things that deserve defending, even if it comes at a high cost" (as cited in Grossman & Christensen, 2008, p. 180). Police officers, then, stand united in that cause, having accepted for themselves and their families a vocation that asks so much of them. It is this common dilemma, the shared goals, and dedication to vocation that bring law enforcement officers together like family.

Servant-Leadership

In his call for a new style of leadership, Greenleaf (1998) acknowledged that "the outlook for our civilization at this moment is not promising, probably because not enough of us care enough for our fellow humans" (p. 22). As Tutu (1999) points out, "We are experiencing a radical brokenness in all of existence. . . . Ours has been the bloodiest century known to human history" (p. 264). And in this world, police officers agree to stand between those who would do harm and those who would be harmed, using whatever means necessary to keep society safe and peaceful. These officers accept this obligation willingly, but at the same time, law enforcement "must reckon with the fact that [the average, healthy officer] comes from a civilization in which aggression . . . is prohibited and unacceptable" (Grossman & Christensen, 2008, p. 163). "Because if we did not have warriors, men and women willing to move toward the sounds of the guns and confront evil . . . our civilization would no longer exist" (p. 5). In order to reconcile these feelings, the law enforcement profession has adopted a culture that serves to separate "us" from "them"; in the words of Grossman and Christensen (2008), "sheepdogs" and "sheep." It is no wonder society often questions, fears, and even hates that which they believe law enforcement represents.

By the very nature of their mission to serve and protect, though, police officers have chosen to serve their fellow humans, and so are in a unique position to build community and promote healing. Greenleaf (1977/2002) wrote that "the servant leader is servant first. . . . It begins with the natural feeling that one wants to serve" (p. 27). In addition to emphasizing service to others, servant-leadership calls for "a holistic approach to work, building a sense of community, and a sharing of power" (Spears, 2002, p. 4). As community protectors and stewards, police officers are role models, community leaders, and servants of the greater good.

Law enforcement agencies in today's society are also limited by their largely pyramidal hierarchical structures, a traditional form of organization that "weakens informal links, dries up channels of honest reaction and feedback, and creates limiting chief-subordinate relationships" (Greenleaf 1977/2002, p. 76). In addition, the bitterness and anger we hold on to in response to police officer assaults and murders holds us back. Spears (2002) argues that today's organizations must transition from this command-and-control structure of organization into a newer type of leadership, "one based on teamwork and community, one that seeks to involve others in decision making, one strongly based in ethical and caring behavior, and one that is attempting to enhance the personal growth of workers while improving the caring and quality of our institutions" (p. 2).

By adopting a servant-leadership approach to organizational structure, leadership, and community, the law enforcement profession—our peace-keepers—could have great power to help turn this bloodiest of centuries into a time of peace and healing. As Spears (2002) points out, "A particular strength of servant leadership is that it encourages everyone to actively seek opportunities to both serve and lead others, thereby setting up the potential for raising the quality of life throughout society" (p. 13).

Greenleaf (1998) posits that "the strongest, most productive institution over a long period of time is one in which, other things being equal, there is the largest amount of voluntary action in support of the goals of the institution" (p. 51). In the same way, the strongest society is one in which its members voluntarily support the greater good; "caring for persons, the more able and the less able serving each other, is the rock upon which a good society is built" (Greenleaf 1977/2002, p. 62). Police officers, then, must not only show strength in enforcement of laws but must also seek to gain voluntary compliance through love, compassion, and caring. As Martin Luther King Jr. said, "I believe that unarmed truth and unconditional love will have the final word in reality" (as cited in Ferch, 2012, p. xvii).

Take the many brave and dedicated police officers who patrol the roadways, writing tickets or making arrests in order to keep motorists safe by ensuring that motorists understand the consequences of their choice to endanger themselves and others. Now imagine what our roadways would be like if the police stopped enforcing traffic laws. The goal of speeding enforcement is not to punish those who choose to violate the law but instead to encourage voluntary compliance through education and deterrence. Many police agencies today have embarked on public education campaigns, working with communities and citizens to instill in them an understanding of the dangers of speeding. This is only one example among many in law enforcement today of a holistic view of service to and within our communities, an example that can and should provide a model for the enforcement of all laws.

Now imagine if fewer officers were killed each year because America's citizens understood and believed in the service they provided, and wanted to keep them safe? Greenleaf (1977/2002) criticized the traditional perspective of society's laws. "When any action is regulated by law," he wrote, "the incentive for individual conscience to govern is diminished—unless the law coincides with almost universally held moral standards (p. 148). Law enforcement is in a position, through servant-leadership, to help heal the rift between society's conscience and those laws that are necessary for a whole society.

Forgiveness

Tutu (1999) argues that "we cannot go on nursing grudges even vicariously for those who cannot speak for themselves any longer" (p. 279). In order to build community and have a hopeful future, he says, we must learn to forgive (Tutu, 1999). In my experience, though, the law enforcement community has a difficult time with this notion of forgiveness. By the very nature of the job that we do in bringing justice to victims and criminals to justice, we are not prone to forgive easily. And when a member of our community is murdered, we feel a collective loss, and that pain carries us forward to try and prevent that evil from happening again, as I did after the murder of my friend Kris. Ferch (2012) writes, "When a death comes to a family, a kind of fierce grip on that which transcends all of us can sometimes be a potent and unifying force below everything" (p. xxi). At the same time, such loss provides us with an opportunity to become closer to one another, to heal and restore our relationships: "to be alive is to know an ever-present cycle of recovery and loss" (p. xxii).

As servant-leadership is focused on love and caring for those within an organization—or a society—so must a servant-leader accept "that imperfections are part of the human condition" (Williams, 2002, p. 68). A capacity to both ask forgiveness and grant it must be at the heart of such service. As Martin Luther King Jr. wrote, "We must develop and maintain the capacity to forgive. [The one] who is devoid of the power to forgive is devoid of the power to love" (as cited in Ferch, 2012, p. 7).

Asking Forgiveness

Tutu (1999) asserts that when a relationship has been damaged, the only possible way toward the future is through forgiveness: "the truth hurts, but silence kills" (p. 107). Both parties, the wronged and the perpetrator, must be willing to reconcile, and asking forgiveness—stepping forward and being willing to humbly look inside oneself—is a first step in this process; forgiveness follows confession (Tutu, 1999).

What does it mean to ask forgiveness? If I am asking that law enforcement officers fill their hearts with forgiveness and grace, then I must be willing to first explore my own capacity for forgiveness. Forgiveness is an integral step toward healing a relationship, and I would argue that the relationship between law enforcement and the citizens they are sworn to protect is broken and in need of repair. Forgiveness is not an easy task, but is a way of "declaring our faith in the future" (Tutu, 1999, p. 273), that we can once again be whole. My own personal story of forgiveness illustrates this point.

I'm not sure I realized the need for a healing in my relationship with my sister until I invited her to visit last winter. I was home for the holidays, and my sister found a babysitter for my niece so that we could have time just for the two of us. As we sipped our wine, our conversation started out lighthearted but quickly moved into more difficult territory. My sister is five years my junior, and our childhood was an interesting one. While the details of our story are deeply personal, what is important is that when I left home at the age of 16, I left my eleven-year-old sister behind, and our relationship suffered. As the older sister, I found myself between my parents and their youngest child, and as a result, I tried to take on a more mature role than I was perhaps ready for. In an attempt to be a mentor, I became arrogant, feeling superior in my career and my life, and so closed myself off to things I could have learned from my younger sibling. Although we had eventually come to a place where we loved and tolerated each other, bad blood lingered between us.

As we talked on this cold Alaskan winter night, a feeling of deep humility and shame came over me as I verbally acknowledge the harm

I had caused my sister and our relationship. I realized how I had externalized the causes for our conflict, either blaming her or blaming our parents. My language changed. I began to tell her my story from my perspective, taking ownership for the first time of the harm I had caused her. There was silence, and there were tears, and there was more wine. I asked for her forgiveness. She nodded, and we hugged. Today my sister is one of the people I admire most in this world. I often feel that her wisdom, her perspective on life, and love, and family, is deeper and more real than mine. She grounds me, and supports me, and her friendship is more important to me than most other things in this world.

Asking for forgiveness, for me, was an unfolding of brutal truth, a breaking down and rebuilding that was painful but cleansing. I hadn't realized that our relationship needed repairing, but after that night, having finally brought so much out into the open, we began to take a new and better path. As Tutu (1999) writes, our forgiveness created a more "robust and resilient relationship" (p. 20). It is true that "forgiveness asks us to love our way through a little bit of messiness" (p. 17), but in the end, the future of my relationship with my sister—one of the most important people in my life—is stronger and healthier than it has ever been.

It is in this spirit that I ask other law enforcement officers to open their hearts to the possibility of forgiveness—not in order to forget wrongs that have been done but to acknowledge them, face them head on, and in doing so become capable of letting go of the bitterness that would otherwise reside in our hearts.

Granting Forgiveness and Restorative Justice

Tutu (1999) differentiates retributive justice, "whose chief goal is to be punitive" (p. 54) from restorative justice, in which "the central concern is the healing of breaches, the redressing of imbalances, the restoration of broken relationships, a seeking to rehabilitate both the victim and the perpetrator" (p. 55). Although I am a part of the "justice system," as a law enforcement officer, I have always felt disconnected from the end result of those actions I take in the field. I arrest someone for a wrong they've done, I book them into jail, and sometimes I testify in court. Their fate, though—their future within the penal system—is something I have not spent much time considering. I do my job, and "the system" does its part. If I am to ask Americans to increase their awareness of the battles that police officers face, however, I must also increase my own awareness by facing the realities and failings of the American justice system of which I am a part.

If I am to consider, then, that true justice relating to the enforcement of laws should be restorative rather than retributive, I must factor the longer-term consequences of my police actions into my decision making on the job. It also means that, with forgiveness in my heart, I must never lose sight of the humanity and worth of those I come in contact with, regardless of the wrongs they may have done. As Tutu (1999) found during his time on the Truth and Reconciliation Commission in South Africa that "however diabolical the act, it did not turn the perpetrator into a demon" (p. 83). When a police officer fails to respect a person they come in contact with, they not only dehumanize that person but risk dehumanizing themselves; "anger, resentment, lust for revenge, even success through aggressive competitiveness, are corrosive" (p. 31).

In considering forgiveness in the case of a fallen officer, one must ask who the injured party is. In responding to Wiesenthal's (1998) story of a Nazi soldier asking forgiveness of a Jew for his crimes, several scholars argue that murder cannot be forgiven because the wronged person is no longer able to grant that forgiveness. In any murder, though, are there not other victims? Certainly in the case of a fallen officer, not only are immediate friends and family are harmed but also coworkers, the community he or she protected, and beyond. Chris Cosgriff, founder of the Officer Down Memorial Page, which records and remembers fallen officers each day and throughout history, says that "when a police officer is killed, it's not an agency that loses an officer, it is an entire nation" (Officer Down Memorial Page, 2012). I would argue, then, that there are many people who might be in a position to forgive.

Forgiving Murder

An even more difficult question must be asked: is murder forgivable? The Dalai Lama argues that we should forgive those who have committed even the worst atrocities (Wiesenthal, 1998, p. 129). However, Fox (1998) argues that "some sins are too big for forgiveness" (p. 145), and Ozick (1998) echoes that "murder is irrevocable" and that "there are spots forgiveness cannot wash out" (p. 215). I am reminded of the story that Tutu tells of the mother of a girl, Suzie, who was murdered in South Africa, and who had forgiveness in her heart for those who committed the murder. The mother wrote, "Anger, hatred, resentment, bitterness, revenge—they are death dealing spirits, and they will 'take our lives.' . . . I believe that the only way we can be whole, healthy, happy persons is to learn to forgive" (Goulden, 1998, p. 156).

In stark contrast to this mother's sentiment, I see posts on social media on a regular basis urging those of us in law enforcement to speak out when a "cop killer" is up for parole. "No parole for cop killers!" the posts exclaim, asking that we write letters and deny their release. Tutu (1999), however, asks us to "condemn the sin while being filled with compassion for the sinner" (p. 83). For what do we gain by hating the man who kills a police officer? For the man with the business card, he has gained nothing but lost his identity in the process. Heschel (1998) asks whether the issue is even really one of forgiveness, or whether it is instead "how the victims . . . can live without bitterness and vengeance, without losing their own humanity" (p. 173).

I believe that the key understanding here is, as Tutu and his colleagues believed during the Truth and Reconciliation Commission proceedings in South Africa after the fall of apartheid, that people do have the ability to change, show remorse, and even reenter society. To believe otherwise would be to dehumanize the perpetrators of crimes, and in doing so, dehumanize ourselves. By instead focusing on partnerships between public servants and the communities they police, through educational and outreach efforts, the mutual humanity and health of the community as a whole are improved.

I want to make two important points here. First, police officers are some of the most honorable, honest, caring people I have ever met. My argument is not that police officers are in the business of dehumanizing people, or that they do not appropriately care for their communities. Quite the opposite; police officers have dedicated their lives to the service of others, even at the expense of their own families and their own lives. I believe, however, that law enforcement agencies can do more to share these successes with their communities, and can include communities as partners in collaboration for the common good. Second, I believe that while many police agencies are very caring organizations, few of them, in my experience, have wholly adopted a servant-leadership way of being. While many leadership scholars acknowledge that there are times—in states of emergency, in states of war—when an authoritarian, top-down leadership format is called for, it is becoming clear that strict command-and-control leadership is "an outmoded, inaccurate, and dangerous model" (as cited in Braye, 2002, p. 296). Retired Lieutenant Colonel Ruby Braye argues that a servant-leadership model would be effective in today's military, and I posit that, by extension, it would also be effective—and is needed—in today's law enforcement. "Because soldiers are expected to make the supreme sacrifice—give their lives, if necessary, in defense of the nation and all that we stand for," she writes, "it has become clear that today's soldiers are not as willing to blindly follow leaders without question" (p. 296). Braye (2002) continues to illuminate the need to become aware of the concerns and pain in the lives of those who are served through acts of love and caring.

Moving Forward

Littell (1998) writes that one of the keys to achieving a higher level of human interaction is "in the enforcement of law by reliable stewards of public power" (p. 200). In my experience, anger and resentment at officer deaths is holding the ranks of those public stewards back from their true potential. Consider what might be accomplished if that bitterness were turned toward good? Forgiveness, as Tutu reminds us, does not mean that we forget or make light of the crime done. Instead, it requires that we face those wrongs but do not dwell on them or let them bring us down as well.

On January 1, 2012, park ranger Margaret Anderson attempted to stop a man in a vehicle who failed to stop at a chain checkpoint on Mount Rainier, in Washington State. Before she was even able to get out of her vehicle, Anderson was confronted with a hail of gunfire, one round striking her in the head and killing her. She was the mother of two young children. The man who committed this horrible act subsequently died of exposure as he fled through the snow from the officers who tracked him. The National Park Service cried in collective agony when this tragedy occurred, just as it did in 2002 when my friend Kris was killed. Anderson's widower and children will be among the survivors at National Police Week in 2013.

I believe that one of the reasons so many police officers are assaulted and murdered is that society has accepted—either through the implicit endorsement of such acts as we see in music and video games that make light of such violence, or through silence and lack of outrage—the murder of these servants of public peace. While I agree that "nothing should happen that would let haters or murderers off the hook by assuring them that grace is readily available" (Marty, 1998, p. 211), I also believe that, as Kushner (1998) argues, we only hurt ourselves by holding on to our resentment of these wrongdoers. It is time we as a society agree to protect those who protect us. We must see these murders for what they are, and never forget them, but use the energy and passion they create for good and positive things.

A new initiative called "Below 100" is an example of such action, a program in which the responsibility for many officer deaths is taken by the officers themselves, who focus on the decision making and mindset that put them into the situations in which they found themselves in danger. Other examples from around the country illustrate the powerful role police agencies can play in bringing about community reconciliation and healing. Examples of this type of "community oriented policing," in which law enforcement partners with its constituents to gain voluntary compliance, include police officers conducting career fairs for Muslim youth in inner-city New York, officers reading to children in Las Vegas classrooms, and officers teaching families about bicycle safety in neighborhoods across the country. Programs such as these show the positive and healing nature of love and forgiveness, and the benefits of power sharing.

In the spirit of such positive and hopeful programs as those mentioned above, I invite police leaders to join me in partnering with our communities to bridge the growing gap between protectors and protected. Here are a few action items that might begin to move us in that direction:

1. Implement a servant-leadership approach both within law enforcement organizations and between these agencies and their constituencies. Be the first to reach out to those who would distrust the police.

2. Empower law enforcement officers to become involved in their communities as servants and friends; practice community-oriented policing. Work to eliminate the oversimplified us-versus-them mentality that separates us.

3. Hold law enforcement officers to a high standard of accountability; ensure that complaints of misconduct are immediately and thoroughly investigated.

4. Encourage awareness of cultural norms within law enforcement agencies. Provide training to officers and police leaders

in justice and forgiveness; work to eliminate vengeance as a motivator, instead promoting healing and reconciliation.

5. Never accept that law enforcement deaths are acceptable, that they are to be expected, or that they will always happen. Every officer death hurts not only the law enforcement family but also the communities they serve.

Greenleaf (1998) argues that the best test of servant-leadership's effectiveness is whether "those being served grow as persons: do they, while being served, become healthier, wiser, freer, more autonomous, more likely themselves to become servants? And what is the effect on the least privileged in society; will she or he benefit, or, at least, not be further deprived?" (p. 43). In this test, Greenleaf (1977/2002) continues to ask if anyone will be hurt by the actions a leader or organization takes. He quotes Shakespeare, saying that true servants are "they that have power to hurt and will do none" (p. 56). Police officers are in a position to do either great harm or great good, and thus have the potential to become loving servants, moving our society forward toward wholeness and health.

Conclusion

Kushner (1998) writes that "forgiving happens inside us. It represents a letting go of the sense of grievance, and perhaps most importantly a letting go of the role of victim" (p. 186). If police agencies adopt a servant-leadership approach to organization based on "harmony, friendliness, [and] community" (Tutu, 1999, p. 31), setting aside the traditional autocratic, pyramidal form of organization, will not the officers grow and themselves become true servants? If each police officer learns to accept love and forgiveness into his or her heart, will not the culture of law enforcement begin to shift from one of retributive justice toward one of reconciliation and positive action? And if we see that culture shift, will not the citizens of America begin to see law enforcement not as an enemy but as a healing, unifying force?

Tutu (1999) speaks about the idea of *ubuntu*, the interconnectedness of all humanity. Law enforcement, rather than seeing itself as tasked with rooting out evil from the populace, should begin to understand its capacity for community building and reconciliation. Through his participation in the Truth and Reconciliation Commission, Tutu recognized that every human being has the capacity for both good and evil. It is in that spirit that I believe police officers around the country can collaborate with the people of the United States to ensure that violence—not only against officers but against citizens as well—becomes socially unacceptable, and thus that these atrocities cease to occur in our society.

Almost every other day, year-round, families of fallen officers gather in churches, in fields, and at gravesides. A flag is folded, edges and points crisp, white gloves and heel taps marking time. Three rifle shots pierce the air, bystanders wincing, jumping ever so slightly with each report. And echoing through trees off of buildings and stained glass, the notes of "Amazing Grace" ring out, the words on the lips of all who can hear: "Amazing Grace, how sweet the sound, that saved a wretch like me." As I strive to serve to the best of my ability my community, my society, and my world, I ask forgiveness of those I have wronged, and have forgiveness in my heart for those who have wronged. "I once was lost, but now am found. Was blind but now I see."

Note

1. "End of watch" refers to the date an officer was killed.

References

Balic, S. (1998). In H. J. Cargas & B. V. Fetterman (Eds.), *The sunflower: On the possibilities and limits of forgiveness* (pp. 109–110). New York, NY: Schocken.

Braye, R. H. (2002). Servant-leadership: Leading in today's military. In L. C. Spears & M. Lawrence (Eds.), *Focus on leadership: Servant-leadership for the twenty-first century* (pp. 295–304). New York, NY: John Wiley & Sons.

Ferch, S. R. (2012). *Forgiveness and power in the age of atrocity.* Lanham, MD: Lexington Books.

Fox, M. (1998). In H. J. Cargas & B. V. Fetterman (Eds.), *The sunflower: On the possibilities and limits of forgiveness* (pp. 143–148). New York, NY: Schocken.

Goulden, M. (1998). In H. J. Cargas & B. V. Fetterman (Eds.), *The sunflower: On the possibilities and limits of forgiveness* (pp. 154–157). New York, NY: Schocken.

Greenleaf, R. K. (1998). *The power of servant-leadership.* L. C. Spears (Ed.). San Francisco, CA: Berrett-Koehler.

Greenleaf, R. K. (2002). *Servant leadership: A journey into the nature of legitimate power and greatness* (25th anniversary ed.). L. C. Spears (Ed.). New York, NY: Paulist Press. (Original work published 1977).

Grossman, D., & Christensen, L. W. (2008). *On combat: The psychology and physiology of deadly conflict in war and peace* (3rd ed.). Millstadt, IL: Warrior Science Publications.

Heschel, S. (1998). In H. J. Cargas & B. V. Fetterman (Eds.), *The sunflower: On the possibilities and limits of forgiveness* (pp. 172–173). New York, NY: Schocken.

Kushner, H. S. (1998). In H. J. Cargas & B. V. Fetterman (Eds.), *The sunflower: On the possibilities and limits of forgiveness* (pp. 183–186). New York, NY: Schocken.

Littell, F. H. (1998). In H. J. Cargas & B. V. Fetterman (Eds.), *The sunflower: On the possibilities and limits of forgiveness* (pp. 197–200). New York, NY: Schocken.

Marty, M. E. (1998). In H. J. Cargas & B. V. Fetterman (Eds.), *The sunflower: On the possibilities and limits of forgiveness* (pp. 208–213). New York, NY: Schocken.

National Highway Traffic Safety Administration. (2005). *Traffic safety facts: Speeding.* Retrieved from http://www-nrd.nhtsa.dot.gov/ Pubs/809915.pdf

Officer Down Memorial Page. (2012). Retrieved July 6, 2012, from www.odmp.org

Ozick, C. (1998). In H. J. Cargas & B. V. Fetterman (Eds.), *The sunflower: On the possibilities and limits of forgiveness* (pp. 213–219). New York, NY: Schocken.

Patrick, U. W., & Hall, J. C. (2005). *In defense of self and others-issues, facts, and fallacies: The realities of law enforcement's use of deadly force.* Durham, NC: Carolina Academic Press.

Spears, L. C. (2002). Introduction: Tracing the past, present, and future of servant-leadership. In L. C. Spears & M. Lawrence (Eds.), *Focus on leadership: Servant-leadership for the twenty-first century* (pp. 1–16). New York, NY: Wiley.

Thompson, C. M. (2000). *The congruent life: Following the inward path to fulfilling work and inspired leadership.* San Francisco, CA: Jossey-Bass.

Tutu, D. (1999). *No future without forgiveness.* New York, NY: Doubleday.

Wall, T. F. (2008). *Thinking critically about moral problems.* Wadsworth Cengage learning.

Wiesenthal, S. (1998). *The sunflower: On the possibilities and limits of forgiveness.* New York, NY: Schocken.

Williams, L. E. (2002). Fannie Lou Hamer, servant of the people. In L. C. Spears & M. Lawrence (Eds.), *Focus on leadership: Servant-leadership for the twenty-first century* (pp. 65–88). New York, NY: John Wiley & Sons.

Chapter 12

Forgiveness

A Humble Path to Servant-Leadership for Police

MARK WHITSON

In an attempt to make sense of the often difficult task of being called to "protect and serve" society, I begin this article by setting the stage for servant-leadership as vital to the police endeavor. The world is ever changing. It is becoming more complex and diverse. In an effort to manage better in a multicultural environment, leadership styles are evolving. Researchers Mayer, Bardes, and Piccolo (2008) indicate "a growing interest in ethical styles of leadership" (p. 180), and one such leadership style is servant-leadership. In my thirty-two years as a public servant, I have found that servant-leadership is an ideal model for police officers, and complements their "serve and protect" attitude. The term *servant-leadership* was conceived by Robert K. Greenleaf (1903–1990). The term was revealed in his article "The Servant as Leader" (1970). Greenleaf (1977/2002) proposed that a leader is one who serves his or her followers, and spent most of his sixty-five-year career as a researcher in the fields of management, development, and education. He believed that a servant-leader first makes sure that "other people's highest priority needs are being served" (p. 27).

For centuries, leadership was cloaked in the suit of command and control. Transforming this style of leadership into one of serving others is difficult. The transition from a hierarchical organization to a community of equality and respect "starts small, goes slow and is very underfunded" (Block, 2011, p. xv). A servant-leadership-focused community builds on one-on-one interaction. It spreads slowly. The members become independent, stronger, knowledgeable, and increasingly destined to becoming servant-leaders. Greenleaf's servant-leadership vision "was to stimulate thought and action for building a better more caring society" (Spears, 1995, p. 3). Ferch (2011) compares servant-leadership to a light in the darkness. He writes that "light is vision, clarity and hope [for the future]" of humanity (p. 21). Greenleaf's proposed servant-leaders put others first. In a workplace atmosphere, servant-leaders are challenged to put "employees, customers and community as number one priority" (Spears, 1995, p. 3).

Spears (1995) suggests ten critical characteristics of servant-leadership:

1. Listening: listening intently to others and oneself

2. Empathy: understanding others and respecting them as individuals

3. Healing: forgiving others in order to restore community

4. Awareness: being conscious of ethical values and concerns

5. Persuasion: leading with influence, not authority

6. Conceptualization: considering the bigger vision

7. Foresight: understanding the consequences of a decision

8. Stewardship: being open and trustworthy

9. Commitment to the growth of people: valuing people and their potential

10. Building community: constructing strong relationships and kinships

In their recent book *Lead with LUV*, Blanchard and Barrett (2011) define *servant-leadership* as "love in action" (p. 104). They quote the Bible to define *love*:

> Love is patient, love is kind
> It does not envy, it does not boast, it is not proud
> It is not rude, it is not self-seeking
> It is not easily angered; it keeps no record of wrongs
> Love does not delight in evil, but rejoices with the truth.

It always protects, always trusts, always hopes, always serves.
Love never fails.
1 Corinthians 13. (as cited in Blanchard & Barrett, 2011, p. 104)

Servant-leadership is based on interpersonal relationships. It is a human-to-human exchange. Magnuson and Enright (2008) posit forgiveness as essential for the maintenance and growth of these types of relationships. *Forgiveness* is defined as "the cessation of resentment . . . or resumption of a beneficent response toward an offender" (p. 114). They also offer the moral principle of beneficence which "may include compassion, unconditional worth, generosity and moral love" (p. 114). Forgiveness is a gift of goodwill. It results in returning humanity to someone who has wronged you. Forgiving does not "condone, excuse, forget or even reconcile" (p. 114). Love, mercy, and forgiveness are at the center of servant-leadership.

Having given a brief introduction to some of the foundational thoughts that define servant-leadership, I want to detail some of my own struggles to draw closer to the tenets of forgiveness and healing found in servant-leadership. In so doing, I hope to illumine some of my own weaknesses and help draw myself and others toward greater health.

My Personal Story of Forgiveness and Healing

I have a daughter, now sixteen years old, who is the love of my life. She is a treasured gift, who over the past couple of years has struggled with growing up. Her struggles led to depression. In a depressed state, she experimented with marijuana and alcohol, trying to self-medicate her pain. I am proud to say she has recovered nicely and no longer uses either drug. She is still trying to cope, and her battle has left her with the scars of frustration and anger. I have supported her, and I struggle with how much I should get involved.

One morning, she was obviously having a bad day. I attempted to get her to talk and open up to me. The more I questioned her, the angrier she got. I just wanted her to vent. I got what I asked for. She vented and placed the burden of her frustration on me. I was unprepared for this weight placed on my shoulders, and I lashed out at her. She yelled that I was an inadequate father, and that she hated me. She also complained that I didn't understand her. I responded with white-hot anger. I told her that she was a mean and vicious girl. Things got out of control, and to this day I don't remember what exactly was said. In the heat of the argument, auditory exclusion and tunnel vision took over. I do remember that hateful words exploded like grenades, and we were both wounded. We got away from each other, and passions subsided. I began to calm down and start thinking normally. I soon experienced a second phase of anger when I recognized my immaturity. I directed this anger at myself for not being the adult. I should have been a better person. I should have been more mature and healthy. I know humans are emotional. I understand that sometimes emotions overwhelm all cognitive processes. That is when anger gets out of control. Barriers are removed and anger is unleashed. Unfortunately, this can result in violent outbursts.

I decided I needed to step forward. I needed to put my ego aside and look to the future. This incident could have destroyed my relationship with my daughter. I didn't want that to happen. I decided to ask for forgiveness from my daughter. I asked her to sit down with me. I looked her in her eyes and said, "I am sorry. Will you forgive me?" I apologized for my angry reactions and the way I had spoken to her. I explained to her that I was not apologizing for being a father and telling her how I felt. I was apologizing for the words I used to communicate those feelings. I explained that she was growing and learning to be an adult, just as I am growing and learning to be a parent. She accepted my apology. I told her I would be respectful to her and understand when she didn't want to talk. We agreed that our future talks would be tempered with love and respect for each other.

I remember how calming it was to decide to ask for forgiveness. I unburdened the load of guilt and shame. When my daughter accepted my apology, all tension left the room. I felt close to her again. Our broken relationship was restored and became whole. Anger fled and a warm feeling of love filled the void. I learned that anger is a barrier to love and compassion. I learned a new pathway of communication with my daughter. I could talk to her more as a loving father rather than as the angry parent. I felt more positive and hopeful about our relationship in the future. This personal forgiveness and healing story reminds me how important forgiveness is in all of our relationships. As a police officer, I came to realize that forgiveness is a path to building partnerships within our communities. Forgiveness will allow me to serve others better.

A Time to Kill and a Time to Heal:
Police and Forgiveness

During the interview process to become a police officer, I was asked, "Why do you want to become a police officer?" I wanted to serve. I wanted to help people and keep them safe from harm. All police officers are asked this question when they apply for the job, and 99 percent will give the same answer. When you transition from civilian to commissioned police officer, you raise your right hand and take an oath to serve with honor and integrity.

I have been a police officer for more than 32 years. For 16 years of those 32 years, I was assigned as a negotiator in my department's Tactical Operations Unit. On one particular callout, our team responded to a barricaded suspect holding another person hostage. The suspect was armed and was wanted for several robberies and shootings. The hostage he held was his mother. During the negotiation, our team managed to rescue the mother and then made plans to deal with the suspect. My hope was that he would choose compliant, peaceful surrender. But the plan, by necessity, included all options. At one point, the man entered the bathroom off the main bedroom. Suddenly he emerged, gun in his right hand, pointed to the floor. He walked slowly toward our containment positions at the door. I talked to the man as our team responded. For a moment I stopped hearing my voice, but I heard the familiar sound of a spoon releasing from a "flash bang" diversionary device. As it went off, I heard a loud explosion, and a bright light temporarily blinded me. I heard a shotgun go off twice as our less lethal operator attempted to get the man to drop the gun. He fired two "bean bag" rounds. We were hoping the man would drop his gun. Instead, I watched him slowly raise his right hand, placing the muzzle of the gun to his right temple. I remember in detail, to this day, seeing his head rock to the left and his body drop to the floor.

Over the next three days, the team and I relived the events of that morning. Our team debriefed the incident and completed an after-action report. We relived the callout in our training the next week. During this time, I felt several emotions. I felt guilt for not being able to stop this man from killing himself. I felt loss at seeing another human's life end tragically. I felt failure for violating an oath to keep everyone safe—even if it means protecting someone from himself. And I felt overwhelming anger because this man had made me feel these emotions. Every member of our team was touched by this incident. We all changed that morning.

This is just one example of the many traumatic and potentially threatening incidents that jar the psyches of police officers each day. These incidents are relived each night in the officers' dreams. The world is a violent place. Grossman and Christensen (2004) state,

> We are arguably in the most violent time in peacetime history. The murder rate is being held down by medical technology, but the aggravated assault rate, the rate at which we are trying to kill or seriously injure each other, might be the highest in peacetime history. (p. 3)

Seeing this human-on-human violence can be an extreme stressor for police officers. Human aggression toward another human is very personal. For people who are victims or witnesses to such aggression, it can be traumatic. It is something that changes the very being of each of us. Police officers' trauma can lead to hostility and anger. This anger includes the perception that many officers have of not being supported by citizens and the media, whom they resent for such attitudes. Anger leads to resentment. Meffert et al. (2008) define *hostility* as "an attitude with a predisposition to dislike and mistrust others, and interpret others behavior as egoistic and hurtful" (p. 410). Notably, mistrust "increases the frequency of anger" and shows "that measures of hostility and anger have overlapping content" (Meffert et al., 2008, p. 410).

According to Sherman (2005), Plato described anger with the word "thumos, the spiritual part of the soul" (p. 68). Roman stoic philosophers believed that all emotions are cognitive and thus controllable. Police officers are expected to control their emotions. Anger is an emotion police officers are expected to keep in check. "Police officers are expected to act personably, but in a detached manner, rather than becoming personally involved when dealing with distressing operational instances, with effectiveness being compromised if they fail to maintain that distinction" (Brown, Fielding, & Glover, 1999, p. 315). Brown et al. (1999) state that "emotional control is an important part of the officer's occupational identity, both in terms of the public's expectation and demands of the informal culture" (p. 315). Am I not human? Am I not supposed to feel? One emotion I feel while at work is anger. Personally, I feel that anger can be a positive emotion. If I do not feel anger after seeing the inhumanity that I witness, it sometimes seems to me as if I do not care. Police officers cannot allow the buildup of negative emotions, a buildup that often ensures that anger will morph into hate or revenge. I know that at times I have felt anger and the desire for revenge. This feeling is sometimes personal, but it can also come in the form of seeking justice. Sadly, I've sometimes felt I was in search of justice in the form of vengeance. It would be payback for all of the victims of crime. All officers must avoid this transition to revenge, which can result in an officer's excessive use of force or verbal abuse. Police officers should use anger to motivate and not express it in the form of excess retribution. When anger becomes hate, it turns emotion into a runaway train. It becomes sudden out-of-control fury, and everyone is a potential target.

I discovered an answer to anger in Ramsey and Ramsey's (n.d.) article "Forgiveness: A Response for Therapists in Dealing with Empathy Fatigue, Vicarious Trauma and Suffering in the Therapeutic Relationship." Ramsey and Ramsey (n.d.) note that "to be human is to suffer" (p. 4). They state humans are "vulnerable to all types of fears, anxieties and distresses that result in significant mental anguish or suffering" (p. 4). Suffering has been described as "a strong emotional response caused by anything that threatens the self or integrity of a person, whether physical, emotional or spiritual" (p. 5). In addition, "Suffering can be experienced vicariously[,] as in the empathetic response of a person seeing another emote anguish or distress" (p. 5). Brown et al. (1999) agree that police officers could be primary victims of these stressors as well as of "policing tasks that expose officers as secondary victims to the trauma of others" (p. 324). Weiss et al. (2010) confirm that "the dangerous aspects of being a first responder (e.g., exposure to life threat) increase the likelihood that these individuals will experience trauma-related symptoms" (p. 734). Asmundson and Stapleton (2008), in a study of 138 police officers, indicated that "all officers reported having experienced trauma" (p. 72). Ramsey and Ramsey (n.d.) state that, just as hostility forms an attitude of displeasure and doubt, "learning of other people's acts of cruelty, deception, betrayal and violation can cause therapists to have their own serious issues of trust, making them cynical, suspicious of people's motives, or perceiving others as untrustworthy" (p. 8). According to Asmundson and Stapleton (2008), one of the symptoms of post-traumatic stress disorder includes "emotional numbing" (p. 66). Ramsey and Ramsey (n.d.) agree that therapists can be vulnerable to emotional numbing. They state, "Sometimes we become desensitized by human emotion, experience and acute overdose of feelings; we turn

ourselves off" (Ramsey and Ramsey, n.d., pp. 9–10). Ramsey and Ramsey
describe a defense mechanism used by people who experience trauma as
disparagement. As a result of trauma, a person's "view of the world and
values changes" (p. 10). He or she "can become cynical and lose a sense
of hope and optimism in humanity" (p. 10). In my experience, this loss
of hope tends to generate anger that has no healthy outlet.

Like therapists, police officers are expected to be stoic and suck it
up, which can be dangerous for the officer and the public the he or she
serves. "Elevated anger has been found to be linked to adverse individual
and public health outcomes" (Meffert et al., 2008, p. 415). Post-traumatic
stress disorder and anger "could lead to increased community problems
with physical health, interpersonal relationships and violence" (p. 415).
Sherman (2005) describes anger as a state of being "thirsty for bloody
revenge . . . an urge to 'lash and lacerate' to seek retribution not for
its own sake but for pleasure. . . . In short, anger terrorizes others as it
torments us" (p. 83).

What is the solution to this serious problem for our law enforcement
officers? What is the solution for potential individual and public health
issues? Sherman (2005) states, "We are to learn to ignore, endure or forgive. We may access, punish and reeducate wrongdoers, but we are to do
so without any angry feelings" (p. 83). He continues, "The urge toward
forgiveness and reconciliation, in some cases independent of a change of
heart by the wrongdoer, may be a response to one's urgent need to find
time to move on and heal, even if those who have committed the wrong
have not repented for their sins" (p. 83). Glaeser (2008) notes, "Forgiveness is one of the key concerns in Judeo-Christian tradition" (p. 337).
Forgiveness has been defined as an "overcoming of resentment toward an
offender . . . one merciful response to someone who unjustly hurts us"
(Ramsey & Ramsey, n.d., p. 13). Cicero reminds us that "we must exercise
respectfulness towards humans, towards the best of them and also towards
the rest" (as cited in Sherman, 2005, p. 56). It is through the process
of forgiveness that the victim releases the hateful thoughts that lead to
revenge. Sherman (2005) assures us that "to forgive is to move beyond
or overcome punishing anger for moral reasons" (p. 85). It is through
empathy, walking in another's shoes, and seeing others as equals that we
are able to forgive. We see the good and positive in others, and for moral
reasons move beyond our anger. This is different from forgetting and
acceptance. Sherman reminds us, "Forgetting is something that happens to

us over time . . . but it is not something we do for moral reasons" (p. 85). Forgiveness "increases emotional and physical benefits, including relief of chronic pain, cardiovascular difficulties and violent behavior" (Ramsey & Ramsey, n.d., p. 15). Forgiveness reduces anger and resentment. It allows a person to release "negative behaviors such as revenge seeking or retaliation towards a transgressor" (Ramsey & Ramsey, n.d., p. 16).

Personally, I believe I am responsible for my attitude toward others. When I see others in a negative light, it is easy to dehumanize them. Anger that I have as a result of their conduct or actions can be replaced by hate and resentment of them personally. All people are made in God's likeness, and, I believe, are equal. My duty is to "temper control with forgiveness, soldierly strength with tolerance for human frailty" (Sherman, 2005, p. 12). My responsibility includes knowing that I share "human frailty" with those who offend me. I must make a conscious choice to have an attitude of forgiveness. Ramsey and Ramsey (n.d.) ask us to "internalize the act of forgiving and visualize absorbing the suffering . . . holding it in a meaningful place, and then letting it go" (p. 18). It is a process that takes time, and I need not rush. Over time, I believe the process of for-giveness will allow me to vanquish the trauma other police officers and I experience in our jobs every day. The forgiveness process is something I need to understand and use so I perform my job in a professional manner, with respect for others. In fact, I've found that forgiveness is a vital necessity for officers. It is not only crucial for our jobs but for our health as well. Forgiveness is important for our relationships at home and with others in the communities we serve.

Forgiveness, Humility, and Servant-Leadership

> Anger is a heavy burden to carry but Dad realized that revenge didn't make it any lighter . . . forgiveness did.
>
> —Gregory Thomas Garcia, *My Name Is Earl*

One's ability to forgive offers benefits to one's emotional and physical health. Forgiveness offers "significant reductions to anger, depression, anxiety, grief and post traumatic stress symptoms and increases in . . . self esteem, hope, positive attitudes, environmental mastery and finding meaning in suffering"

(Magnuson & Enright, 2008, pp. 114–115). It helps erase from the mind the painfulness of trauma and allows for relationships to be rebuilt. Solomon, Dekel, and Zerach (2009) stated that "forgiveness may be important for individuals suffering from PTSD to overcome their fears and memories of certain events and can ultimately affect not only their well-being but their personal relationships" (p. 548). In the Christian tradition, Saint Paul explained that Jesus died on the cross to gain forgiveness for our sins. Jesus subjected himself to humiliation and death because of his love for man. Saint Paul notes that Jesus's followers "forgive one another because they themselves had been forgiven by God through Christ" (as cited in Magnuson & Enright, 2008, p. 114). Humility is part of forgiveness. Sandage and Wiens (2001) advance humility as a way "to view others as one's equal" (p. 205). At Philippi, Saint Paul urged humility and that one "consider others better than yourselves" (as cited in Sandage & Wiens, 2001, p. 205). Saint Paul equated humility with being unselfish. Sandage and Wiens (2001) write, "Paul is encouraging the Philippians to humbly care for others and to put their concerns ahead of their own" (p. 206). Saint Paul believed that humility and putting others first promoted unity in a diverse Christian community.

Humility is "an understanding of one's imperfections, and to be free of arrogance and low self-esteem" (Sandage & Wiens, 2001, p. 207). Bethel (2009), in *A New Breed of Leader*, states that humility is the opposite of arrogance. Arrogance is the fear of one's inadequacies, and the fear of being open and vulnerable (Bethel, 2009). Low self-esteem can obstruct being altruistic to others. Sandage and Wiens (2001) indicate that low self-image can lead to defensive narcissism that is "contrary to humility, empathy and forgiveness" (p. 207). Empathy is vital to humility and to the ability to recognize others' need for forgiveness. It takes strength and courage to be humble. T. S. Eliot wrote, "Humility is the most difficult of virtues to achieve" (as cited in Bethel, 2009, p. 336). Just as humility is important to forgiveness, it is also necessary to servant-leaders.

Hunter (2004) states that humble leaders "listen to the opinions of others" (p. 95) and view leadership "as a position of trust and stewardship" (p. 96). Humble leaders are open and confident. A confident leader understands that mistakes are learning opportunities. A confident leader who is humble and possesses the ability to forgive and to ask for forgiveness for mistakes allows the learning process to advance, which results in growth for individuals and the organization. Collins (2001) describes a "Level 5" leader as an executive who "builds enduring greatness through a paradoxical combination of personal humility and professional will" (p. 70). The practice of humility and forgiveness opens our eyes to the humanness of others and is "related to psychological healing and releasing feelings of vengeance and anger" (Solomon et al., 2009, p. 548). This results in the practitioner becoming more human. Freire (2000) points out that "the pursuit of full humanity, however, cannot be carried out in isolation or individualism, but only in fellowship and solidarity" (p. 85). Police officers seeking "fellowship and solidarity" with the communities they patrol can use servant-leadership to obtain this goal.

Police and Servant-Leadership

Miller, in "Police Leadership in the 21st Century," states,

> The future of police leadership cries for openness, vision, wisdom, compassion and men and women of goodwill. If you love public service, are willing to generously share your talent and time with the department and the community, value the dignity of others and decree a sense of purpose—answer the call. (as cited in International Association of Chiefs of Police, 1999, para 9)

The "call" Bill Miller is referring to is a leadership that treats others equally. He believes that to be effective in the new millennium, law enforcement agencies need to partner with the citizens of the communities they serve. In 1999, at the International Association of Chiefs of Police first "President's Leadership Conference," several recommendations were made on the subject of police leadership. The International Association of Chiefs of Police (1999) suggested the development of an "Every Officer as a Leader" training program (sec. I, para. 1). Another recommendation was that law enforcement prioritize "communication, collaboration, partnership development, and understanding of and responsiveness to the needs" of the community (International Association of Chiefs of Police, 1999, sec. II, para. 3). Community needs require that police officers prioritize equal treatment and fairness. Tyler (2001) suggests that the public judge "the fairness of procedures used by authorities" (p. 215) in two ways: "(1) how people were treated by legal authorities with whom they deal[,] and (2) whether people think that those legal authorities make their decisions fairly" (p. 215). Tyler (2001) further proposes that

> all residents—majority and minority—are very concerned about how the police generally treat people. They make their evaluations of the police not primarily in terms of whether the police are effective in solving community problems or by whether they make good decisions when they are regulating public behavior. Instead, residents are strongly influenced by whether or not the police and courts treat people with respect, dignity and fairness. (pp. 218–219)

Every police officer in the community is a leader. To meet the expectations of equality and fair treatment, law enforcement would be wise to lead in the style of Robert Greenleaf. Police servant-leaders should partner with the community and lead with an attitude of influence and not authority. The successful police servant-leader must be humble, see humanity in others, and forgive. Listening, openness, empathy, healing, awareness, persuasion, conceptualization, foresight, stewardship, commitment, and community are qualities that characterize servant-leadership. These words also describe the skills required for accommodating communication. According to Giles et al. (2006), police officers using accommodating communication can obtain positive satisfaction in their interactions with civilians. Police officers displaying accommodating communication in their servant-leadership practices will achieve cooperation and a willingness to follow, and will obtain the positive opinion of citizens. As I conclude my reflections here on the anger officers experience and on the forgiveness that can set us free, I turn to the beautiful thoughts of Freire (2000), who posits that there are two dimensions within all words: "reflection and action" (p. 87). He also suggests, "There is no true word that is not at the same time praxis" (p. 87). For me, this means that the way we speak is also the way we live. Law enforcement can find the true word in servant-leadership, and apply this in the daily experience of seeking to protect and serve society. In the true word is social change. I believe that as police servant-leaders, we must remember that "to speak the true word is to transform the world" (Freire, 2000, p. 87).

Look with favor upon a bold beginning

—Virgil, *Georgics*

References

Asmundson, G. J. G., & Stapleton, J. A. (2008). Associations between dimensions of anxiety sensitivity and PTSD symptom clusters in active duty police officers. *Cognitive Behavior Therapy, 37*(2), 66–75.

Bethel, S. M. (2009). *A new breed of leader: 8 leadership qualities that most matter in the real world.* New York, NY: Berkley Books.

Blanchard, K., & Barrett, C. (2011). *Lead with LUV: A different way to create real success.* Upper Saddle River, NJ: FT Press.

Block, P. (2011). Foreword—servant-leadership: Creating an alternative future. In S. R. Ferch, & L. C. Spears (Eds.), *The spirit of servant-leadership* (pp. xiii–xxvi). New York, NY: Paulist Press.

Brown, J., Fielding, J., & Grover, J. (1999). Distinguishing traumatic, vicarious, and routine operational stressor exposure and attendant adverse consequences in a sample of police officers. *Work & Stress, 13*(4), 312–325.

Collins, J. (2001, January). Level 5 leadership: The triumph of humility and fierce resolve. *Harvard Business Review, 79*(1), 66–76.

Ferch, S. R. (2011). Servant-leadership and the interior of the leader: Facing violence with courage and forgiveness. In S. R. Ferch & L. C. Spears (Eds.), *The spirit of servant-leadership* (pp. 21–49). New York, NY: Paulist Press.

Freire, P. (2000). *Pedagogy of the oppressed.* New York, NY: Continuum.

Garcia, G. T. (Executive producer). (2005). *My name is Earl.* 20th Century Fox Television.

Giles, H., Fortman, J., Dailey, R. M., Barker, V., Hajek, C., Anderson, M. C., & Rule, N. O. (2006). Communication accommodation: Law enforcement and the public. Retrieved from https://escholarship.org/uc/item/52d406tv

Glaeser, M. (2008). What does it take to let go? An investigation into the facilitating and obstructing factors of forgiveness—the therapist's perspective. *Counseling Psychology Quarterly, 21*(4), 337–348.

Greenleaf, R. K. (2002). *Servant leadership: A journey into the nature of legitimate power and greatness* (25th anniversary ed.). L. C. Spears (Ed.). New York, NY: Paulist Press. (Original work published 1977).

Grossman, D., & Christensen, L. W. (2004). *On combat: The psychology and physiology of deadly conflict in war and peace.* Washington, DC: PPCT Research Publications.

Hunter, J. C. (2004). *The most powerful leadership principle: How to become a servant-leader.* New York, NY: Crown Business.

International Association of Chiefs of Police. (1999). *Police leadership in the 21st century.* Recommendations from the president's first leadership conference, May 1999. Alexandria, VA: International Association of Chiefs of Police.

Magnuson, C. M., & Enright, R. D. (2008). The church as forgiving community: An initial model. *Journal of Psychology & Theology, 36*(2), 114–123.

Mayer, D. M., Bardes, M., & Piccolo, R. F. (2008). Do servant-leaders help satisfy follower needs? An organizational justice perspective. *European Journal of Work & Organizational Psychology, 17*(2), 180–197.

Meffert, S. M., Metzler, T. J., Henn-Haase, C., McCaslin, S., Inslicht, S., Chemtob, C., & Marmar, C. R. (2008). A prospective study of trait anger and PTSD symptoms in police. *Journal of Traumatic Stress, 21*(4), 410–416.

Ramsey, M. I., & Ramsey, C. L. (n.d.). Forgiveness: A response for therapists in dealing with empathy fatigue, vicarious trauma, and suffering in the therapeutic relationship. Retrieved from Gonzaga University ORGL 532 course resources.

Sandage, S. J., & Wiens, T. W. (2001). Contextualizing models of humility and forgiveness: A reply to Gassin. *Journal of Psychology & Theology, 29*(3), 201–211.

Sherman, N. (2005). *Stoic warriors: The ancient philosophy behind the military mind.* New York, NY: Oxford University Press.

Solomon, Z., Dekel, R., & Zerach, G. (2009). Posttraumatic stress disorder and marital adjustment: The mediating role of forgiveness. *Family Process, 48*(4), 546–558.

Spears, L. C. (1995). Introduction: Servant-leadership and the Greenleaf legacy. In L. C. Spears (Ed.), *Reflections on leadership* (pp. 1–16). New York, NY: John Wiley & Sons.

Tyler, T. R. (2001). Public trust and confidence in legal authorities: What do majority and minority group members want from the law and legal institutions? *Behavioral Sciences & The Law, 19*(2), 215–235.

Weiss, D. S., Brunet, A., Best, S. R., Metzler, T. J., Liberman, A., Pole, N., . . . Marmar, C. R. (2010). Frequency and severity approaches to indexing exposure to trauma: The critical incident history questionnaire for police officers. *Journal of Traumatic Stress, 23*, 734–743. doi: 10.1002/jts.20576

Part III

Servant-Leadership, Forgiveness, and Family

Chapter 13

Servant-Leadership, Forgiveness, and Unlimited Liability

Fathers and Sons

Keith Allan

I don't pretend to be an expert on forgiveness. In fact, most of my life I have nursed bitterness against my own father. Recently, however, I have begun to be convinced of the interior depth of the servant-leader and of how far I've been from that depth at certain crucial times in my life. In noticing this distance, and wanting to close the gap and become more whole and more loving as a man and as a leader, I've recently been led to consider my life in relationship to the life of my father.

I also don't claim to be mature about forgiveness. In fact, I'm just beginning. I feel confident that the overexacting or linear way in which I describe the work of forgiveness and reconciliation in this chapter is unlikely to be the form the actual work will take. I did, however, feel led to make a start on the work, and wanted to record these first steps toward the possibility of something good both in my life with my son and in my life with my father.

To describe and interpret justice and forgiveness from a personal perspective is not only foreign to our modern way of life but often also brings about an intense nexus of fear, anxiety, and lack of hope. The desire that forgiveness be asked for and simultaneously the unwillingness to forgive provides a poignant backdrop to the need for fathers and sons to seek restorative justice rather than retributive action.

I will provide an account of my relationship with my father in order to detail a history of events throughout my life that have left me void of respect, honor, and regard for him. My intent is not to discredit him; rather, the introspection and catharsis that have resulted from my readings and thoughts around the idea of unconditional forgiveness have opened my heart. Where there was once a heart that was bruised and torn are now openness and the desire to understand. Palmer (2005) expressed his own personal pain, sense of woe, and broken heart when he stated, "To grow one must experience profound disappointments." In the case of my father, his profound disappointments never seemed to result in personal growth; the growth that did occur was almost by chance. The profound disappointments he lived through, and which I witnessed, motivated me to avoid the mistakes he had made and to create a home environment that was built on love, appreciation, nurturing attention, and harmony.

I have looked back many times in my life, searching for memories of love, caring, and commitment. My father provided a home, meals, and a high school education. I recognize that there are others who had far less, and I am grateful for what he did provide. I now recognize that the occasional searching for moments of love, caring, and commitment represents my internal desire to forgive my father without his needing to ask me for forgiveness, although for forgiveness to be complete, each of us must extend forgiveness accordingly. Ferch (2004) states, "One of the defining characteristics of human nature is the ability to discern one's own faults, to be broken as the result of such faults, and in response, to seek a meaningful change" (p. 225). In this chapter I hope to recognize my own side of the equation, and see how, despite my father's weaknesses, I am at fault for nurturing the schism that exists between us. But to recognize alone is not enough. As a leader, I hope I can express my shortcomings, ask for forgiveness, and persevere by walking the difficult road the future asks of me.

I grew up in an upper-middle-class neighborhood with a middle-class income. The disparity between the two served as the platform for alcoholism, abuse, neglect, fear, confusion, and lack of personal guidance. All of this was compounded by the fact that our extended family and community were acutely aware of my father's inadequacies. I remember thinking at an early age that I needed to protect him personally and professionally. After holiday dinners, my uncle would drive us home, but not before Dad fell into the bushes. "He's just tired," I was told. Once home, the physical abuse would start, with my mother being the object of my father's attention. As I turned thirteen, Dad turned his violent attention on me. This typically occurred if he had lost his job or wrecked the car, or, in one case, if he suspected that I was using drugs. I remember thinking how ironic this was, being falsely accused as a substance abuser by a substance abuser who was presently under the influence. I summed it up as moronic. Yet I do remember being awakened late that night by my father. He was sitting on the edge of my bed. He whispered, "I am sorry." I turned away from him in the dark, not saying a word.

Retributive justice extended? Yes. His ability to ask for forgiveness was forever lost that night as a result of my rejecting his apology. Tutu (2000) writes, "Thus to forgive is indeed the best form of self-interest since anger, resentment, and revenge are corrosive of that summum bonum, that greatest good, communal harmony that enhances the humanity and personhood of all in the community" (p. 35). I am now an adult with my own family, working hard in a fast-paced industry. It has been some decades since I left home. My father and I spend our holidays apart, and phone conversations serve as our only communication, which is limited at best.

As a result of learning about forgiveness and justice, I feel I have come to a different place. I also recognize that the journey is far from over. As Greenleaf (1995) stated so eloquently, "Begin now to prepare for what can best be done in old age" (p. 19). I have a personal motto that is a result of my own life experiences: "Time is short; life is long." I believe I have a responsibility to my father to ask for his forgiveness for being a son who rejected him instead of supporting him despite his personal problems. Life is long, but time goes by quickly, so my decision to reconcile needs to be acted upon in a nurturing way. Forgiveness can serve as the embodiment of restorative justice and true leadership. I never saw these qualities in my father, and yet I believe they may very well become evident as a result of developing servant-leadership roles with one another.

In my goal to forgive unconditionally, I will reflect on and implement a plan of action using the ten characteristics of the servant-leader as referenced by Spears (1995), which I will list here. This plan of action will incorporate the tenets of servant-leadership, personal introspection, and an understanding of what specific strategies I hope to employ to nurture the forgiveness process.

Listening: As described by Spears, listening involves the ability to listen with one's body, spirit, and mind. In the case of my father and I, we rarely engaged in meaningful conversation. Perhaps my asking for forgiveness will encourage this. I will apologize for rejecting his apology that night long ago when he sat on the edge of my bed.

Empathy: I will identify those talents my father never had the opportunity to express or enjoy. I will recognize that his talents are innately expressed in me (he is currently 73 years old) and that I am an extension of him. In essence, my achievements in life should be shared as our achievement together as father and son.

Healing: "There is something subtle communicated to one who is being served and led if, implicit in the compact between servant-leader and led, is the understanding that the search for wholeness is something they share" (Spears, 1995, p. 5).

Awareness: I feel I have a strong sense of awareness as a result of experiencing "profound disappointments" in my relationship with my father. Awareness serves as an example of one of the gifts I received as a result of my relationship with him. This heightened sense of awareness is best used as a means to listen attentively and with compassion.

Persuasion: The building of our relationship needs to be recognized as our need to be whole. We cannot each do it alone, as I have often striven to do and my father has often resigned himself to doing. Rather, the concept of *ubuntu* can be a good initial ground: "My humanity is caught up, is inextricably bound up, in yours" (Tutu, 2000, p. 35). *Ubuntu* will inform and surround a spirit of change in my way of viewing my father: no longer holding him in a dark light, refusing my own cynicism, surrounding myself with others to help and guide me along the way, and persevering in love as continued failures of our relationship ensue.

Conceptualization: Here it is necessary for both my father and for me to see beyond our relationship to each of our relationships with my son. My son observes how I interact with my father. Despite the fact that I interact with my son differently than my father did with me, I need to consider how and to what extent my son will communicate with me after he becomes an adult.

Foresight: I try to refer to experiences in the past and apply correlations where applicable. Here again, the relationship I wanted to have with my father I currently have with my son. The lack of communication I have had with my father is not what I want with my son. Forgiveness and restorative justice are what I want for my son to witness between my father and me.

Stewardship: Unconditional trust will need to be established. I feel that listening will serve as the catalyst between us that will promote healing and the desire to serve each other.

Commitment to Growth: I will ask for my father's advice. This alone is a gift a son can give to his father. Acknowledgment that my father is recognized as valued and respected for his opinion and his wisdom is a gift.

Building Community: For me, and in my relationship with my father, community is best represented by family. Through my nurturing of a servant-leader relationship with my father, other members of my family will observe and respond with respect for our relationship that may result in harmony expressed among us all.

Every accomplishment begins with a dream and a vision. I am encouraged by Greenleaf's bright notion that behind every great achievement is a dreamer of great dreams. The successful servant-leader has visions that promote growth, understanding, and harmony. Before my father dies, I hope my gift to him will be what we could not attain between us previously: harmony.

References

Ferch, S. R. (2004). Servant-leadership, forgiveness and social justice. In L. C. Spears & M. Lawrence (Eds.), Practicing servant-leadership: Succeeding through trust, bravery, and forgiveness (pp. 225–240). San Francisco, CA: Jossey-Bass.

Greenleaf, R. K. (1995). Life's choices and markers. In L. C. Spears (Ed.), *Reflections on leadership* (pp. 17–21). New York, NY: John Wiley & Sons.

Palmer, P. (2005). Servant-leadership interview: Online mentor gallery. [Video file]. Retrieved from Gonzaga University course notes.

Spears, L. C. (1995). Introduction: Servant-leadership and the Greenleaf legacy. In L. C. Spears (Ed.), *Reflections on leadership* (pp. 1–16). New York, NY: John Wiley & Sons.

Tutu, D. (2000). *No future without forgiveness.* New York, NY: Doubleday.

Chapter 14

Servant-Leadership and Forgiveness Asking

Two Personal Narratives and a Discussion

MADUABUCHI LEO MUONEME

Robert Greenleaf coined the term *servant-leader* in the 1960s and 1970s after his involvement with tertiary institutions (Greenleaf, 1977/2002). Larry Spears (2004), a close disciple of Greenleaf, extracted the ensuing ten characteristics as essential to the development of servant-leadership: listening, empathy, healing, awareness, persuasion, conceptualization, foresight, stewardship, commitment to the growth of people, and building community. Awareness, persuasiveness, foresight, stewardship, and a desire for healing are qualities that can motivate individuals to seek reconciliation. There is a nexus between servant-leadership, the philosophy of nonviolence, and forgiveness. Just as a servant-leader first desires to serve, he or she must also first desire to ask forgiveness instead of waiting for the other to ask.

    This chapter will reflect on forgiveness asking at a personal level. I will recount two scenarios in my life (my biological family and my Jesuit family) in which I personally sought reconciliation. The focus of these two scenarios is to disclose how sour incidents were altered through the application of forgiveness asking, and to articulate the grace, restoration, and growth that these encounters of forgiveness asking brought to my life. I will finish with a characteristic analysis of the insights I gained from the experience of forgiveness asking.

Servant-Leadership and the Superiority of Nonviolence

In describing a servant-leader, Greenleaf emphasizes that the first step to becoming a servant-leader is the natural desire to serve (Greenleaf, 1977/2002). This conscious choice is followed by a conscious aspiration to lead (Greenleaf, 1977/2002). The gulf between the leader-first and the servant-first is wide; the servant-first has a greater proclivity to persevere in paying attention to another's needs (Greenleaf, 1977/2002). Leaders who "sustained intentness of listening" can get invaluable insights and ideas that assist them in leading the way for a family or an organization (Greenleaf, 1977/2002, p. 30). Greenleaf (1977/2002) also finds that servant-leaders are highly intuitive, have foresight, and are prudent: "The prudent [person] is one who constantly thinks of the 'now' as the moving concept in which the past, the present moment, and the future are an organic unity" (p. 38). He distinguishes between the formal and the informal structures in organizations. The formal structures are like a paved pathway, with specified authorities, routine operations, and rules to follow, and does not provide sufficient room for leadership; leadership takes place more powerfully in informal structures in which there is room for creativity, "constructive interpersonal relationships," calculated risk taking, well thought-out induce-ment, and the judicious regulation of priorities (p. 38).

Kathleen Patterson uses the category of "virtues" to speak of the dimensions of servant-leadership (van Dierendonck, 2010; Wallace, 2007). Agape love, humility, vision, altruism, empowerment, service, and trust are seven virtues of a servant-leader (Wallace, 2007). Servant-leadership is an ethical form of leadership, which also promotes compassion, justice, stewardship, community, human dignity, personal responsibility, and char-acter (Wallace, 2007). Instead of focusing on the self, the servant-leader focuses on others (Stone, Russell, & Patterson, 2003). Servant-leaders are motivated to meet the needs of their followers so that the followers can prosper (Wallace, 2007). By nature, these servant-leaders have a procliv-ity to raise others up and help them become wiser, freer, and healthier (Greenleaf, 1977/2002).

Similarities between servant-leadership and transformational leadership include people-oriented leadership; vision; the generation of trust, respect, and credibility; influence; risk sharing; delegating; role modeling; mentoring; teaching; communication; listening; and empowering and valuing followers (Stone et al., 2003). Both spectra of leadership emphasize "individualized consideration and appreciation of followers" (Stone et al., 2003, p. 4).

The theories of servant-leadership and transformational leadership are complementary rather than opposed. Van Dierendonck (2010) sees an overlap between servant-leadership and transformational leadership, and demonstrates that Spears advanced ten characteristics of servant-leadership, Laub (1999) expounded six clusters, Russell and Stone (2002) differentiated nine functional characteristics and eleven additional characteristics, and Patterson (2003) gave seven dimensions based on virtue ethics. Out of a plurality of different portrayals of servant-leadership, van Dierendonck (2010) discerns six characteristics: empowering and developing people, humility, authenticity, interpersonal acceptance, providing direction, and stewardship. He came up with his six characteristics using empirical methods based on the measurements of servant-leadership and discriminating "between antecedents, behavior, mediating processes and outcomes" (p. 5).

From the foregoing description, one can surmise that a servant-leader readily forgives and seek forgiveness, since he or she is a good listener, empathic, aware, and persuasive. A servant-leader is also committed to the growth and freedom of others, and to building a community of love, and possesses foresight. Martin Luther King Jr. and Nelson Mandela had foresight of a new United States and a new Republic of South Africa, respectively. Rather than resort to violence or retaliation to achieve their ends, they turned toward nonviolence, love, and reconciliation. Foresight involves thinking about the long-term consequences of one's decisions (Gunnarsson & Blohm, 2011). A leader who promotes compassion, justice, stewardship, community, human dignity, personal responsibility, and character will more likely generate peace, healing, and goodwill in relationships and organizations. Since servant-leaders focus on others instead of themselves, they are motivated to meet the needs of others. I think this spirit of wanting the best for others disposes servant-leaders to seek reconciliation, forgiveness, and restoration rather than discord, resentment, and retribution. When a family or organization is based on discord, the tension will infect the relationships and create a dysfunctional structure of interactions. In contrast, harmony will lead to smooth and meaningful relationships in a family or organization. A servant-leader refuses the praxis of domination. Freire (1993) stated, "Domination reveals the pathology of love: sadism in the dominator and masochism in the dominated" (p. 89).

Mahatma Gandhi had a heart full of love and forgiveness, and he adopted satyagraha (soul force) in galvanizing the Indian people to seek liberation through nonviolence. Gandhi said that he believed nonviolence was infinitely superior to violence, and that forgiveness was more heroic than retribution or punishment (King, 1969). During a visit to India, King learned that patience was a virtue in the praxis of nonviolence. In this regard, there is a nexus between a servant-leader and nonviolence. A servant-leader avoids the impatience of a dominant leader. In the strategy of nonviolence proposed by King (1969) for the civil rights movement, the practitioner seeks justice and reconciliation rather than victory. He or she also sacrifices personal wishes so that all persons might be free (King, 1969). There is hence a desire to make others more free. This desire for the psychic liberation of others is a tenet of servant-leadership.

King's nonviolent strategy also exhorts practitioners to perform regular service for others and to desist from the violence of fist, tongue, or heart (King, 1969). Service is accordingly another link between the philosophy of nonviolence and servant-leadership. In practicing nonviolence, we are also exhorted to seek justice and reconciliation and not victory (King, 1969). This dovetails with restorative justice. Walking and talking in the manner of love and making personal sacrifices for the freedom of others are also part of the dictates of nonviolent movement (King, 1969). Love, sacrifice, and concern for the freedom of others all fit the characteristics of a servant-leader. Satyagraha is the basic idea of Gandhi's nonviolence or civil resistance (King, 1969). Retribution, resentment, and unforgive-ness are based on a heart of violence, while restoration, forgiveness, and compassion toward oneself and one's offenders are rooted in a nonviolent heart and spirit. King practiced personal forgiveness. According to his wife, Coretta Scott King, whenever King did something wrong, it pricked his conscience, and if it were possible, "he would always make apologies and seek forgiveness" (King, 1969, p. 59).

Like Gandhi and Mandela, in his rhetoric and in his deeds King was a servant-leader of the nonviolent civil rights movement. King redefined leadership in a speech he once gave a speech on the subject of greatness and service in which he told of two of Christ's disciples, James Zebedee and John Zebedee, who wanted to hold places of importance in the King-dom. The other ten disciples were indignant. King went on to remind his audience to be careful not to condemn the disciples, saying that if we were to inspect our hearts and minds, we would notice that we all have that desire to be great (King, 1998). This is evidenced in the Olympic world, the business world, and the political world. King quoted the psychoanalyst Alfred Adrian in contending that the will to importance or greatness is the dominant impulse driving humans (King, 1998). Hence, when babies are born, they cry for attention (King, 1998). Nietzsche taught that the will to power is the essence or metaphysics of one's existence, and is defined in one's being as one's striving to become (Coffeen, 2010). King reminds us that Jesus did not condemn his disciples' desire for greatness, saying, "If you want to be great—wonderful. But recognize that he who is greatest among you shall be your servant. That's the new definition of greatness" (King, 1998, p. 182).

King's point is that Christ exhorted everyone to transform the desire for greatness into the desire for greatness in service, greatness in love, greatness in humility, greatness in truth, greatness in justice, greatness in generosity, and greatness in forgiveness. Greatness in service became King's new definition of greatness, and he believed that we all could be great because we can all serve (King, 1998). King's (1998) metaphor for the desire to be in front in the parade of life was the "drum major instinct" (pp. 170–171). This instinct is a powerful force that can be self-destructive and destructive of others if not harnessed but becomes meaningful and purposeful if transformed into service. Robert Greenleaf's idea of servant-leadership is reminiscent of King's definition of greatness. If we really desire to lead, we must first desire to serve. Service is what inspires authentic leadership, which is selfless, liberating, and empowering of others. King (1998) instructs us that in becoming servants, we simply need a "heart full of grace and a soul generated by love" (p. 183). Mother Teresa of Calcutta, like King a Nobel Peace laureate, was another servant-leader who cheerfully gathered broken babies, mothers, and fathers from the slums of Calcutta and brought them to a place of remedy, rest, and redemption. She has inspired millions of people across religious boundaries because to a world full of indigence caused by domination she brought empowerment, meaning, and liberation through love and service.

Personal Forgiveness Asking Experiences: Two Narratives

First Narrative: With My Dad

It is essential that I provide a brief historical, biographical, and geographical frame for this narrative. My parents, Leonard and Cecilia, got married on October 25, 1969. My dad was a high school biology teacher, while my mum was a civil servant. They brought up their five children in Jos, Plateau State (North Central Nigeria), and Ilorin, Kwara State (western Nigeria). My dad relocated to Ilorin first with three of my siblings, while my mum, my youngest brother Joe, and I remained in Jos, pending the right time for the whole family to be reunited.

While I was finishing high school in Jos, I became a lapsed Catholic. One day, my mother asked me to follow her to church for a Confirmation mass at a military school, to be celebrated by the then Catholic bishop of Jos, the late Archbishop Gabriel Gonsum Ganaka, a close friend of my dad. I told Mum I would come for mass that day but on the condition that we go to our regular parish (simply because I was also interested in catching sight of a lady friend). Mum said, "Fine, come into the car." But she could not imagine not attending the bishop's Confirmation mass, and so along the way, she took a diversion and drove me and my youngest brother to the mass I was not interested in attending. I was exasperated, but I had no alternative at that point but to attend the mass. I listened intently to the bishop's sermon, and it changed my life. To this day, it remains the best sermon I have ever heard.

This powerful sermon, which I never intended to hear, moved me to read the Gospel of Matthew and caused a deep religious conversion in me. Eventually, I was spurred on to read the entire New Testament. My passion then was to study medicine, but I also began to think of the priesthood. It eventually became a tug of war: doctor of the soul or doctor of the body? I was glad to know that there was a possibility of following both vocations at the Society of Jesus. Leaving zoological studies at the University of Jos, I joined the Jesuits in Nigeria. After some years of formation in Nigeria, I was missioned to Loyola University Chicago, where I did a degree in philosophy and theology. Subsequently, I returned to Nigeria for regency, a period of apostolic work and teaching.

The next stage of formation (ministry studies in theology) took place at the Hekima Jesuit School of Theology in Nairobi, Kenya. Following that, I was ordained a priest on July 14, 2001, in Lagos, Nigeria. All of my family members were present. After serving in two Jesuit apostolates in Nigeria, I was missioned to Boston College, where I studied for a master of science in teaching in physics. After completing the degree program, the provincial missioned me to pastor a Jesuit parish in Lagos, Nigeria, where I also taught physics at a Jesuit high school. Lagos is in the southwestern part of Nigeria. That is where my sister Ngozi currently lives with her husband, Chibuike, and three children. Ben, my immediate younger brother, lives in Edo State, central southern Nigeria, with his wife, Judith, and three children. Ugo lives in Jos with his wife, Adesua, and three children, while Joe lives in the Federal Capital Territory (north-central geopolitical zone of Nigeria) with his wife, Kelechi, and two children.

In June 2007, while I was the parish priest of St. Francis Catholic Church in Lagos, I once had the responsibility of hosting the diaconate ordination of nine deacons of Archdiocese of Lagos. We had never had such a ceremony in our parish before. We anticipated that many lay people and priests of the Lagos archdiocese were going to flood our parish. There was an archdiocesan planning committee, but since our parish was the hosting parish, I was expected to ensure that things went well. My parents (who were residing in Jos at this time) were in Lagos visiting with my sister and her husband during this period. In the midst of the hectic planning for the ordination, I had gone over to my sister's home to welcome my mum and dad. They told me they would be coming for the diaconate ordination. I was glad they would be coming to witness the ceremony, but I warned them that I might not be a great host to them in the parish because I would be very busy with the events of the ordination ceremony.

On the day of the diaconate ordination, I bore a lot of burden before, during, and after the ceremony. I was anxious trying to ensure that the ceremony was perfect. The sanctuary was filled with about ninety priests, and the mass lasted about three hours. After the mass, a reception was to immediately follow in the parish hall. As pastor of the parish, I was supposed to escort and be with the ordaining prelate. Meanwhile, I realized that things were not quite ready at the parish hall (the reception venue). In the midst of the tension, my parents wanted my attention. The big error on my part was that I failed to give proper attention to them. After the ordination, instead of catching my breath and being fulfilled that the ceremony had gone well, I took a long walk, disappointed with myself that I had let worries and busyness shield me from welcoming my parents. I was angry about the fact that I was leading under stress. I went to my sister's house the following day (after Sunday mass) to visit with my parents.

Somehow, I was feeling righteous because I had indicated to my parents that I would be occupied on the day of the ordination. My dad made it clear to me that he was not happy with me. I tried to argue in my defense, and my mum tried to make peace between my dad and me. I left my sister's house displeased. That same evening, I took a day off from my parish and went to our other Jesuit parish in Lagos. The whole ordination ceremony was a paradox. I gave all of my energy to the planning and the execution, and the ceremony went well. Everybody was happy, but here I was stressed out and having issues with my dad.

In retrospect, I think the overload of work in the parish exposed how I was engaged in below-the-line thinking. I was working under stress and anxiety. Ferch (2012) refers to the work of leadership consultant Paul Nakai, who says that feelings such as anxiety, stress, anger, and fear immerse one at the troubled level or at a lower level of consciousness—below-the-line thinking. I felt I needed reconciliation, and later on I met with the pastor in another Jesuit parish that I had gone to for a day off and shared with him this disenchanting experience I had had with my dad. He recommended that I take time to travel to Jos (where my parents had returned after their time in Lagos) and reconcile with my dad, and that I could present a symbolic gift to my dad. It took me a long time to create time for this journey. I was consumed with pastoral work, but on a deeper level, I think I was struggling to overcome the inertia around asking for forgiveness. The next month (July), my dad called me to wish me a happy birthday. Later that month, on July 31 (the feast of Saint Ignatius), my parish broke ground to commence construction of the Mother Teresa Medical Centre and Cultural Centre. August, September, and October got so busy that I kept procrastinating traveling to Jos.

In November, I finally made the move. I boarded a bus to Abuja to first visit my younger brother Joe. The next day, after celebrating mass at his home, I got in a taxi and traveled to Jos. I wanted it to be a surprise visit. On reaching Jos, my younger brother Mike and his wife, Sandra, picked me up. To my surprise, they told me that my parents had gone to our hometown in the south. I got scared. Now that I had taken time to travel such a long distance to ask my dad and mum for forgiveness, they were not around. I became desperate, but I persisted. The following day, I boarded a bus for the eight-to-nine-hour journey to southern Nigeria.

Before arriving at the bus station at my destination, I had been able to make phone contact with my dad. He and mum came to pick me up. I was so pleased to see them. I did not tell them why I had traveled down. But after dinner, the moment of "forgiveness asking" dawned. With just the three of us in the living room, I summoned my courage and brought back the events of June. I asked for their forgiveness. As I did so, a load was removed from my heart. My dad and mum were very happy and accepted my apology, and at the same time offered words of advice regarding my pastoral duties. I opened the gifts I had brought and presented them to my parents. They were very appreciative of the visit, the reconciliation, and the gifts. The following day we went back to the bus station. My dad was wearing the shirt I had brought for him. We took a photograph together before I embarked on the journey back to Lagos.

This experience of hurt and reconciliation catapulted me toward being more evenhanded in my pastoral work. After my pastoral mission in that parish, my parents came to celebrate with me during a send-forth party. I showered them with great hospitality. I could not afford to let any form of responsibility prevent me from spending each available moment with them. My next assignment after St. Francis Parish in Lagos was Loyola Jesuit College in Abuja, where I served as a vice principal and teacher. It was during my time in Abuja, at the height of the Christian-Muslim strain in Jos, that my siblings and I made efforts to relocate my aging parents from Jos to Abuja. I personally traveled with them to help move some of their property from Abuja to Jos.

On October 25, 2009, my parents celebrated their fortieth wedding anniversary. I mobilized my siblings, and we were able to plan a beautiful commemoration for Dad and Mum. Since the ceremony took place in Abuja, most of the weight of planning the ceremony was on me, but I was delighted to give my heart and soul to it in gratitude for my parents' love for us. Although I was meticulous in preparing for their ruby anniversary, it was less tedious than my preparation for the ordination ceremony in Lagos. Looking back, I think my level of consciousness at Abuja was above-the-line thinking, not because I do not like Lagos but because the magnitude of my responsibilities in Abuja was not so great. Using above-the-line thinking, one feels contentment, ease, gracefulness, gratitude, optimism, forgiveness, inspiration, love, and humor in the midst of challenge (Ferch, 2012). I acknowledge I did have these feelings in Lagos, but my anxieties and workload conspired to drown them.

After the forgiveness-asking experience, I became more sensitive to the needs of my parents. I am so grateful to God that my parents are alive. During my time in Abuja, before tertianship (a stage of Jesuit formation), I fought for my parents' pension funds. Because of corruption in the civil service, some staff members at the federal secretariat in Abuja were dillydallying with the pensions of retired civil servants. This is one of the results of the massive top-to-bottom corruption. I had to personally make many visits to the civil service office to fight for my parents, who are pensioners and whose pensions were denied them for a long time. Thankfully, the government finally approved their pensions. After my tertianship, my provincial missioned me to serve as pastor in another Jesuit parish in Benin City. During my time there, I made arrangements for surgical procedures for my dad through the help of a parishioner in the medical profession. My dad and mum stayed in our parish during my dad's surgery. Subsequently, I spent quality time with my parents in May before my new mission to Spokane, Washington, for doctoral studies in leadership last year. We went to the Millennium Park in Abuja to be with nature. I celebrated daily masses for them. They pray daily for me, and I pray daily for them. This is an excerpt of a tribute I wrote in the program for their ruby wedding anniversary in October 2009:

> Dad, whenever I went to you for advice I came out with insights and a better direction. . . . Beaming with smile, you are a man of peace. . . . You gave us moral lessons of life in many stories you told. . . . Wherever you go, fruits, flowers, crops and trees were planted. . . . Mum, you are the first to take me to school (Corona, Bukuru). You gave me depth and vision in the basics of mathematics and English. . . . You radiate joy, warmth, goodness, and tender love. . . . Your deep sense of history broadened my vision. . . . Papa and Mama: You both pray together and taught the family the importance of prayer. You are both the first to get up and the last to go to bed. You used a family bicycle bell to wake us up to prayer, and when the bell was not around you used a gong. You are the first to teach me about God, and you quietly sowed the seeds of my vocation to the Catholic priesthood. You are our first role models, and you were truly dedicated to God, family, and work. Your words of wisdom gave direction to our lives. The family motto "Goodness for happiness" has challenged us to be people of conscience. You could both imagine a good future when the present was gloomy. You always encouraged going to church together, traveling together, and helped us to imbibe the power of positive thinking. Your desire for family unity ushered in oneness of mind and harmonious living.

SECOND NARRATIVE: WITH A JESUIT COMPANION

The other story of asking forgiveness that I would like to share occurred at Gonzaga University. The conflict developed in a flash, with one of my finest Jesuit companions. Intriguingly, it stemmed from our different views on the conflict between Galileo Galilei and the Catholic Church. Father Michael Maher is a brilliant historian and is the chair of the Catholic Studies Department. He is also the chaplain of the Knights of St. Columbus. I have a lot of respect for him, and I appreciate his insightful perspectives on history. Currently, one of the courses he has designed to teach students at Gonzaga is the history of the Society of Jesus. Whenever people make controversial historical statements, he is one person I can confidently go to for clarification.

However, during a lively conversation at lunch on February 25, 2013, I asked Maher about his views on the controversy surrounding Pope Pius XII and the Jews. Maher used historical facts to explain that Pius XII was not anti-Semitic but loved the culture of the German people. I was satisfied with his argument. As our conversation progressed, I brought up the Galileo controversy with the certitude that the Church was absolutely wrong in this controversy. My premises were Galileo's heliocentric view of the universe and the posthumous apology of Pope John Paul II in 2000. Maher cautioned me about the certitude of my position and said that I should not conclude that Galileo had been right. I got emotional, thinking Maher was blindly defending the Church, but he was simply trying to let me know that the Galileo controversy was more complex than it might appear. He argued that the Galileo affair has to be juxtaposed with the models of the universe at that time.

Maher's point was that the Church had been wrong, but so had Galileo, whose circular theory was wrong. However, I took the view that the Church officials did not accept the heliocentric view. This unplanned conversation generated more tension than insight. The tension forced me to do more research on the affair of Galileo and the Church, and to review the models of the universe designed by Ptolemy, Nicolaus Copernicus, Tycho Brahe, Galileo, and Johannes Kepler. I found out that even though John Paul II had apologized, the Galileo affair was indeed more complex than it seemed. Oops! Maher had been right. Though no major rift between us had occurred, I felt a need to apologize to him immediately. I imagined the context for the forgiveness asking. I also contemplated what words of apology I would say.

Before leaving my room for community dinner that day, I was hoping I would see Maher at dinner. As I went in to get my meal, Maher also came in to get his. After saying hello, I quickly seized the opportunity and asked forgiveness for the argument that afternoon. My apology changed the tone of our relationships, tensions immediately dissolved, and our defenses were dropped. We sat at a new table and had a wonderful dinner. A community member who had witnessed the afternoon controversy just hours earlier was not sure if he was seeing correctly and kept staring at us now having a peaceful conversation. To me, this was an experience of a dramatic shift from conflict to grace.

The following day, on February 26, Maher and I met again at another table for dinner. As my other Jesuit companions left for other businesses for the evening, Maher and I remained and kept chatting. Our rich and interesting conversations took us to different topical landscapes. He shared with me about his experience on the day Martin Luther King Jr. was assassinated. This fateful day had been Maher's birthday, April 4, 1968, at the time he was living with his parents in Wisconsin. He shared how due to the tensions in the city, his dad, a medical professor at Marquette University, had had to drive their black maid home. There were fears of riots in Wisconsin, which were eventually realized. We chatted about the history of the Jesuits and shared many anecdotes and jokes. I cannot remember laughing more loudly with Maher than I did at this meal.

The next day, Maher presided at our Jesuit community mass and gave an inspiring sermon in which he wove together the topics of leadership, service, and Pope Benedict's last day as pontiff. He and I met again for dinner in the dining hall, and I complimented him on his brilliant sermon. I began to wonder if my constant uncalculated meetings with Maher after our debate at lunch and my forgiveness asking were mere coincidences or the fruits of forgiveness asking. It seems to me it was the latter. On March 2, Maher and I met again on the second floor. I had tickets to the Gonzaga-Portland basketball game, but with so many fish to fry, I was contemplating whether to watch the first or the second half. My intuition told me that Maher was looking for a ticket to the game. I asked him if he wanted my ticket. He was hesitant, since he did not want to deprive me of seeing the game. Finally I brought out the ticket and said, "If you want to see the whole game (first half and second half) then you should have my ticket." He replied, "Are you sure?" I said, "Yes." And that settled it. After he took the ticket, I was immediately reminded of the ongoing phenomenon I saw as a manifestation of forgiveness asking. There was a change in the dynamics of my interactions with Maher that caused me to meet Maher at the right time, made me aware to the fact that he was looking for a basketball ticket, and made me generous to offer my ticket to him. I ended up watching the second half of the basketball game on television with some other Jesuit companions.

Conclusion: Insights Gained and a Discussion

Martin Luther King Jr. (1998) said, "Within the best of us there is some evil, and within the worst of us, there is some good" (p. 46). He also said that when we look in the face of every person and see deep down in that person "the image of God," we begin to love him or her in spite of what he or she does (p. 46). I believe that one of the challenges for every servant-leader is to recognize and promote the element of good in others. Abraham Lincoln demonstrated this goodwill during his presidency. Where his friends saw only the bad in Lincoln's former adversary Edwin Stanton, Lincoln saw a quality of good leadership in him and made Stanton the US Secretary of War. I think that seeing the other side of the coin (both our own coin and the coins of the other) can lead us to seek forgiveness as well as to forgive others. When we know that we ourselves and others are in need of redemption, forgiveness becomes a mutual redemptive act. Experiences of asking for forgiveness help me to realize my shadows. Gaining the light of forgiveness energizes me to also pass on the light of forgiveness to others who hurt me or may hurt me.

The Greek verb *aphiemi* means "to give up a debt" or "to let go" (*Aphiemi*, n.d.). In the Hebrew language, forgiveness (*nasa, ns'*) means "to lift away," "to carry away," or "to remove" (Walts & Gulliford, 2004). When one is forgiven, he or she is untied and lifted. This description of forgiveness matches my experiences of forgiveness asking. When I recognize my need to ask for forgiveness, I recognize that my heart is tied and needs to be untied. I need the person that I hurt by omission or commission to lift up my burden and free my heart. The times that I asked for forgiveness from my dad and from Maher, their acceptance helped to unbind me, and I felt lifted and free to fly again.

Looking back, I feel the experience of moving from conflict to grace with Maher was providential, as it occurred while I was writing this chapter. Insights about forgiveness and restorative justice motivated me to immediately ask for forgiveness instead of permitting fate to evaporate the strings of friction that were quickly being knit through dispute. I think every debate and discussion about life should continually move us toward a return to our common brotherhood and sisterhood. That is our strength. Our lives are meant to be lives of grace, not conflict. If I had not decided to apologize, I would have missed an opportunity. One of the insights I gained from my experience of forgiveness asking is that I took total responsibility in asking for pardon. I could not pass that responsibility to someone else. I took responsibility in owning my fault.

A pit of conflict can turn into a mecca of life and grace. In reflecting on and articulating my experience of forgiveness asking, I observed my growth in humility, wisdom, freedom, authenticity, and wholeness. Forgiveness asking has the power to transform a person, leading them to adopt the attitude of a servant-leader. Forgiveness asking is also a process. In my asking forgiveness of my dad and Maher, the process was both physical and spiritual. As I reflected on these experiences, I was reminded of the journey of Victor and Thomas in the film *Smoke Signals* (Estes & Eyre, 1998) by the great American poet and screenwriter Sherman Alexie, a man of Native American (Spokane and Coeur d'Alene) descent who has faced his own generational demons in the context of the colonization of Native Americans, and of liberation through story and journey. Victor and Thomas were both physically traveling and on an interior journey, and Victor eventually experienced inner healing. Healing, which is "to make whole," is what motivates a servant-leader (Greenleaf, 1977/2002, p. 50).

Forgiveness asking was redemptive and restorative for me, for my dad, and for my Jesuit companion. I observed profound interior changes in my relationship with my dad and with Maher. We began to see ourselves in a new light. One key to forgiveness asking is a recognition of our shadows. The search for light and making amends gave me the impetus to overcome the inertia of protracted procrastination and excuses, especially with my dad. Understanding the past, engaging the future, and recognizing blind spots are paramount in developing foresight (DeGraaf, Tilley, & Neal, 2004). Forgiveness asking is not something we leave to chance, luck, or fate. Ferch (2012) says that Carl Jung believed that the denial of our shadows is a human weakness that causes us to project blame on others, away from ourselves, and thereby to undercut the opportunity for self-growth. Blaming leads us to mediocrity (Ferch, 2012). This weakness can be overcome through insight and knowledge, and goodwill and love (Ferch, 2012). I believe forgiveness asking is inspired by insight and goodwill. Tyrell (1999) wrote, "Man is made to know and to love" (p. 136). Knowing is cognitive self-transcendence, while loving is self-transcendence and entrance into communion with the other (Tyrell, 1999). It is in the self-transcendence of love that we discover ourselves and realize our true identities (Tyrell, 1999).

There is also a form of discernment involved in forgiveness asking. Reflecting on my experiences, I wished to know whether I was right in my stances. Sometimes the false feeling of righteousness blocks the move toward forgiveness asking. Saint Ignatius of Loyola, in his second rule for the discernment of spirits, says that it is characteristic of the evil spirit to cause anxiety, discouragement, and obstacles for those who are progressing from good to better (Ignatius, 1992, #315). However, the good spirit stirs up courage, strength, consolation, tranquility, and inspiration, which move a person toward good (Ignatius, 1992, #315). I noticed the oscillation between these two spirits in my decision to ask for forgiveness. I also learned from my reflections that it is important to keep in mind Loyola's fifth rule for the discernment of spirits: after resolving to move toward forgiveness asking, one should avoid the temptation to make a change in a time of desolation.

Saint Ignatius also warns that the evil angel can appear as an angel of light (Ignatius, 1992, #332). Metaphorically, my shadows in a relationship might appear as lights, and consequently lead to pride and make me wait for the other to ask for forgiveness of me instead of my making the first move. I believe that prayer is important for the ritual of forgiveness asking. It is also important to use our contemplative imagination to prepare ourselves for the forgiveness-asking ritual. Praying to have the heart and mind of a servant-leader and praying to say the right words are essential to transform conflict into an opportunity for new life. I am reminded of how Tutu (1997) and the members of his Truth and Reconciliation Commission had a prayerful interfaith service in the town where the first hearing of the committee was to take place.

Forgiveness asking also restores trust and dignity in our relationships. The truth sets one free (John 8:32), and forgiveness asking is a confession based on truth. Asking for forgiveness is like designing and building a bridge that connects the heart to the mind. Reyes (n.d.) said that if a person's heart is not connected to his or her mind, he or she will hurt others. In addition, if we do not have freedom from the compulsion to seek retaliation or the freedom to ask forgiveness, then we need to pray for that freedom. "I am sorry" or "Will you forgive me?" is difficult to say (Tutu, 1997, p. 269). It requires freedom and humility. Ferch (2012) believes that the servant-leader is a person of persuasion and not coercion. He adds, "A rich sense of persuasion in everyday life can change the world" (p. 148).

In my experience, the words "I am sorry" or "Please forgive me" have a powerful and persuasive force that lead the other to offer forgiveness. After all, we do not force another person to forgive; we beg him or her to forgive. Forgiveness asking also requires dialogue rooted in love and not coercion. Freire points out that love is the foundation of true dialogue (Freire, 1993). The logical consequence of dialogue that is based on a relationship of love and humility is mutual trust (Freire, 1993). It is this mutual trust that allows souls to transcend the nights of discord and see a rising sun of harmony on the horizon. I also think that the quest for forgiveness is easier if one's consciousness is at the above-the-line level of thinking. For Václav Havel, leader of the Velvet Revolution, consciousness foreshadows being; and reflective consciousness and the human heart are seedbeds for human liberation (Ferch, 2012; Palmer, 2000). The way to reconciliation and freedom is through the practice of consciousness. Ferch (2012) said, "Servant-leadership echoes Havel's refreshing sense of the sacred with regard to consciousness and being" (p. 123). Those whose level of consciousness is above the line are servant-leaders (Ferch, 2012). They motivate others through love, discernment, peace, forgiveness, humility, self-responsibility, and service (Ferch, 2012).

Forgiveness asking is also a redemptive and life-giving experience. But it takes interior self-knowledge, self-introspection, self-awareness, and self-evaluation for one to see the need for and embrace the possibility of redemption. Furthermore, forgiveness asking is a phenomenon that takes place in the spirit and philosophy of *ubuntu*. In this spirit, each person's existence and humanity becomes meaningful in the eyes of another (Ferch, 2012; Tutu, 1997). I resonate with the power and meaning of the words in the title of Tutu's (1997) book *No Future without Forgiveness*; I too believe that a good future is founded on restorative justice. For our lives to flourish and become meaningful, the spirit of forgiveness must live in our hearts. Forgiveness asking is an act of love, and overcoming the inertia that prevents us from extending love to others can be challenging. Loving the other is a disposition that demands from us vulnerability, humility, and surrender (Ferch, 2012).

Ferch (2012) sees a progression in the realm of forgiveness. When we think of forgiveness, we resist the idea. When this resistance is broken, we have a desire to forgive someone. But the real revolution comes when we pass this stage and begin to "affirm the need to ask for forgiveness" (Ferch, 2012, p. 46). At this stage, we are ready to swallow our pride and walk toward others to ask for forgiveness, leading to change and healing in ourselves and in the other person. In my experience of forgiveness asking, I went through these phases, albeit uniquely for each scenario. If we cannot ask for forgiveness, we will find it difficult to forgive others. We really have nothing to lose by asking for forgiveness. Rather, we have enlightenment and transformation to gain. Being able to see our shadows can drive us to seek forgiveness. My experience of conflict (no matter how small) is an experience of darkness. Forgiveness asking helps me to shine light into my life. Just as a servant-leader first desires to serve, I also think that he or she must also first desire to ask forgiveness instead of waiting for the other to ask forgiveness first.

Remembering, mulling over, and sharing my experiences of forgiveness asking are what Palmer (2000) describes as an "inner work" (p. 91). Reflection, journaling, meditation, spiritual friendship, and prayer are forms of inner work (Palmer, 2000). Exploring my shadows and my interior life are also good preparation for better servant-leadership in family, communal, and organizational settings. Palmer (2000) testified that the experience of telling the truth about dark experiences helped him stay in the light. I also think that the experience of articulating the truth of our failures and our forgiveness asking encounters strengthens us and allows us to stay in the light. Palmer (2000) sees authentic leaders as those who lead from within. In a similar vein, I think forgiveness asking makes leaders able to lead more authentically from the power of their inner life and from the depth of their minds and hearts. Emotional and social sacrifice pilot leaders to ask forgiveness and to forgive others, thereby bestowing moral authority on leaders (Covey, 2002).

Reflecting on my forgiveness asking experiences, I think there was depth of listening involved. I listened to my conscience, listened again to what transpired, and reconsidered what the other was saying or feeling. This then created an interior instability that needed to be resolved through forgiveness asking. I experienced a restoration of order and harmony in my relationships with my dad and Maher. An implication of this insight, for me, is that a servant-leader, who is characteristically a good listener, has the advantage of having a disposition that allows him or her to easily ask forgiveness of others. By listening to the disharmony in his or her heart, the servant-leader seeks to restore relational tranquility, and this restoration establishes deeper meaning in the organizational life in which he or she is involved. Consequently, I am challenged to develop better listening skills and to aspire to attain the qualities of a servant-leader.

Frankl (2000) said that the fundamental driving force in us is the will to meaning: "Therefore man is originally characterized by his 'search for meaning' rather than his 'search for himself'" (p. 84). Frankl also believed that the more we forget ourselves and give ourselves to a cause or to another person, the more human we become. My own experience of forgiveness asking is that it positively affected my humanity, as well as the humanity of the other, and established a deeper meaning in my relationship with others. There was also a transformation in the dynamics of my relationships. I could no longer take the gift of relationship for granted. Another benefit of forgiveness asking is that it breaks down walls and builds bridges across our common humanity. When I was reflecting on my experiences of forgiveness asking, I noticed that reconciliation went beyond saying, "I am sorry" (as is indicated by my stories above). Ongoing transformations continue after forgiveness asking. This confirms for me what Tutu (1997) meant when he said that reconciliation is an ongoing process. It is also insightful to know that the work of reconciliation is God's dream for humanity (Tutu, 1997). Therefore, in asking for forgiveness, I am participating in God's dream.

References

Aphiemi. (n.d.). Blue Letter Bible. Retrieved from https://www.blueletterbible.org/lang/lexicon/lexicon.cfm?Strongs=G863&t=KJV

Coffeen, D. (2010). Nietzsche's Will to Power. Retrieved from http://www.youtube.com/watch?v=pOzYZmUtbKY

Covey, S. (2002). Foreword. In L. C. Spears (Ed.), *Servant-leadership: A journey into the nature of legitimate power and greatness* (pp. 1–13). New York, NY: Paulist Press.

DeGraaf, D., Tilley, C., & Neal, L. (2004). Servant-leadership characteristics in organizational life. In L. C. Spears & M. Lawrence (Eds.), *Practicing servant-leadership: Succeeding through trust, bravery, and forgiveness* (pp. 133–166). San Francisco, CA: Jossey-Bass.

Estes, L. (Producer), & Eyre, C. (Director). (1998). *Smoke signals* [Motion picture]. Los Angeles, CA: Miramax.

Ferch, S. R. (2012). *Forgiveness and power in the age of atrocity: Servant leadership as a way of life.* Lanham, MD: Lexington Books.

Frankl, V. E. (2000). *Man's search for ultimate meaning.* New York, NY: Perseus.

Freire, P. (1993). *Pedagogy of the oppressed* (30th anniversary ed.). New York, NY: Continuum.

Greenleaf, R. K. (2002). *Servant leadership: A journey into the nature of legitimate power and greatness* (25th anniversary ed.). L. C. Spears (Ed.). New York, NY: Paulist Press. (Original work published 1977).

Gunnarsson, J., & Blohm, O. (2011). The welcoming servant-leader: The art of creating hostmanship. In S. R. Ferch & L. C. Spears (Eds.), *The spirit of servant-leadership* (pp. 68–85). New York, NY: Paulist Press.

Ignatius. (1992). *The spiritual exercises of saint Ignatius.* (G. Ganss, Trans.). Chicago, IL: Loyola Press.

King, C. S. (1969). *My life with Martin Luther King, Jr.* New York, NY: Puffin Books.

King, M. L., Jr. (1998). *A knock at midnight: Inspiration from the great sermons of Reverend Martin Luther King, Jr.* C. Carson & P. Holloran (Eds.). New York, NY: Warner Books.

Laub, J. A. (1999). *Assessing the servant organization: Development of the servant organizational leadership assessment (SOLA) instrument* (Doctoral dissertation). Retrieved from http://foley.gonzaga.edu/

Palmer, P. J. (2000). *Let your life speak: Listening for the voice of vocation.* San Francisco, CA: Jossey-Bass.

Patterson, K. A. (2003). *Servant leadership: A theoretical model* (Doctoral dissertation). Regent University, Virginia.

Reyes, R. (n.d.). *Conflict.* [Video file]. Retrieved from Gonzaga University course notes.

Russell, R. F., & Stone, A. G. (2002). A review of servant leadership attributes: Developing a practical model. *Leadership & Organization Development Journal, 23*(3), 145–157.

Spears, L. C. (2004, Fall). Practicing servant-leadership. *Leader to Leader, 34,* 7–11.

Stone, A. G., Russell, R. F., & Patterson, K. (2003). Transformational versus servant-leadership: A difference in leader focus. Servant-Leadership Research Roundtable, August 2003. Virginia Beach, VA.

Tutu, D. M. (1997). *No future without forgiveness.* New York, NY: Image Doubleday.

Tyrell, B. (1999). *Christotherapy I: Healing through enlightenment.* Eugene, OR: Wipf and Stock.

van Dierendonck, D. (2010). Servant-leadership: A review and synthesis. *Journal of Management, 20,* 1–34.

Wallace, J. R. (2007). Servant-leadership: A worldview perspective. *International Journal of Leadership Studies, 2*(2), 114–132.

Walts, F., & Gulliford, L. (2004). *Forgiveness in context: Theology and psychology in creative dialogue.* New York, NY: T & T Clark.

Chapter 15

Justice and Forgiveness in the Family

JOHN R.

The presence of a committed alcoholic/addict in the midst of a family has
a profound effect on the family's structure and dynamic. Over time in such
an environment, a web of frustration, disappointment, shattered hope, bitter
resentment, unmet expectations, and mutually debilitating codependency is
woven, enmeshing equally the alcoholic and his loved ones. This pattern
is nearly universal, and yet many if not most alcoholics proceed for years
thinking that it does not apply to them. I was no different.

For fifteen years, from my first drink at age fifteen until my last at
age thirty, my progressive alcoholism was a continuing source of chaos and
discord not only for me but in the lives of all those who love me. My
journey through recovery has been one of stages: from awareness of my
problem to acceptance of its stark reality to a dawning understanding of
its huge scope to the powerful desire to get help to full-blown metanoia
catalyzed by a bona fide spiritual experience to a sustained commitment
to living according to the principles laid out in the Twelve Steps of Alcoholics Anonymous (Alcoholics Anonymous, 2001, pp. 59–60).

Along the way, there have been many opportunities to be a participant
in the life-restoring process of both forgiving and being forgiven. In this
chapter, I will explore some of the damage caused by my alcoholism and
addiction, followed by an examination of the restorative power wrought
by the applied solution of the Twelve Steps, with a particular focus on
the sponsorship relationship and the amends-making process of Step 9
(Alcoholics Anonymous, 2001, pp. 76–84) and their resonance with the

ideas of Robert Greenleaf. As a part of this examination, I will explore the forgiveness dialogue that took place with my father during the Ninth Step process as a representative example of the regenerative power of forgiveness asking.

The Problem

When my addiction is viewed through the lens of its negative effects on the family dynamic, there are two primary issues that leap to the fore. The first is integrity, and the second is health. An unpacking of these two broad concepts will show how pervasively and insidiously addiction affects each aspect of a family's relationship with its addict, and how harmful the addiction is to the overall family environment.

It is said that relationships are built on trust. Ultimately, this axiom is impossible to fulfill when one of the parties to the relationship is an alcoholic. The alcoholic is serving a higher master. My own integrity, my capacity to engender trust in others, was severely diminished during the last decade of my drinking and using. I was unreliable and known at times to be a liar, a dissembler, and, if things were bad enough, even a thief. I could not be trusted to hold newborn nieces and nephews, and I was regretfully left off many party invitations. These realities, however, were a far cry from my perception of myself. I considered myself a bit down-and-out. Maybe. But for the most part I operated under the delusion that I was the same upstanding near-superhero I had always been.

The erosion of my physical, mental, and spiritual health was the other wedge that my alcoholism created within the family. Alcoholics often operate under the much-quoted persistent delusion "I am only hurting myself!" The South African understanding of the universal truth that is *ubuntu* (Tutu, 1999, p. 31) reveals this to be a lie. The family is intimately interconnected, and that which sickens one sickens the whole. As my own alcoholism and drug abuse progressed, it took an ever-worsening toll on my body, mind, and spirit. Near the end, I gained forty pounds while ignoring myriad other signs of bodily breakdown, totally neglected my spiritual development, and consistently engaged in behavior that suggested the presence of a death wish. Watching me visibly destroy myself in this way was an incredible burden for my family to bear, and even today I shudder to think of the heartache I put them through during the worst of those times.

The Solution

As the saying goes, eventually things get bad enough that you either get help or you die. Lots of people die. By the grace of God, when things finally got bad enough for me, that same family I had been turning my back on for all of those years was right there to help me. They mustered the fortitude for an(other) intervention. They made the arrangements for the inpatient facility. They wrote me constantly while I was there, and they were there to pick me up the day I got out, hoping against hope that this time, things were going to be different. This time, things were.

Peck (1995), in his chapter featured in Larry Spears's *Reflections on Leadership*, describes the Twelve Steps of Alcoholics Anonymous as a world-class "technology for peacemaking" (p. 88). In the same collection, Ken Blanchard exhorts all managers to take to heart the principles of the Twelve Steps (Lee & Zemke, 1995, p. 105). In his introduction to the later collection *Insights on Leadership*, Spears (1998) singles out Alcoholics Anonymous and the Twelve Step approach as exemplifying the principles of servant-leadership (p. 10). Greenleaf (2002) himself pointed to AA as an organization responsible for unparalleled healing (p. 50). I am heartened to hear of the respect that these eminent writers and thinkers hold for the Twelve Steps. It reinforces my understanding that servant-leadership is real and practically viable, since I know from direct personal experience that the Twelve Steps are.

Marietta Jaeger tells us that real justice is not punishment but restoration (Tutu, 1999, p. 155). Restoration is the purpose of the Twelve Steps. Restoration of relationship, restoration of health, restoration of integrity, restoration of hope, and the restoration of the capacity for joy. This restoration occurs through the application of twelve living principles, which constitute a spiritual program of action to be embodied for a lifetime. Lee and Zemke (1995) give a concise encapsulation of Steps 1 through 3: admit vulnerability, acknowledge there is a Higher Power, and get aligned with that power (p. 105). Step 4 is the first of the so-called action steps, in which the alcoholic sets to work making a list of all of the people he has harmed. This list will be used during Step 9, when the actual amends-making process begins.

My own relationship to AA and to the Twelve Steps goes back to 1995, when as a senior in high school I was forced to attend meetings after getting in trouble with alcohol and drugs. Ten years later, I returned to meetings at the pointed request of a girlfriend who demanded I get sober. Even during those periods when my presence at AA's tables was not my idea, I had always respected the sincerity of the people in the meetings, and when my time finally came, I knew right where to go. As prodigal sons perennially are, I was welcomed back into the AA fold immediately, with one difference: this time I got connected with a sponsor.

The Sponsorship Relationship in AA

Nowhere in the Alcoholics Anonymous *Big Book* does one find reference to formal sponsorship, but the importance of the sponsorship relationship within the Twelve Step methodology is primary and unquestioned. What is understood by those who know is that the practical wisdom inherent in the steps can be properly transmitted only from one alcoholic to another. It cannot be learned from a book. In fact, it is the awareness of and focus on this very truth that represents AA's singular advantage over every other treatment modality before or after it, of which Greenleaf (2002) was aware (p. 50). Spurred by the realization of this truth's power, AA cofounders Bill Wilson and Dr. Bob Smith in effect sponsored each other as AA was birthed in Akron, Ohio, in 1935. The understanding that talking with another alcoholic about their experience, strength, and hope was foundational to recovery eventually became codified in the Twelve Steps. This understanding was the root of the first AA meetings, which took place in the living rooms of the founders and other early adherents. At these meetings, the sponsorship tradition of one-to-one transmission of these hard-won but simple truths was established.

Echoing Jesus's own statements that sinners paradoxically find the way to redemption more easily than their righteous brethren, Greenleaf (2002) writes,

> No one can judge, from where one now stands, how difficult the next step along the road of spiritual growth may be. Those of good works . . . may find the next step of staggering proportions. Their seeming opposites—the unsuccessful, the misfit, the unlovely, the rejected—may take the next step with ease. (p. 339)

Many who fit this description—unsuccessful, unlovely, rejected misfits—having finally suffered enough to be teachable, find themselves recipients of that greatest of gifts, serenity. The gift comes as a result of rigorous engagement with the spiritual program of action called the Twelve Steps, as mediated by a sponsor. And indeed, many of these former misfits, having had the spiritual awakening promised in Step 12 (Alcoholics Anonymous, 2001, p. 60), will take the next step with ease: perpetuating the sponsorship chain of humble, grateful service by going on to sponsor other alcoholics in need.

The servant-leader acknowledges that his or her own healing is the motivation for the work that they do (Greenleaf, 2002, p. 50). So too does the alcoholic in recovery acknowledge explicitly that he helps other alcoholics for the sake of his own sobriety and sanity. Here, we are again witness to the reality of *ubuntu*, whereby we know that through helping others to heal, we ourselves are healed, and vice versa. Of the innumerable pithy sayings, acronyms, and aphorisms that abound in the halls of AA, perhaps none better sums up the heart of the matter than that perfect paradox "You've got to give it away to keep it."

And so those who find themselves gifted by grace in turn give the gift away, so that they might retain it. This process takes place most healthily and effectively in the form of the sponsor/sponsee relationship, an arrangement into which each newcomer is encouraged to enter. There are an infinite number of approaches to the transmission of AA wisdom, each as unique as the dynamic between the sponsor and the sponsee. It is here, in this relationship, that we most clearly see AA's prototypical servant-leadership shining through. Though it is quoted often enough in the servant-leadership literature so as to be blunted of its impact, I nevertheless call attention to Greenleaf's (2002) initial definition of servant-leadership, as I can think of no other relationship that embodies its tenets in such a verifiable fashion as that of the AA sponsor and sponsee:

> The servant leader is servant first. It begins with the feeling that one wants to serve, to serve first. Then conscious choice brings one to aspire to lead. . . . The best test . . . is this: do those served grow as persons? Do they, while being served, become healthier, wiser, freer, more autonomous, more likely to themselves become servants? (p. 27)

Here, the sponsor is servant first because he has had an attitude of service instilled in him since he first began working the steps. Service is a principal cornerstone of AA, along with unity and fellowship. A spirit of service pervades AA, and newcomers gradually internalize the service mentality as they see its tangible effects on those they wish to emulate, those who "have what they want." As they mature in their recovery and deepen in their commitment to service, it is likely that opportunities to sponsor newcomers will present themselves. Now, as sponsors (servant-leaders) leading their sponsees through the steps, they serve as catalysts for growth. Their sponsees, to whom they are pledged in service, often quickly and in dramatic fashion become healthier, wiser, freer, more autonomous, and more likely to become servants. And as a part of the process, the sponsor's own spiritual life is enriched and strengthened. The privilege of witnessing the mutually enriching transformation take place in a sponsee, servant-led by a sponsor from utter sickness to radiant health, stands today as one of life's most sublime joys.

It happened like that for me. There is no rule that says you will get the sponsor you expect or think you deserve. In fact, there are no rules at all, and the allocation of newcomer to sponsor is something that happens differently everywhere, since each meeting of Alcoholics Anonymous is autonomous on such matters. My sponsor didn't fit any of my preconceived notions about who he should be. But why should he? He was, and is, in "a role . . . uniquely appropriate for him as an individual, that drew heavily on his strengths and demanded little that was unnatural for him" (Greenleaf, 2002, p. 49). He was a union crane operator with five years' sobriety and a story that surpassed mine in nearly every level of severity, and what mattered was that emotionally and spiritually we had both been bankrupt in the same way. We connected on a suprarational level, and he offered to take me through the steps. I gratefully accepted, and we set to work.

Here again, before ever hearing the term *servant-leadership*, I experienced it in its purest form. This man, a virtual stranger, agreed to take me through the steps in the same way that his sponsor had done for him. What this meant was that he offered to me at least five hours of his time per week for nearly four months. He invited me into his home and we read through the *Big Book* out loud, stopping often to discuss and underline passages. We went to many meetings together, and he began easing me into service by taking me with him to his commitments. As we worked through the steps, we became friends, though friendship per se is not at all a prerequisite of a healthy sponsorship relationship. We finished the book and made our way through the first seven steps, and throughout he would remind me of how much he was being transformed by the process even as I was, for he had worked with other newcomers before, but none had completed the steps.

At this stage, I was on fire, and the people around me could see it. I was working the steps, and I was an active participant in my life. Everything was changing for me, and it was a heady feeling not just for me but for my entire family. For the first time ever, I was taking action in my life on behalf of the good. The pinnacle of this action was the restorative work I was doing as a component of the steps, particularly Steps 8 and 9, which tell us that with the guidance of our sponsor we:

8. Made a list of all people we had harmed, and became willing to make amends to them all.

9. Made direct amends to such people wherever possible, except when to do so may injure them or others. (Alcoholics Anonymous, 2001, p. 59)

And so I began making Ninth Step amends to people: old friends, girlfriends, my mother, my brothers, former employers, and others. Some were difficult; all were redemptive.

When you are working the steps sincerely and in earnest, magic can start happening very quickly. A palpable sense of spirit will begin to animate your life as you move through the process of cleaning up your side of the street and setting right old wrongs. There is great humility required, but with perseverance the rewards are many. Indeed, the so-called "Ninth Step Promises," each predicated on taking an active stance of forgiveness, resulting in a realization of faith, and often read aloud in AA meetings, are bold enough to quote in their entirety:

If we are painstaking about this phase of our development, we will be amazed before we are half way through. We are going to know a new freedom and a new happiness. We will not regret the past nor wish to shut the door on it. We will comprehend the word serenity and we will know peace. No matter how far down the scale we have gone, we will see how our experience can benefit others. That feeling of uselessness and self-pity will disappear. We will lose interest in selfish things and gain interest in our fellows. Self-seeking will slip away. Our whole attitude and outlook upon life will change. Fear of people and of economic insecurity will leave us. We will intuitively know how to handle situations which used to baffle us. We will suddenly realize that God is doing for us what we could not do for ourselves. (Alcoholics Anonymous, 2001, pp. 83–84)

Are these extravagant promises? We think not. They are being fulfilled among us—sometimes quickly, sometimes slowly. They will always materialize if we work for them.

Greenleaf (2002) echoes the penultimate and cumulative Ninth Step Promises in his own writings on the subject of foresight:

Living this way [simultaneously as a historian, contemporary analyst, and prophet] is partly a matter of faith. Stress is a condition of most modern life, and if one is a servant leader and carrying the burdens of other people—going out ahead to show the way, one takes the rough and tumble (and it really is rough and tumble in some leadership roles)—one takes this in the belief that, if one enters a situation prepared with the necessary experience and knowledge at the conscious level, in the situation the intuitive insight necessary for one's optimal performance will be forthcoming. Is there any other way, in the turbulent world of affairs (including the typical home), for one to maintain serenity in the face of uncertainty? (p. 39)

Greenleaf is saying the same thing that AA's founders are saying: a person moving through life animated by the principles of servant-leadership will be further guided by an inner and inerrant voice. This is the sort of permanent guidance I was seeking: access to and relationship with the source of that inerrant voice. I still had work to do.

Ninth Step in the Microcosm

Those first several Ninth Step dialogues I initiated, while certainly valid, necessary, and redeeming in their own right, also served as practice for the big one. My relationship with my father had been rocky since I could remember, and had worsened as my disease had progressed. My father was a very successful and driven physician, and my perceived lackadaisical approach toward life infuriated him to no end. For healing to happen, we first had decades of frustrated attempts at communication to contend with.

I was frightened because I knew that I still had hidden resentments toward my father. I needed to be free of these, and to that end I waited for a while to initiate the conversation. I waited, too, because he had heard too many empty apologies from me in the past. Too many empty promises. There needed to be some small foundation of credibility to stand upon for the dialogue to be meaningful.

An opportunity presented itself whereby I convinced my dad to join me on a five-day retreat in the woods with the Franciscan writer, teacher, jail chaplain, and mystic Richard Rohr, himself no small proponent of Twelve Step spirituality, which he referred to in a personal anecdote as "America's great gift to world spirituality." This was out of character for my dad, and I felt the spirit at work even with his acceptance. During the retreat, he and I were not often together, due to the gathering's format. This gave us each opportunities to reflect separately on the retreat's purpose and content, which was concerned primarily with grief and loss.

After the retreat, we were both in a pregnant liminal space. In a restaurant at O'Hare airport, I bought my father dinner, maybe for the first time. I had been sober for nine months. I poured my heart out, I poured my guilt out, I poured my shame out, I poured my confusion out, I poured my directionless dying hatred out. I told him that I had always loved him and that I knew that he loved me. I asked him for forgiveness for all of my transgressions, which I named. I shared aloud a representative litany of my sins against him, letting us both look the beast in the eye (Tutu, 1999, p. 28). I told him that I had emptied my heart of all hatred and anger toward him, which was finally true. We talked for three hours, the most transparent, vivifying conversation I've ever had with him. It was transformational and transcendent for both of us, and that night we shared a hotel room at O'Hare and slept like babies.

Today my father and I have a wonderful relationship. We still disagree; we have very different approaches to life, different ways of prioritizing things in our worlds. But we respect each other and love each other. It is amazing how the newfound, or perhaps rediscovered, love between us has trickled down and expanded outward into the rest of the family. This didn't happen overnight, but rather followed something like Pawlikowski's (1998) phased alchemical formula consisting of stages: repentance, contrition, acceptance of responsibility, healing, and finally reunion (p. 221). I know that a major part of the success of this healing operation was bound up in the willingness to ask for forgiveness, the willingness to go first, and the willingness to embrace the humility that such a stance entails.

Conclusion

For fifteen years, my alcohol and drug addiction presented an impassable obstacle to a healthy family life. Alcoholism destroys relationships even as it destroys people, reducing alcoholics to shells of their former self physically, spiritually, and mentally. The effect that this degradation has on families is horrific, as the interconnected reality of the family unit is made manifest in the pain they visibly share and collectively bear.

My alcoholism, though a source of great pain for both myself and for my entire family, is also something for which I am paradoxically grateful. Through it, I have been guided, finally, to a place of humility, healing, and immense gratitude. Alcoholism has brought me into relationship with the Twelve Steps of AA, and with the fellowship of men and women who practice its principles. Through these steps, and this fellowship, I have learned of a new way of living predicated on acceptance, willingness, gratitude, humility, and forgiveness. I have learned these things through actually experiencing them, which is a different category of learning altogether. This way of life has helped bring about a new era of love and connection in my family, for which we are all eternally grateful.

As my relationship to the Twelve Steps has evolved into a deep awareness of their value as a lifelong spiritual program of action, I have become aware of the parallels between the Twelve Step approach and servant-leadership. In fact, as Greenleaf and others have recognized, the Twelve Steps are a process through which servant-leaders are created and then nurtured as they retransmit that which was freely given to them. The relationship between a sponsor and a sponsee is as close to the pro-totypical servant-leader/follower relationship as any I am aware of, and it is worthy of further study as a servant-leadership model.

The power of forgiveness, of asking for forgiveness, was made manifest in life-giving ways through the course of my Ninth Step work. The forgiveness-asking dialogue I shared with my father stands as the most perpetually life-giving communication channel I have ever opened with anyone. Its fruits continue to be borne. My experiences with asking for (and receiving) forgiveness over the past several years, exemplified by the ongoing relationship with my father, leave me with no doubt that Tutu (1999) is correct: there is no future without forgiveness. With it and through it, however, miracles are possible in our lives, families, and communities.

Editor's Note

In keeping with AA's 11th and 12th Traditions, this article has been published under the author's first name and the initial of his last name.

References

Alcoholics Anonymous. (2001). *The story of how many thousands of men and women have recovered from alcoholism* (4th ed.). New York, NY: AA World Services.

Greenleaf, R. K. (2002). *Servant leadership: A journey into the nature of legitimate power and greatness* (25th anniversary ed.). L. C. Spears (Ed.). New York, NY: Paulist Press. (Original work published 1977).

Lee, C., & Zemke, R. (1995). The search for spirit in the workplace. In L. C. Spears (Ed.), *Reflections on leadership* (pp. 99–112). New York, NY: John Wiley & Sons.

Pawlikowski, J. T. (1998). In H. J. Cargas & B. V. Fetterman (Eds.), *The sunflower: On the possibilities and limits of forgiveness* (pp. 220–225). New York, NY: Schocken.

Peck, M. S. (1995). Servant-leadership training and discipline in authentic community. In L. C. Spears (Ed.), *Reflections on leadership* (pp. 87–98). New York, NY: John Wiley & Sons.

Spears, L. C. (1998). Introduction: Tracing the growing impact of servant-leadership. In L. C. Spears (Ed.), *Insights on leadership* (pp. 1–14). New York, NY: John Wiley and Sons.

Tutu, D. (1999). *No future without forgiveness.* New York, NY: Doubleday.

Part IV

Servant-Leadership, Forgiveness, and Personal Applications

Chapter 16

The Image of God, Servant-Leadership, and Forgiveness

Karen Petersen Finch

The image of the leader as servant has come to exercise a profound influence within secular organizations (Spears, 1995). Yet one can argue that its antecedents are in the religious world. Servant-leadership is a major theme in the Judeo-Christian tradition, from a weeping Joseph embracing his brothers (Genesis 45:15, *New Oxford Annotated Bible*) to Jesus washing the feet of his disciples (John 13:5). The image also figures in Islam, Zen, and Taoism (Vanourek, 1995). Greenleaf (1977), whose writings brought the image of the servant-leader into the public imagination, was a Quaker; his seminal essay on servant-leadership was inspired by Herman Hesse's *Journey to the East*, in which the hero is ultimately revealed as the head of a religious order (Spears, 1995).

The image of the leader as servant also resonates for people who are not visibly connected to any religious tradition. Peters and Waterman (1982), whose writings on leadership are well-known, expresses suspicion of the contemporary movement to bring spirituality into secular arenas such as the workplace. Vanourek (1995) urges managers to develop a caring attitude toward employees and to "shun the glory that feeds our insecure egos" (p. 301). Vanourek's perspective is very near to that of Greenleaf (1977), who insisted that "the only authority deserving one's allegiance is that which is freely and knowingly granted by the led to the leader in response to, and in proportion to, the clearly evident servant stature of the leader" (pp. 9–10).

It is significant that a leadership model with religious roots could have settled so comfortably into the public imagination, especially given the intense focus of many Americans today on preserving the separation of church and state (Boston, 2005, p. 1). I believe the success of this model has to do with its implicit commentary on the value of human beings. To voluntarily serve another person is to acknowledge that he or she is worthy of effort, attention, and respect. As Spears (1995) wrote, "Servant-leaders believe that people have an intrinsic value beyond their tangible contributions as workers" (p. 7). Moreover, Greenleaf (1977) maintained that the value of service was not in the act itself as much as in its effect on the recipient. He asked,

> Do those served [meaning all or almost all of the people touched by that influence] grow as persons? Do they, while being served, become healthier, wiser, freer, more autonomous, more likely themselves to become servants? And, what is the effect on the least privileged in society; will they benefit, or, at least, not be further deprived? (pp. 13–14)

Greenleaf's (1977) call for leaders to consider the effect of their influence on the people they serve, especially the least fortunate, resonates with Jesus's command to "love your neighbor as yourself" (Mark 12:31). In Greenleaf's (1977) words, "Caring for others, the more able and the less able serving each other, is the rock upon which a good society is built" (p. 49). Yet I would argue that the roots of Greenleaf's call to care for others go back even further in the Judeo-Christian tradition, back to the early chapters of Genesis. "So God created humankind in his image, in the image of God he created them; male and female he created them" (Genesis 1:27). From the biblical point of view, to consider people as worthy of care is not just one possible anthropological stance among many. Rather, it is the only response commensurate with God's work in creation, in which God imprinted the divine image on Eve and Adam and, through them, on every human being.

Inherent in this biblical doctrine, however, is a paradox: those who are made in the image of God do not always exhibit the beauty and splendor of God's character (1 Chronicles 16:29). As Greenleaf (1977) wrote, "Anybody could lead perfect people—if there were any. But there aren't any perfect people" (p. 21). Therefore servant-leadership involves the acceptance of "the halt, the lame, half-made creatures that we are"

(Greenleaf, 1977, p. 21). At no time are "the vagaries of human nature" more visible than when communities are in conflict, whether that conflict be personal, familial, national, or global (Greenleaf, 1977, p. 20). In conflict, servant-leadership must grapple with the dark side of human nature and the reality that human beings, while made in God's image, have a long history of hurting one another. According to Greenleaf (1977), the true servant "always accepts and empathizes, never rejects" (p. 20).Yet are people who have actively harmed others, ranging from manipulative coworkers to participants in mass atrocity, still worthy of acceptance and empathy?

In this chapter I examine the biblical idea of creation in the image of God with particular reference to the practice of forgiveness. As Ramsey (2006) affirms, forgiveness is a logical extension of the values embedded in servant-leadership (p. 5). A leader who is dedicated to serving others naturally focuses on healing, which Greenleaf (1977) defines as "making whole" (p. 36). In the biblical tradition, the word *shalom* signifies the peace of God that is rooted in God's own wholeness or holiness, and is God's intention for human life (Feinberg, 1984, p. 833). To forgive is to acknowledge that, although genuine harm has been done, a return to shalom is possible if both victim and perpetrator can turn away from the wrongs of the past and begin a new relationship, one that is based on honesty and growing trust. The concept of human beings as made in the image of God can fuel the practice of forgiveness by reminding leaders of the transcendent aspect of human nature by affirming the creation unity that people share, whatever their differences may be, and by encouraging us to view individuals and communities through the lens of hope. By practicing forgiveness, servant-leaders can lead persons in conflict, as well as the community around them, toward the shalom that is God's intention for human life (Feinberg, 1984).

The Image of God and Transcendence

The creation of human beings in God's image has been a subject of Christian reflection since the early days of the church (Motyer, 1984). Theologians across the centuries have agreed that although God's imprint is on all of creation, humanity reflects God's character in a unique way; this reflection gives women and men permanent worth and dignity (Henry, 1984, p. 546). Christian theologians have, however, hotly debated the question of which aspect of human personhood in particular contains the divine image, be it rational intelligence, moral choice, or religious openness (Henry, 1984). In recent years, a kind of consensus has emerged that highlights the human capacity for relationship as the best reflection of God's image in us, for that capacity involves and depends upon the other proposed answers of "rational understanding, moral obedience, and religious communion" (Henry, 1984, p. 548). In other words, humanity "is made for personal and endless fellowship with God" and with one another (p. 548). Frankl (2000) agreed with this consensus when he spoke of

> that fundamental characteristic of the human reality which I have come to term its self-transcendent quality. I thereby want to denote the intrinsic fact that being human always relates and points to something other than itself—better to say, something or someone. . . . Man [*sic*] is oriented toward the world out there, and within this world, he is interested in meanings to fulfill, and in other human beings. By virtue of what I would call the pre-reflective ontological self-understanding he knows that he is actualizing himself precisely to the extent to which he is forgetting himself, and he is forgetting himself by giving himself, or loving a person other than himself. Truly, self-transcendence is the essence of human existence. (p. 138)

The self-transcendence of humanity suggests that we are most authentically human (and, paradoxically, closest to the divine image) when we are stretching toward loving relationship with God and others. On these grounds, there is nothing trivial about the way in which human beings deal with one another. To actively harm another person is to violate the image of God in that person and in myself; it is "like spitting in the face of God" (Tutu, 1999, p. 93). Both Frankl (1974) and Tutu spoke with authority on the subject of "man's inhumanity to man," having witnessed the atrocities of Auschwitz and apartheid-era South Africa, respectively. It is significant that, given their experience, both men strongly affirmed the existence of a transcendent element in human nature that remains, no matter how an individual's actions may defile it. According to Frankl (1974), the strange fact of human existence is that we are both bearers and violators of God's image:

> In concentration camps . . . we watched and witnessed some of our comrades behave like swine while others behaved like

saints. Man [sic] has both potentialities within himself. . . . Our generation is realistic, for we have come to know man as he really is. After all, man is the being who has invented the gas chambers of Auschwitz; however, he is also that being who has entered those gas chambers upright, with the Lord's Prayer or the Shema Yisrael on his lips. (pp. 212–213)

In situations of deep conflict, it is tempting for leaders to collapse Frankl's (1974) paradox and consider participants in the conflict as either heroes or monsters (Tutu, 1999). Leaders who identify themselves as servants may feel this temptation with particular intensity because of an orientation toward healing the wounded and creating justice for victims. The concept of persons as bearers of the image of God, however, suggests that leaders ought to consider the well-being of both victims and perpetrators as they strive to bring about healing in communities. According to Tutu (1999), the members of South Africa's Truth and Reconciliation Commission (TRC) benefited from this theological perspective on offenders:

We . . . were quite appalled at the depth of depravity to which human beings could sink and we would, most of us, say that those who committed such dastardly deeds were monsters because the deeds were monstrous. But theology prevents us from doing this. Theology reminded me that, however diabolical the act, it did not turn the perpetrator into a demon. We had to distinguish between the deed and the perpetrator . . . to hate and condemn the sin while being filled with compassion for the sinner. (p. 83)

Furthermore, Tutu (1999) recognized that creation in the image of God includes moral responsibility (Henry, 1984, p. 548). Therefore, failing to identify perpetrators as bearers of God's image was a way of "letting accountability go out the window" (Tutu, 1999, p. 83). "If perpetrators were to be despaired of as monsters and demons, then . . . we were then declaring that they were not moral agents to be held responsible for the deeds they had committed" (p. 83).

The leaders of the TRC chose to extend compassion and forgiveness as a way of reminding perpetrators that they were in fact human beings, made for relationship with God and with others, with all the transcendent requirements of that identity. Some critics of the commission identified the TRC's approach as "cheap grace" and a miscarriage of justice. Yet I believe that reminding perpetrators of their essential humanity through forgiveness is (paradoxically) the most effective way of demonstrating how despicable their actions have been, and how great a responsibility they now hold for healing the damage that has been done in their community. In other words, because they offered amnesty to offenders, the leaders of the TRC made it safe for feelings of repentance and responsibility to emerge:

> I say we are sorry. I say the burden of the Bisho massacre will be on our shoulders for the rest of our lives. We cannot wish it away. It happened. But please, I ask specifically the victims not to forget, I cannot ask this, but to forgive us, to get the soldiers back into the community, to accept them fully, to try to understand the pressure they were under then. This is all I can do. I'm sorry, this I can say, I'm sorry. (Col. Horst Schoberberger, as cited in Tutu, 1999, pp. 150–151)

In postapartheid South Africa, Tutu (1999) and the other members of the TRC exemplified the caring that Greenleaf (1977) identified as the heart of servant-leadership. Victims experienced the TRC's care as empathy and support; perpetrators experienced it as empathy and forgiveness (Ramsey, 2006). In both cases, the TRC treated their fellow South Africans as bearers of God's image and invited them to express that identity in a new relationship with one another and with God, for the healing of their nation and as a sign to the world that the shalom of God is possible (Tutu, 1999).

The Image of God and Creation Unity

In the context of servant-leadership, the goal of forgiveness is unity between persons who were formerly enemies (Tutu, 1999, p. 280). Muck (2006) distinguished between three different types of unity that appear in biblical history: creation unity, affiliation unity, and relationship unity. Both affiliation and relationship unity have to do specifically with the Christian church; however, creation unity refers to the ontological oneness that humanity experienced in the early chapters of Genesis, prior to our expulsion from the Garden of Eden. This unity was based on the shared image of God and did not rule out difference; in fact, "to have unity, you must first of all have difference" (Muck, 2006, p. 1). Muck (2006) asserted that beneath the many divisions apparent in today's world, this creation unity still exists and will one day be restored in the kingdom of God.

Based on Muck's (2006) schema, one could argue that forgiveness is best understood not as the creation of a new relationship but as the expression of an ontological unity that continues to exist among human beings, however great the apparent alienation between them. Tutu (1999) referred often to this creation unity using the African term *ubuntu* (also called *botho*), which means "a person is a person through other persons" (p. 31). *Ubuntu* reflects shalom, or "the primordial harmony that was God's intention for all creation" (Tutu, 1999, p. 263). It assumes that human beings were designed to live in community with one another. Even when that community is damaged by disrespect or violence, some vestiges of it remain: so much so, that whenever we harm another person, we also harm ourselves (Muck, 2006). In other words, the concept of *ubuntu* parallels what Frankl (2000) affirmed as the essence of human existence: our orientation toward relationship with God and with others.

Greenleaf (1977) identified servant-leaders as builders of community, since "only community can give the healing love that is essential for health" (p. 37). Muck's (2006) concept of creation unity suggests a paradigm shift for servant-leaders who are seeking to build and sustain community: from the superhuman task of creating unity to the more manageable vision of restoring a unity that is already inherent in creation. In today's world, however, servant-leaders must build community across divisions that seem nearly as ancient as the Garden of Eden. Some of these divisions have been solidified by centuries of persecution and violence, as is the case with the division between Jew and Gentile (Wiesenthal, 1998). The brutalities of the Holocaust have had the double effect of making community between Jews and Gentiles unthinkable without forgiveness, while being so heinous as to make forgiveness seem impossible. In his book *The Sunflower*, Wiesenthal (1998) described an encounter between a Jew and a Gentile that perfectly illustrates this double effect. Wiesenthal was a prisoner in a Nazi camp in Poland when he was called to the bedside of a dying SS officer who wished to confess his war crimes to a Jew. During the encounter, Wiesenthal expressed compassion to the dying soldier, yet when he was asked directly for words of absolution, he walked quietly from the room and never returned. So unnerved was Wiesenthal (1998) by this encounter that he ended his narrative with the question, "Was my silence at the bedside of the dying Nazi right or wrong?" (p. 97).

In the symposium of responses that follows, many commentators expressed the conviction that Wiesenthal (1998) was justified in withholding forgiveness. He had no right to forgive on behalf of his fellow Jews, for one can only reasonably forgive sins against oneself (Alkalaj, 1998; Bejski, 1998; Heschel, 1998). However, while he did not want to minimize Wiesenthal's dilemma, Tutu (1999) took issue with this perspective (p. 275). He compared the SS officer's confession with the apology from Dr. Willi Jonker (representing the Dutch Reformed Church) to the victims of apartheid in 1990:

> One could well ask whether [Dr. Jonker] could claim to speak for past generations of [the DRC's] members, though it would be an oddly atomistic view of the nature of a community not to accept that there is a very real continuity between the past and the present and that the former members would share in the guilt and the shame as in the absolution and the glory of the present. . . . They too are part of who we are, whether we like it or not. . . . That is what makes a community a community or a people a people—for better or for worse. (pp. 276–279)

One can extend Tutu's (1999) argument even further on the basis of *ubuntu*. Deeper than the continuity between members of a community is the creation unity that extends between everyone made in the image of God, such that all of us belong to one community, the human community (p. 265). In this sense Wiesenthal and the dying SS officer were members of the same community due to "a certain basic human equality as common both to 'victim' and 'perpetrator' " (Pawlikowski, 1998, p. 221). Stein (1998) argued that the compassion Wiesenthal displayed at the officer's bedside was an act of solidarity with him; for "he did not treat the man as a monster who had committed monstrous deeds. Rather, he honored the humanity of a man who had lost his humaneness" (p. 253). I respectfully submit that had Wiesenthal chosen to speak words of forgiveness, they would have been justified on the same basis.

No servant-leader will find it easy to encourage unity between persons who are divided from one another along ethnic or religious lines, especially when those divisions have been hardened by violence. Yet the concept of creation unity can inspire servant-leaders both to ask for and to grant forgiveness, ideally allowing them to serve as models to others in their community. From the perspective of creation unity, asking for and granting forgiveness begin with the acknowledgement that I, too, am, in Frankl's (1974) terms, both a bearer and a violator of the divine image (pp. 212–213). In other words, I forgive "because I fear not to be forgiven" (Cargas, 1998, p. 124). Creation unity is a powerful spur toward forgiveness because it reminds us that all persons, myself as well as others, are capable both of the greatest heroism and the deepest depravity (Tutu, 1999).

The Image of God and Hope

According to Greenleaf (1977), hope for the future is an important aspect of servant-leadership—especially with regard to the next generation. Servant-leaders are called to "raise the spirit of young people, help them build their confidence that they can successfully contend with the condition [of society], work with them to find the direction they need to go and the competencies they need to acquire, and send them on their way" (p. 172). Tutu (1999) maintained that in our divided world, one of the core competencies we need to instill is the ability both to ask for and grant forgiveness:

> If we are going to move on and build a new kind of world community there must be a way in which we can deal with a sordid past. The most effective way would be for the perpetrators or their descendants to acknowledge the awfulness of what happened and the descendants of the victims to respond by granting forgiveness, providing something can be done, even symbolically, to compensate for the anguish experienced. . . . True forgiveness deals with the past, all of the past, to make the future possible. (pp. 278–279)

Tutu's (1999) statement that forgiveness "makes the future possible" is based on the recognition that if violence continues to grow in our world, there may well be no future for our children to inherit. Yet forgiveness also expresses hope for the future in its assumption that both individuals and communities are capable of responding to "the better angels of our nature" (Lincoln, 1861, para. 35). As Tutu (1999) summarized, "In the act of forgiveness we are declaring our faith in the future of a relationship and in the capacity of the wrongdoer to make a new beginning on a course that will be different from the one that caused us the wrong. . . . It is an act of faith that the wrongdoer can change" (p. 273). For Tutu, the basis of this faith is the lingering presence of the image of God, even in the worst perpetrator.

In calling the next generation to take up the discipline of forgiveness, Tutu (1999) was issuing a call for transformational leadership, of which hope is a necessary ingredient (Spears, 1995). According to Northouse (2001), transformational leadership is the process by which a leader "engages with others and creates a connection that raises the level of motivation and morality in both the leader and the follower" (p. 132). It assumes that even in situations of intense conflict in which persons have committed great wrongs, those wrongs do not prevent community members from embracing change (Northouse, 2001). The hope that characterizes transformational leadership has a firm foundation if one accepts the biblical idea of a transcendent aspect of human nature that is not defaced even by the grossest moral failure (Henry, 1984, p. 547). Forgiveness then can serve as a powerful expression of this hope, and a mechanism for transformation in which both leader and followers become "healthier, wiser, freer, more likely themselves to become servants" (Greenleaf, 1977, pp. 13–14).

Finally, the concept of human beings as made in the image of God suggests that servant-leaders need not assign arbitrary limits to the transformational power of forgiveness. If there are no conditions under which God's image in a person may be defaced, then forgiveness is appropriately unconditional (Enright, 1991). Ramsey (2006) found empirical support for this hypothesis in her study on the experiences of former perpetrators in postapartheid South Africa. She concluded that "in an environment where human beings practice the principles of servant-leadership, empathy, forgiveness, and healing, there is hope for redemption in the hearts of some of the most hardened persons, the most unrepentant perpetrators, and hope for the restoration of community" (Ramsey, 2006, p. 26). Interestingly, perpetrators experienced the most transformation when the forgiveness offered them was "not bound by the remorse or denial of the perpetrator" (Ramsey, 2006, p. 26).

The Divine Image

I began by observing that servant-leadership, a concept with roots in the religious world, has had great influence among persons who do not embrace any form of religious tradition. I end with a parallel observation. The concept of the divine image in human beings, which is an important cornerstone of Jewish and Christian theology, can be instructive for anyone who contemplates asking for or granting forgiveness, whether or not that person is actively religious. It is instructive because forgiveness begins and ends with a recognition of shared humanity, and a sense that the shalom of the community is of greater value than one's personal well-being. Such are the core convictions of servant-leadership (Spears, 1995).

References

Alkalaj, S. (1998). In H. J. Cargas & B. V. Fetterman (Eds.), *The sunflower: On the possibilities and limits of forgiveness* (pp. 101–105). New York, NY: Schocken.

Bejski, M. (1998). In H. J. Cargas & B. V. Fetterman (Eds.), *The sunflower: On the possibilities and limits of forgiveness* (pp. 111–118). New York, NY: Schocken.

Boston, R. (February, 2005). Pennsylvania school district's 'Intelligent Design' policy violates church-state separation, says Americans United lawsuit. Washington, DC: Americans United for Separation of Church and State. Retrieved from http://www.au.org/site/News2?page=News Article&id= 7192&abbr=CS

Cargas, H. J. (1998). In H. J. Cargas & B. V. Fetterman (Eds.), *The sunflower: On the possibilities and limits of forgiveness* (pp. 124–126). New York, NY: Schocken.

Enright, R. D. (1991). *Handbook of moral behavior and development*. Hillsdale, NJ: Lawrence Erlbaum Associates.

Feinberg, C. (1984). Peace. In W. A. Elwell (Ed.), *Evangelical dictionary of theology*. Grand Rapids, MI: Baker Book House.

Frankl, V. (1974). *Man's search for meaning: An introduction to logotherapy*. New York, NY: Pocket Books.

Frankl, V. (2000). *Man's search for ultimate meaning*. New York, NY: Basic Books.

Greenleaf, R. K. (1977). *Servant-leadership: A journey into the nature of legitimate power and greatness*. Mahwah, NJ: Paulist Press.

Henry, C. (1984). Image of God. In W. A. Elwell (Ed.), *Evangelical dictionary of theology*. Grand Rapids, MI: Baker Book House.

Heschel, S. (1998). In H. J. Cargas & B. V. Fetterman (Eds.), *The sunflower: On the possibilities and limits of forgiveness* (pp. 172–174). New York, NY: Schocken.

Lincoln, A. (1861, March 4). First inaugural address, New York, NY. Bartleby.com. Retrieved from http://www.bartleby.com/124/pres3 1.html

Motyer, S. (1984). Man, doctrine of. In W. A. Elwell (Ed.), *Evangelical dictionary of theology*. Grand Rapids, MI: Baker Book House.

Muck, T. S. (2006, May). That they may be one: John 17: 11a in the context of other religions. Symposium conducted at the meeting of the Mountain States Wee Kirk Conference of the Presbyterian Church (USA), Glorietta, NM.

Northouse, P. (2001). *Leadership: Theory and practice* (2nd ed.). Thousand Oaks, CA: Sage.

Pawlikowski, J. T. (1998). In H. J. Cargas & B. V. Fetterman (Eds.), *The sunflower: On the possibilities and limits of forgiveness* (pp. 220–225). New York, NY: Schocken.

Peters, T., & Waterman, R., Jr. (1982). *In search of excellence: Lessons from America's best-run companies.* New York, NY: Harper and Row.

Ramsey, M. (2006). *Servant-leadership and unconditional forgiveness: The lives of six South African perpetrators.* Walla Walla, WA: Walla Walla Community College.

Spears, L. (1995). Introduction: Servant-leadership and the Greenleaf legacy. In Larry C. Spears (Ed.), *Reflections on leadership* (pp. 1–16). New York, NY: John Wiley & Sons.

Stein, A. (1998). In H. J. Cargas & B. V. Fetterman (Eds.), *The sunflower: On the possibilities and limits of forgiveness* (pp. 250–255). New York, NY: Schocken.

Tutu, D. (1999). *No future without forgiveness.* New York, NY: Doubleday.

Vanourek, R. A. (1995). Servant-leadership and the future. In Larry C. Spears (Ed.), *Reflections on leadership* (pp. 298–307). New York, NY: John Wiley & Sons.

Wiesenthal, S. (1998). *The sunflower: On the possibilities and limits of forgiveness.* New York, NY: Schocken Books.

Chapter 17

Servant-Leadership, Regenerative Love, and Forgiveness

Harris W. Fawell

Servant-Leadership—"None Dare Call It Religious?"

Christine Wicker, a senior religion reporter for the *Dallas Morning News*, in her essay "Seeking the Soul of Business" captures an intriguing aspect of the spirit of Robert Greenleaf and the servant-leadership movement he created. Wicker (1998) observes, "None dare call it religious! But a management philosophy catching on at companies across America sounds so much like religion that adherents are sometimes at pains to make the difference clear. This is spirituality. Ethics. Values. Common sense. And market imperative, they say" (p. 246). But not necessarily the domain of religion.

The prologue to Wicker's essay states that Wicker (1998) is writing a book on "individualistic spirituality, a trend that University of Chicago church historian Martin Marty calls one of the three greatest changes happening in American religion today" (p. 247).

It is important to note that there is indeed an elementary rebirth of the power and practicality of love as incorporated, for instance, in Greenleaf's servant-leadership writings as well as other writings in a variety of fields, that is perhaps best described as a rise of consciousness or "individual spirituality." But it is important to note that this rebirth of the power of love is not led by any specific religious organization. In fact, the reference to religion is placed in the context of honoring both the individual person's identity and the collective's choice to pursue wholeness within the context of religion, or outside of that context. For instance, though

305

the image of Christ washing the feet of his disciples was a central image to Greenleaf regarding the power, beauty, and love evoked by servant-leadership, Greenleaf did not impose his own personal beliefs on others, and in fact encouraged a graceful, open sense of mutuality for humanity as a whole, regardless of religious tradition. In later life Greenleaf often lived in community as a Quaker, and was blessed with an iconoclastic, often countercultural persona. He appeared to foresee and thus discard the heavy baggage religious, gnostic, atheistic, or even irreligious biases and ideological colorations often carry, and he forwarded a kind of elegant and disciplined view of the regenerative powers of love for all people.

Thus, servant-leadership appears to fit comfortably in the description of individual spirituality, or "individualistic spirituality," to borrow Martin Marty's words, as a part of a growing worldwide consciousness of the practical power of love and forgiveness both within the context of religion and outside of religious contexts.

Laszlo (2002), the founder and president of the Club of Budapest and author of the books *The Choice* and *Macroshift*, writes in the magazine *IONS Noetic Sciences Review*, "Behind the global cacophony of terrorism, war, social, economic, and ecological upheaval, something else is happening. A quiet but significant groundswell of consciousness is arising perhaps just in time to save us a sustainable niche on this still-beautiful planet" (p. 9). Laszlo (2002) adds,

> Perhaps the most promising aspect of the people involved in this groundswell of consciousness is their spirituality. This need not mean adherence to a formal religion or organized church. It can be an inner-directed attitude, a search for personal identity and meaning in life. Spirituality[,] unlike religion[,] is a private matter, penetrating the relationship between the individual and the cosmos. Unlike religion, it does not require a particular place for its exercise, nor does it require a priesthood. Its temple is the mind of the individual, and its altar is the state of consciousness that comes about through deep meditation and prayer, art and literature in their many forms[,] and the remarkable fact that science is evolving in a holistic way of thinking about the world. (pp. 14–15)

Laszlo (2002) also reports that addressing a joint session of Congress in Washington in February 1991, Czech writer-president Václav Havel said,

Without a global revolution in the sphere of human consciousness, nothing will change for the better . . . and the catastrophe
towards which this world is headed—the ecological, social,
demographic, or general breakdown of civilization—will be
unavoidable. (p. 15)

Laszlo (2002), however, while admitting that "Havel's view is well taken,"
writes,

but it is not a ground for pessimism. The breakdown of civilization is not unavoidable: Our consciousness can be evolved.
In a significant number of people it is evolving already. If each
of us would evolve his or her consciousness, today's stream of
what I call "Holos-consciousness" would swell into a mighty
tide that could change the world. (p. 15)

Scott (2001), editor of the magazine *Spirituality and Health*, which deals
with the soul-body connection, expressed similar sentiments in an article
about a cultural revolution he too sees taking place:

Two years ago, we founded this magazine on a simple premise.
Namely, that all of us are living in an era of such profound
and hopeful change that it is not an exaggeration to call it a
renaissance. The word, of course, means "rebirth." What's being
reborn is our sense of ourselves as spiritual beings, deeply
connected and open to one another and to something greater
than ourselves. These are exciting times, and whether that's a
blessing or a curse is up to us. The first step in realizing our
potential may lie in recognizing what's going on around us.
(p. 26)

Unleashing the Amazing Powers of Love

Peter Block, a supporter of servant-leadership and a well-known business
consultant and author, is quoted by Wicker about the religious aspects of
servant-leadership and Greenleaf's philosophy. Wicker tells a story about
Block, a Jew, who was once complimented after a speech about servant-
leadership and told he sounded like a good Christian. His reply was, "I'm

just trying to figure life out" (as cited in Wicker, 1998, p. 247). And then he added the telling words so many people feel about servant-leadership: "It's pure pragmatism for me" (as cited in Wicker, 1998, p. 247).

Individual spirituality and servant-leadership are founded upon a very simple yet profound basis, to wit, the expansion of the power of our love and the respect it builds in our relationships with others. It assumes that we are here in this time-and-space experience to love and serve, and that the only thing that really matters is that we love each other.

Unfortunately, the expansion of our love is conditioned by differences of religion, nationality, race, tribe, gender, cultures, skin color, social class, money, ego, politics, ad infinitum. Chopra (1994) writes that only when we "drop the terrific burdens and encumbrances of defensiveness, resentment and hurtfulness" can we "become lighthearted, carefree, joyous, and free" (pp. 36–37). That is not an intricate concept. Love is very learner-friendly.

The notion of deep learning presents itself: that only love and forgiveness have any chance of ridding our human ego of the many judgments, criticisms, and hatreds that divide humanity. Jampolsky (1979) writes,

> If we love, we tend to forgive, and forgiveness is the vehicle for changing our perceptions and letting go of our fears, condemning judgments and grievances. We need to remind ourselves constantly that love is the only reality there is. Anything we perceive that does not mirror love is a misperception. Forgiveness, then, becomes the means of correcting our misperceptions; it allows us to see only the love in others and ourselves and nothing else. (p. 65)

The more we expand love and forgiveness, the more we realize their practical power.

When I was in my first year of college many years ago, student attendance was required at weekly chapel services. At that time, I had never been a member of any church. I found, however, that I enjoyed these services. At one of these chapel events an elderly preacher rose to speak. After surveying the student body, he opened his sermon by quietly saying, "Never criticize." He paused, took his time to again view his audience, and quietly repeated his admonition: "Never criticize." He then suddenly pounded the podium with the flat of his hand, making a very loud thud (awakening many students in the process), and thundered the words, "No, never!" Most of us were startled.

His message was elementary: "The power of love in your life is what you are. So don't compromise it by negative judgments, resentments and criticisms."

Although those thoughts didn't sink in right away, the seeds were planted.

I have come to believe, after 14 years in our nation's government, that eventually we all must learn that we need to develop the ability, indeed, perhaps better referred to as a "response-ability," to drop our negative judgments, defensiveness, resentments, hatreds, and criticisms, which serve only to short-circuit our natural gifts of love. We do, indeed, need to remind ourselves constantly that love is the only reality there is and that we are all here to love and serve. Conscious thinking often sees only distorted visions. Love is ever true. Goldsmith (1961) writes, "We are admonished to withhold all judgments because if we judge by appearances the world is filled with skies that sit on mountains and car tracks that come together" (p. 63). Most people wouldn't go so far as Goldsmith, nor would they agree with Shakespeare's (1998) Hamlet that "there is nothing either good or bad, but thinking makes it so" (p. 29). But we all know in our better moments that much of what we see is an illusion and that there is so much bad in the best of us and so much good in the worst of us it hardly behooves any of us to judge or criticize each other, lest we become and be known, over time, as all judgment but not much of love.

Each time we catch ourselves criticizing and hating, our better selves remind us that someone so taught us as a child and that only the miracles of love and forgiveness can undo such behavior.

That seems to me to be what Greenleaf also was writing about when he urged employers to abandon command-and-control leadership for a servant-leadership that validates the worth and dignity of employees with a love that is free of criticism, command, and judgment. Greenleaf (1977) writes,

> Love is an indefinable term and its manifestations are both subtle and infinite. But it begins, I believe, with one absolute condition: unlimited liability. As soon as one's liability for another is qualified to any degree, love is diminished by that much. (p. 38)

Unlimited liability to love, of course, is unconditional love.

This kind of love is usually held up for ridicule in the "real world." Good for poets and philosophers, dreamers, perhaps, but not practical. But this is beginning to change.

In Larry Spears's interview of Margaret Wheatley, he mentioned that in her book *Leadership and the New Science* she wrote, "Love in organizations is the most potent source of power we have available." Spears then asked her, "What do you think that servant-leaders inside our many organizations can do to unleash love in the workplace?" Wheatley replied,

> It's simple: just be loving. Why has expressing love become such
> a problem when it is a fundamental human characteristic? This
> is where I think we have overanalyzed and overcomplexified
> something that is known to everyone alive. Babies know how
> to unleash love. (Spears & Noble, 2005, p. 62)

We should all pause to let Wheatley's words sink in. Wheatley is not a philosopher. She is a business consultant of renown. She gives practical, commonsense advice to business people who seek her help and advice. Well, there it is. In practical, commonsense English. There's nothing mysterious about love. It is simple. It is practical. It is a "fundamental human characteristic." Yet too often it is imprisoned deep within us.

Robert Browning (1948) wrote,

> Truth is within ourselves; it takes no rise from outward things.
> There is an inmost center in us all where truth abides in full-
> ness—and to know rather consists in finding a way whence the
> imprisoned splendor from within may escape, than in effecting
> entry of a light supposed to be without. (p. 431)

Yet we all seem to "seek without" for the great truths, for our light. But, alas, our light is never without. It is instead the imprisoned splendor of love and compassion always within and always ready for its miraculous use. It binds us together with all mankind, always reminding us that wholeness is indeed our natural state.

Albert Einstein, perhaps the greatest scientist of the twentieth century, put it this way,

> A human being is part of the whole, called by us "Universe,"
> a part limited in time and space. He experiences himself, his

thoughts and feelings, as something separated from the rest—a kind of optical delusion of his consciousness. This delusion is a prison for us, restricting us to our personal desires and to affection for a few persons nearest to us. Our task must be to free ourselves from this prison by widening our circle of compassion to embrace all living creatures and the whole nature in its beauty. (as cited in Baxter, 2015)

We all have to free ourselves from the prison of our illusions and the insecurities of our freedom by simply being still and quiet and widening our circle of compassion and love so that at least as we enter old age—and hopefully before—we can free that imprisoned splendor of love within us.

We all know better than we do. If we knew "back then" what we know now, our circles of compassion would be wider. Yet life is nothing if not a learning process. There is an old German saying "We get too soon old and too late smart." But one never gets too old to continue learning. The opportunity to love and serve is always there.

Heschel (1967) writes in *Insecurity of Freedom*,

The years of old age may enable us to attain the high values we failed to sense, the insights we have missed, the wisdom we ignored. They are indeed formative years, rich in possibilities to unlearn the follies of a lifetime, to see through inbred self-deceptions, to deepen understanding and compassion, to widen the horizon of honesty, to redefine the sense of fairness. One ought to enter old age the way one enters the senior year at a university. (p. 78)

Das (2006), one of the foremost teachers of Buddhism in the West, after quoting Heschel, goes on and says, "Pablo Casals at the age of 93 was practicing the cello five or six hours a day. Someone asked him, 'Pablo, why are you still practicing the cello?' Casals answered: 'Because I think I'm making progress'" (p. 85).

The Wonderful Gifts of Religion?

The wonderful gift of religion is the message that we are spiritual in nature. A major drawback, however, to religion is expressed in the magazine

Spirituality and Health by Lesser (2001), cofounder of the Omega Institute, the nation's largest holistic education and retreat center. Lesser (2001) writes, "We've had thousands of years of rule-based theologies that demand love and proscribe hatred, envy and inhumanity" (p. 37). In response to that accusation, her close friend Smith, author of *The World's Religions*, asked,

> How much of the damage you are thinking of was due to Christianity and how much to the fact that the people who perpetrated it happened coincidentally to be Christian and behaved in the way greedy and power-hungry people tend always and everywhere to behave? (as cited in Lesser, 2001, p. 38)

To which Ms. Lesser (2001) replied,

> But I don't think it is enough to say that the shadow side of a religion is activated coincidentally; that the greedy and pow-er-hungry people within a certain religion would be greedy and power-hungry regardless of religious affiliation. I think that religions have to take more responsibility than that. (p. 39)

Lesser and Smith are great friends and have a strong mutual respect for each other's views. Religions can be good or bad and at times ridiculous, and so can people pursuing spirituality independent of religion. Obviously, good teachers such as Lesser and Smith—teachers who strive to free their students even of the teacher's own philosophical preferences—abound both within and without formal religion. Condemnation of a given religion is like condemnation of the self: it is worthy, if received well and authen-tically acted upon. Let's take, for example, two of the major religions of the ancient and contemporary world, and one ideology. In the name of both Islam and Christianity, and what many call "the new religion," an ideology called science, dastardly deeds have been perpetrated throughout history. Now let's extend this thought. Both within and outside the con-text of Islam, Christianity, and science, whole cultures have perpetrated massacres, mass bloodshed, genocide, and human atrocities of every form. Even so, there is a sense of illumination that accompanies all great spiritual traditions, as well as all great cultural traditions, and yes, all great ideas, which we might also call great dreams. And within such traditions, ideas, and dreams, a transcendent understanding tends to rise from the ashes of our human frailties and failures.

Unconditional Love Thrives without Organization, Rules, or Regulations

Many religions, however, still have significant problems in conditioning love on the basis of religious affiliation. Neither can many religions affirm other religions as authentic ways of salvation or liberation on their own terms. History is replete with thousands of years of religious discrimination between and within religions, as well as against those who profess no religious faith. Even in the twenty-first century there remains a great deal of misunderstanding, hatred, vengeance, and the conditioning of love by those who lead or profess to represent world religious faiths. In addition, there is little effort among the world's religious leaders to address what Lesser refers to as that "shadow side" of religion. Why haven't religious leaders sought an international body of religions that would at least affirm the free flow of love and the sanctity of human life as everyone's right—especially the world's war-ridden children's? Who is at fault for this elementary neglect?

A friend of mine was part of a group that traveled to Israel and to the West Bank of Palestine to view the walls the Israelis have built to shut out the Palestinians. The group heard from Dr. Jad Isaq, a Palestinian who heads the Applied Research Institute of Jerusalem; he talked about the pain of being a Palestinian whose land has been stolen. Here is what my friend reported that Dr. Isaq said to this group of Christians:

> Dr. Isaq said he had no use for religion. He said he sees three kinds of religious people: Christians—like George Bush who woke up one morning and said he dreamed that God told him to invade Iraq. So he did. And next week he might say God told him to invade Iran. Jewish—like Ariel Sharon[,] who said this is the land God gave him, so it's all right for him to take it from the Palestinians. Muslims—like the suicide bomber who does not like what is going on so he kills himself and others with him. Between these three crazies, I cannot live. If these are the three religions, Christianity, Islam and Judaism, then to hell with religion. (personal communication)

I do not validate Dr. Isaq's conclusions as to who are the "crazies" in the Middle East (there are enough of them to share the blame), but I do agree with Lerner (2006) "that we cannot continue using violence against violence as a way to end violence" (p. 11).

Honoring the History of the Great Spiritual Traditions

I also believe that Robert Greenleaf, Mahatma Gandhi, Martin Luther King Jr., Nelson Mandela, Václav Havel, Bishop Desmond Tutu and many new leaders of the twentieth century have honored the history of the world's great spiritual traditions by demonstrating that the regenerative power of love can nullify vengeance and terrorism. There is an old saying that "he who uses vengeance must remember to dig two graves: one for his enemy and one for himself."

That, I believe, is the strong and unified message capable of being delivered by all of our great religions to the "crazies" of this beleaguered world who espouse terrorism in all of its sophisticated and not-so-sophisticated forms. If political and religious leaders fail to speak out about the regenerative power of love as a natural antidote to vengeance, then others who are individually spiritual must do so. Love, in the final analysis, is simply treating people with respect, that is, validating their worth and dignity. The roots of violence are always found in disrespect and despair.

In an article in the *Christian Science Monitor*, Lampman (2006) writes,

> Respect is one of the most widely shared yearnings among human beings, and it touches the emotional core of people in profound ways. Respect given can be powerful and transformative. The results of respect withheld can be painful or even explosive. At a time when civility seems to be diminishing, some see the power of mutual respect as a way to break through cultural stereotypes and religious prejudices. (para. 3)

Lampman (2006) also quotes Akbar Ahmed, professor of Islamic studies at American University in Washington, DC, who points out, "Cultures are rubbing against each other more than ever before in history. . . . We need to be sensitive to . . . respect, honor, dignity, and how they are viewed in different societies" (para. 4).

Obviously, the simple power of love can demonstrate respect for a person who may be viewed as an enemy. Lampman (2006) quotes Rabbi Marc Gopin, director of the Center for World Religions, Diplomacy and Conflict Resolution at George Mason University in Arlington, Virginia, as stating that when such a demonstration of the power of love occurs, "it's a shock," and that "respect can have remarkable effects" (para. 9).

It's not as though the world has not recently experienced national leaders who have embraced and successfully used the practical power of love in meeting hatred, vengeance, and terrorism. Examples abound in leaders such as Gandhi of India, who championed love, nonviolence, forgiveness, and peaceful civil disobedience as a response to unjust laws in successfully leading India in a largely bloodless revolution against England.

And a youthful-hearted though physically aged Nelson Mandela, the liberator of South Africa from brutal terrorism and apartheid, followed Gandhi's advice and used the power of love and nonviolence to convince President F. W. de Klerk of South Africa to announce to a startled world that the best interests of the white community of South Africa would be served by negotiating themselves out of the exclusive control of political power. King also replicated Gandhi's reliance on the power of love and forgiveness in his successful civil rights revolution in America in the 1960s. And there were many more world leaders in the brutal and bloody twentieth century who recognized the practical powers of love and that using violence against violence is no way to end violence.

We live in a fast-shrinking world of time and space. As Havel expressed it, time may be running out unless there is "a global revolution in human consciousness" (as cited in Laszlo, 2002, p. 15).

Today there is growing evidence of such a global revolution in the sphere of human consciousness. After all, the human spirit is freer today than ever before, and the potential of the evolving human spirit—that imprisoned splendor within us all—is boundless. Under these circumstances, movements such as servant-leadership and individual spirituality encourage us to lead by emphasizing the amazing regenerative powers of love in all our lives.

And why not? After all, the idea is hard to escape, that we are all here to love and serve. For some, that's what life is all about. For many, the beauty of love is what makes life worth living. Everyone knows its touch; some more than others; some in a highly conditioned form. But we all know it exists. No one has to take it on faith. It is the universal, golden rule of life that is increasingly being verified by high-quality science. No one, religious or not, can copyright love, for love crosses all the many boundaries, prejudices, religions, politics, tribes, and cultures with ease.

Love sells only itself and is easily felt and identified. No broker is necessary. It validates the interconnectedness of us all.

In a real sense, no political or theological walls can be erected that fence out love. Charles Schultz, a practicing Christian and the creator of "Peanuts" and Charlie Brown, reportedly said after having taught Methodist Sunday school for ten years, "The best theology is probably no theology: Just love one another."

The story told of the well-known teaching of Hillel, the celebrated first-century rabbi for whom Jewish campus organizations today are named, illustrates this simple point. A man approached Hillel and said, "If you can teach me the whole truth of the Torah while I stand on one foot, you can make me a Jew." Hillel replied, "What is hateful to you, do not do to your neighbor. This is the whole Torah; the rest is commentary" (Kimball, 2002, p. 131). That is a good description of unconditional love, and is at the center of all of our great religions and thoughts, yet it is often buried in the commentaries, regulations, dogmas, and cultures of organized religions or in the disorganized methodologies of thought found both within and outside religion. Fortunately, as was expressed by Wheatley, it is also "a fundamental human characteristic-babies know how to unleash love" (Spears & Noble, 2005, p. 62). Is it any wonder that Hillel's fame with young people has lasted over the centuries?

A Gentle Chiding of Religion

It is interesting to note that even the Dalai Lama has gently chided organized religions. In a review of two of the Dalai Lama's best-selling books, *Ethics for a New Millennium* and *The Art of Happiness* in the *New York Times*, Bernstein (1999) quotes the Dalai Lama as stating, "I sometimes say that religion is something we can perhaps do without" (para. 14). Bernstein (1999) comments,

> One wonders if that is not part of his appeal, a call for a "spiritual revolution" that does not depend on the idea of a Supreme Being. It is perhaps the perfect way to satisfy the spiritual hunger of people living in a scientific and secular age. (para. 14)

Bernstein (1999) further comments, "The Dalai Lama refreshingly claims no unusual spiritual powers. He identifies himself as an ordinary man, prone to the same troubles as the rest of us, but one who has learned something about conquering the impulses that make us unhappy" (para. 5).

In the same article, Bernstein (1999) quotes the Dalai Lama as stating,

> Generally speaking, one begins by identifying those factors which lead to happiness and those factors which lead to suffering. Having done this, one then sets about gradually eliminating

those factors which lead to suffering and cultivating those that lead to happiness. That is the way. (para. 1)

"Happiness comes . . . from cultivating the traits of selflessness, generosity and compassion for others" (para. 16), which gently relieves one of the burdens of judgments, criticisms, and defensiveness, hence breeding happiness.

I see these words of the Dalai Lama as part of a not-so-quiet cultural and spiritual revolution of the practical powers of love—perhaps part of the reinvention of spirituality that Greenleaf was referring to in his views of servant-leadership, which aim to simply validate the worth and dignity of people. How refreshing.

A story told by Huston Smith in *Spirituality and Health* is revealing about the Dalai Lama's refusal to judge others (Lesser, 2001). Mr. Smith writes that a Hindu swami tried several times to get the Dalai Lama to say that Buddhism was a more peaceful religion than Christianity. When the Dalai Lama dodged the questions and it was put to him a third time, the Dalai Lama said (no doubt with a twinkle in his eye), "If I say anything against someone else's religion, the Buddha would scold me" (as cited in Lesser, 2001, p. 38).

This simple message that our judgments (such as the one proposed to the Dalai Lama) often get in the way of, and dilute, our love is a big part of the driving force of the individual spirituality renaissance that Greenleaf, Block, Wheatley, Laszlo, Scott, and so many others appear to be articulating. We all may have separate views of life, but that doesn't mean that judgments and criticisms have to get in the way of our extending love and kindness.

The noted American poet Wilcox (1942) expressed these sentiments:

> Don't look for the flaws
> As you go through life;
> And even though you find them,
> It is wise and kind to be somewhat blind,
> And look for the virtue behind them. (p. 105)

There is an old saying that if one has a choice of being right or kind, one should always opt to be kind. Few of us can follow that admonition. But there is wisdom in it.

In fact, one of the most self-serving things one can do for mind and body is to love others "no matter what," that is, by dismissing our judgments and criticisms that only serve to drag us down and dilute our energies.

If that sounds difficult to do, it's because as simple and as beautiful as unconditional love is, it involves changing our customary frames of reference. This is not easy. Consider Fosdick's (2002) words said of Henry Ward Beecher: "No one ever felt the full force of his kindness until he did Beecher an injury" (p. 30). With Beecher, unkindness was met not with judgments, unkindness, or vengeance but with more love, no matter what. Obviously, Beecher had a different frame of reference than most. And it included the immense power of loving unconditionally.

Fosdick (2002) also wrote, "We can never forgive as much as we have been forgiven" (p. 27) and quoted Booker Washington as saying, "I will not let any man reduce my soul to the level of hatred" (p. 31). Fosdick quoted Abraham Lincoln's words on several occasions:

> No man resolved to make the most of himself can spare the time for personal contention. Still less can he afford to take all the consequences, including the vitiating of his temper, and the loss of self-control. . . . You have more of that feeling of personal resentment than I have . . . perhaps I have too little of it; but I never thought it paid. . . . I shall do nothing in malice. What I deal with is too vast for malicious dealing. (as cited in Fosdick, 2002, pp. 30–31)

Lincoln obviously knew that ill judgments, criticisms, and loss of one's temper serve only to dilute the power of one's love, or, as the Dalai Lama might express it, serve only to produce impulses that make us unhappy.

The Beauty and Simplicity of Love

The beauty of love is that it is not a matter of intellect. It has only to be released. Das (2006) seems aware of this when he writes, "Wisdom tells me I am nothing; love tells me everything" (p. 85).

Nor is the power of love as impractical as it may seem when one realizes that quantum physics is now verifying that the physical appearances reported by our limited human receptors can be highly illusory. Indeed, subatomic particles, of which we are all constructed, act and react in accordance with the attitude and feelings of the scientific observer. We are finally beginning to be aware that most people tend to be as good or as bad as we choose to see them as being.

We have begun to understand Henry Ward Beecher, Booker T. Washington, Mahatma Gandhi, Mother Teresa, Martin Luther King Jr., Will Rogers, Albert Schweitzer, Nelson Mandela, Bishop Tutu, Václav Havel, Corazon "Cory" Aquino, and countless others who have discerned the elementary power of love and forgiveness when it is not conditioned by the heavy baggage of endless judgments and criticisms. Were these people saints? By no means. But they have evolved in consciousness enough to realize how painful it is to their souls to let their love be conditioned by the acts or words of others. Covey (2004), in his *Seven Habits of Highly Effective People*, also affirms that the simple, universal principles of unconditional love

> are not esoteric, mysterious or "religious" ideas. There is not one principle taught in this book that is unique to any specific faith or religion, including my own. These principles are a part of most every major enduring religion, as well as enduring social philosophies and ethical systems. They are self-evident and can easily be validated by any individual. It's almost as if these principles or natural laws are part of the human condition, part of the consciousness, part of the human conscience. They seem to exist in all human beings, regardless of social conditioning and loyalty to them, even though they might be submerged or numbered by such conditions or disloyalty. (p. 34)

Using today's high-tech verbiage, one could say that we are all "hardwired" for love. I am convinced that this is what fires the engines of our world's greatest leaders. It is part of an evolution of consciousness, a transformational bridge to authenticity and service without a purely personal agenda. And that's why so many people are interested in it. In its essence, love makes complex things simple.

Ornish (1999), a cardiologist and author of the book *Love and Survival*, is one of the many writers who speaks about the practical power of love from the viewpoint of the complexities of medicine and new science. He writes,

> This book is based on a simple but powerful idea: Our survival depends on the healing power of love, intimacy, and relationships. Physically. Emotionally. Spiritually. As individuals. As communities. As a country. As a culture. Perhaps even as

a species. . . . Love and intimacy are at a root of what makes us sick and what makes us well, what causes sadness and what brings happiness, what makes us suffer and what leads to healing. If a new drug had the same impact [as love and intimacy], virtually every doctor in the country would be recommending it for their patients. It would be malpractice not to prescribe it—yet, with few exceptions, we doctors do not learn much about the healing power of love, intimacy, and transformation in our medical training. Rather, these ideas are often ignored or even denigrated. (pp. 1–3)

Ornish (1999) further writes,

I am not aware of any other factor in medicine [that has a greater impact on our survival than the healing power of love and intimacy]—not diet, not smoking, not exercise, not stress, not genetics, not drugs, not surgery—that has a greater impact on our quality of life, incidence of illness, and premature death from all causes. (pp. 2–3)

He continues,

Put in another way, anything that promotes feelings of love and intimacy is healing; anything that promotes isolation, separation, loneliness, loss, hostility, anger, cynicism, depression, alienation and related feelings often leads to suffering, disease, and premature death from all causes. While the evidence on the relationship of psycho-social factors to illness is controversial, most scientific studies have demonstrated the extraordinarily powerful role of love and relationships in determining health and illness. (Ornish, 1999, p. 29)

Ornish (1999) adds,

I am learning that the key to our survival is love. When we love someone and feel loved by them, somehow along the way our suffering subsides, our deepest wounds begin healing, our hearts start to feel safe enough to be vulnerable and to open a little wider. We begin experiencing our own emotions and the feeling of those around us. (p. 96)

Love and the Pointing Finger of "Touchy-Feely"

Of course, despite the growing support of the power of unconditional love, community, relationships, bonding, and connectedness, there will always be doubters of the power of love as a natural cosmic law.

Dr. Rachel Naomi Remen, associate clinical professor of medicine at the University of California, San Francisco, School of Medicine and author of *Kitchen Table Wisdom*, addresses such doubters from the viewpoint of medicine and science. Dr. Remen cautions,

> Anything that is not intellectual is seen as a weakness in this culture—the intuition, the spirit, the soul, the heart. Up until very recently, people devalued these things. It still opens one up to the pointing finger of touchy-feely. (as cited in Ornish, 1999, p. 208)

Dr. Remen, however, adds,

> But I don't care about the pointing finger anymore. Often, people who point that finger have no idea what human strength looks like. These things that are seen as so soft are far more powerful, when the chips are down, than the ideas and the intellect, all these things we respect so much. They are what enable us to meet the events of our lives and not be trampled by them. Ideas are not as powerful as the heart and the soul. Love is more powerful than ideas. (as cited in Ornish, 1999, pp. 208–209)

Immediately upon the tragic occurrences of September 11, 2001, when our nation's feelings were suddenly and catastrophically "down," the soft values of love, community, relationships, and connectedness all immediately surfaced across America to unite and strengthen our nation. It is, indeed, these softer values that enable us in troubled times to experience what human strength is and how important our relationships and connectedness with each other are.

It appears at times that those involved in administering health care often go to great lengths not to talk about love and affection in healing. Somehow, the words *love* and *intimacy* are hard to say, for fear, I suppose, of that pointing finger.

Chopra (1992), in *Unconditional Life*, tells the story of a hospital's treatment of premature babies. One group of babies was given normal

treatment in the hospital's intensive care unit for neonates. The other group
was scheduled for fifteen minutes of special attention, in which someone
reached in through the portholes of their sealed cribs to stroke them
and gently wiggle their arms and legs. Dr. Chopra (1992) reported that

> the result of such a simple addition to the usual hospital formula
> was striking. The stroked babies gained 47 percent more weight
> per day than the control group; they were more alert and started
> to act like normally delivered babies sooner. Finally, they left
> the hospital a week ahead of schedule, allowing the authors
> of the study to note a savings of $3,000 per infant. . . . Here,
> the contrast between life and antilife seems almost too obvious
> to point out. Scientific medicine has reached the stage where
> it is not respectable to call stroking by its right name—much
> less love and affection. Stroking has to go by the Orwellian
> "tactile/kinesthetic stimulation." (pp. 14–15)

Chopra (1989), in *Quantum Healing*, also told the interesting story of an
Ohio University study of heart disease in the 1970s that was conducted
by feeding quite toxic, high-cholesterol diets to rabbits in order to block
their arteries, duplicating the effect that the diet has on humans. Dr.
Chopra (1989) reported,

> Consistent results began to appear in all the rabbit groups, except
> for one[,] which strangely displayed 60 percent fewer symptoms.
> Nothing in the rabbits' physiology could account for their high
> tolerance to the diet, until it was discovered by accident that the
> student who was in charge of feeding these particular rabbits
> liked to fondle and pet them. . . . This alone seemed to enable
> the animals to overcome the toxic diet. (pp. 30–31)

Dr. Chopra added that repeat experiments in which one group of rabbits
was treated neutrally while the others were loved came up with similar
results.

Love: The One Creative Force

Butterworth (1993) tells the story of a distinguished professor of sociol-
ogy who conducted a study to determine the effects on children living

in an environment that was ravaged by warlike conditions and economic uncertainty. He gathered 200 young boys from the most impoverished and violent areas of Baltimore and sent a group of eager graduate students to interview them. Sadly, but not surprisingly, his researchers' evaluation of each boy's future was "He hasn't got a chance for success." They could see only despair ahead of them.

Twenty-five years later, another professor, intrigued by the study, conducted follow-up research to see exactly what had happened to those 200 boys. Had their lives turned out as dismally as they had feared? Surprisingly, they had not. Of the 200 original research subjects, 180 were located, and of these 180 nearly all of them had grown up to be successful, healthy, happy adults who were contributing positively to their communities (Butterworth, 1993).

What had happened between the time of the original research study and adulthood? The follow-up research could find only one common factor that linked all of the boys. All of them reported that they had been profoundly affected by the same teacher. When this teacher was located, now much older, and asked to tell what remarkable things she had done to change the course of these children's lives, her eyes sparkled and her lips broke into a gentle smile. "It's really very simple," she said. "I loved those boys" (Butterworth, 1993, p. 3).

She just loved them. That was the very practical and in-common treatment that teacher gave to her students that brought unanticipated success to their lives.

Some would say that to extend love unconditionally to others is weakness, a retreat from the realities of life. But it is the weak who retreat from the deep realities. Love and gentleness can be expected only from the strong. Truly successful people are aware that their primary responsibility in life is to love and serve others.

Evolving humanity is beginning to realize that anything that gets in the way of loving and serving—be it political, social, religious, tribal, racial, or whatever—is a misuse of our consciousness, and, indeed, consciousness is what we are.

Implications for the Education of Our Children

In our children's formal education, we stress all kinds of achievements to be attained in terms of grades, athletic prowess, academic laurels, attending the finest schools, and so forth, with the implication that ultimately they will bring important jobs, material comforts, increased social advantages, and meaning and purpose to life.

But as alluring as these achievements are, in the final analysis, they are of secondary importance for our children in terms of their experience, from mature, transparent, authentic adults, as we are here in this fragile time-and-space experience to love and serve humanity. The world's most revered leaders have always been servant-leaders, from Gandhi and Mother Teresa to Greenleaf and many more. This kind of a focus in life always produces people on the front lines of serving humanity.

We all might consider anew how children would react during their formative years if they were advised that their basic purpose in life, their road to true greatness, is simply to love and to forgive (themselves and others) and to serve humanity.

Perhaps children would be impressed by the very practical approach of a highly regarded and successful American football coach, Vince Lombardi. Marinho (2006) quotes Lombardi as saying, "I don't necessarily have to like my players and partners. But as a leader I must love them. Love is loyalty, love is teamwork, love respects dignity and individuality. This is the strength of any organization" (p. 261).

Recognizing how powerful love is, of course, is very challenging for most of us, but giving love and forgiveness in our daily lives is not complex. It is a universal power bestowed at birth, and it is a practical necessity of life. It can be liberally dispersed or grossly limited by our own conditions or racial, religious, cultural, tribal, social, economic, and many more man-made restrictions.

Consider how Martin Luther King Jr. felt about the power and accessibility of love. King (1998) wrote about greatness and simply related it to love:

> Everybody can be great . . . because anybody can serve. You don't have to have a college degree to serve. You don't have to make your subject and verb agree to serve. You only need a heart full of grace. A soul generated by love. (p. 183)

Dr. George Wald, a Harvard biologist who won the Nobel Prize, writes, "What one really needs is not Nobel laureates, but love. The Nobel laureate is a consolation prize. What matters is love" (as cited in Kornfield, 1984, p. 97).

And consider too what King (1968) said about terrorism, certainly the antithesis of love and service, on the night before he was assassinated: "It is no longer a choice between violence and nonviolence in this world; it's nonviolence or non-existence" (para. 7). One has only to look at terrorism and the growing hate and vengeance that are popularized by the world's political leaders, entertainment industries, news media, extremist religions, amoral philosophies, and overly reductionistic scientist-atheists to see how important King's message of love, nonviolence, and forgiveness is.

If challenged by parents and educators, children could be led to focus on how they can best use their unique talents of love and forgiveness to serve people and a frightened world. And why not? Love is natural to children, especially to very young children. A one-year-old baby will immediately give back smile for smile and love for love because that is his nature. While all children may not continue to respond with love, depending on conditions at birth and their early environment, most of them have that potential, which could be brought out by parents and teachers who are not afraid to talk openly about those words *love* and *forgiveness*. Who knows how many Gandhis, Lincolns, Martin Luther Kings, Coretta Kings, Corazon Aquinos, Albert Schweitzers, Henry Ward Beechers, Desmond Tutus, Nelson Mandelas, Mother Teresas, and Robert Greenleafs are potentially within our children just waiting to be drawn forth?

The Turning of Violence and Hate into Tolerance, Love, and Forgiveness

In January 2006, Michelle Bachelet was elected as the first woman president of Chile. She was also the first woman to rise to political prominence by her own merits rather than the political power of her husband. Bachelet also bears her own scars from the dark years of massive human rights abuses during Augusto Pinochet's coup in 1973. Her father, an air force general who opposed Pinochet, died after being tortured in one of Pinochet's prisons. Bachelet and her mother were also arrested by the Pinochet government, tortured, and forced into exile. At Bachelet's inauguration as president of Chile, she spoke of life and healing, not death and revenge, "Violence entered my life, destroying what I loved. Because I was a victim of hate, I have dedicated my life to turn that hate into understanding, into tolerance and, why not say it, into love" (as cited in Reel, 2006, para. 7). The power of love was waiting within her to be tapped. How encouraging and unique it is to hear a prominent politician, a victim of hate, dedicate her life to "turning hate into understanding and tolerance and, why not say it, into love."

Yes, why not say it? Again, as Margaret Wheatley asks, "Why has expressing love become such a problem when it is a fundamental human characteristic?" (Spears & Noble, 2005, p. 62). Is it not a powerful human instinct in all of us? And as such a deep human instinct, shouldn't it be more popularly expressed?

The Power of Forgiveness

Michelle Bachelet is not your ordinary political leader. Her insights reflect a growing awareness by world leaders that forgiveness allows, indeed, encourages leaders to turn "hate into understanding, into tolerance and, why not say it, into love." She understands that in failing to forgive by cherishing our grievances, we only dilute our most valuable resource, our power of love.

Jampolsky (1979), advances the same insight in his definition of *forgiveness*:

> Forgiveness then becomes a process of letting go and over-looking whatever we thought other people may have done to us, or whatever we may think we have done to them. When we cherish grievances we allow our mind to be fed by fear and we become imprisoned by these distortions. When we see our only function as forgiveness, and are willing to practice it consistently by directing our minds to be forgiving, we will find ourselves released and set free. Forgiveness corrects the misperception that we are separate from each other, and allows us to experience a sense of unity and at-one-ment with each other. (pp. 65–66)

In other words, forgiveness frees up our dormant love. Mrs. Bachelet has found her real self, her purpose in life, and that's good news for the people of Chile.

Desmond Tutu, the South African Anglican bishop who helped lead the opposition to apartheid and decades of black and white terrorism in South Africa, also spoke eloquently and bravely about the power of forgiveness. After the creation of democracy in South Africa, Bishop Tutu chaired the Truth and Reconciliation Commission. The TRC was designed to grant forgiveness and amnesty for all acts of terrorism, for blacks and whites who admitted their guilt for actions committed during the South African apartheid nightmare and sought forgiveness. In Tutu's (1977) book, aptly titled *No Future without Forgiveness*, he writes,

> Thus, to forgive is indeed the best form of self-interest since anger, resentment, and revenge are corrosive of the summum bonum, the greatest good, communal harmony that enhances the humanity and personhood of all in the community. (p. 35)

Tutu (1977) states further,

> Forgiveness is not being sentimental. The study of forgiveness has become a growth industry. Whereas previously it was something often dismissed pejoratively as spiritual and religious, now because of the Truth and Reconciliation Commission in South Africa it is gaining attention as an academic discipline studied by psychologists, philosophers, physicians and theologians. In the United States there is an international Forgiveness Institute attached to the University of Wisconsin, and the John Templeton Foundation, with others, has started a multimillion-dollar Campaign for Forgiveness research. (pp. 271–272)

Lampman (2007) tells the story about the immense power of forgiveness that reshaped the life of investment banker Azim Khamisa, whose only son, Tariq, a student at San Diego State University, was shot and killed by a 14-year-old gang member as he was delivering pizzas for a part-time job. Khamisa recounted that when he learned of his son's death, it "felt like a nuclear bomb detonated inside of me" (as cited in Lampman, 2007, para. 2). He reported that he was filled with extreme grief for a long time but eventually experienced a very profound "vision that there were victims at both ends of the gun" (as cited in Lampman, 2007, para. 2).

That led him to make a crucial choice of forgiveness of the murderer and his family. It also led him to create an antiviolence program that measurably altered attitudes among youths in San Diego and other cities. After his son's death, Khamisa created the Tariq Khamisa Foundation to develop and hold antiviolence forums in elementary and middle schools throughout San Diego. Seeking to inspire youths to choose nonviolent alternatives for solving their differences, he invited the father of his son's killer to join him in this work. The father accepted, and Khamisa asked himself this utterly striking question: "Would he have become my friend if I'd wanted revenge? Revenge is never the right response. Conflict will never go away, but from conflict, brotherhood and unity are possible" (as cited in Lampman, 2007, para. 13).

How many of us would have asked such a question? It is difficult for most of us to realize how necessary it is to practice love and forgiveness in our lives. Yet we really have no choice. Sooner or later the necessity is like a clarion call: we are here to love and serve. It's really just that simple if humanity is to save itself a place on this still-beautiful planet.

The world badly needs people like Bishop Tutu, Michelle Bachelet, and Azim Khamisa who are not afraid to speak out about the practical power of forgiveness. These are just three of the not-so-rare new leaders of our age who have learned not to let other people's wrath and vengeance control their actions or dilute their love or cause them to follow the road to still more vengeance.

Conclusion

There is an emerging global awareness in human consciousness today sparked by prophetic new and exciting voices. These voices are grounded on a growing belief in one's individual spirituality, the wholeness of our natural state, and, as Greenleaf expressed it, in the simple and regenerative forces of love and forgiveness.

Over the centuries, common folk lived with a simple and often hidden faith in the power of love and forgiveness, and we are all the better for their unrecorded lives that were challenged by so many counterproductive cultures, clans, dogmas, and beliefs. Eliot (2003), in her novel *Middlemarch*, seems to recognize this:

> For the growing good of the world is partly dependent on unhistoric acts; and that things are not so ill with you and me as they might have been, is half owing to the number who lived faithfully a hidden life, and rest in unvisited tombs. (p. 838)

Growing numbers of people, worldwide, however, now live not in faithfully hidden lives but in open and global revolutions of profound changes that challenge our clashing cultures and disparate religious and nonreligious beliefs. Increasingly, the common and caring folk see themselves, as Scott (2001) expressed it, "as spiritual beings deeply connected and open to one another and to something greater than ourselves" (p. 26).

That something "greater than ourselves" requires the granting of universal human rights to all people on our good earth regardless of gender, race, religion, or nationality. This may be a struggle for some of our political and religious leaders, but these are values sorely needed by much of humanity. Fortunately, they are easily available to anyone through giving love and forgiveness, because these are our most fundamental human characteristics, and they are inexhaustible and easily shared. They simply require, in the words of Greenleaf, that we validate the worth and dignity of the people with whom we interrelate. And remembering that we are here to love and serve. And that love alone makes life sweet.

And the crucible of life is love. No more. No less.

Tielhard de Chardin agreed,

The day will come when, after harnessing space, the winds, the tides and gravitation, we shall harness for God the energies of love. And on that day, for the second time in the history of the world, we shall have discovered fire. (as cited in Canfield & Hansen, 1993, p. 1)

References

Baxter, P. (2015). *Finding perace in life and death* (Kindle ed.). Bloomington, IN: Balboa Press.

Bernstein, R. (1999, Oct. 7). A monk's keys to happiness, and to the best-seller list. *New York Times*. Retrieved from https://archive.nytimes.com/www.nytimes.com/library/books/100799dalai-book.html

Browning, R. G. (1948). *Paracelsus: Part I. In Masterpieces of religious verse*. New York, NY: Harper & Brothers.

Butterworth, E. (1993). Love: The one creative force. In J. Canfield & M. V. Hansen (Eds.), *Chicken soup for the soul* (pp. 2–3). Deerfield Beach, FL: Health Communications.

Canfield, J., & Hansen, M. V. (1993). *Chicken soup for the soul*. Deerfield Beach, FL: Health Communications.

Chopra, D. (1989). *Quantum healing*. New York, NY: Bantam Books.

Chopra, D. (1992). *Unconditional life*. New York, NY: Bantam Books.

Chopra, D. (1994). *The seven spiritual laws of success*. San Rafael, CA: Amber-Allen and New World Library.

Covey, S. R. (2004). *The 7 habits of highly effective people*. New York, NY: Free Press.

Das, S. (2006, Jan.–Feb.). Ripening over time: The art of becoming a wise elder. *Spirituality & Health*.

Eliot, G. (2003). *Middlemarch*. London: Penguin Group.

Fosdick, H. E. (2002). *The manhood of the Master: The character of Jesus Christ*. M. W. Perry (Ed.). Seattle, WA: Inkling Books.

Goldsmith, J. S. (1961). *Living the infinite way*. New York, NY: Harper & Row.

Heschel, A. J. (1967). *The insecurity of freedom: Essays on human existence*. New York, NY: Noonday.

Jampolsky, G. G. (1979). *Love is letting go of fear*. Berkeley: Celestial Arts.

Kimball, C. (2002). *When religion becomes evil*. New York, NY: Harper San Francisco.

King, M. L. Jr. (1968). I've been to the mountaintop. Retrieved from https://www.afscme.org/union/history/mlk/ive-been-to-the-mountaintop-by-dr-martin-luther-king-jr

King, M. L., Jr. (1998). *A knock at midnight: Inspiration from the great sermons of Reverend Martin Luther King, Jr.* C. Carson & P. Holloran (Eds.). New York, NY: Warner Books.

Kornfield, J. (1984). The smile of the Buddha: Paradigms in perspective. In S. Grof (Ed.), *Ancient wisdom and modern science* (pp. 94–109). New York, NY: SUNY.

Lampman, J. (2006, Feb. 23). Roots of violence found in disrespect. *Christian Science Monitor*. Retrieved from https://www.csmonitor.com/2006/0223/p14s01-lire.html

Lampman, J. (2007, Jan. 25). A drive to help others forgive. *Christian Science Monitor*. Retrieved from https://www.csmonitor.com/2007/0125/p13s02-lihc.html

Laszlo, E. (2002, March–May). The quiet dawn. *IONS Noetic Sciences Review, 59*.

Lerner, M. (2006, March–April). *Tikkun*, 21(2): n.p.

Lesser, E. (2001, Spring). Do we have to choose? Huston Smith and Elizabeth Lesser hash it out. *Spirituality & Health*, 37–39.

Marinho, R. (2006). The servant-leader and the team: Love without measure! *The International Journal of Servant-Leadership, 2*(1), 261–285.

Ornish, D. (1999). *Love & survival. New York, NY*: HarperCollins.

Reel, M. (2006, Jan. 16). Chile elects first female president Bachelet, a former political prisoner, will keep socialists in power. *The Washington Post*. Retrieved from https://www.washingtonpost.com/archive/politics/2006/01/16/chile-elects-first-female-president-span-classbankheadbachelet-a-former-political-prisoner-will-keep-socialists-in-power-span/3342d9a6-d3a2-4c63-8094-c0a55855812d/

Scott, R. O. (2001, Spring). Are you religious or are you spiritual? *Spirituality & Health*, 26–28.

Shakespeare, W. (1998). *The tragedy of Hamlet, prince of Denmark* (Sylvan Barnet, Ed.). Signet Classic. Minneapolis, MN: Tandem Library.

Spears, L. C., & Noble, J. (2005). The servant-leader: From hero to host. *The International Journal of Servant-Leadership, 1*(1), 47–73.

Tutu, D. M. (1977). *No future without forgiveness*. New York, NY: Doubleday.

Wicker, C. (1998). Seeking the soul of business. In L. C. Spears (Ed.), *Insights on leadership: Service, stewardship, spirit, and servant-leadership* (pp. 246–250). New York, NY: John Wiley & Sons.

Wilcox, E. W. (1942). *Kingdom of love and how salvator won*. Whitefish, MT: Kessinger.

Chapter 18

Finding the Way Home

The Emergence of a Servant-Leader through the Power of Forgiveness

MARK T. McCORD

Sitting at a corner table in a small café in the Plaka neighborhood of Athens, Greece . . . Afghanistan seemed to be a million miles away and yet it had followed me there. Like an unseen vapor, Afghanistan permeated my every thought, causing words to catch in my throat and my body to be in constant motion. Even then, more than three months after I had completed an almost-four-year posting, I could not seem to shake Afghanistan. The result was an awkward silence, and fractured thoughts. My wife sat across from me, the look on her face belying her frustration. She did not know what to do for me . . . after all this time apart when she had subjugated her needs and desires to become my lifeline to the rest of the world . . . she had run out of answers. I was lost, and for the first time in twenty-one years of marriage, she could not help me find the way home. As raindrops dripped slowly down the windowpanes, I began to ask myself how things had come to this.

The seeds of what Debbie and I now refer to as "the Athens Incident" had actually began many years earlier, when I left the economic development business in the United States to accept a position as country director of the Center for International Private Enterprise in Romania.[1] In 2000, our family left behind everything we had ever known to embark on a global adventure to implement US government–funded programs to build the economy of developing countries, commonly called emerging markets. As an economic development specialist, I was well positioned to lead such programs. What I was not prepared for, however, was the exponential change that this move would make in my life and that of my family. Our experience in Romania was profound, with the project earning accolades from the Romanian government, stakeholders, and our client alike for its impact on the country's economy and the lives of its people. Yet, as with all initiatives of this type, it had to end, so in October 2003 the center appointed me its country director for Afghanistan. This began an odyssey of nearly four years, which culminated in dramatic success from the standpoint of the impact our projects made on the country's economy and citizens, but which also eroded my spirit, placing me in a dark and unforgiving mental state.

Throughout my years in the international development business, I not only led long-term economic growth projects in a number of countries but also provided short-term assistance to private sector and government institutions around the world as requested by my organization. This took me to some of the most troubled areas of the world, where building the economy was a high-stakes game fraught with political, ethnic, and educational challenges. None of these experiences would fully prepare me for Afghanistan, however, as the level of destruction in the country upon my arrival in 2003 was staggering. As a postconflict specialist,[2] I felt fully capable of embracing the challenge. Yet all my training and experience had not prepared me for the magnitude of the task, as it required more than rebuilding buildings and infrastructure . . . it required rebuilding lives.

Afghanistan's sad history is etched on the faces of its people. Friends, enemies, tycoons, and paupers have all been affected by the scourge of violence dating back to the overthrow of His Majesty Mohammad Zahir Shah in 1973. Working in Afghanistan is an exercise in perseverance; it has worn down even the strongest leaders and organizations. When the center sent me to open an office in Kabul in October 2003, I did what I always had done on international assignments. I went to work. Fourteen- to sixteen-hour days were common, most with little electricity, even less hot water, and nascent communications apparatus. I soon realized, though, that those inconveniences paled in comparison to those in the lives of the majority of Afghans, including members of my own team.

I have long considered myself a servant-leader, having built high-performing teams throughout my career. I prided myself on working side by side with my team members, getting to know them, listening to them, and empowering them to achieve their goals. This is the attitude with which I approached our work in Afghanistan, and it resonated with our team and our stakeholders alike. Over time, though, servant-leadership was replaced by an unwavering focus to succeed where others had failed . . . to achieve dramatic results in a place where incremental victories were lauded as significant . . . to leave a legacy that would be respected by all those with whom I came into contact. In short, the longer I stayed in Afghanistan, the more it became about me rather than about them. The fact is that success was achieved, the impact was dramatic, and a legacy was built, but in doing so I became obsessed with processes and results instead of people. I became so lost in the work that I forgot why we were doing the work in the first place. In short, I forgot the "power of the hyphen," meaning I placed emphasis on leadership rather than service.[3]

In his seminal work on the topic, Greenleaf (1977/2002) stated, "The servant-leader is a servant first. . . . It begins with the natural feeling that one wants to serve, to serve first. Then conscious choice brings one to aspire to lead" (p. 27). Greenleaf expanded on this thought in his later writings. Spears (2005) pointed out that "servant-leadership emphasizes increased service to others; a holistic approach to work; promoting a sense of community; and the sharing of power in decision-making" (p. 32). My initial focus in Afghanistan was as a servant, but all too soon the difficult circumstances and daily challenges caused me to revert to my natural predilection to control my environment, making servant-leadership a style rather than a core belief.

I should have seen warning signs of this transformation, but it happened so gradually I failed to notice that the more we achieved, the more driven and unhappy I became. Relationships crumble when there is an absence of joy, when unhealthy reality hits so hard and so often that happiness is snuffed out like a candle. This is the situation in which I found myself in Afghanistan, and while one could argue it was normal given the circumstances, it negatively affected my relationships with people who were empowered to and wanted to help me. The seeds of discontent were sown early, growing into a briar that ensnared us all.

The first part of my story here deals with my relationships within my own organization, outlining how my embracing of "the other path" led to forgiveness and ultimately reconciliation. The narrative would not be complete, however, without including my personal relationship with my wife, which had to be reconstructed even after the restoration of my work relationships had taken place. My wholeness is very much interwoven into the overall story, as it represents the compass with which I found my way home.

Sowing the Seeds of Discontent: The Beginning of Conflict

Greenleaf (1998) contended that optimal organizational performance rests at least in part on the ability of a leader to accept the existence of a shared vision of which he is part but not parcel. It was a difference in philosophy over organizational vision, which sowed the seeds for discontent early on in my tenure as country director for my organization's US government–funded programs in Afghanistan. The organization's vision, as crafted by its executive director (and the organization's founder), was singularly focused on building democracy around the world by supporting transparent elections, freedom of the press, and corporate governance. My philosophy, and functionally what we were required to do in Afghanistan as part of our contract, was vastly different in that it focused on economic growth as a catalyst for the development of a stable society. In short, the foundation of our organization's philosophy was to build democracy and good governance first, which would lead to the creation of economic growth. My approach from 25 years as an economic developer, as well as the mandate from our client, was to generate economic growth as a way to buoy the country's movement toward democracy. This difference in vision created conflict from the beginning, which resulted in a power struggle that shook the organization to its core. In essence, over time I became a "hero-as-leader," as discussed by McGee-Cooper and Trammel (2002), in that I fed off of conflict, acting decisively, rolling over all obstacles, and achieving significant results—all the while leaving a trail of fractured relationships and acrimony in my wake.

As our projects in Afghanistan gained greater success in terms of both results and accolades from our client, my relationship with our executive director and senior management team at our Washington office was gradually reduced to a test of wills. For every push from the home office to comply with what I believed were inane regulations or to change our program to be more "democracy"-focused, I pushed back, contending that our results and client relationship proved that our vision and approach were sound. This led to a series of actions by our senior management, which tracked along with Greenleaf's (1977/2002) dimensions of power, namely being coercive, manipulative, and persuasive. First, our deputy director used coercive power, letting me know that if our office did not comply with organizational regulations, even though they were not required by our client, as well as alter the program to focus more on governance and democracy, she would be forced to "write a letter of reprimand and put it in my file." As it happened, this call came a few hours after a suicide bombing had taken place just a block from our office in Kabul, injuring a good friend of mine. I was in no mood for coercion and replied, "Here's what you need to do. Write the letter of reprimand, copy it a hundred times, and put all of them in my file, because I am not going to alter a program that is successful and making our organization money because you feel the need to have us do more paperwork." I reminded her that every time we left our compound we could die, so she was the least of my worries. My response was emotional and made the situation worse. Her request might have been inappropriate for the situation, but my response provided little room for negotiation. Raymond Reyes (n.d.), vice president of diversity at Gonzaga University, contends, "You can't give what you don't have. If you want peace, you have to give peace." Neither one of us was in a place where we could give peace because we did not possess it ourselves.

In *No Future without Forgiveness*, Tutu (1999) says that when a relationship has been damaged or made impossible, the perpetrator should apologize. In this case, we were both unwilling to acknowledge our error, dogmatically clinging to our own views of the organization. This led to the use of manipulative power, in which both the organization's senior leaders and I attempted to force compliance through the use of powerful intermediaries (Greenleaf, 1998). In my case, it was then Afghan minister of commerce Sayed Mustafa Kazemi, who informed our organization's leadership that our program's efforts in the country were "exactly right" and needed no alteration or distraction. In the case of my executive director, the manipulation came in the form of the vice president of a powerful US-based counterpart organization who visited us in Afghanistan to make the case for democracy building as a path to economic growth, instead of vice versa. Powerful forces were at play, but these attempts only worsened the situation within the organization at a time when our programs continued to achieve success. Ferch (2012) states, "One of the defining characteristics of human nature is the ability to discern one's own faults, to be broken as the result of such faults, and in response, to seek meaningful change" (p. 17). With neither party able to accept their faults, the situation was destined to get worse.

A final effort to bridge the ideological and communication gap between our leadership in the field and in the home office was the use of persuasive power (Greenleaf, 1998). The organization's executive director traveled to Afghanistan in an effort to persuade me and our client that the philosophy behind our implementation of the program was flawed, that democratic actions buoyed economic growth, not the other way around. He failed to make headway in either case, which was frustrating for all concerned. In fact, our client commented at one point during a contentious meeting, "Your organization is making money. . . . You have a leader here who is making an impact on this country during a time of real danger and difficulty. . . . Why are you trying to ruin a good thing?" This visit, more than anything that had occurred prior, caused both me and our executive director to lose faith in the system, thereby creating mistrust.

The power struggle going on within the organization reinforced Greenleaf's (1977/2002) contention that organizations are seen too often as a means to end, entities to be exploited that are devoid of humanity. The struggle became a test of wills that had less to do with results than with victory, which led to mistrust and ultimately to a failure within the organization's systems.

The Path to Mistrust: Losing Faith in the System

Sipe and Frick (2009) describe the dimensions of a system in the form of a pyramid formed of events, strategy, culture, and beliefs. Beliefs constitute the pyramid's foundation, as they are the critical factor in the development of systems. Using this pyramid, one can readily identify the stress that our differing beliefs put on our organization as a whole. This divergence of beliefs about economic development and democracy, combined with cultural differences germane to working in Afghanistan, negatively affected our organization's strategy. This, of course, instigated a series of events that augmented the overall disconnect throughout the system.

Greenleaf (1977/2002) viewed formal and informal organizational structures as both necessary elements for governance and as potential stressors. However, when rigid formal structures clash with informal structures that respond more to leadership, friction is likely to occur. This is especially true when the former undermines the latter, meaning that leadership breaks down because of conflict over elements of the formal structure.

In my mind, the formal system was inflexible and had to change, yet the harder I pushed against it, the harder the system pushed back. This resulted in our Afghanistan team losing faith in the home office system, focusing instead on what we needed to do at the country level to serve our client. At the other end of the spectrum, the home office leadership continued its attempts to force the Afghanistan office into the system it had developed for its other programs in the United States and around the world. Instead of reevaluating the system and making adjustments, it attempted to "cure" the situation by changing the scope of the project, which resulted in major pushback from our client and stakeholders in Afghanistan. In short, the cure, as highlighted by Sipe and Frick (2009), was worse than the disease. By late 2006, there was little trust and even less cooperation between our field office and our headquarters, which widened the communications gap. It was, for all intents and purposes, a war of attrition.

The Path to Gridlock: Overcoming System Failure

It became apparent in early 2007 that the system was broken and someone had to intervene in order to repair it. Greenleaf (1977/2002) pointed out in *Servant Leadership: A Journey into the Nature of Legitimate Power and Greatness*, "No matter the competence or intentions, if trust is lacking nothing happens" (p. 83). This lack of trust had to be overcome, and in order for the gridlock within our organization to be broken, one side or the other had to seek reconciliation. After spending many hours evaluating my own belief system, along with my actions over the previous years, which had contributed to the internal conflict, I realized the need to accept responsibility for my own decisions and generate momentum toward reconciliation. Ferch (2012) notes, "Usually the leader who commands and controls has good intentions, while failing to see the impact of diminishment he or she is having on others" (p. 73). I realized my intentions had been good, but my unwillingness to cede control had, if not caused, at least inflamed the disintegration of trust between our field and home office leadership. Because of the stress compounded by the isolation, danger, and politics surrounding the daily implementation of our work in Afghanistan, I had resorted to "below the line" thinking, using retribution, control, and dominance in dealing with our organization's leadership and colleagues at the home office (Ferch, 2012, p. 124). In essence, I became the ultimate critic, spending much of my time, as Greenleaf (2002) pointed out in his essay "The Essentials of Servant-Leadership," dissecting the organization's wrongs instead of building on its strengths. In essence, I had begun to "hear the analyst too much and the artist too little" (p. 23). The time had come for forgiveness and reconciliation, and the process had to begin with me.

The Other Path: Forgiveness and Reconciliation

Tutu (1999) contends that true forgiveness deals with the past in order to lay the foundation for the future. To create a better future, I reached out to everyone at our home office, beginning with our executive director, and asked for forgiveness. In *American Masculine*, Ray (2011) relays a story about reconciliation between a husband and wife, in which the protagonist says, "I have loved you with an everlasting love, I have drawn you with loving-kindness" (p. 13). This is what occurred through my act of contrition. Not only did I ask for forgiveness, I adopted an attitude of love that, while not erasing the hurt of the past, laid the foundation for a future. When I asked my colleagues for forgiveness, they almost universally responded by asking my forgiveness for their actions.

Tutu (1999) also argues that forgiveness is not an end state but rather the beginning of a process of reconciliation. This being the case, I initiated dialogue with our home office leadership to comprehensively and constructively address the issues that had contributed to the systems failure. In doing so, we worked together to find a workable solution. Within less than a month, a system was in place that allowed us to serve our client, comply with home office procedures, and maintain strong communication ties. It took many more months for the reconciliation to be complete, but the initial traction gained from a simple act of contrition was nothing short of miraculous. For two years, we had jointly chosen a path of conflict, stubbornness, and mistrust, but now we embraced another path, the one to reconciliation, and it made all the difference.

Over the final years of the Afghanistan program, our team in the field and the home office leadership reconciled our beliefs, culture, and actions, reaching a state of tolerance in which we came to understand and appreciate the differences between us. It also led to a state of personal and professional healing, as we were able not only to forgive each other but to forgive ourselves as well. We learned, we grew, and we established "the other path" as the standard by which we would deal with each other.

At the end of 2007, I was recruited by my current company, a large multinational consulting firm, and after a great deal of soul searching I decided to accept its offer of employment, therefore becoming leader of a major program to support peace and reconciliation in Cyprus. Before accepting the offer, however, I sat down with my organization's executive director during his final visit to Afghanistan in order to discuss this opportunity. His response was overwhelming. "Mark," he said with more sincerity than I had ever seen him exhibit,

> we don't want you to leave. You are more than part of our team; you are part of our family. Family members don't always get along . . . and heaven knows we haven't . . . but we are in a good place now. I know I have no right to ask you to stay, but you need to know that if you do we will do everything we can to ensure it is a good decision. If you decide to take this offer, we will be disappointed but you will no less be part of our family.

I cried because of his sincerity and because of my own feelings of loss and remorse. He cried because he knew things could have been different had we not stubbornly held to our points of view for so many years. In the end, I determined that four years in Afghanistan away from my wife and family was enough, and the ability to be part of the peace negotiations in Cyprus was too compelling. Even now, however, I have good relations with my former colleagues. The war is over, as we embraced "the other path," which led to understanding, reconciliation, and ultimately restoration.

In *Forgiveness and Power in the Age of Atrocity: Servant-Leadership as a Way of Life*, Ferch (2012) asks an important question: "Can we notice where we are causing harm and at least try to do no harm?" (p. 209). I have embraced this philosophy, looking within myself and monitoring my actions to determine if I am doing harm, causing others to stumble. As a servant-leader, I embrace my responsibility to be flexible, facilitate empowerment, and promote fairness. To do this, I have had to focus on being a servant first, no easy task, since I have always valued leadership above all else. By stepping back and empowering others, by giving up some control, I was able to move forward. Of all I learned during my four years in Afghanistan, this was by far the greatest epiphany. Yet, to make this so, I had to face an even larger challenge in the reconstruction of the relationship with my wife. After almost four years apart, seeing each other only for a week or two every quarter, a fissure had developed that I had not been able to see, a fracture that made itself apparent in a graphic way on a cold, rainy night in Athens.

The Athens Incident:
A Collision of Leadership and Conscience

In his novel *Fools Crow*, Welch (1986) interweaves the story of Fast Horse, a warrior from the Lone Eaters band of the Blackfeet tribe who through a series of events alienated himself from his family and his community. He lived an isolated life, joining other bands of Blackfeet but belonging to none of them. When he was at home, his guilt and anger made him a stranger, and when he was with others, the fact that he was a stranger exacerbated his guilt and anguish. It was a vicious cycle that he could not break but for an act of contrition, specifically, retrieving the body of his old friend Yellow Kidney, who had been killed in a raid on the Crow tribe years before as a result or Fast Horse's disloyalty. For Fast Horse to find the way home, he had to take Yellow Kidney home.

In recent years, I have found that forgiveness is a pathway for finding the safety and comfort of home. It is my story, yet it is not unique to me. It began in Afghanistan, came to the forefront in Greece, and continues today.

A Stranger in a Strange Land

The Sunflower recounts Wiesenthal's (1976) experiences as a Holocaust survivor, specifically his encounter with a dying SS soldier who asked him for forgiveness. Wiesenthal listens to the dying soldier's confession but declines to forgive him, later asking whether or not this was the right thing to do. Scholars the world over have attempted to answer his question. Fox (1976) stated, "Forgiving and forgetting are two separate acts. One should forgive—not out of altruism but out of the need to be free or get on with one's life—but we ought not forget" (p. 148). This statement encapsulates the many issues that kept me from finding my way home. During my time in Afghanistan, I felt I had seen too much, accomplished too little, and worked too hard. Physically and emotionally, I was spent, and even the eight cups of coffee I drank before noon each day could not lift the mental fog that engulfed me.

Greenleaf (1977/2002) expounded on the issue of care, calling it "an exacting and demanding business," which requires "wisdom and tough-mindedness and discipline" (p. 255). While I possessed tough-mindedness and discipline, wisdom had eluded me, as I had for years focused on leadership and control as means to an end versus servanthood as a path to lasting impact.

As a postconflict specialist, I had seen the worst the world had to offer. I had stood at the sites of mass graves in Cambodia, Kosovo, Rwanda, and Sierra Leone. I had seen the sick and dying and I had heard the stories of those who had survived. Even so, I had been able to compartmentalize, to do my job with compassion yet detachment. Yet, because of the nature of our work, the length of time I served there, and the intense pressure under which we operated, Afghanistan was different. The enormity of the task weighed on me, taking precedence over everything else in my life. As the pressure to rebuild the country's economy and social structure increased, my ability to remain detached became acute, causing me to psychologically pull away from everything and everyone that was not associated with the work I had to do. This manifested itself in a rigid structure, an almost insatiable desire to achieve results, and the development of a communication and support network that was all about me instead of about those who were trying to reach out. The result was that every conversation with my wife became focused on how I was doing, without a thought as to how her life was unfolding. This created resentment within her that was never articulated, but it seethed under the surface as she bore the weight of not only her own life but mine as well.

I failed to acknowledge during this period that joy, sadness, pleasure, and pain are choices. Greenleaf (1977/2002) put it succinctly but powerfully when he said, "The forces of good and evil in the world are propelled by the thoughts, attitudes, and actions of individual beings" (p. 28). At this stage in my life I had made a choice to be unhappy, which permeated my thoughts, attitude, and actions. I had made my peace with those in my organization that I had wronged in my myopic pursuit of results, but I had not done so with the one person who had been my ballast through it all—my wife.

In Ferch's (2012) research on forgiveness, one of his research participants revealed, "When resentment is going on, I think it dehumanizes, destroys. . . . You are feeding on each other's weaknesses and there are shrugs, and look aways, the evil eye . . . sarcasm. . . . No intimacy" (p. 189). When I left Afghanistan, honors were bestowed on me by the

Afghan people and by James Wood, the US ambassador to Afghanistan, for the success our organization had achieved in rebuilding the country's economy and physical infrastructure. I was lauded for the intense focus had I brought to the work and for the "unyielding tenacity" with which I had reached out to the Afghan people—but no one gave my wife an award for buoying me up during the times I wanted to quit, during the long nights alone in the dark with nothing but her voice to guide me, during the long winters when there was no heat or electricity, or during the intense summers when a cool breeze was as scarce as a stream in the desert. She had always been there, even when thousands of miles away, and yet her role in my success had gone unnoticed and unappreciated.

Another Holocaust survivor, Nobel Prize winner Wiesel (2003), provided a transparent and poignant view of how constant pressure and conflict can create a level of detachment whereby even those one loves the most are subjugated to one's own basic desires. In Wiesel's case, sharing food and providing comfort to his dying father became a chore, something he did not out of love or understanding but out of duty. Throughout my years in Afghanistan, my relationship with my wife had become the same. Her needs became distractions that I could ill afford, burdens I could not or would not carry in addition to those of keeping my team and myself alive while achieving results.

When one is immersed in a situation that consumes him, it is difficult to see beyond the enormity of the issues that are readily apparent. An example is *My Father's House*, in which Fraser (1988) describes having spent much of her life confronting her own demons caused by sexual abuse by her father while ignoring the plight of those around her. This was never more apparent than in her relationship with her mother, who had also suffered physical and psychological abuse from Sylvia's father, which was made exponentially worse by the knowledge that she had done nothing to protect her children. She had not been there for Sylvia, but Sylvia likewise had not been there for her, as she was singularly focused on rebuilding her own life. In hindsight, I understand that I adopted this mentality in dealing with my wife, as in my altered state of consciousness I did not consider what my words, actions, and neglect were doing to her.

As my years in Afghanistan progressed, my compartmentalization and detachment manifested themselves in a lack of concern for my own safety. I took chances that others would not take, I went where others would not go, all the while convincing myself that it was my job. The low point was when I called my wife in the middle of a firefight that had erupted in our neighborhood between progovernment soldiers and Taliban militants. It was time for me to call her, so I did, never thinking about the psychological effect it would have on her to hear gunfire and explosions in the background. I had reached the point where I did not care about anyone but myself and those around me who contributed to our work.

Throughout this period, I was under the illusion that I was not just a leader but a servant-leader, having empowered those around me and affected the lives of the Afghan people. This belief became like a blindfold, blacking out the glaring deficiencies in my leadership brought on my single-mindedness and hubris. Greenleaf (1977/2002) contended that a servant as leader "always empathizes, always accepts the person, but sometimes refuses to accept some of the person's effort as good enough" (pp. 33–34). In this case, my actions did not meet the standard of a servant, let alone a servant-leader, but my wife's did. Had my focus been outward instead of inward, I would have realized it was her patience and grace that kept me going during my time in Afghanistan.

In his short story "How We Fall," Ray (2011) provides insight into the toll that compartmentalization and detachment play in the creation of resentment. Through the story of a married couple, Benjamin and Sadie, who are divided by communications dissonance and abusive behavior, Ray sheds light on the loss of intimacy that occurs when communication breaks down and self-indulgent behavior becomes an obstacle to understanding. Until restoration is achieved through forgiveness, the natural predilection of individuals is to want emotional and physical separation, because acts of tenderness and compassion are expressions of the heart. These expressions become too painful and are thus relegated to silence, or worse yet, emotional and/or physical detachment.

It took a night in Athens for the wall between my wife and me to crumble, for me to see for the first time since my departure for Afghanistan the true effect it had on her. As we finished our meal, a rainstorm moved through Plaka, drenching the ancient streets and sending tourists and locals alike running for cover. We could have stayed at the restaurant until the storm subsided, but my skin was crawling. I wanted to leave, and as usual my wife silently complied. Our driver began navigating the narrow streets, turning onto one of the main avenues of the city, snaking toward our hotel near Syntagma Square in bumper-to-bumper traffic. As our car lurched to a stop and we were surrounded by other vehicles, I was overwhelmed by the urge to get away, as getting caught in traffic in Afghanistan made one vulnerable to suicide bombers and other types of attacks. I told Debbie that we had to get moving, that it was unsafe—we had to get back to the hotel. She patted my arm and said, "It is okay. We are in Athens. You are not in Afghanistan. Nothing will happen here. Just relax and enjoy the ride." But alas, I could not, and a few moments later I jumped out of the stopped car in the middle of traffic and began walking in the torrential rain toward our hotel.

Debbie caught up with me in half a block, soaked to the skin and angrier than I had ever seen her. "This is it," she screamed against the wind and rain. "I can't take any more. You don't care about me . . . you don't care about anyone but yourself. All those years you were in Afghanistan, where we met once every three months somewhere in the world, I was dying inside. I had no peace, I had no joy. . . . I had nothing but shiny baubles all around me to remind me of your success. I gave up everything—my career, my friends, my volunteer work—just so I could be exactly where you needed me to be when you called and what you wanted me to be when you were home. I can't do it anymore. I'm done. I am through trying to fix everything. This is your mess, you fix it." With that, she stormed down the street, where our driver was waiting, and they drove off into the rainy night. For the first time in years, I realized I had no home that I felt was my own. I was a stranger in a strange land, alienated even from the one person who had supported me through everything.

Finding the Way Home:
Restoring Intimacy and Peace

Reviewing Greenleaf's writings over a long period of time, Spears (1998), the CEO of the Greenleaf Center for Servant Leadership, developed ten characteristics of a servant-leader, two of which are empathy and healing. Until I began to move past my own needs and have empathy for my wife's, healing could not occur. Empathy and healing are indelibly connected by a cord of understanding, for it is through understanding that one can truly empathize, therefore leading to healing.

Debbie returned to our hotel room hours later and sat on the edge of the bed. She looked at me with eyes that were no longer angry, but sad. "What I said on the street was wrong," she said with her voice quivering, "this is not your problem to fix, it is ours. We have always been able to talk to each other and I need you to talk to me now." It was like a dam broke—we talked all night. There were tears and raised voices, but the end result was forgiveness.

In asking Debbie's forgiveness, I acknowledged my unfeeling actions, my detachment, and my narcissistic tendencies, but I also expressed the willingness to change. It was the latter that most resonated with her. She said, "I want my husband back. I want the man I married twenty-one years ago to come home." In a powerful gesture that broke down the last of my defenses, she touched my face and said, "This is home. Home is where I am. Home is where your son is. Forget about our house and what we have to show for our success. Home is us . . . everything else is secondary."

In a movie, this would have been the end of the story, but reality requires a much longer process for reconciliation and healing. It is apparent, however, that even if forgiveness occurs, one cannot "unring the bell." Forgiveness is part of the restoration process, but it is not the parcel. Restoration takes time, effort, and open communication that rebuilds trust. This was certainly the case with our relationship, as Debbie and I worked intensely for the next two years to regain the peace and trust that had previously surrounded us. In essence, we found our "forgiving touch" by taking the opportunity to (1) restore a loving bond, (2) restore our character, (3) move beyond past relational pain, (4) lift the burden of shame, and (5) restore oneness (Ferch, 2012). This process allowed both of us to find our way home, using introspection to examine our motives and actions. What we came to realize coincides with Thompson's (2000) statement, "The problems you encounter in your world are problems that are within you—change yourself and the world around you has to change" (p. 151). I knew I had to change within before I could change from without. This took time, effort, and asking for forgiveness, but the effort resulted in the restoration of our marriage as well as of our relationships with others.

Finding my way home was a journey of discovery that included tragedy and comedy, joy and tears, laughter and sadness. The importance of this journey cannot be overstated, however, in that it allowed me not only to find my way home but to find myself along the way. It was as though the fog lifted, not all at once but gradually, as the sunlight of a new consciousness shone through. For Debbie and me, the experience was not unlike the final paragraph of the Ray's (2011) short story "How We Fall," in which Benjamin and Sadie's restoration took them to new heights from which they overcame the past and "rose again on vigorous wing beats all the way to the top of the sky where they met one another and held each other fiercely, and started all over, falling and falling" (p. 14).

We rose, we fell, we clung to each other, and through that process the forgiving touch was restored. Debbie forgave me, I forgave myself, and in doing so I found my way home, to her, to the center of my universe. Finally, after everything, there was peace.

Notes

1. The Center for International Private Enterprise is an affiliate of the United States Chamber of Commerce that promotes democracy, good governance, and economic growth around the world.

2. A postconflict specialist is a person who implements complex programs within an environment that has recently suffered from internal conflict. Typically, this requires a high degree of diplomacy, negotiating skill, and cultural sensitivity, as even small issues are magnified due to the political and economic circumstances.

3. Wallace (2011) discusses the importance of the "hyphen" in servant-leadership, as it takes the emphasis off leadership and denotes it as an expression of servanthood.

References

Ferch, S. R. (2012). *Forgiveness and power in the age of atrocity: Servant leadership as a way of life*. Lanham, MD: Lexington Books.

Fox, M. (1976). In H. J. Cargas & B. V. Fetterman (Eds.), *The sunflower: On the possibilities and limits of forgiveness* (pp. 143–148). New York, NY: Schocken.

Fraser, S. (1988). *My father's house: A memoir of incest and of healing* (1st American ed.). New York, NY: Ticknor & Fields.

Greenleaf, R. K. (1998). *The power of servant-leadership*. L. C. Spears (Ed.). San Francisco, CA: Berrett-Koehler.

Greenleaf, R. K. (2002). Essentials of servant-leadership. In L. C. Spears & M. Lawrence (Eds.), *Focus on leadership: Servant-leadership for the twenty-first century* (pp. 19–26). New York, NY: John Wiley & Sons.

Greenleaf, R. K. (2002). *Servant leadership: A journey into the nature of legitimate power and greatness* (25th anniversary ed.). L. C. Spears (Ed.). New York, NY: Paulist Press. (Original work published 1977).

McGee-Cooper, A., & Trammell, D. (2002). From hero-as-leader to servant-as-leader. In L. C. Spears, & M. Lawrence (Eds.), *Focus on leadership: Servant-leadership for the twenty-first century* (pp. 141–152). New York, NY: John Wiley & Sons.

Ray, S. (2011). *American masculine: Stories*. Minneapolis, MN: Graywolf Press.

Reyes, R. (n.d.). *Conflict*. [Video file]. Retrieved November21, 2010, from Gonzaga University course notes.

Sipe, J. W., & Frick, D. M. (2009). *Seven pillars of servant leadership: Practicing the wisdom of leading by serving*. New York, NY: Paulist Press.

Spears, L. C. (1998). Introduction. In L. C. Spears (Ed.), *The power of servant-leadership* (pp. 1–16). San Francisco, CA: Berrett-Koehler.

Spears, L. C. (2005). The understanding and practice of servant-leadership. *The International Journal of Servant-Leadership, 1*(1), 29–45.

Thompson, C. M. (2000). *The congruent life: Following the inward path to fulfilling work and inspired leadership*. San Francisco, CA: Jossey Bass.

Tutu, D. (1999). *No future without forgiveness*. New York, NY: Doubleday.

Wallace, D. (2011). The power of a hyphen: The primacy of servanthood in servant-leadership. In S. R. Ferch & L. C. Spears (Eds.), *The spirit of servant-leadership* (pp. 166–169). New York, NY: Paulist Press.

Welch, J. (1986). *Fools crow*. New York, NY: Penguin Books.

Wiesel, E. (2003). *Night: With related readings*. Saint Paul, MN: EMC/Paradigm.

Wiesenthal, S. (1976). *The sunflower: On the possibilities and limits of forgiveness*. New York, NY: Schocken.

Chapter 19

The Bull, the China Shop, and Forgiveness

MARYALICE GIROUX VILJOEN

Although empirical data supporting the significance of servant-leadership abounds, in practice it is often an intangible art, a carefully executed dance of persuasion and stewardship, of empathy and healing, woven together with grace and humility. When the steps of this dance fall out of sync with the music of the community, alienation occurs, to the detriment of both the leader and the led.

In 2004 I was recruited to work at a resort on an island in the Caribbean. The managing director of the island was a gentleman who had been a mentor during the early days of my hospitality career. Over the years we had become quite close, and I considered him to be more family than friend. His request that I go to the island and "straighten things out" was a great professional compliment. However, instead of accepting the employment offer in a spirit of humility and service, I neglected to consider the impact of my arrival on the existing staff. This misstep resulted in a difficult experience riddled with dissonance and degradation, for both my colleagues and myself.

Shelter Cove (a pseudonym) is a small, private island in the Caribbean. The sole occupant of this island is a resort of the same name. The resort is made up of hotel rooms, beach-front villas, private homes, and a world-class spa. When the private homes are not in use by their owners, they are part of the rental pool for resort guests. The average daily rate for a hotel room starts at $500 per night, and for the villas, $3,000 per night. The resort guests are "A-list" corporate executives, Hollywood stars, international sports icons, and other notable (and notorious) members of worlds of fashion, politics, journalism, and literature. A staff village set in the center of island houses approximately 100 expatriate workers from Australia, Great Britain, Bali, and the United States. The managing director (MD) had arrived approximately six months prior, replacing a very popular but ineffective predecessor. Over the course of his six months, the staff community went from having no Americans to having Americans installed in all but one senior position. I was the last piece of the puzzle to arrive. My position was newly created; capitalizing on my background in both operations and sales, I was to develop a new division on the island that focused specifically on the private homes. Therefore I would be taking slivers of work from various departments, including guest service, sales and reservations, food and beverage, boat transportation, building maintenance, and spa operations.

Whether it's a small business group around a conference table, an extended family around a dinner table, or a group of colleagues thrust together in a small-town environment, simply bringing a group of people together does not in and of itself create a community. Forming a community requires shared values and an appreciation of the importance of "working cooperatively and caring about one another" (Kouzes & Posner, 2003, p. 129). Trust is a core construct in a healthy and effective leader-constituent relationship (Caldwell & Dixon, 2010; Kouzes & Posner, 2007). The constituents of such a community are best served with a leader who is servant before leader, who shows the way through nurturing relationships, one person at a time (Spears 2004), and who is willing to be vulnerable (van Dierendonck, 2011).

Using servant-leadership and restorative justice as a framework, this chapter explores the alienation I experienced in this work environment, the leadership errors that I made, and the breakdown in my relationship with the MD. I will also describe the role of forgiveness and restoration in the aftermath of our separation, and the subsequent healing that has taken place.

The Bull

Arriving on Shelter Cove was a heady experience. I was tackling my first five-star luxury property, and although I had several years' experience in living as an expatriate in a spousal role, this was my first international work experience. On my arrival it became clear that the MD was under a great deal of pressure to make some significant changes at the resort. The financial situation was not a good one, but despite the removal of the previous MD, the staff seemed to be content with the current state of affairs. The MD was not the patient, fun-loving man I had come to be close friends with. Instead, the pressures of the situation had added an autocratic edge to his leadership style. In a servant-leadership model, change is driven in a relationship hallmarked by trust between leader and constituent. This atmosphere of trust assumes that leaders will act in the best interest of the follower, and in turn, followers will act in the best interest of the organization (Melchar & Bosco, 2010). Autocratic leadership can work well with new employees who are being trained in very specific tasks (Yukl, 2010). However, when it is used exclusively, trust evaporates and the potential for dehumanization and oppression increases. Freire (2000) observes in *Pedagogy of the Oppressed*, "The oppressor consciousness tends to transform everything surrounding it into an object of its domination" (p. 58). He adds, "The dominant elites, on the other hand, can—and do—think without the people—although they do not permit themselves the luxury of failing to think about the people in order to know them better and thus dominate them more efficiently" (p. 131).

Uncharacteristically, and rather unwittingly, I began to adopt that same autocratic edge to my own leadership style. Gone was the understanding that my role as a leader was to grow people into becoming healthier, stronger, and more autonomous (Greenleaf, 1977). As the leader of the private estates, I would be dealing with the resort's most VIP residents and guests. I failed to recognize the resentment that existing staff members would feel toward me personally because I had been selected for a prize position. Although an experienced manager, I had yet to develop to the level of leader whose actions were reflexively those of a servant-leader, and therefore failed to submit to "voluntary subordination" (Phipps, 2010, p. 157). Instead I was serving others only when it was "convenient or personally advantageous" (p. 157). In addition, I had completely failed to understand the impact that having a minority group take control, particularly a group of Americans—viewed as Freire's (2000) "dominant elites"—would have on this multicultural organization. And most importantly, I did not take the time to share myself with the others, to show that "my humanity is caught up, is inextricably bound" (Tutu, 1999, p. 31) with theirs. I had become "bloated with an exaggerated sense of self" (Kouzes & Posner, 2007, p. 347), thus earning the distrust of the staff I had come to lead.

The China Shop

Because of its remoteness, Shelter Cove is not only a workplace but a society as well. A conflict with a coworker did not necessarily conclude at the end of a shift. After-hours time was spent in communal dining and recreation areas. This delicate balance meant that its leaders needed to extend themselves beyond the day-to-day operations and influence the well-being of the community as a whole. This organizational stewardship is best carried out in an environment of prosocial and altruistic behavior (Barbuto & Gifford, 2010), and when this does not happen, as Greenleaf (1977) has observed, trust, respect, and ethical behavior are difficult to maintain. Given the small size of the island population, it was highly susceptible to the negativity of gossip, politics, and backstabbing. As a leader, my role was to build a healthy community (Melchar & Bosco, 2010). Instead, my poor leadership of the project I was brought to spearhead contributed to the communal tendency toward negativity and tore at the fabric of the entire community.

My social isolation grew quickly. The second-in-command on the island was the hotel manager (HM), a gentleman from Great Britain who was the only non-American still in a leadership role. Two months after my arrival, he invited me to dinner. Despite my clumsy entry, he saw that I had intrinsic value beyond my operational contributions as a worker (Spears 2010), value that had not begun to flourish. He kindly and frankly addressed my situation, explaining the bigger picture to me, including the resentment of key staff members who felt they should have had the position, the overall anti-American feelings, and, most painful for me to hear, the staff's perception that I was arrogant. The HM was taking an important step in building community through essential dialogue. As a person of influence on the island, his willingness to build a bridge through "the will to listen and to evoke listening" (Ferch, 2012, p. 162) was a critical turning point in my experience there. I left the dinner with a new friend and a fresh outlook. I will forever be grateful to him for that dinner. The HM displayed a great deal of love for me that evening. As a true servant-leader he looked past the political trouble he would have from staff that might view him as a traitor. He showed a commitment to me as an individual and as a valued partner, rather than an inconvenience (Caldwell & Dixon, 2010). He reached out and made taking care of me his highest priority, seeking my growth with compassion and empathy (Sipe & Frick, 2009). From that night forward, he and I became community partners. By giving me his public "seal of approval" for the rest of the staff to see, it was clear that we were not enemies, and in Lincoln's words, "If you make a friend of an enemy, do you have an enemy any longer?" (as cited in Ferch, 2012, p. 163).

At his suggestion, I sought out some of the key staff members who were particularly wounded by my arrival. During these conversations I worked toward interpersonal acceptance: to understand their feelings and admit my wrongdoings, even when met with anger and hostility (van Dierendonck, 2011). Although I am an extremely private person, I tried hard to open myself and provide unlimited liability of love (Greenleaf, 1977), just as the HM did for me. I had no clear successes here. I was met with a great deal of suspicion because of the way I had been brought in, because I was American, and because of my own behavior. My overtures to my colleagues were met with mixed results, in that some said they were willing to restart our relationship with a clean slate. But others, the vast majority, found it difficult to move from their "stance of . . . bitterness" toward a stance in which they were "no longer focused on how [they've] been wronged" (Ferch, 2012, p. 46). I had no choice but to demonstrate my remorse through my behavior, adjusting my style to one of community building and consensus. In short, I was shaking off the cloak of autocracy that had enveloped me from the beginning of my time at Shelter Cove.

In the midst of this, my relationship with the MD deteriorated. He had counted on me to deliver the results, quickly and efficiently. My stumble had made his life difficult, and his style continued to worsen into the depths of autocracy. Even as I began to amass small wins, my success was not enough to balance what he perceived as a threat to my loyalty to him—my friendship with the HM. Whereas the HM was leading altruistically, the MD, with his need for power focused on the institution, was leading egotistically with a high need for personal power (Whittington, 2004). In years past I had been able to walk into his office and have frank discussions with him. I tried this on several occasions, to share the insights my steps toward reconciliation had provided me regarding the culture on the island. I wanted to provide the same type of loving servant-leadership that had set me on a more peaceful path. However, he was growing more and more isolated, arrogant, and coercive; discussions such as this became impossible. Metzger (2010) compares this to Shakespeare's King Lear. A powerful man comes to a tragic end because he surrounds himself only with people who flatter him. He slowly but surely banishes the friends who try to tell him the unvarnished truth. Although the MD did not come to a tragic end, our friendship did. At the end of my contract at Shelter Cove, I did not ask for a renewal, nor was one offered. I was banished.

Forgiveness

During my experience at Shelter Cove, I failed to see my own impact on others, and my own faults, and did not take responsibility for the hurt I had caused and for which I needed to seek forgiveness (Ferch, 2012). Because of the transient and global nature of the community, the "fluid and natural act" (p. 46) of granting forgiveness had not been achieved with my peers. In the short life of our respective contracts with the organization, we simply did not have the time to develop the depth of relationship and interpersonal trust (van Dierendonck, 2011) that would allow me to properly demonstrate my remorse and commitment to real change. However, the primary casualty of the experience, my relationship with the MD, was within reach and deserved attention. A little over a year after my departure, I returned to Shelter Cove. I hoped to free both of us from the burdens of our recent past and the mistakes that so characterized it. During our earlier time, when he had been a mentor to me, he had willingly met my errors with empathy and the understanding that growth required failure and failure required forgiveness (Caldwell & Dixon, 2010). We had had no contact during the previous year; my email advising him of my arrival and request for some private time was met with a polite response saying he looked forward to having a quiet drink, which had been our custom for many years.

In Wiesenthal's *The Sunflower*, Pawlikowski (1998) makes a distinction between forgiveness and reconciliation. Pawlikowski describes a structure that requires repentance, contrition, acceptance of responsibility, healing, and reunion (p. 221). In preparing for our time together, I considered all that had occurred between us and realized the provoking event was my inability to successfully build a team and effectively lead the project. The MD had used a great deal of political and cultural capital in bringing me to Shelter Cove, and my actions made his life more difficult, not less. Thus, asking for forgiveness began with an expression of true regret for my actions that started us down the slippery slope of alienation. He shared his anger and frustration with me, not in the harsh tones that characterized our final months together but in quiet words cloaked in the affection that had once been the hallmark of our relationship. In the cool darkness of a Caribbean night, the journey toward healing and light began. After the visit, our communication returned, tentatively at first, and then in a more robust manner, as we shared emails and telephone conversations. We are on opposite ends of the world now, but we are restored to a greater intimacy than we shared prior to our estrangement.

Conclusion

When the artful dance of servant-leadership falls out of step with the music of the community, dissonance and discord result. My experience at Shelter Cove was a watershed moment in my professional life that demonstrated the remarkable power of well-executed servant-leadership. Whereas I sought to focus on the organizational objectives set forth by the MD, the HM sought to focus on being of service to me, and to the rest of the staff, by taking steps to create a collaborative culture (Sipe & Frick, 2009). It was my failures there that marked the beginning of a transition that would lead me to the Organizational Leadership program at Gonzaga University, and to a level of professional success that I have not previously reached. As Ferch (2012) asks, so I too must consider on a daily basis, "Am I shaking off my blindness and committing to the long good road of change and reconciliation?" (p. 123). Indeed, it is the ironic truth of servant-leadership that when one ceases to operate from a motive based in ego and personal power, one may achieve the greatest professional, and personal, success (Whittington, 2004). I have not forgotten the other people at Shelter Cove, those with whom I have not been able to attain a restored relationship. It is something I revisit on a regular basis, to see if I can learn where they are now, what they are doing, and if they would consider hearing from me. Most importantly, this experience guides my daily leadership life. I am acutely aware of the fine line I walk every day between humility and hubris, arrogance and service. I have seen my worst attempt at leadership, and I now seek my best attempt on a daily basis.

References

Barbuto, J. E., & Gifford, G. T. (2010). Examining gender differences of servant leadership: An analysis of the agentic and communal properties of the servant leadership questionnaire. *Journal of Leadership Education, 9*(2), 4–21.

Caldwell, C., & Dixon, R. D. (2010). Love, forgiveness, and trust: Critical values of the modern leader. *Journal of Business Ethics, 93*, 91–101.

Ferch, S. R. (2012). *Forgiveness and power in the age of atrocity.* Lanham, MD: Lexington Books.

Freire, P. (2000). *Pedagogy of the oppressed.* New York, NY: Continuum.

Greenleaf, R. K. (1977). *Servant leadership: A journey into the nature of legitimate power and greatness.* New York, NY: Paulist Press.

Kouzes, J. M., & Posner, B. Z. (2003). *Credibility: How leaders gain and lose it, why people demand it.* San Francisco, CA: Jossey-Bass.

Kouzes, J. M., & Posner, B. Z. (2007). *The leadership challenge.* San Francisco, CA: John Wiley and Sons.

Melchar, D. E., & Bosco, S. M. (2010). Achieving high organization performance through servant leadership. *The Journal of Business Inquiry, 9*(1), 74–88.

Metzger, M. (2010). *Sequencing: Deciphering your company's DNA.* Waukesha, WI: Game Changer Books.

Pawlikowski, J. T. (1998). In H. J. Cargas & B. V. Fetterman (Eds.), *The sunflower: On the possibilities and limits of forgiveness* (pp. 220–225). New York, NY: Schocken.

Phipps, K. A. (2010). Servant leadership and constructive development theory: How servant leaders make meaning of service. *Journal of Leadership Education, 9*(2), 151–167.

Sipe, J. W., & Frick, D. M. (2009). *Seven pillars of servant leadership: Practicing the wisdom of leading by serving.* Mahwah, NJ: Paulist Press.

Spears, L. C. (2004). Practicing servant leadership. *Leader to Leader, 4,* 7–11.

Spears, L. C. (2010). Character and servant leadership: Ten characteristics of effective, caring leaders. *The Journal of Virtues and Leadership, 1*(1), 25–30.

Tutu, D. (1999). *No future without forgiveness.* New York, NY: Random House.

van Dierendonck, D. (2011). Servant leadership: A review and synthesis. *Journal of Management, 37*(4), 1228–1261.

Whittington, J. L. (2004). Corporate executives as beleaguered rulers: The leader's motive matters. *Problems and Perspectives in Management, 3*, 163–169.

Yukl, G. (2010). *Leadership in organizations.* Upper Saddle River, NJ: Pearson Prentice Hall.

PART V

SERVANT-LEADERSHIP, FORGIVENESS, AND CONTINUING RESEARCH DEVELOPMENT

Chapter 20

Development of a
Leadership Forgiveness Measure

ANNELIES VAN POELGEEST AND DIRK VAN DIERENDONCK

In a sense, organizations are communities formed out of relationships between the people working there. As such, leaders are faced with the challenge of creating a culture where people get along and stay on good terms with one another. However, mistakes and faults—sometimes even offenses—are an inevitable part of working together. It is a fact of life that relating to others inevitably exposes people to the risk of being offended or harmed by those other people (McCullough, 2001). People are not perfect, which can cause friction. There are different ways in which people can react to potential negative situations caused by the mistakes of others. When harm is the greatest, when injury is most noticeable, or when offense is most intentional and pointed, responses such as retribution and vengeance are more likely than forgiveness (Cameron & Caza, 2002). It shouldn't come as a surprise that when it comes to social relationships, Berry and Worthington (2001) found that the quality of the relationship can be predicted significantly by two dispositional attributes: unforgiveness and forgiveness. Where unforgiveness is a trait reaction of anger, forgiveness is a response with love and empathy. They stated that the more a relationship is characterized by forgiveness, the healthier this relationship will be. For the people involved, physical, mental, emotional, and social health have been associated as long-term benefits of working with forgiveness.

Until now, forgiveness has mostly been studied at the individual and dyadic level. However, as was argued by Madsen et al. (2009), forgiveness can and should also be studied at organizational level. This level logically includes the other levels, for each organization is formed of individuals and the relationships between those individuals. The practice of forgiveness supports the development of organizational cultures characterized by greater internal harmony and healing (Stone, 2002). Lack of forgiveness, especially at the team level, however, may produce internal competition, which can lead to kingdom building within an organization, with potential negative results for performance.

Organizational forgiveness is a way for individuals to repair damaged workplace relationships and overcome debilitating thoughts and emotions resulting from interpersonal injury (Aquino et al., 2003). Interpersonal workplace forgiveness is a process whereby the injured colleague overcomes negative emotions toward his or her offender, and refrains from causing the offender harm even when he or she believes it is morally justifiable to do so. Cameron and Caza (2002) define *organizational forgiveness* as the capacity to foster collective abandonment of justified resentment, bitterness, and blame, and instead adopt positive, forward-looking approaches in response to harm or damage. To allow this to happen, people must be aware of the virtue of forgiveness, and know how to handle it. It should be known how to practice the art of forgiveness, for the lack of forgiveness could have impact at each level within the organization (Stone, 2002).

Leaders play an important role in cultivating forgiveness as part of the organizational and team culture. They function as role models, and by showing intentional forgiveness, they help build an open, noninvasive, and consistent dialogue in the organization regarding conflict issues (Ferch & Mitchell, 2001). *Intentional forgiveness* is defined as the deliberate decision to work through debilitating emotions and choose relational justice. In such cases a leader chooses to create an environment in which forgiveness can be asked and granted. Leaders can play two vital roles in fostering forgiveness and, consequently, in the healing that allows the organization to move forward (Cameron & Caza, 2002). One vital role is to provide meaning and vision around forgiveness. Provision of legitimacy and support is also essential. Leaders can exemplify, highlight, and celebrate virtuous actions such as forgiveness by initiating and supporting organizational structures, systems, and resources that are aligned with forgiveness and other important virtues (Madsen et al., 2009).

Forgiveness is particularly relevant for servant-leaders because of their primary focus on followers (Van Dierendonck, 2011). This link can be directly extrapolated from Patterson's model (2003) of servant-leadership, which consists of *agapao* love, humility, altruism, trust, serving, and having vision for and empowering followers. It can be argued that *agapao* love and humility are essential for forgiveness. *Agapao* love is love in a social or moral sense. A leader considers each person as a complete person, with needs, wants, and desires (Winston, 2002). Forgiving another person is also a social or moral action, and *agapao* love can be a helpful ingredient. True humility means that the leader is not self-focused but rather focused on others, the followers. Humility is not having a low view of oneself or one's self-worth viewing oneself as no better or worse than others. To forgive is an expression of humility, for it is retreating into the background in case of hurt by the other party; it shows modesty as an aspect of humility (Van Dierendonck & Heeren, 2006).

Leadership forgiveness is expected to be related to ethical leadership. According to Brown, Trevino, and Harrison (2005), employees can learn about ethical conduct via role modeling, and leaders are an important and likely source of such modeling. When the leader is an ethical leader, he or she nurtures followers, empowers them, and promotes social justice (Yukl, 2000). Brown et al. (2005) define *ethical leadership* as "the demonstration of normatively appropriate conduct through personal actions and interpersonal relationships, and the promotion of such conduct to followers through two-way communication, reinforcement, and decision-making" (p. 120). So, ethical leadership is about relationships within the organization, and the behavior of the leader toward followers, which should be morally justifiable.

In conclusion, leadership forgiveness is a challenging but essential element of attaining a more nurturing and fulfilling climate at work, and it is proving itself to be a promising area of research. Presently, only a few researchers have reported the direct and indirect effects of forgiveness on job performance and well-being at work. The purpose of this chapter is to introduce a short measure that will allow future studies on the influence of forgiveness by leaders. The theoretical foundation of this measure is the interpersonal forgiveness literature. As such, the measure aims to provide an empirical bridge between the servant-leadership field and insights gained from forgiveness theory and research.

Methods

Participants

The survey was an open online survey conducted within the network of the first author. One-hundred and ten persons filled out the survey, 51 percent men and 49 percent women. Their mean age was 27.5 years (SD = 7.0). Forty-eight percent worked in a nonprofit organization, 52 percent in a profit organization. Their leaders were 72 percent men and 28 percent women.

MEASURES

Leadership Forgiveness. Forgiveness is mostly studied as forgiveness toward oneself and toward others. Thompson et al. (2005) extended this perspective to forgiveness of situations. They developed a new measure of dispositional forgiveness of self, others, and situations: the Heartland Forgiveness Scale. The eighteen items of their measure were reformulated for the purpose of this study to acknowledge the perspective of the leader as experienced by followers. All questions were answered on a Likert scale, with six categories ranging from "hardly ever" to "practically always."

Ethical Leadership. Ethical leadership was measured by the scale developed by Brown et al. (2005). This measure consists of twelve items, and internal consistency is .92.

Servant-Leadership. The *agapao* love and humility elements of servant-leadership were measured with scales from the Dennis and Bocarnea (2005) measure. Each scale consists of five items. Internal consistencies are .86 and .76, respectively.

Results

Exploratory factor analysis was used to determine the dimensional structure of the scale. First, the conditions were checked to see if they allowed for a stable factor structure. Although the sample size is relatively small, with 110 it is still above the absolute minimum of 100 respondents mentioned in the literature, and the subject-to-variables ratio is 6.1:1, which is above the accepted minimum of 5:1 (Ferguson & Cox, 1993). Skewness and kurtosis of all items was between the +/− 2.0 range, confirming that they were normally distributed. The appropriateness of the correlation matrix to produce a factor structure not found by change alone was confirmed by the Kaiser-Meyer-Olkin test of .777 (minimum is .5) and a significant Bartlett's test of sphericity (645.817, df=153, p < .001).

Second, to determine the number of factors underlying the items, we used the scree test together with a conceptual check of the resulting rotated solution. The scree test suggested that either two or three dimensions would fit best (eigenvalues: 5.03, 2.34, 1.45). The three-dimensional structure did not replicate the structure reported by Thompson et al.

(2005) in terms of self, other, and situation. It also was less interpretable than the two-dimensional structure. The division of the items within the two-dimensional structure suggested a positive-oriented factor, and a negative-oriented factor. Varimax rotation was used to determine the items that best exemplified each factor. To be included, an item had to have a minimum factor loading of 0.4 on one factor only, and a minimum difference with the other factor of 0.3 (Ferguson & Cox, 1993).

Eight items were excluded from the final version. Table 20.1 shows the items and factor loadings. Each dimension consists of five items. Based

Table 20.1. Leadership Forgiveness Measure, Items, and Factor Loadings

	I Reconciliation	II Retaliation
1. If things go wrong for reasons that can't be controlled, my supervisor gets stuck in expressing him/herself negatively about it.	−.20	.75
2. With time, my supervisor develops an understanding for mistakes made by employees.	.79	−.21
3. When my supervisor is disappointed by uncontrollable circumstances in the organization, he/she continues to express negatively about them.	−.11	.80
4. With time, my supervisor can be understanding of bad circumstances in the organization.	.78	−.26
5. My supervisor continues to be hard on employees who have hurt him/her.	−.20	.63
6. Learning from mistakes that my supervisor has made helps him/her to get over them.	.71	.01
7. If employees mistreat my supervisor, he/she continues to treat them negatively.	−.24	.63
8. With time, my supervisor develops a better understanding of the mistakes he/she has made.	.79	−.13
9. It is really hard for my supervisor to accept negative situations that aren't anybody's fault.	−.02	.63
10. When somebody disappoints my supervisor, he/she can eventually move past it.	.64	−.22

Source: Verdoold & van Dierendonck, 2010.

Table 20.2. Descriptives and Intercorrelations of Leadership Forgiveness, Ethical Leadership, and Servant-Leadership (N =110)

	M	SD	1	2	3	4
1. Reconciliation	4.05	1.01				
2. Retaliation	2.13	.88	−.39			
3. Ethical Leadership	4.55	.84	.55	−.43		
4. Humility	3.92	1.04	.38	−.37	.59	
5. Agapao Love	4.04	1.06	.54	−.31	.81	.54

Note: All correlation significant $p < .01$. M = Mean; SD = Standard Deviation.
Source: Verdoold & van Dierendonck, 2010.

on the item content, we called the first dimension "reconciliation" and the second "retaliation." Internal consistencies are .81 and .78, respectively. Their intercorrelation is −.39.

Table 20.2 shows the intercorrelations between ethical leadership and servant-leadership. As expected, these are moderately strong, and in the expected positive and negative directions. Most striking are the strong correlations between reconciliation and ethical leadership and the *agapao* love element of servant-leadership. This indicates that both forgiveness dimensions have conceptual overlap with these leadership theories, but that the measure also contributes unique variance.

Conclusion

This study set out to introduce a measure for leadership forgiveness grounded in the personality and social psychological theory of forgiveness and linked to key elements of servant-leadership theory. Building on the measure of Thompson et al. (2005), a short ten-item measure was developed consisting of two subdimensions: reconciliation and retaliation. Our operationalization is in line with the two interpersonal dimensions described by Aquino, Tripp, and Bies (2006): revenge and reconciliation. The psychometric properties in terms of factorial validity and reliability are promising. Our measure contributes to the servant-leadership field by specifically focusing on this mostly neglected aspect of servant-leadership.

References

Aquino, K., Grover, S. L., Goldman, B., & Folger, R. (2003). When push doesn't come to shove: Interpersonal forgiveness in workplace relationships. *Journal of Management Inquiry, 12*(3), 209–216.

Aquino, K., Tripp, T. M., & Bies, R. J. (2006). Getting even or moving on? Power, procedural justice, and types of offense as predictors of revenge, forgiveness, reconciliation, and avoidance in organizations. *Journal of Applied Psychology, 91*(3), 653–668.

Berry, J. W., & Worthington Jr., E. L. (2001). Forgivingness, relationship quality, stress while imagining relationship events, and physical and mental health. *Journal of Counseling Psychology, 48*(4), 447–455.

Brown, M. E., Trevino, L. K., & Harrison, D. A. (2005). Ethical leadership: A social learning perspective for construct development and testing. *Organizational Behavior and Human Decision Processes, 97*, 117–134.

Cameron, K., & Caza, A. (2002). Organizational and leadership virtues and the role of forgiveness. *Journal of Leadership and Organizational Studies, 9*(1), 33–48.

Dennis, R. S., & Bocarnea, M. (2005). Development of the servant-leadership assessment instrument. *Leadership & Organization Development Journal, 26*(7/8), 600–615.

Ferch, S. R., & Mitchell, M. M. (2001). Intentional forgiveness in relational leadership: A technique for enhancing effective leadership. *The Journal of Leadership Studies, 7*(4), 70–83.

Ferguson, E., & Cox, T. (1993). Exploratory factor analysis: A users' guide. *International Journal of Selection and Assessment, 1*(1), 84–94.

Madsen, S. R., Gygi, J., Hammond, S. C., & Plowman, S. F. (2009). Forgiveness as a workplace intervention: The literature and a proposed framework. *Journal of Behavioral and Applied Management, 10*(1), 246–262.

McCullough, M. E. (2001). Forgiveness: Who does it and how do they do it? *Current Directions in Psychological Science, 10*(6), 194–197.

Patterson, K. (2003). *Servant-leadership: A theoretical model.* Unpublished doctoral dissertation, Graduate School of Business, Regent University.

Stone, M. (2002). Forgiveness in the workplace. *Industrial and Commercial Training, 34*(7), 278–286.

Thompson, L. Y., Snyder, C. R., Hoffman, L., Michael, S. T., Rasmussen, H. N. Billings, L. S., . . . & Roberts, D. E. (2005). Dispositional forgiveness of self, others, and situations. *Journal of Personality, 73*(2), 313–359.

Van Dierendonck, D. (2011). Servant leadership: A review and synthesis. *Journal of Management, 37*(4), 1228–1261. doi:10.1177/0149206310380462

Van Dierendonck, D., & Heeren, I. (2006). Toward a research model of servant-leadership. *The International Journal of Servant-Leadership, 2*(1), 147–164.

Verdoold, A., & van Dierendonck, D. (2010). Development of a leadership for-
    giveness measure. *The International Journal of Servant-Leadership,* 6(1), 285–
    292.
Winston, B. (2002). *Be a leader for God's sake.* Virginia Beach,VA: Regent University.

Chapter 21

The Principles of Servant-Leadership =
The Principles of Forgiveness

Paul Nakai

On an overcast summer day in 1944, Sgt. Jimmy Makino was with his squad on patrol in a field outside of Livorno, Italy. Suddenly, they were under heavy German cannon fire. To Jimmy's right, Pfc. Kiyoto Nakai fell to the ground. Shrapnel had entered Nakai's left eye socket, torn out the bridge of his nose, and continued on through his right eye. Another piece of shrapnel injured his left ear as well as wounding him in a number of other areas of his body. That field in Italy would be the last thing that Nakai would see. Kiyoto Nakai was my dad.

For the next two years, Kiyoto would focus on healing physically. He was then sent to Hines VA Hospital in Chicago, Illinois, to further his rehabilitation. From there, our family moved to Exeter, New Hampshire, where my father learned his trade as a furniture and cabinet maker.

In 1972, during my wedding reception celebration in Hawaii, I noticed a small group of my dad's army buddies talking among themselves and casting disparaging looks at one of the guests. I must admit that I could recognize only half of the people who joined us that night. The rest were distant relatives or family friends I had not met. This fellow who stood alone and under the disgusted gaze of my dad's friends was someone I had placed in that category of "unknown."

Unable to get an explanation from any of my dad's buddies, I asked my dad about this person. He immediately knew who I was talking about.

My dad had invited a few people he felt close to from his rehabilitation days. The fellow's name was Willits. Willits had been an orderly in Hines' "blind ward" and had been assigned to take care of the blind veterans. He was caught pilfering the veterans' packages and then passing on to them whatever he did not take.

When this was discovered, the ward administrator spoke to the affected patients. My dad was one of two who did not want to press charges. He went on to say that Willits was a good friend and companion during his stay at Hines. The two of them would talk together through both the sad times as well as the fun times. Willits would read him his mail and showed a sincere interest in my dad's family. He would take my dad for walks around the facilities as well as take his breaks with him.

As my dad would constantly tell me, "Not all bad people are all bad . . . and not all good people are all good." He would say that if you need to forgive, you've already let it get too far. Yes, there will be times when a person or circumstances hand you a thoroughly rotten situation and you will have to find your way to forgiveness, but in many normal day-to-day situations, you can see it coming and can resolve it in your heart before it implodes.

Before the hospital administrator let him go, Willits asked that he have an opportunity to apologize to the GIs. It was then that Dad asked Willits that they stay in touch. I haven't seen Willits again since that night at my reception. He did send his condolences when Dad died a couple of years later.

Interestingly enough, it's taken me most of my life to comprehend the three stances that Dad had toward life that enabled him to forgive, achieve what he achieved, and keep moving forward.

First and foremost, he had a deep acceptance and appreciation of people. Although my dad was rather quiet and unassuming most of the time, many found it difficult to be around some of his friends because of his friends' personalities and apparent flaws. Some of his friends would occasionally "stretch the truth" or exaggerate their accomplishments. Others would borrow his tools and then lose them. They would come over and empty the refrigerator of beer. But throughout this, my dad always saw their humor and their commitment to his and our welfare. He never judged them, and accepted their completeness.

This capability to truly accept others because of their basic character endeared him to his friends when others rejected them. More importantly, he held this stance when the rejection occurred not because of irritating traits but for reasons of race, religion, or standing in the community. He saw people as people. Today, I wish that I had been listening more intently back then.

One thing that I do recall is how impressed I was about his second trait, namely, his humility, his curiosity, and his desire to do things regardless of his blindness. He stretched the apparent boundaries of his talent as a furniture maker when he decided to build a four-poster bed for my mom. As he turned out each section on his lathe, the only assistance that he asked of me was to identify the color of the wood and the coarseness of the grain. He would surprise me with an occasional statement such as "I wonder how good I could be at bowling?" or "I've always wanted to try golf." He did both.

Finally, although my dad was not a religious man, I believe that he was a generous and purposeful man. Being the surviving "eldest son" of the "eldest son" of a traditional Japanese family, his purpose was to take care of the extended family. He not only furnished our home with furniture that he built but you could also find his furniture in every relative's home, as well as in the homes of his closest friends. I only started to realize how prolific he had been as his friends and our family members started to age and pass on. We would receive phone calls about dining room sets, dressers, chairs, stools, and end tables that Dad had built without charge that had been in their homes for decades. Our family and the families of his deceased friends now thought that it was only fitting that these pieces were returned to the family of the man who built them. As I mentioned, Dad was a quiet and unassuming man who had a simple sense of purpose and meaning . . . and he lived his life accordingly.

Life's Clues from Forgiveness

A few years ago, a horrendous tragedy occurred in Nickel Mines, Pennsylvania. A deranged gunman entered an Amish schoolhouse and shot ten young school girls, killing five. But "perhaps even more startling than the violence was the quiet yet powerful response of the Amish community offering unconditional forgiveness to the murderer. They reached out to his family with baskets of food and warm welcomes into their homes" ("Jonas Beiler: Think no evil," n.d.).

As much of the world was amazed by this response and tried to understand how a community could respond with such forgiving solidarity, I was struck when Caroline Myss (2006) commented on the Amish response of truly forgiving by saying, "Forgiveness is irrational. It is the most irrational thing that most people will ever, ever attempt in their life." This caused me to pause and reflect. I wondered, "What makes forgiveness an irrational act?" Is it because it is contrary to our inbred or learned reaction for revenge, retribution, or justice? Is it irrational because it indicates that we condone the act? Or is it because it doesn't fit within a simple or linear solution? Perhaps I needed to explore another way of seeing life.

I realized that much of my life has been spent being rational and objective. I believed that viewing things and laying them out rationally was the best way (the only way) to do things. I was convinced that there was an order to maximizing learning and performing. I believed in prerequisites—101 needed to occur before 201, "basic" needed to be learned before "advanced." I studied Latin to improve my English. I studied physics before I studied fluid dynamics.

Perhaps this is true in many objective, mature, and static learning situations. But perhaps this approach also limited my ability to truly forgive, love, lead, and be with others. I believed that a simple statement would lead to the necessary and profound epiphany. I noticed that this belief was at the foundation of my blindness to a more synergistic understanding of how life worked.

Up until then, I could not understand those people who learned another language not by merely memorizing words or learning sentence structure but through the multidimensional and at times "irrational" emersion in the culture of the language. I failed to see that great achievers and great achievements could come from those who didn't draw on previous credentials or experiences. I did not fully understand the entrepreneurial spirit or the eureka moment. I could not fathom how leaders could hold two or more conflicting ideas in their mind until an insight occurred. These results challenged my rational and linear objectivity.

If in fact forgiveness was irrational, I decided, it might be more effective to explore forgiveness in an irrational fashion than in the rational approach that I had taken. Perhaps I needed to explore this notion by holding it lightly on my fingertips and looking at it holistically. It occurred to me that rational forgiveness is called *tolerance*—a reasonable substitute more available to most of us. I can tolerate the offender while still holding negative feelings toward them, but I am free of those feelings when I forgive. Perhaps achieving tolerance would be an easier place for me to start this journey than forgiveness. Perhaps reconciliation comes from tolerance . . . and true acceptance comes from forgiveness.

Instead of seeing the state of forgiveness as a goal, it may be wiser to see forgiveness as a journey. Instead of seeing forgiveness as the intention of our efforts, it may be wiser to reflect on forgiveness as a mechanism for discovery. What can we learn when we've been in a state of forgiveness? What can we learn when we find the forgiveness mind-set impossible to achieve or revolting to our desire for revenge or our need to be "right?"

Are there clues to be found with those who have forgiven in the direst circumstances?

There are so many "larger than life" examples of forgiveness in the personas of Mahatma Gandhi, Mother Teresa, the Dalai Lama, Nelson Mandela, and Martin Luther King Jr. Perhaps it is because of their tremendous impact that we find ourselves quietly whispering, "I could never do that."

However, all that you need do is to listen to and embrace the stories of everyday people who forgave when they had every reason not to do so. I am moved and inspired by those members of the Amish community in Nickel Mines and by the journeys of individuals such as Linda Biehl and Azim Khamisa.

In 1993, Linda Biehl and her husband, Peter, learned that their daughter, Amy, a Fulbright scholar working in South Africa against apartheid, was beaten and stabbed to death in a black township near Cape Town. In 1998, the four youths convicted of Amy's murder were granted amnesty by the Truth and Reconciliation Commission after serving five years of their sentence—a decision that was supported by both Peter and Linda. At the amnesty hearing, Peter and Linda clasped the hands of the families of the perpetrators. Peter then quoted from an editorial Amy had written for the *Cape Times*: "The most important vehicle of reconciliation is open and honest dialogue," he said. "We are here to reconcile a human life which was taken without an opportunity for dialogue. When we are finished with this process we must move forward with linked arms" (Biehl, n.d.). Easy Nofemela and Ntobeko Peni, two of the convicted men, now work with Linda for the Amy Biehl Foundation Trust in Cape Town, a charity that dedicates its work to putting up barriers against violence. Since Peter's sudden death in 2002, Linda regularly returns to Cape Town to carry on her work with the foundation.

Azim Khamisa was a successful international investment banker when his son, Tariq, was murdered by a 14-year-old gang member. For Azim, this set off a two-year journey of trying to find peace and conciliation for the pain in his heart and the turmoil in his head. He actively read books, sought counsel, prayed, and spoke with others who had suffered similar losses. However, at the end of each day, the thought demons would return in force, and at the beginning of each day, he had to "will" himself to get out of bed.

As Khamisa (2012) tells it, finally, after two years, spiritually spent and emotionally bankrupt, he completely surrendered himself into the embrace of his God. Instead of moving forward from the moment of his sadness, he returned to a state of grace and acceptance from which he could renew his journey of forgiving. By stepping onto this path, Azim started to work with the murderer's grandfather, Ples Felix. The two delivered their message to elementary school children, warning them of the terrible price that gets paid because of gang life. Azim has also long forgiven his son's murderer, Tony Hicks, and frequently meets with him in prison. Azim is also leading the effort for Tony's parole so that Tony can join him and his grandfather in their campaign to work with the youth of Southern California.

True forgiveness seems to be best understood when experienced in a nonlinear holistic fashion. Forgiveness starts to reveal itself as one spends more time in the confluence of vitality, discovery, and purpose, that is, when we spend more of our time in our psychological and spiritual "sweet spot."

A dear friend who is an accomplished artist and author and a sought-after counselor likens these moments to an "opening portal." She notices that whatever she does takes on a special dimension if she does it while this "portal" is open. Her art is more inspiring, heartfelt, and complete. Her counseling is more gentle, effective, and profound. She attracts people to her, and opportunities to contribute appear miraculously. When she forces her performance—when the portal is closed—she notices that her work is good—but not spectacular. This phenomenon is also true of forgiveness.

When Azim surrendered himself, he allowed his "portal" to open. It was then that forgiveness fully displayed itself to him through this opening. He regained his state of vibrancy and resilience. He partnered with Ples Felix and engaged Tony Hicks in his journey. He immersed himself in learning and deciphering the attraction that gang existence had for the youth of his community. From this exploration, he realized that gang living was actually a social reality that took the life of his son. As a member of society living in that social reality, he played a role both in its existence and in its demise. From his "research," he realized that the majority of children make the decision to become a part of a gang around the time that they are in the third grade. He became inspired to reach out to as many children as he could to help prevent such choices from being made. This became his purpose and what provided meaning to his life.

Life is often viewed as a journey. One of my early mentors told me, "From the moment we are born to the moment that we die, we are constantly trying to make sense of life." At any given moment in time, we are either moving forward or we are stuck. Forgiveness is the mind-set that frees us from the anchor-like effects of our past. Fresh starts enable us to step enthusiastically into our future.

Ask yourself, how well do you forgive and forget? Can you see the life-affirming and freeing effects of our ability to forgive? Or do you find yourself burying your hurtful feelings within you or find yourself taking these feelings out on those around you? Do you have a familiarity with feelings of judgment and distrust? Does your life feel as though it is constricting around you and becoming more rigidly defined?

If you notice that forgiveness is not a path that you frequent or even consider, the next thing to do is to ask yourself if that is something that you want to explore and change. If so, there may be a clue for you in reflecting on any of the three stances we've mentioned.

Living a More Forgiving and Thriving Life

Based on extensive research initially conducted by the University of Michigan and by the University of Southern California, my colleagues and I discovered three elemental stances toward life that are universally shared by effective and thriving individuals (Nakai, 2009). Since publishing those results, we have continued on the journey to better understand each of these stances as well as how they manifest when they are in concert with one another. Taken collectively, the resulting capability that comes from this synergy contributes to our "being at our best" and is at the foundation of our interconnectedness with one another.

When I consider my dad's journey of forgiveness with those of Linda Biehl and Azim Khamisa, they are all reflective of the three stances toward life uncovered by this recent research.

The three stances are:

1. An openness to exploration and growth. A hunger and
    humility for learning. Holding "lightly" what one already
    knows or has experienced. A high regard and gratitude
    for epiphanies. Being able to simultaneously hold two or
    more conflicting thoughts in your mind until an insight
    occurs. Seeking and discovering simpler, more profound,
    and creative ways to get things done.

2. A life's journey of vibrancy, vitality, and resiliency. A per-
    sonal ownership of and appreciation for one's vitality and
    vibrancy. Seeing the oneness of us all. A respect for rapport
    and collaboration. A sense of dignity born from a personal
    journey of values. Resiliency born in forgiveness and a fresh
    start.

3. Being guided by purpose, focus, and contribution. A clear
    and evolving sense of meaning, purpose, mission, and direc-
    tion. A growing sense of authenticity and grace. Valuing
    deep and natural connections with one another. Gratitude
    for inspiration and wisdom. A connection with something
    larger than the self.

Taken separately, each of these stances holds the promise of providing tremendous perspective, heartfelt compassion, and hopeful certainty. However,
the profundity of these three stances occurs in those moments when they
operate simultaneously, when there appears an exponential magnification
that surpasses anything that results from the sum of the three parts. When
we experience this moment, we often refer to it as being in our "sweet
spot," performing beyond ourselves but not so much beyond so as to
jeopardize our authenticity.

Metaphorically speaking, these three dimensions parallel the three
forces of powered flight, namely, thrust, lift, and drag. However, what
enabled the Wright brothers to succeed where others had failed was their
discovery of a fourth element. This fourth element enabled them to access
the simultaneous effects of the first three forces. This fourth element is
what makes stable flight possible, that is, the ability to instantaneously
and appropriately adjust to and accommodate any and all changes in the
moment.

How, then, do we fully embrace and benefit from these three elements and from their collective influence? As I mentioned earlier, for most

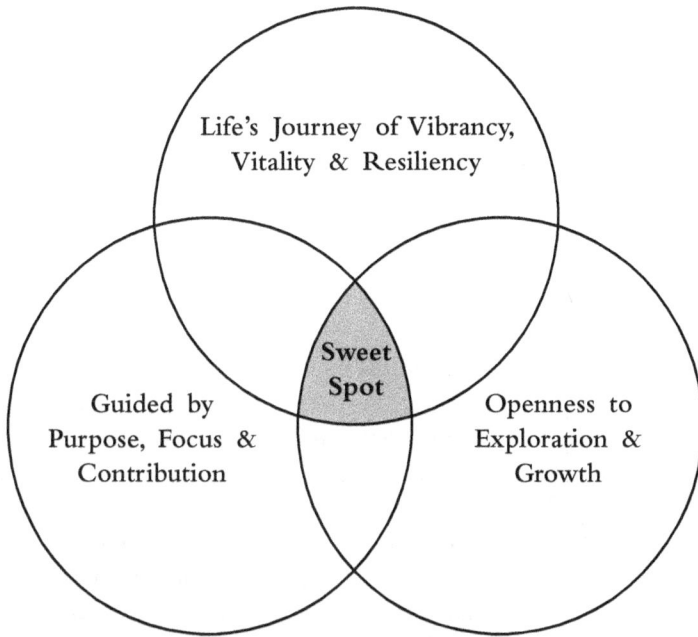

Figure 21.1. Sweet spot. *Source:* Nakai, 2010.

of my life I have followed a linear process of learning, understanding, and performing. I've frequently asked myself which elements am I most comfortable with, and which I am least comfortable with. The feedback that I've received is very much along these lines as well, that is, what am I good at and where do I need to improve? My journey of improvement was to hold fast to my strengths and to strengthen my weaknesses. Unfortunately, this did not work as well as I had hoped.

Recently, I've noticed that much of this approach comes from an assumption that I am a certain way all of the time, that my comfort and proficiency level are relatively static and accurate indicators.

Interestingly enough, we have discovered that at any given moment in time, we may vary within these three elements. The three stances are not static descriptions of character or style. There may be times and situations in which we are open to discovery and growth (the learning stance), and times when we are not. We can also see the openness and closedness of our mind-sets change even within the boundaries of an ongoing conversation.

In fact, we can experience the same phenomenon occur within the single stance of vitality. Our moods and attitudes will change at any given moment in time. The more we try to control them, the more ineffective and self-conscious we become. There are times when we see the innocence in ourselves and others, and times when we easily impugn less-than-noble motives to others' actions. There are times when we fully experience our dignity and resilience, and times when we take things too personally and harbor hurt and resentment.

As for our purpose stance, there are times when our self-centeredness, self-interest, or greed gets the better of us. We lose sight of why we are here or how we can contribute to a greater good. And there are times when we find ourselves chasing short-term fixes to the problems of the day. There are times when we are inspired and aligned with our purpose, and times when we feel the drudgery, obligation, and boredom of life.

Instead of taking this linear approach or looking at how we can improve ourselves, why not look at how we can be more sensitive to where we are on this continuum at any given moment in time, and then how we can be more adaptive and flexible to that moment in our life. If this is too big an arena for you to play in, try to find that area of reality for you that presently lies on the continuum between benefit-to-self and benefit-to-humanity. If we can keep this essence and intention in our hearts, we cannot help but contribute at a higher level. Although we are not always one way or the other, the promise of servant-leadership is not only to achieve great things but also to engage with others in a contributory fashion and to do so in such a way as to uplift the spirits of all involved.

The Principles of Forgiveness = The Principles of Servant-Leadership

The mind-sets of forgiveness and servant-leadership are lofty and magnificent. They are not hypothetical notions but real ideals that manifest when we are in a state in which the three stances of vitality, openness to discovery, and purpose are very much alive and active. If I were to paraphrase Caroline Myss, in many instances servant-leadership, too, is an "irrational" act and one of the most "irrational" things that a person can attempt. The additive effect of the three stances in unleashing the state of forgiveness have the same effect on the notion of servant-leadership.

As an example, I want to share with you my long-time work relationship and close friendship with a hospital CEO. This leader has frequently led from this "sweet spot" state and has been a positive catalyst in many lives. Having worked with him for more than a decade, I'm grateful for being able to share the discoveries and achievements of his journey. (An agreement of confidentiality prevents me from disclosing his name.)

As long as I've been working with this leader, I've appreciated his capacity to manifest his loftiest purpose-driven intentions and his insatiable curiosity and desire to consistently grow. His efforts in creating a "magnet" hospital system were born from his motivation to provide quality healthcare to everyone in the area that they served regardless of whether they could afford it or not (the purpose mind-set). In addition, he was constantly exploring and reinventing himself and wanted to find ways to awaken this desire to learn in those around him (the learning mind-set).

However, when we first met, his vitality and vibrancy were in a fragile state. He felt emotionally tossed about by some of his relationships, both personal and professional. Regardless of his efforts, his marriage was coming to an end. His corporate boss and the people that his boss surrounded himself with treated people as expendable commodities and would regularly insult if not violate the dignity of those around them. The driving orders that came from the corporate offices were duplicitous and misleading. And he had been ordered to achieve maximum profits while promoting the optics of a caring, people-first organization.

In addition, this man had inherited much of his senior team from a recent merger. This president based his fundraising approach on extravagant events, favoritism, and political maneuvering. Regardless of the coaching that the CEO gave the president to inspire greater values-based substance as well as provide more countywide services and benefits, the president kept his focus on playing to the chosen few.

This CEO's COO / chief nursing officer had put her name in for the CEO's job. When she did not get it, out of disappointment, she would withhold information whenever she and the CEO would get together. She had a difficult time with the cultural values that this CEO wanted to make a way of life and would control everyone around her with an "iron fist."

The CEO could rely on a few members of his team who were aligned with his purpose, values, and mission and who consistently performed in an admirable way. Because of their results, these individuals found themselves being promoted to the corporate headquarters shortly after the CEO took the reins of the hospital.

As long as I've known this CEO, his strength has been his sense of purpose and his authenticity (purpose). He has always looked to discover and internalize new and better ways to get things done (learning). However, during the early days of our working together, this leader's initial response to the turmoil and misalignment in his team was to try to placate or cater to the upset and skepticism instead of dealing with the source of the skepticism, namely, how they thought and felt. Because of his strong sense of accountability, he found himself taking these attitudinal and values issues on himself. He tried to calm the troubled waters. He became the referee between key executives who could not get along on their own. He found himself choreographing activities and taking on himself the role of coordinator. He started to demand the attitudes that he wanted to see from those around him. After a while, he found himself being the "hub" through which all major activities had to flow. This not only slowed down progress but necessitated his working twice as hard. As a result, when he was fatigued or disheartened, he would lecture and tell his people what to do. He was caught in a continuous loop of stimulus-reaction.

However, shortly after we started working together, as a testament to his sense of character and humility, he could see the pivotal role that his feelings and his thinking played in assessing and responding to any situation. He discovered his capacity to strengthen and weatherproof his personal sense of vitality and resilience (vitality). His state of mind was no longer victimized by others' negative attitudes or points of view. For the first few years, he and I not only worked together but I also introduced him to another consultancy that I felt could better accompany him and his organization on this journey.

His strengthening stance of vitality combined with his already strong stance of purpose and learning yielded a highly effective and profound leadership. He held himself and his team to high yet realistic standards of performance. He also held everyone to expectations of consistent improvement, learning, and growth. Finally, he held himself and everyone on his team to high standards of dignity and resilience. From this grounding, he proactively coached and mentored those around him in daily dialogue. To this day, he fluidly integrates the three dimensions of servant-leadership as he fulfills his role as CEO.

Since that time, this CEO and his organizations have been consistently accelerating in their sense of service, in the quality of their offerings, and in the substance of their culture. They have been recognized not only within their community but also in the broader world of organizational excellence and quality healthcare.

The three elements that contribute to a state of forgiveness are the same three elements that contribute to the effective servant-leader. Interestingly enough, it has been my experience that for many servant-leaders the "front burner" elements seem to consistently be purpose-driven and open to learning. They share an inspiration born from contribution and a never-ending curiosity and desire to discover and grow. This is the stance with which they consistently raise their sense of vitality and resilience, and with which they become clearer and more inspired by how they can contribute and be of service to others as well as to the world in general.

The Journey for the New Year

The three stances of vitality, learning, and purpose are key not only to forgiveness and servant-leadership but also to understanding and internalizing life's other "ideals," such as interconnectedness (monism), freedom, peace, love, and fresh starts.

Although at times forgiveness is difficult to truly achieve, it appears to be a natural and innate state. As we've mentioned, it is an internal state that you return to instead of an external state you learn about. As such it's not "special" within our nature, however, it appears "special" because of its infrequency. The effort and angst we appear to expend to get to that point is not necessary to create forgiveness; rather, the effort allows us to get past the thought habits and personal obstacles that we place in our way. We do not create forgiveness; we allow the gift of forgiveness to reappear. It's a state that is always there.

The same is true of servant-leadership, that is, leading through being of service. True servant-leadership may be as simple as living by the following principles as often as possible:

Forgiving
Leading through service
Being at peace
Loving
Experiencing awe
Showing gratitude
Exercising freedom
Stepping into new moments

References

Biehl, L. (n.d.). Linda Biehl and Easy Nofemela. Retrieved from https://www.theforgivenessproject.com/linda-biehl-easy-nofemela

Jonas Beiler: Think no evil. (n.d.). Retrieved from https://www1.cbn.com/700club/jonas-beiler-think-no-evil

Khamisa, A. (2012). *From murder to forgiveness*. Bloomington, IN: Balboa Press.

Myss, C. (2006). Countdown with Keith Olbermann for Oct. 5. Retrieved from http://www.nbcnews.com/id/15156514/ns/msnbc-countdown_with_keith_olbermann/t/countdown-keith-olbermann-oct/#.XjM85nt7lhF

Nakai, P. (2009). Receiving the gift of servant-leadership. *The International Journal of Servant-Leadership, 5*(1), 347–369.

Nakai, P. (2010). The principles of servant-leadership = the principles of forgiveness. *The International Journal of Servant-Leadership, 6*(1), 295–308.

About the Editors

Jiying Song, PhD, PMP

After earning her master of engineering in China and working in the field of IT for fourteen years, Jiying (Jenny) came to the United States to pursue a master of divinity from George Fox University. After completing her second master's degree, she earned a PhD in leadership studies from Gonzaga University. Through this process, she has discovered that she has a passion for both effective leadership and academic work.

During her career in China, she served as the operation director of an IT company and managed the operation service center and marketing department for seven years. She obtained a project management professional certification and an IT service management certification and worked as a project manager for more than ten years. During her graduate study at George Fox University, she worked as teaching assistant for Dr. MaryKate Morse, teaching and tutoring graduate students in New Testament Greek. She has been active in ministry to international students and visiting scholars at George Fox University since 2013. She graduated from George Fox University and received the dean's award for "superior academic achievement, exemplary Christian character, and extraordinary potential for service as a Christian scholar." At Gonzaga University, she worked with Dr. Chris Francovich as a data analyst for National Science Foundation's ADVANCE project. She taught project management and spiritual formation at George Fox University. Currently she is assistant professor of business and economics at Northwestern College and serving as associate editor with Dr. Shann Ray Ferch and Larry C. Spears for *the International Journal of Servant-Leadership*.

Dung Q. Tran, PhD

Dr. Dung Q. Tran is an assistant professor of organizational leadership in the School of Leadership Studies at Gonzaga University. Working at the intersection of organizational leadership, communication, and Jesuit higher education, his scholarship has appeared in the *International Journal of Servant-Leadership*; *Communication Research Trends*; the *Journal of Catholic Education*; and (with M. R. Carey) in the following anthologies: *Evolving Leadership for Collective Wellbeing: Lessons for Implementing the United Nations Sustainable Development Goals*; *Breaking the Zero-Sum Game: Transforming Societies through Inclusive Leadership*; and *The Palgrave Handbook of Workplace Spirituality and Fulfillment*.

Shann Ray Ferch, PhD

In his work as professor of leadership with the internationally recognized PhD program in leadership studies at Gonzaga University (www.gonzaga.edu/doctoral), Dr. Shann Ray Ferch considers how servant-leadership honors personal and collective responsibility, and self-transcendence across the disciplines. As a poet and prose writer, his work has appeared in *Poetry*, *McSweeney's, Narrative Magazine, Story Quarterly, Best New Poets*, and *Poetry International* (www.shannray.com). He is a National Endowment for the Arts fellow and the author of the American Book Award–winning collection of short stories *American Masculine: A Book of Creative Nonfiction and Political Theory*; *Forgiveness and Power in the Age of Atrocity: Servant Leadership as a Way of Life*; the Western Writers of America Spur Award–winning novel *American Copper*; the High Plains Book Award–winning poetry collection *Balefire*; the poetry collection *Sweetclover*; the collection of short stories *Blood Fire Vapor Smoke*; and two books coedited with Larry C. Spears, *The Spirit of Servant Leadership* and *Conversations on Servant-Leadership*. Dr. Ferch has also served as a research psychologist with the Centers for Disease Control, as a panelist for the National Endowment for the Humanities, and is a systems psychologist in private practice.

    As a leadership consultant, Dr. Ferch has led initiatives in business, health, government, and public service organizations in the United States, South America, Europe, Asia, and Africa. The editor of *the International Journal of Servant-Leadership*, Dr. Ferch, in collaboration with senior advisory editor Larry C. Spears and associate editor Jenny Song, publishes essays, science, and scholarly work dedicated to the wisdom, health, autonomy, and freedom of others.

Larry C. Spears

Larry C. Spears has spent thirty years as a global advocate of servant-leadership. He met Robert K. Greenleaf in 1990 and served as president and CEO of the Robert K. Greenleaf Center from 1990 to 2007. In 2008, Spears founded the Larry C. Spears Center for Servant-Leadership (www.spearscenter.org), where he now serves as president, and also began to teach graduate courses in servant-leadership for Gonzaga University, where he serves as servant-leadership scholar. Larry Spears and Shann Ferch cofounded *the International Journal of Servant-Leadership* in 2005 (www. gonzaga.edu/ijsl), where he serves as senior advisory editor. Spears is a noted writer and editor of over a dozen books on servant-leadership. He served as editor or coeditor of all five of Robert Greenleaf's posthumously published books, including *On Becoming a Servant-Leader* (1996), *Seeker and Servant* (1996), *The Power of Servant-Leadership* (1998), *Servant-Leadership: 25th Anniversary Edition* (2002), and *The Servant-Leader Within* (2003). Spears is also coeditor and contributing author to a series of servant-leadership anthologies that include *Reflections on Leadership* (1995), *Insights on Leadership* (1998), *Focus on Leadership* (2002), *Practicing Servant-Leadership* (2004), *The Spirit of Servant-Leadership* (2011), and *Conversations on Servant-Leadership* (2015). In addition, he has contributed chapters on servant-leadership in seventeen books edited by others.

As a popular speaker on servant-leadership, Spears has given hundreds of talks in numerous countries since 1990 in which he has encouraged others in their own understanding and practice of servant-leadership. A 2004 television broadcast interview of Spears by Stone Phillips on *NBC's Dateline* was seen by ten million viewers.

Contributors

Keith Allan is owner of VinPure Services and Napa Cider Company. VinPure Services provides wine purification to over four hundred client wineries throughout California, Oregon, and Washington. Annual production is five million gallons of wine per year and over one million gallons of cider and nonalcoholic beverages. After developing training, leadership, and management programs within the pharmaceutical industry for over twenty-three years, applying these skills to Keith's day-to-day business relationships and employee development has contributed to a year-over-year growth of over 34 percent gross sales annually since 2010. For Keith it has always been both a pleasure and goal to contribute to the success of another individual's personal and professional objectives. Understanding an individual's career desire, skill set, and preferred learning style has resulted in a mentorship style that is collaborative and sensitive to the work environment and development. Secondarily, Keith's mentorship style truly supports the servant-leadership construct expressed at VinPure Services and Napa Cider Company. To date, Keith has assisted employees in transitioning to other career positions, and in completing their undergraduate and graduate degrees at both the masters and PhD level. Keith currently resides in Napa, California, with his wife, Mary, and their son, Chase, is a lieutenant in the US Navy, stationed in Crete. Keith holds a bachelor's degree in psychology from California State University at Long Beach, a master's degree in organizational development and leadership from Gonzaga University, and a master's in business administration from Saint Joseph's College of Maine.

Christian B. Cabezas obtained his degree in psychology at the Pontificia Universidad Católica del Ecuador, where he currently teaches graduate and undergraduate courses in psychometrics and quantitative research methods. His main research interests and publications include leadership, personality, motivation, perceptual biases, and higher education. He obtained a masters degree in psychology at the University of Idaho, and later a masters of business association at the University of Alcalá in Madrid, Spain. He obtained his PhD in leadership studies at Gonzaga University in Washington State, where he learned about the theory and practice of servant-leadership.

Andrew Campbell is the director of the International Peace and Leadership Institute. He provides emerging leadership research and leadership development and training programs about a leader's role in the international, national, and nongovernmental organization designed for conflict prevention—specifically for conflict resolution practitioners conducting and executing peacemaking, peacekeeping, and peace-building activities within postconflict resolution and peaceful leadership. In addition, as a retired senior military officer, Dr. Campbell works for the Department of Defense specializing in counterterrorism and global security cooperation. Dr. Campbell possesses a doctorate in global leadership from the Institute of Indiana Technology, Fort Wayne, Indiana, and a master's degree in diplomacy in international conflict management from Norwich University, Northfield, Vermont. He is an adjunct professor for the Air Force Command and Staff College, Norwich University, and for the Federal Executive Institute. Dr. Campbell is a recognized national and international speaker on peace leadership, and addressed the World Society of Victimology at The Hague in 2012, the Peace Leadership Conference in 2017, the International Leadership Association in 2011–2018, and the European Consortium for Political Research in 2015–2017. He is widely published in both national and international journals, with articles in the *International Journal of Servant-Leadership* on such topics as *"Leadership Education in Transitional Justice in Promoting Global Peace," "Civic Engagement through Education,"* and *"Forgiveness and Reconciliation as an Organizational Leadership Competence in Transitional Justice."* He recently published a book titled *Global Leadership Initiatives for Conflict Resolution and Peacebuilding and Peace Leadership: Self-Transformation to Peace* that explores leadership theories and practice models to conceptualize the intersection of leadership within conflict management and peacebuilding.

Rakiya Farah lives in England, where she is reading for the bachelor of civil law (a postgraduate degree in English law) at the University of

Oxford. Rakiya has degrees in various disciplines from the University of Cambridge, the London School of Economics, and University College London. She completed a master of arts in organizational leadership at Gonzaga University in 2013, a program that galvanized her passion for social justice. Before returning to education in the United Kingdom, Rakiya spent eight years working in communications consultancy in Qatar. She enjoys keeping fit, rowing, and clay pigeon shooting.

Harris W. Fawell served in Congress from 1985 to 1999, where he chaired the House Employer Employee Relations subcommittee in the 104th and 105th sessions. Prior to his election to Congress he spent fourteen years in the Illinois State Senate. He lives in Naperville, Illinois, where he and his wife have raised their three children. In support of his belief that the religions of the world could unite on the common theme of love and forgiveness, he has collected ideas from twentieth-century leaders, scholars, philosophers, and prophets, ranging from the eminent to the obscure. His writings also reflect a lifetime of, as he would say, quoting *The Wizard of Oz*, "meditating, cogitating, and otherwise hobnobbing with the gods."

Karen Petersen Finch is associate professor of theology at Whitworth University. She is also a minister of Word and Sacrament in the Presbyterian Church (USA). Karen earned her master of divinity from Princeton Theological Seminary, and her doctorate from Gonzaga University. She is also a fellow of the Lonergan Institute of Boston College. Karen looks at ecumenical dialogue through the lens of Bernard Lonergan's theological method, particularly dialogue between Roman Catholic theology and her own Calvinist/Reformed tradition. She is currently writing a manual for local dialogue between Presbyterian and Catholic laypeople.

Mark T. McCord is an international development executive with more than thirty-five years of experience in leading organizations and consulting with governments. From 2007 to 2017, Mark was a director at Deloitte Consulting LLP and was one of their key practice leaders in leadership, innovation, organizational transformation, economic development, competitiveness, governance, fundraising, and trade development. Prior to that, he served as an international director for the Center for Private Enterprise (a division of the US Chamber of Commerce) and as president and CEO of several metropolitan Chambers of Commerce in the United States. He is also cofounder and technical director of the Carthage Institute, which implements youth leadership and economic development programs in conjunction with the US and foreign governments. In 2017, Mark was named a Senior Policy Fellow for Youth Leadership and Empowerment by the Rockefeller Foundation and asked to participate in its prestigious program in Bellagio, Italy. Mark received his undergraduate degree in social sciences at Southwestern Oklahoma State University, and a master of arts in organizational leadership at Gonzaga University. He and his wife, Debbie, have been married for thirty-five years and have one son, Daniel, who is thirty-two years old.

Maduabuchi Leo Muoneme, a Jesuit priest, is the author of *The Hermeneutics of Jesuit Leadership in Higher Education.* He entered the Society of Jesus in 1988 and was ordained a priest in 2001. He received his PhD from Gonzaga University in Spokane, Washington. He did his bachelor's studies at Loyola University of Chicago and graduated with first class honors and a double major in philosophy and theology. He was a pioneer member of the staff of Loyola Jesuit College in Abuja, Nigeria. After regency, he was missioned to the Hekima Jesuit School of Theology, at the Catholic University of East Africa in Nairobi, Kenya, where he received a degree in theology for ecclesiastical ministry. Subsequently, he did a master of studies in physics at Boston College, Massachusetts. Muoneme served as a visiting chaplain at Wellesley College, Massachusetts. He has pastored two Jesuit parishes in Nigeria (St. Francis Catholic Church in Lagos and St. Joseph Catholic Church in Benin City), and served as an interim pastor in a Jesuit parish (Holy Family Catholic Church) in Monrovia, Liberia. He taught physics at Loyola Jesuit College in Abuja and also served as the vice principal for university admissions. He once served as Chaplain of St. Francis Catholic Secondary School, where he also taught physics. He taught physics and mathematics at the Government Secondary School Karshi, Federal Capital Territory. He served as the special adviser to the vice chancellor of the Catholic University of Nigeria, Abuja (Veritas University), and a lecturer at the same university. Additionally, he served as the director of general studies at Veritas University. He was appointed as the administrator of St. Francis Catholic Secondary School, Idimu, Lagos, on July 15, 2017.

George Patrick Murphy began his business career working for Scott Paper Company Worldwide (acquired by Kimberly Clark Corporation in 1995). He eventually assumed the roles of vice president of sales and business integration at Sani-Fresh International (a Scott Paper Worldwide Subsidiary); North America vice president of sales and channel development, Away From Home Division; vice president–business leader, Asia Pacific Region (headquartered in Hong Kong); and later as a Kimberly-Clark North America vice president, Away From Home Division, and as a corporate officer. After George retired from Kimberly-Clark, he served as president and CEO of Technical Concepts Worldwide for over eight years (prior to the company's acquisition by Newell-Rubbermaid Corporation). George next became a limited partner, operating partner, executive adviser, and/or board member for several private equity enterprises, including Atlas Paper Mills LLC, where he was elected chairman. Until recently, he served on the board of directors of Wausau Paper Corporation, a NYSE Public Company. Murphy currently serves as the founder and chairman of Blue Venture Advocates (BVA) and as chairman emeritus and current board member of Altitude Medical. He also serves as strategic adviser, principal, and/or board member at several of BVA's consortium member enterprises, including Canadian Private Company CRAiLAR FTI. Active in nonprofits, Murphy serves as vice chairman of the Spitzer Center for Visionary Leadership, as a member of the board of directors at the Catholic Leadership Institute, and as a founding member of the executive advisory board at the USC Marshall School of Business–Neely Center for Ethical Leadership and Decision Making, and at the Gonzaga University School of Leadership Studies. He also serves on the parish council at Saint Mary's Catholic Church in Park City, Utah. Murphy received his undergraduate and graduate degrees from the University of Southern California, where he graduated with honors. He and his wife of forty-four years, Bonnie, have three daughters and six wonderful grandchildren.

Paul Nakai is the founding partner and principal of Leadership Spirit International LLC. Leadership Spirit International is a consulting group specializing in developing and deepening the servant-leadership capacity of executives in teambuilding, optimizing performance-based relationships, and shaping the thriving servant-leadership culture to sustainably be more agile in achieving organizational objectives. Paul was formerly a managing partner and executive vice president with Senn Delaney, where he specialized in executive coaching and leadership development to support and lead the organization through crucible challenges such as mergers and acquisitions, shifting corporate cultures, leadership shortages, downturns or upturns in business, debilitating internal strife, constant disruption, and the need for transformation. Paul has consulted for and led major cultural processes in numerous industries, including crucial engagements at Three Mile Island Nuclear Generating Stationand for NASA in response to critical challenges. Through Leadership Spirit International, Paul is dedicated to healthy, thriving servant-leadership in order to assist executives in unleashing the spirit behind their personal leadership as well as unleashing the collective spirit of their organizations. Paul currently lives in Marin County, California, with his wife Nancy and his immediate family.

Lena Pace is the branch chief of law enforcement for the Intermountain Region of the National Park Service (NPS). She was born and raised in small-town Alaska just outside Glacier Bay National Park, where she developed a great appreciation for environmental protection and the mission of the NPS. She got her bachelor's degree in environmental studies and politics from Whitman College and attended the Federal Law Enforcement Training Center just after she graduated. In 2012, she received her masters in organizational leadership from Gonzaga University, where she first studied servant-leadership. She has subsequently coordinated servant-leadership training for other law enforcement leaders in the NPS. In 2017, Lena attended the FBI National Academy, a ten-week leadership academy for law enforcement leaders from around the world. Lena currently lives in Denver, Colorado, with her husband and is a CrossFit coach in her spare time.

Eleni Prillaman (Kametas) works at Loyola University Chicago as the manager and adviser for the campus radio station, WLUW 88.7 FM. Eleni is a 2011 graduate of Gonzaga University, where she earned a master's degree in communication and leadership. In no particular order, Eleni is a mother, wife, avid concertgoer, champion for animals, and food documentary enthusiast, and enjoys long walks on the beach.

John R. is married with three beautiful children. He is currently the director of cybersecurity at a large organization and has held executive positions in multiple corporations. He has been clean and sober for more than eleven years.

Marleen Ramsey has worked in a variety of roles in counseling, teaching, and administration at the collegiate level and feels very fortunate to have spent her entire professional career in academia. She retired in December

2017 from her positions as vice president of Instruction (VPI) and chief academic officer (CAO) at Walla Walla Community College. Prior to being the VPI and CAO, she was the director of transitional studies, a tenured faculty member, and a counselor in the Student Affairs Department. Her primary research interest has focused on the impact of empathy and forgiveness and the relational dynamics between perpetrators and those who have extended forgiveness to them. She enjoys spending time with her husband, their daughters, sons-in-law, and three grandsons, a.k.a. "the three scampering squirrels."

Mark Whitson is currently employed as an executive protection specialist at Bayer AG. Previously, he was employed by the St. Louis County (MO) Police Department. During his time as a police officer, he served in patrol, drug enforcement, and criminal investigation divisions. He was also assigned to the Tactical Operations Unit, where his principle assignment was as a negotiator. In 2014, Mark retired as a sergeant after thirty-four years of service. In 2012 he graduated from Gonzaga University with a masters of art degree in communications and leadership. He resides in Saint Charles, Missouri, and can be reached at markwhitson2@gmail.com.

Dirk van Dierendonck is professor of human resource management, particularly leadership and management development, at Rotterdam School of Management, Erasmus University. His areas of expertise include human resource management, (servant) leadership and leadership development, positive organizational scholarship, and measurement development. Dirk van Dierendonck is the author of a number of books and book chapters, as well as over seventy scholarly articles published in major academic journals, including the *Journal of Management*, the *Journal of Applied Psychology*, the *Academy of Management Journal*, the *Journal of Organizational Behavior*, and the *European Journal of Work and Organizational Behavior*.

Annelies van Poelgeest graduated at the Rotterdam School of Management, Erasmus University, the Netherlands, where she received her MScBA in human resource management. Her thesis focused on the leader's propensity to forgive and its influence on a culture of openness and fairness within a team. For a couple of years, she worked as a job coach at a foundation that focuses on the reintegration of homeless people in Rotterdam. Presently, she is developing a workbook about prayer, in addition to serving in her role as a stay-at-home mom for her family of two kids.

Maryalice Giroux Viljoen has over twenty-five years' experience in providing service in various industries, most notably the hospitality sector. As the first vice president of organizational development for Modus Hotels in Washington, DC, she was part of a team that guided a rebranding effort focused on the core tenets of servant-leadership. After Modus, Maryalice moved to Honduras, where she assisted in the development of a bilingual high school hospitality management program, along with training local residents to run a full-service hotel nestled in the mountains of Gracias, Lempira. After a battle with breast cancer that taught Maryalice the grace of being served, she now focuses her attention on infusing all industries with the spirit of hospitality through workshops in servant-leadership, service and service recovery, and managing multicultural teams. She is an adjunct professor at Trinity Washington University in Washington, DC, and provides concierge support to high-tier executives in the DC area. Maryalice earned a master's degree in organizational leadership at Gonzaga University.

Index

power, 199, 223, 231–232, 336–338,
355, 357; power politics, xxiv, 136,
139, 150; white power, 214–215
pragmatism, 308
prayer, 52, 79, 126–127, 145, 170,
177–178, 189, 201, 203, 206, 268,
273, 275, 297, 306; The Lord's
Prayer, 126, 297; Shema Yisrael, 297
privilege, x, 12, 41, 61, 67, 108, 203,
233, 284, 294
productivity, xxv, 23, 84, 120–121,
140, 149, 151
professional outsource service provider,
75
proportionality and desert, 89, 96
PTSD (post-traumatic stress disorder),
46, 243–244, 246
purpose, 371, 374–381

Qatar, 88
Quaker, 11, 293, 306
Quantum Healing, 322
quick-fix, 12, 63, 73, 78
Quran, 179

racism, 2, 39, 105, 216, 222
reconciliation, 339, 365–366;
ceremony, 57; definition of, xxiv,
141; forgiveness and, xx, xxiii, xxv,
3, 52, 129, 141–142, 144, 158–159,
205, 244, 255, 276, 340, 356, 373;
two levels of, xxiv, 143
reflection, 22–23, 73, 81, 357
reflexivity, 23
regret, 52, 213, 356
relatedness, 92, 95–96. *See also*
connectedness; interrelatedness
relationship, 296, 298–299; bilateral,
138; interpersonal, xx, 18, 25–26,
51, 89–96, 119, 121, 142, 227,
239, 256, 320–321, 335–336, 361;
between objects, 16, 90; among

nations, 101; restoring, xx, xxiv, 29,
44–45, 54, 79, 81, 93, 110, 136–
137, 142, 240, 347
reprisal, 94, 168. *See also* retaliation
research methods: confirmatory
factor analysis, 26; exploratory
factor analysis, 364; hermeneutic
phenomenology, xvii–xviii, 28,
45; hermeneutical analysis, 24;
longitudinal study, xxvi–xxviii, 323;
mixed-methods, xx, 14, 16, 24;
qualitative, xiv, xvi, xxxi, 14–16;
quantitative, xiv, 13–16; survey, 363
resentment, xxiii, 27, 89, 92, 110,
124, 135, 137–141, 143, 148, 150,
188, 205, 221, 229–232, 239, 242,
244–245, 255, 261–262, 279, 287,
308–309, 318, 327, 343, 345, 353–
354, 362, 378. *See also* bitterness
resilience, 56, 68, 90, 96, 153, 157,
374, 378, 380–381
respect, xix, 49, 54, 65, 74, 154, 171,
191, 229, 308, 314
responsibility, 22, 24, 65, 72, 84,
100, 105, 108, 113, 136, 141, 150,
152, 178, 198, 206, 223, 232, 255,
265, 267, 271, 297–298, 323, 356;
collective, 221–223; self-, 89–93,
274, 339, 341
restoration, 281, 285, 347
restorative interaction, 27
retaliation, 77, 169, 245, 261, 273,
365–366. *See also* reprisal
risk, xv, xxi, 18, 24, 41, 65, 76, 138,
143, 168–169, 190, 216–217, 229,
260
rituals, 20, 179, 273
Robben Island, 129
Rockwell, Norman, 221
Rohr, Richard, 287
role models, 19, 70, 224, 260, 268,
362–363

Stanton, Edwin, 271
stewardship, 19–20, 100, 238, 354
suffering, 243, 316–317
Sun Yat-sen, 11
Sunflower, The, 299, 342, 356
superiority, 99, 108–109, 260
survival, 65, 73, 76, 151, 319–320
survive and thrive, 61, 69, 73, 77
survivors, 219–220, 342, 344
symbol, xv–xvi, xxxi–xxxii, 57, 172

Talmud, 152
Taoism, 10, 293
Teresa of Calcutta, Saint, 263, 324
thingness, 91–92
thinking: above-the-line, 267, 274;
    below-the-line, 266, 339
Thoreau, Henry David, 119
Three Hermits, The, 125–127
Thuan, Francis Xavier Nguyen Van,
    2–4
Time, 189
tolerance, xxviii–xxix, 17–18, 23,
    26, 153, 181, 245, 325–326, 340,
    372–373
Tolstoy, Leo, 125
Torah, 316
tournaments, 123
Townsend & Bottum, 95
trades, 102, 104, 106
TRC (Truth and Reconciliation
    Commission), xvii, xix, xxiv, 28,
    38–44, 46–50, 56–57, 65, 99, 129–
    130, 181, 184, 229–230, 233, 273,
    297–298, 327, 373
trust, 13–14, 66, 127–128, 137–138,
    143, 153, 155–157, 166, 174, 180,
    183, 191, 193, 196, 198, 202, 222,
    243, 246, 256, 260, 273–274, 280,
    295, 339, 347, 352–354, 356, 362;
    mistrust, 67, 153–156, 173, 222,
    242, 338, 340

Tutu, Desmond, xvii, xxiv, 20, 27–28,
    38, 40, 99, 110, 129–130, 222,
    226–231, 233, 255–256, 273–274,
    276, 280–281, 287, 289, 296–302,
    326–328, 337, 340, 353; *No Future
    without Forgiveness,* 274, 327, 337

ubuntu, 130, 181–182, 233, 256, 274,
    280, 283, 299–300
Uganda, xxiii, 40, 138
Unconditional Life, 321
underdevelopment, 104
unicorn, 90
United Kingdom, 16, 23, 88
United Nations, 141
United States Conference of Catholic
    Bishops, 193–194, 198, 201
unity, 298–301, 328

values, 65–66, 68, 72
vengeance, xxv, 28, 77, 145, 148, 168,
    173, 230, 233, 243, 247, 313–315,
    328, 361
victims, xviii–xx, xxiv, 38, 40, 92,
    135–139, 142, 148, 190–192, 201
Vietnam, 2–4
violence, 241–242, 313, 325; apartheid
    era, 39–40, 46, 105–106; Auschwitz,
    296–297; black-on-white violence,
    xvii; Heidelberg Tavern attack, xvii,
    42–43, 56; Holocaust, 65, 222, 299,
    342; incest, 90; Jos crisis, 172–174,
    177; the massacre of Indians, 102;
    murder, xvii, 2, 42, 46, 107, 145,
    220–221, 223, 225–226, 229–232,
    242, 327, 371, 373–374; Nigerian
    Civil War, 166–168; nonviolence,
    157, 175–177, 179, 182, 259–262,
    315, 325, 328; physical abuse,
    254–255, 344; Saint James Church
    massacre, xvii, 42–43, 47, 56;
    September 11 attacks, 321; sexual

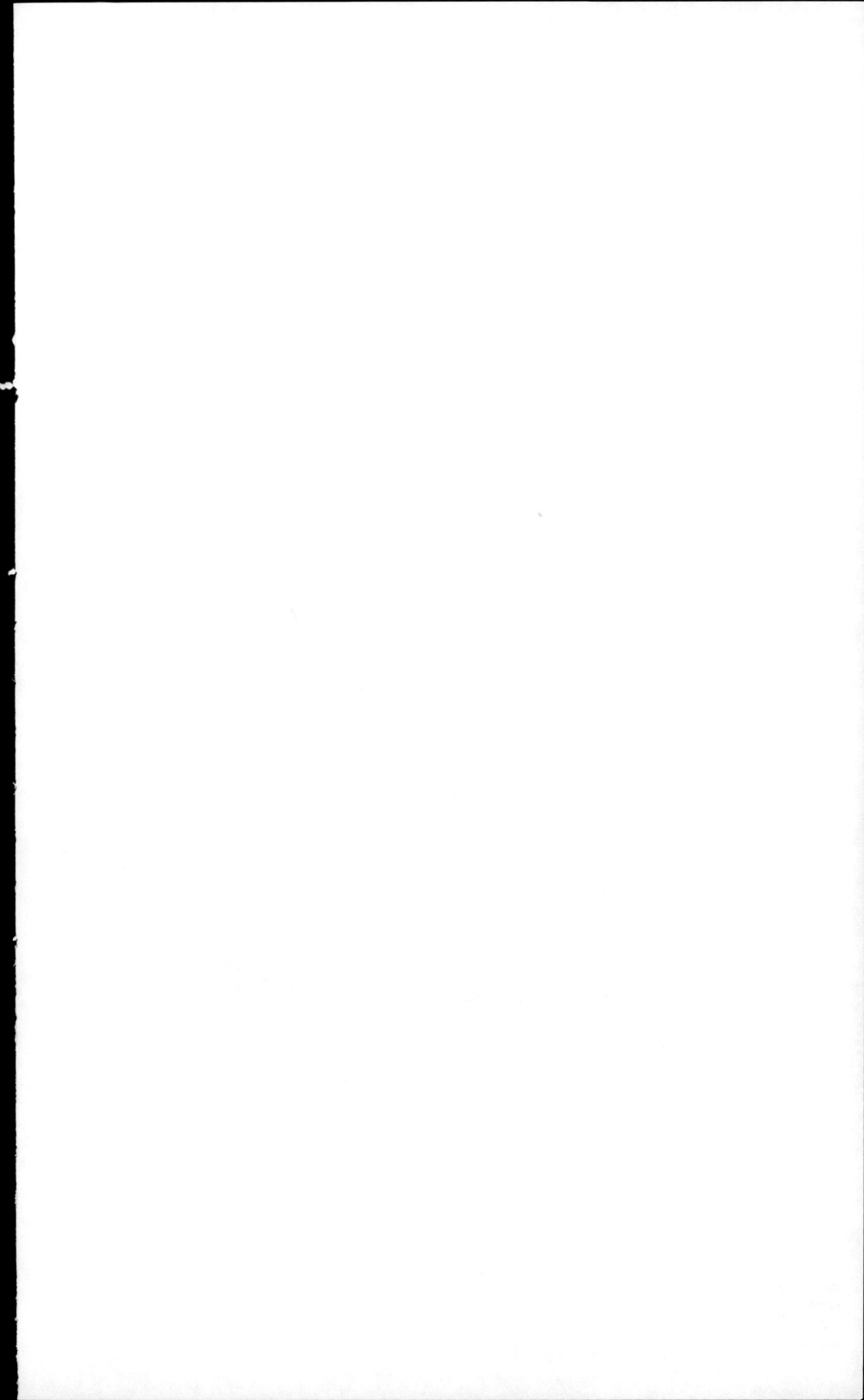

www.ingramcontent.com/pod-product-compliance
Lightning Source LLC
Chambersburg PA
CBHW021545210326
41599CB00010B/320